54th Annual Meeting of the Association for Computational Linguistics (ACL 2016)

System Demonstrations

Berlin, Germany
7 – 12 August 2016

ISBN: 978-1-5108-2761-5

ACL 2016

The 54th Annual Meeting of the
Association for Computational Linguistics

Proceedings of System Demonstrations

August 7-12, 2016
Berlin, Germany

Preface

Welcome to the proceedings of the system demonstrations session. This volume contains the papers of the system demonstrations presented at the 54th Annual Meeting of the Association for Computational Linguistics on August 7-12, 2016 in Berlin, Germany.

The system demonstrations program offers the presentation of early research prototypes as well as interesting mature systems. We received 85 submissions, of which 28 were selected for inclusion in the program (acceptance rate of 33%) after review by three members of the program committee.

We would like to thank the members of the program committee for their timely help in reviewing the submissions.

Organizers:

Sameer Pradhan, cemantix.org and Boulder Learning, Inc.
Marianna Apidianaki, LIMSI, CNRS, Université Paris-Saclay

Program Committee:

Apoorv Agarwal, Columbia University (USA)
Nikolaos Aletras, Amazon (UK)
Simon Baker, University of Cambridge (UK)
Daniel Bauer, Columbia University (USA)
Taylor Berg-Kirkpatrick, UC Berkeley (USA)
Laurent Besacier, LIG, Université Joseph Fourier (France)
Chris Biemann, TU Darmstadt (Germany)
Grzegorz Chrupała, Tilburg University (The Netherlands)
Vincent Claveau, IRISA-CNRS (France)
Anne Cocos, University of Pennsylvania (USA)
Daniël de Kok, University of Tübingen (Germany)
Michael Denkowski, Carnegie Mellon University (USA)
Georgiana Dinu, IBM Watson (USA)
Tomaž Erjavec, Jožef Stefan Institute (Slovenia)
Darja Fišer, University of Ljubljana (Slovenia)
Annemarie Friedrich, Saarland University (Germany)
Dimitris Galanis, ILSP / Athena Research Center (Greece)
Yvette Graham, Dublin City University (Ireland)
Carolin Haas, Heidelberg University (Germany)
Barry Haddow, University of Edinburgh (UK)
David Jurgens, Stanford University (USA)
Valia Kordoni, Humboldt University of Berlin (Germany)
Gerhard Kremer, University of Stuttgart (Germany)
Patrik Lambert, Pompeu Fabra University (Spain)
Philippe Langlais, Université de Montréal (Canada)
Angeliki Lazaridou, University of Trento (Italy)
Joseph Le Roux, Université Paris Nord (France)
John Lee, City University of Hong Kong (Hong Kong)
Alessandro Lenci, University of Pisa (Italy)
Pierre Lison, University of Oslo (Norway)
Nikola Ljubešić, University of Zagreb (Croatia)
Nitin Madnani, Educational Testing Service (USA)
Wolfgang Maier, University of Düsseldorf (Germany)
Suresh Manandhar, University of York (UK)
Benjamin Marie, LIMSI, CNRS, Université Paris-Sud (France)
Stella Markantonatou, ILSP / Athena Research Center (Greece)
Yuval Marton, Microsoft Research (USA)
Pascual Martínez-Gómez, National Institute of Advanced Industrial Science and Technology (Japan)
Saif Mohammad, National Research Council (Canada)
Alessandro Moschitti, Qatar Computing Research Institute (Qatar)
Philippe Muller, IRIT, Toulouse University (France)

Preslav Nakov, Qatar Computing Research Institute (Qatar)
Diane Napolitano, Educational Testing Service (USA)
Hiroshi Noji, Nara Institute of Science and Technology (Japan)
Pierre Nugues, Lund University (Sweden)
Yannick Parmentier, University of Orleans (France)
Mohammad Taher Pilehvar, University of Cambridge (UK)
Stelios Piperidis, ILSP / Athena Research Center (Greece)
Maja Popović, Humboldt University of Berlin (Germany)
Vinodkumar Prabhakaran, Stanford University (USA)
Prokopis Prokopidis, ILSP / Athena Research Center (Greece)
Alessandro Raganato, Sapienza University of Rome (Italy)
Carlos Ramisch, LIF, Aix-Marseille Université (France)
Siva Reddy, University of Edinburgh (UK)
Adithya Renduchintala, Johns Hopkins University (USA)
German Rigau, UPV/EHU, University of the Basque Country (Spain)
Djamé Seddah, University Paris-Sorbonne (France)
Advaith Siddharthan, University of Aberdeen (UK)
Michel Simard, National Research Council (Canada)
Artem Sokolov, Heidelberg University (Germany)
Lucia Specia, University of Sheffield (UK)
Miloš Stanojević, University of Amsterdam (The Netherlands)
Kaveh Taghipour, National University of Singapore (Singapore)
Xavier Tannier, LIMSI, CNRS, Univ. Paris-Sud, Université Paris-Saclay (France)
Christoph Teichmann, University of Potsdam (Germany)
Jörg Tiedemann, University of Helsinki (Finland)
John Tinsley, Iconic Translation Machines Ltd (Ireland)
Nadi Tomeh, Université Paris 13, Sorbonne Paris Cité (France)
Olga Uryupina, University of Trento (Italy)
Lonneke van der Plas, University of Malta (Malta)
Andrea Varga, The Content Group (UK)
Ivan Vulić, University of Cambridge (UK)
Marion Weller-DiMarco, University of Stuttgart (Germany)
Guillaume Wisniewski, LIMSI, CNRS, Université Paris-Sud (France)
Shiqi Zhao, Baidu (China)
Pierre Zweigenbaum, LIMSI, CNRS, Université Paris-Saclay (France)

Table of Contents

Conference Program

Monday, August 8, 2016

18:00–21:00   ***ACL System Demonstrations Session A***

POLYGLOT: Multilingual Semantic Role Labeling with Unified Labels
Alan Akbik and Yunyao Li

Online Information Retrieval for Language Learning
Maria Chinkina, Madeeswaran Kannan and Detmar Meurers

Terminology Extraction with Term Variant Detection
Damien Cram and Beatrice Daille

DeepLife: An Entity-aware Search, Analytics and Exploration Platform for Health and Life Sciences
Patrick Ernst, Amy Siu, Dragan Milchevski, Johannes Hoffart and Gerhard Weikum

Visualizing and Curating Knowledge Graphs over Time and Space
Tong Ge, Yafang Wang, Gerard de Melo, Haofeng Li and Baoquan Chen

A Web-framework for ODIN Annotation
Ryan Georgi, Michael Wayne Goodman and Fei Xia

Real-Time Discovery and Geospatial Visualization of Mobility and Industry Events from Large-Scale, Heterogeneous Data Streams
Leonhard Hennig, Philippe Thomas, Renlong Ai, Johannes Kirschnick, He Wang, Jakob Pannier, Nora Zimmermann, Sven Schmeier, Feiyu Xu, Jan Ostwald and Hans Uszkoreit

TranscRater: a Tool for Automatic Speech Recognition Quality Estimation
Shahab Jalalvand, Matteo Negri, Marco Turchi, José G. C. de Souza, Falavigna Daniele and Mohammed R. H. Qwaider

TMop: a Tool for Unsupervised Translation Memory Cleaning
Masoud Jalili Sabet, Matteo Negri, Marco Turchi, José G. C. de Souza and Marcello Federico

MMFeat: A Toolkit for Extracting Multi-Modal Features
Douwe Kiela

JEDI: Joint Entity and Relation Detection using Type Inference
Johannes Kirschnick, Holmer Hemsen and Volker Markl

OpenDial: A Toolkit for Developing Spoken Dialogue Systems with Probabilistic Rules
Pierre Lison and Casey Kennington

MUSEEC: A Multilingual Text Summarization Tool
Marina Litvak, Natalia Vanetik, Mark Last and Elena Churkin

Language Muse: Automated Linguistic Activity Generation for English Language Learners
Nitin Madnani, Jill Burstein, John Sabatini, Kietha Biggers and Slava Andreyev

ccg2lambda: A Compositional Semantics System
Pascual Martínez-Gómez, Koji Mineshima, Yusuke Miyao and Daisuke Bekki

MeTA: A Unified Toolkit for Text Retrieval and Analysis
Sean Massung, Chase Geigle and ChengXiang Zhai

MDSWriter: Annotation Tool for Creating High-Quality Multi-Document Summarization Corpora
Christian M. Meyer, Darina Benikova, Margot Mieskes and Iryna Gurevych

Jigg: A Framework for an Easy Natural Language Processing Pipeline
Hiroshi Noji and Yusuke Miyao

An Advanced Press Review System Combining Deep News Analysis and Machine Learning Algorithms
Danuta Ploch, Andreas Lommatzsch and Florian Schultze

Tuesday, August 8, 2016

18:00–19:30   ***ACL System Demonstrations Session B***

Personalized Exercises for Preposition Learning
John Lee and Mengqi Luo

My Science Tutor—Learning Science with a Conversational Virtual Tutor
Sameer Pradhan, Ron Cole and Wayne Ward

pigeo: A Python Geotagging Tool
Afshin Rahimi, Trevor Cohn and Timothy Baldwin

POLYGLOT: Multilingual Semantic Role Labeling with Unified Labels

Alan Akbik   **Yunyao Li**

IBM Research

Almaden Research Center

650 Harry Road, San Jose, CA 95120, USA

{akbika,yunyaoli}@us.ibm.com

Abstract

Semantic role labeling (SRL) identifies the predicate-argument structure in text with semantic labels. It plays a key role in understanding natural language. In this paper, we present POLYGLOT, a multilingual semantic role labeling system capable of semantically parsing sentences in 9 different languages from 4 different language groups. The core of POLYGLOT are SRL models for individual languages trained with automatically generated Proposition Banks (Akbik et al., 2015). The key feature of the system is that it treats the semantic labels of the English Proposition Bank as "universal semantic labels": Given a sentence in any of the supported languages, POLYGLOT applies the corresponding SRL and predicts English Prop-Bank frame and role annotation. The results are then visualized to facilitate the understanding of multilingual SRL with this unified semantic representation.

1 Introduction

Semantic role labeling (SRL) is the task of labeling predicate-argument structure in sentences with shallow semantic information. One prominent labeling scheme for the English language is the Proposition Bank (Palmer et al., 2005) which annotates predicates with *frame* labels and arguments with *role* labels. Role labels roughly conform to simple questions (*who, what, when, where, how much, with whom*) with regards to the predicate. SRL is important for understanding natural language; it has been found useful for many applications such as information extraction (Fader et al., 2011) and question answering (Shen and Lapata, 2007; Maqsud et al., 2014).

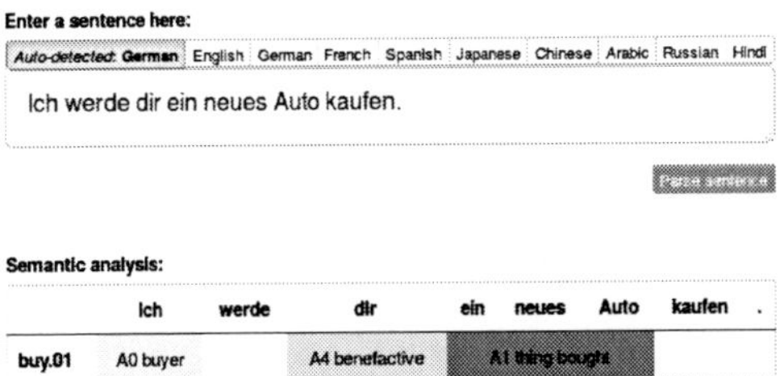

Figure 1: Example of POLYGLOT predicting English Prop-Bank labels for a simple German sentence: The verb *"kaufen"* is correctly identified to evoke the BUY.01 frame, while *"ich"* (*I*) is recognized as the *buyer*, *"ein neues Auto"* (*a new car*) as the *thing bought*, and *"dir"* (*for you*) as the *benefactive*.

Not surprisingly, enabling SRL for languages other than English has received increasing attention. One relevant key effort is to create Proposition Bank-style resources for different languages, such as Chinese (Xue and Palmer, 2005) and Hindi (Bhatt et al., 2009). However, the conventional approach of manually generating such resources is costly in terms of time and experts required, hindering the expansion of SRL to new target languages.

An alternative approach is *annotation projection* (Padó and Lapata, 2009; Van der Plas et al., 2011) that utilizes parallel corpora to transfer predicted SRL labels from English sentences onto sentences in a target language. It has shown great promise in automatically generating such resources for arbitrary target languages. In previous work, we presented an approach based on filtered projection and bootstrapped learning to auto-generate Proposition Bank-style resources for 7 languages, namely Arabic, Chinese, French, German, Hindi, Russian and Spanish (Akbik et al., 2015).

Unified semantic labels across all languages.

One key difference between auto-generated PropBanks and manually created ones is that the former use English Proposition Bank labels for

1

Proceedings of the 54th Annual Meeting of the Association for Computational Linguistics—System Demonstrations, pages 1–6,
Berlin, Germany, August 7-12, 2016. ©2016 Association for Computational Linguistics

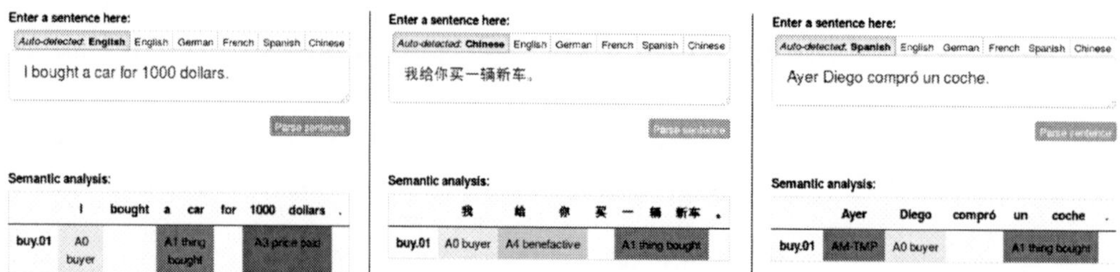

Figure 2: Side by side view of English, Chinese and Spanish sentences parsed in POLYGLOT's Web UI. English PropBank frame and role labels are predicted for all languages: All example sentences evoke the BUY.01 frame and have constituents accordingly labeled with roles such as the *buyer*, the *thing bought*, the *price paid* and the *benefactive*.

all target languages, while the latter use language-specific labels. As such, the auto-generated Prop-Banks allow us to train an SRL system to consume text in various languages and make predictions in a shared semantic label set, namely English Prop-Bank labels. Refer to Figures 1 and 2 for examples of how our system predicts frame and role labels from the English Proposition Bank for sentences in German, English, Chinese and Spanish.

Similar to how Stanford dependencies are one basis of *universal dependencies* (De Marneffe et al., 2014; Nivre, 2015), we believe that English PropBank labels have the potential to eventually become a basis of "universal" shallow semantic labels. Such a unified representation of shallow semantics, we argue, may facilitate applications such as multilingual information extraction and question answering, much in the same way that universal dependencies facilitate tasks such as crosslingual learning and the development and evaluation of multilingual syntactic parsers (Nivre, 2015). The key questions, however, are (1) to what degree English PropBank frame and role labels are appropriate for different target languages; and (2) how far this approach can handle language-specific phenomena or semantic concepts.

Contributions. To facilitate the discussions of the above questions, we present POLYGLOT, an SRL system trained on auto-generated PropBanks for 8 languages plus English, namely Arabic, Chinese, French, German, Hindi, Japanese, Russian and Spanish. Given a sentence in one of these 9 languages, the system applies the corresponding SRL and visualizes the shallow semantic parse with predicted English PropBank labels. POLY-GLOT allows us to illustrate our envisioned approach of parsing different languages into a shared shallow semantic abstraction based on the English Proposition Bank. It also enables researchers to

experiment with the tool to understand the breadth of shallow semantic concepts currently covered, and to discuss limitations and the potential of such an approach for downstream applications.

2 System Overview

Figure 3 depicts the overall architecture of POLY-GLOT. First, we automatically generate labeled training data for each target language with annotation projection (Akbik et al., 2015) (Figure 3 Step 1). We use the labeled data to train for each language an SRL system (Figure 3 Step 2) that predicts English PropBank frame and role labels. Both the creation of the training data and the training of the SRL instances are one-time processes.

POLYGLOT provides a Web-based GUI to allow users to interact with the SRL systems (Figure 3 Step 3). Given a natural language sentence, depending on the language of the input sentence, POLYGLOT selects the appropriate SRL instance and displays on the GUI the semantic parse, as well as syntactic information.

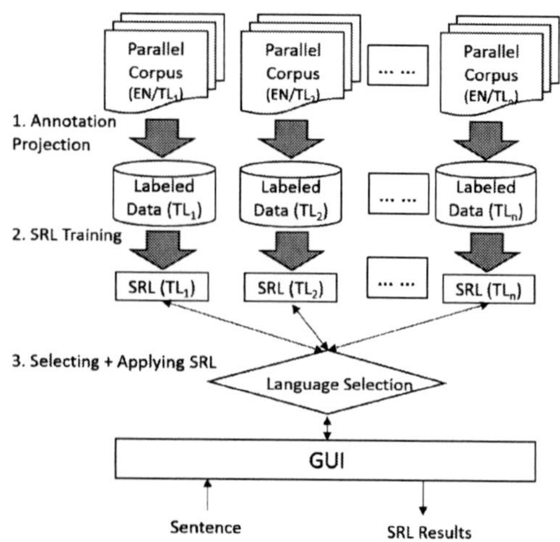

Figure 3: System overview

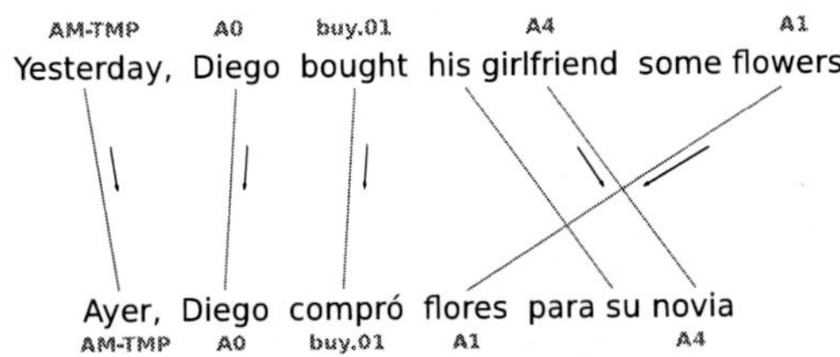

Figure 4: Annotation projection for a word-aligned English-Spanish sentence pair.

In the next sections, we briefly describe the creation of the labeled data and the training of the SRL systems, followed by a tour of the Web UI.

3 Auto-Generation of Labeled Data

We followed an annotation projection approach to automatically generate the labeled data for different languages. This approach takes as input a word-aligned parallel corpus of English sentences and their translations in a target language (TL). A semantic role labeler then predicts labels for the English sentences. In a projection step, these labels are transferred along word alignments onto the target language sentences. The underlying theory is that translated sentence pairs share a degree of semantic similarity, making such projection possible (Padó and Lapata, 2009).

Figure 4 illustrates an example of annotation projection: Using an SRL system trained with the English Proposition Bank, the English sentence is labeled with the appropriate frame (BUY.01) and role labels: *"Diego"* as the *buyer* (**A0** in PropBank annotation), *"some flowers"* as the *thing bought* (**A1**) and *"his girlfriend"* as the *benefactive* (**A4**). In addition, *"yesterday"* is labeled **AM-TMP**, signifying a temporal context of this frame. These labels are then projected onto the aligned Spanish words. For instance, *"compró"* is word-aligned to *"bought"* and thus labeled as BUY.01. The projection produces a Spanish sentence labeled with English PropBank labels; such data can in turn be used to train an SRL system for Spanish.

State-of-the-art. Direct annotation projection often introduces errors, mostly due to non-literal translations (Akbik et al., 2015). Previous work defined lexical and syntactic constraints to increase projection quality, such as filters to allow only verbs to be labeled as frames (Van der Plas et al., 2011), heuristics that ensure that only heads of syntactic constituents are labeled as arguments (Padó and Lapata, 2009) and the use of verb translation dictionaries to guide frame map-

pings. In (Akbik et al., 2015), we additionally proposed a process of filtered projection and bootstrapped learning, and successfully created Proposition Banks for 7 target languages. We found the quality of the generated PropBanks to be moderate to high, depending on the target language. Table 1 shows estimated precision, recall and F1-score for each language with two evaluation methods. *Partial* evaluation counts correctly labeled incomplete constituents as true positives while *exact* evaluation only counts correctly labeled complete constituents as true positives. For more details we refer the reader to (Akbik et al., 2015) .

4 Semantic Role Labeling

Using the auto-generated labeled data, we train the semantic role labeler of the MATE toolkit (Björkelund et al., 2009), which achieved state-of-the-art semantic F1-score in the multilingual semantic role labeling task of the CoNLL-2009 shared task (Hajič et al., 2009). The parser is implemented as a sequence of local logistic regression classifiers for the four steps of predicate identification, predicate classification, argument identification and argument classification. In addition, it implements a global reranker to rerank sets of local predictions. It uses a standard feature set of lexical and syntactic features.

Preprocessing. Before SRL, we execute a pipeline of NLP tools to extract the required lexical, morphological and syntactic features. To facilitate reproducability of the presented work, we use publicly available open source tools and pre-

		PREDICATE			ARGUMENT				
LANG.	Match	P	R	F1	P	R	F1	Agr	κ
Arabic	part.	0.97	0.89	0.93	0.86	0.69	0.77	0.92	0.87
	exact	0.97	0.89	0.93	0.67	0.63	0.65	0.85	0.77
Chinese	part.	0.97	0.88	0.92	0.93	0.83	0.88	0.95	0.91
	exact	0.97	0.88	0.92	0.83	0.81	0.82	0.92	0.86
French	part.	0.95	0.92	0.94	0.92	0.76	0.83	0.97	0.95
	exact	0.95	0.92	0.94	0.86	0.74	0.8	0.95	0.91
German	part.	0.96	0.92	0.94	0.95	0.73	0.83	0.95	0.91
	exact	0.96	0.92	0.94	0.91	0.73	0.81	0.92	0.86
Hindi	part.	0.91	0.68	0.78	0.93	0.66	0.77	0.94	0.88
	exact	0.91	0.68	0.78	0.58	0.54	0.56	0.81	0.69
Russian	part.	0.96	0.94	0.95	0.91	0.68	0.78	0.97	0.94
	exact	0.96	0.94	0.95	0.79	0.65	0.72	0.93	0.89
Spanish	part.	0.96	0.93	0.95	0.85	0.74	0.79	0.91	0.85
	exact	0.96	0.93	0.95	0.75	0.72	0.74	0.85	0.77

Table 1: Estimated precision and recall over seven languages from our previous evaluation (Akbik et al., 2015).

Language	NLP Preprocessing	Parallel Data Sets	#Sentences
Arabic	StanfordCoreNLP, KhojaStemmer, StanfordParser	UN, OpenSubtitles	24,5M
Chinese	StanfordCoreNLP, MateParser	UN, OpenSubtitles	12,2M
English	ClearNLP	n/a	n/a
French	StanfordCoreNLP, MateTransitionParser	UN, OpenSubtitles	36M
German	StanfordCoreNLP, MateTransitionParser	Europarl, OpenSubtitles	14,1M
Hindi	TnTTagger, MaltParser	Hindencorp	54K
Japanese	JJST	Tatoeba, OpenSubtitles	1,7M
Russian	TreeTagger, MaltParser	UN, OpenSubtitles	22,7M
Spanish	StanfordCoreNLP, MateParser	UN, OpenSubtitles	52,4M

Table 2: NLP tools and source of parallel data used for each language. Since English is the source language for annotation projection, no parallel data was required to train SRL.
NLP tools: StanfordCoreNLP: (Manning et al., 2014) , TnTTagger: (Brants, 2000), TreeTagger: (Schmid, 1994), KhojaStemmer: (Khoja and Garside, 1999), StanfordParser: (Green and Manning, 2010), StanfordCoreNLP: (Choi and McCallum, 2013), MateParser: (Bohnet, 2010), JJST: *proprietary system*, MateTransitionParser: (Bohnet and Nivre, 2012), MaltParser: (Nivre et al., 2006).

trained models where available. A breakdown of the preprocessing tools used for each language is given in Table 2.

Data sets. In order to generate training data for POLYGLOT, we used the following sources of parallel data: The UN corpus of official United Nations documents (Rafalovitch et al., 2009), the Europarl corpus of European parliament proceedings (Koehn, 2005), the OpenSubtitles corpus of movie subtitles (Lison and Tiedemann, 2016), the Hindencorp corpus automatically gathered from web sources (Bojar et al., 2014) and the Tatoeba corpus of language learning examples[1]. The data sets were obtained from the OPUS project (Tiedemann, 2012) and word aligned using the Berkeley Aligner[2]. Table 2 lists the data sets used for each language and the combined number of available parallel sentences.

5 POLYGLOT User Interface

The Web-based GUI of POLYGLOT allows users to enter sentences in one of 9 languages and request a shallow semantic analysis. Figure 5 presents a screenshot of the GUI. Users begin by entering a sentence in the text field and clicking on the "parse sentence" button. As indicated in Figure 3, it is then passed to a language-specific NLP pipeline based on the associated language that is detected automatically by default or specified by the user. The pipeline tokenizes and lemmatizes the sentence, performs morphological analysis, dependency parsing and semantic role labeling.

Output. The syntactic and semantic parsing results are displayed below the input field, following the design of (Björkelund et al., 2010): The topmost result table is the semantic analysis, pre-sented as a grid in which each row corresponds to one identified semantic frame. The grid highlights sentence constituents labeled with roles and includes role descriptions for better interpretability of the parsing results.

Below the results of the semantic analysis the GUI shows two more detailed views of the parsing results. The first visualizes the dependency parse tree generated using WHATSWRONGWITH-MYNLP[3], while the second (omitted in Figure 5 in the interest of space) displays the full syntactic-semantic parse in CoNLL format, including morphological information and other features not present in the dependency tree visualization. These two views may be helpful to users that wish to identify possible sources of SRL errors. For instance, a common error class stem from errors in dependency parsing, causing incorrect constituents to be labeled as arguments.

Example sentence. Figure 5 illustrates the result visualization of the tool. A user enters a sentence *"Hier, je voulais acheter une baguette, mais je n'avais pas assez d'argent"* (engl. *"Yesterday I wanted to buy a baguette but I didn't have enough money"*) into the text field. As indicated in the top left corner, this sentence is auto-detected to be French.

The results of semantic analysis is displayed below the input field. The first column in the grid indicates that three frames have been identified: WANT.01, BUY.01 and HAVE.03. The second row in the grid corresponds to the WANT.01 frame, which identifies *"je"* (engl. *"I"*) as the *wanter* and *"acheter une baguette"* (engl. *"buy a baguette"*) as the *thing wanted*. The arguments are color-coded by PropBank argument type for better readability. For instance, in the PropBank annotation scheme,

---

[1] http://tatoeba.org/eng/

[2] https://code.google.com/archive/p/berkeleyaligner/

[3] https://code.google.com/archive/p/whatswrong/

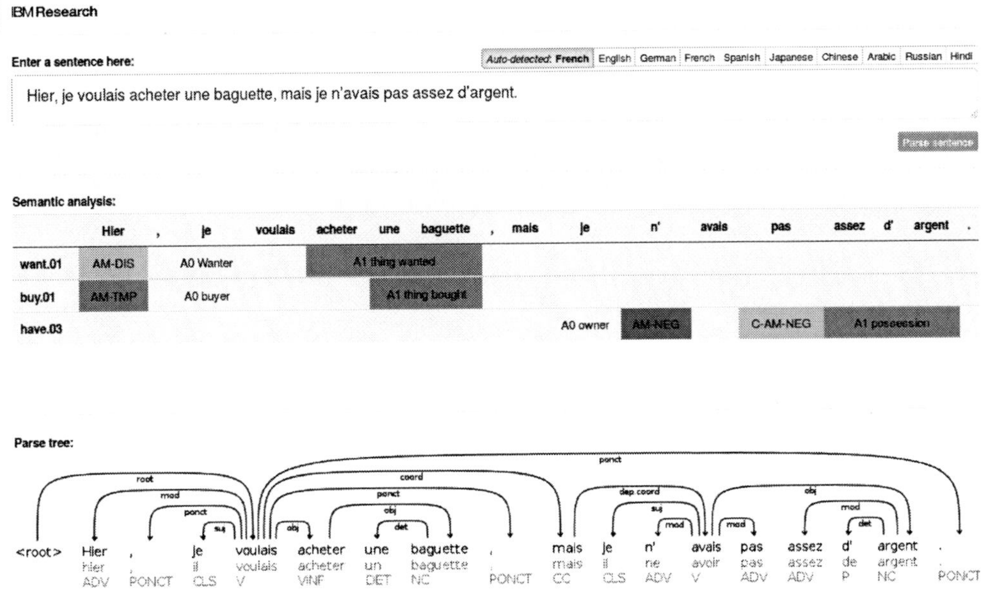

Figure 5: POLYGLOT's Web UI with a French example sentence.

the *agents* of the three frames in the example (the *wanter*, the *buyer* and the *owner*) are all annotated with the same role (**A0**). They are thus highlighted in the same yellow color in the visualization. This allows a user to quickly gauge whether the semantic analysis of the sentence is correct[4].

6 Demonstration and Outlook

We present POLYGLOT as a hands-on demo where users can enter sentences and request shallow semantic analyses. We also plan to make it publicly accessible in the future. We are currently working on improving the annotation projection approach to generate higher quality data by experimenting with further constraints, language-specific heuristics and improved frame mappings. We are particularly interested in how far English Proposition Bank labels are suitable for arbitrary target languages and may serve as basis of a "universal semantic role labeling" framework: we are qualitatively analysing auto-generated PropBanks in comparison to manual efforts; meanwhile, we are evaluating POLYGLOT in downstream applications such as multilingual IE. Through the presentation of POLYGLOT, we hope to engage the research community in this discussion.

---

[4]The example sentence in Figure 5 contains one error: The word "*hier*" (engl. "*yesterday*") should be labeled **AM-TMP** instead of **AM-DIS**. All other labels are correct.

References

Alan Akbik, Laura Chiticariu, Marina Danilevsky, Yunyao Li, Shivakumar Vaithyanathan, and Huaiyu Zhu. 2015. Generating high quality proposition banks for multilingual semantic role labeling. In *ACL 2015, 53rd Annual Meeting of the Association for Computational Linguistics Beijing, China*, page to appear.

Rajesh Bhatt, Bhuvana Narasimhan, Martha Palmer, Owen Rambow, Dipti Misra Sharma, and Fei Xia. 2009. A multi-representational and multi-layered treebank for hindi/urdu. In *Proceedings of the Third Linguistic Annotation Workshop*, pages 186–189. Association for Computational Linguistics.

Anders Björkelund, Love Hafdell, and Pierre Nugues. 2009. Multilingual semantic role labeling. In *Proceedings of the Thirteenth CoNLL: Shared Task*, pages 43–48, Boulder, Colorado, June. Association for Computational Linguistics.

Anders Björkelund, Bernd Bohnet, Love Hafdell, and Pierre Nugues. 2010. A high-performance syntactic and semantic dependency parser. In *Proceedings of the 23rd International Conference on Computational Linguistics: Demonstrations*, pages 33–36. Association for Computational Linguistics.

Bernd Bohnet and Joakim Nivre. 2012. A transition-based system for joint part-of-speech tagging and labeled non-projective dependency parsing. In *Proceedings of the 2012 EMNLP-CoNLL*, pages 1455–1465. Association for Computational Linguistics.

Bernd Bohnet. 2010. Very high accuracy and fast dependency parsing is not a contradiction. In *Proceedings of the 23rd COLING*, pages 89–97. Association for Computational Linguistics.

Ondřej Bojar, Vojtěch Diatka, Pavel Rychlỳ, Pavel Straňák, Vít Suchomel, Aleš Tamchyna, Daniel Zeman, et al. 2014. Hindencorp–hindi-english and hindi-only corpus for machine translation. In *Proceedings of the Ninth LREC*.

Thorsten Brants. 2000. Tnt: a statistical part-of-speech tagger. In *Proceedings of the sixth conference on Applied natural language processing*, pages 224–231. Association for Computational Linguistics.

Jinho D. Choi and Andrew McCallum. 2013. Transition-based dependency parsing with selectional branching. In *Proceedings of the 51st Annual Meeting of the Association for Computational Linguistics*.

Marie-Catherine De Marneffe, Timothy Dozat, Natalia Silveira, Katri Haverinen, Filip Ginter, Joakim Nivre, and Christopher D Manning. 2014. Universal stanford dependencies: A cross-linguistic typology. In *LREC*, volume 14, pages 4585–4592.

Anthony Fader, Stephen Soderland, and Oren Etzioni. 2011. Identifying relations for open information extraction. In *Proceedings of the Conference on Empirical Methods in Natural Language Processing*, pages 1535–1545. Association for Computational Linguistics.

Spence Green and Christopher D Manning. 2010. Better arabic parsing: Baselines, evaluations, and analysis. In *Proceedings of the 23rd COLING*, pages 394–402. Association for Computational Linguistics.

Jan Hajič, Massimiliano Ciaramita, Richard Johansson, Daisuke Kawahara, Maria Antònia Martí, Lluís Màrquez, Adam Meyers, Joakim Nivre, Sebastian Padó, Jan Štěpánek, et al. 2009. The conll-2009 shared task: Syntactic and semantic dependencies in multiple languages. In *Proceedings of the Thirteenth CoNLL: Shared Task*, pages 1–18. Association for Computational Linguistics.

Shereen Khoja and Roger Garside. 1999. Stemming arabic text. *Lancaster, UK, Computing Department, Lancaster University*.

Philipp Koehn. 2005. Europarl: A parallel corpus for statistical machine translation. In *MT summit*, volume 5, pages 79–86.

Pierre Lison and Jörg Tiedemann. 2016. Opensubtitles2016: Extracting large parallel corpora from movie and tv subtitles.

Christopher D. Manning, Mihai Surdeanu, John Bauer, Jenny Finkel, Steven J. Bethard, and David McClosky. 2014. The Stanford CoreNLP natural language processing toolkit. In *Association for Computational Linguistics (ACL) System Demonstrations*, pages 55–60.

Umar Maqsud, Sebastian Arnold, Michael Hülfenhaus, and Alan Akbik. 2014. Nerdle: Topic-specific question answering using wikia seeds. In *COLING (Demos)*, pages 81–85.

Joakim Nivre, Johan Hall, and Jens Nilsson. 2006. Maltparser: A data-driven parser-generator for dependency parsing. In *Proceedings of LREC*, volume 6, pages 2216–2219.

Joakim Nivre. 2015. Towards a universal grammar for natural language processing. In *Computational Linguistics and Intelligent Text Processing*, pages 3–16. Springer.

Sebastian Padó and Mirella Lapata. 2009. Crosslingual annotation projection for semantic roles. *Journal of Artificial Intelligence Research*, 36(1):307–340.

Martha Palmer, Daniel Gildea, and Paul Kingsbury. 2005. The proposition bank: An annotated corpus of semantic roles. *Computational linguistics*, 31(1):71–106.

Alexandre Rafalovitch, Robert Dale, et al. 2009. United nations general assembly resolutions: A six-language parallel corpus. In *Proceedings of the MT Summit*, volume 12, pages 292–299.

Helmut Schmid. 1994. Probabilistic part-of-speech tagging using decision trees. In *Proceedings of the international conference on new methods in language processing*, volume 12, pages 44–49. Citeseer.

Dan Shen and Mirella Lapata. 2007. Using semantic roles to improve question answering. In *EMNLP-CoNLL*, pages 12–21.

Jörg Tiedemann. 2012. Parallel data, tools and interfaces in opus. In *Proceedings of LREC, MAY 21-27, 2012, Istanbul, Turkey*, pages 2214–2218.

Lonneke Van der Plas, Paola Merlo, and James Henderson. 2011. Scaling up automatic cross-lingual semantic role annotation. In *Proceedings of the 49th Annual Meeting of the Association for Computational Linguistics: Human Language Technologies: short papers-Volume 2*, pages 299–304. Association for Computational Linguistics.

Nianwen Xue and Martha Palmer. 2005. Automatic semantic role labeling for chinese verbs. In *IJCAI*, volume 5, pages 1160–1165. Citeseer.

Online Information Retrieval for Language Learning

Maria Chinkina   **Madeeswaran Kannan**   **Detmar Meurers**

Universität Tübingen
LEAD Graduate School
Department of Linguistics
{mchnkina,mkannan,dm}@sfs.uni-tuebingen.de

Abstract

The reading material used in a language learning classroom should ideally be rich in terms of the grammatical constructions and vocabulary to be taught and in line with the learner's interests. We developed an online Information Retrieval system that helps teachers search for texts appropriate in form, content, and reading level. It identifies the 87 grammatical constructions spelled out in the official English language curriculum of schools in Baden-Württemberg, Germany. The tool incorporates a classical efficient algorithm for reranking the results by assigning weights to selected constructions and prioritizing the documents containing them. Supplemented by an interactive visualization module, it allows for a multifaceted presentation and analysis of the retrieved documents.

1   Introduction

The learner's exposure to a language influences their acquisition of it. The importance of *input* in second language (L2) learning has been repeatedly emphasized by the proponents of major Second Language Acquisition theories (Krashen, 1977; Gass and Varonis, 1994; Swain, 1985), with psycholinguists highlighting the significance of frequency and perceptual salience of target constructions (e.g., Slobin, 1985).

In line with this research, a pedagogical approach of input flood (Trahey and White, 1993) is extensively used by L2 teachers. However, manually searching for linguistically rich reading material takes a lot of time and effort. As a result, teachers often make use of easily accessible schoolbook texts. However, this limits the choice of texts, and they are typically less up-to-date and less in line with students' interests than authentic texts. In the same vein, a survey conducted by Purcell et al. (2012) revealed that teachers expect their students to use online search engines in a typical research assignment with a very high probability of 94%, compared to the 18% usage of printed or electronic textbooks.

With this in mind, we developed an online Information Retrieval (IR) system that uses efficient algorithms to retrieve, annotate and rerank web documents based on the grammatical constructions they contain. The paper presents *FLAIR*[1] (Form-Focused Linguistically Aware Information Retrieval), a tool that provides a balance of content and form in the search for appropriate reading material.

2   Overview and Architecture

The *FLAIR* pipeline can be broadly reduced to four primary operations – Web Search, Text Crawling, Parsing and Ranking. As demonstrated by the diagram in Figure 1, the first three operations are delegated to the server as they require the most resources. Ranking, however, is performed locally on the client endpoint to reduce latency.

Web Crawling

We chose to use Microsoft Bing[2] as our primary search engine given its readily available Java bindings. By default, the top 20 results are fetched for any given search query. A basic filter is applied to exclude web documents with low text content. The search is conducted repeatedly until the resulting list of documents contains at least 20 items.

---

[1]The online tool is accessible at: http://purl.org/icall/flair

[2]http://bing.com

Proceedings of the 54th Annual Meeting of the Association for Computational Linguistics—System Demonstrations, pages 7–12,
Berlin, Germany, August 7-12, 2016. ©2016 Association for Computational Linguistics

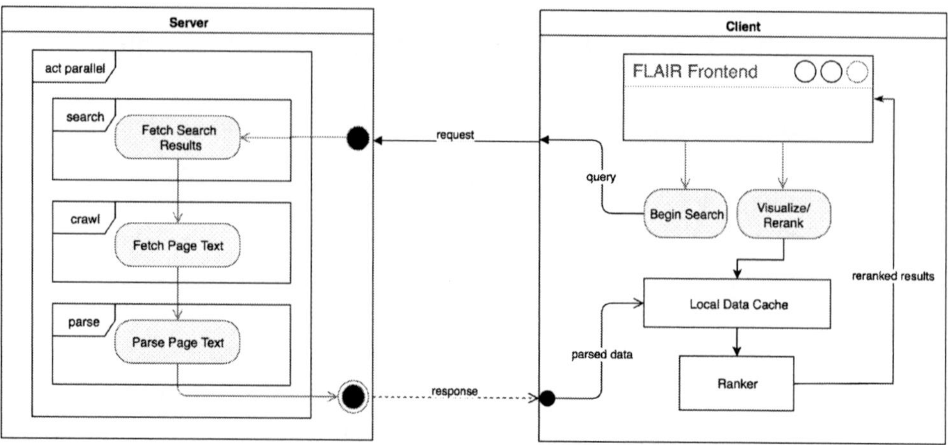

Figure 1: FLAIR architecture.

Text Extraction

The Text Extractor makes use of the Boilerpipe library[3] extracting plain text with the help of its DefaultExtractor. The choice is motivated by the high performance of the library as compared to other text extraction techniques (Kohlschütter et al., 2010).

Parsing

Text parsing is facilitated by the Stanford CoreNLP library[4] (Manning et al., 2014), which was chosen for its robust, performant and open-source implementation. Our initial prototype used the standard PCFG parser for constituent parsing, but its cubic time complexity was a significant issue when parsing texts with long sentences. We therefore switched to a shift-reduce implementation[5] that scales linearly with sentence and parse length. While it resulted in a higher memory overhead due to its large language models, it allowed us to substantially improve the performance of our code.

Ranking

The final stage of the pipeline involves ranking the results according to a number of grammatical constructions and syntactic properties. Each parameter can be assigned a specific weight that then affects its ranking relative to the other parameters. The parsed data is cached locally on the client side for each session. This allows us to perform the ranking calculations on the local computer, thereby avoid a server request-response roundtrip for each re-ranking operation.

We chose the classical IR algorithm BM25 (Robertson and Walker, 1994) as the basis for our ranking model. It helps to avoid the dominance of one single grammatical construction over the others and is independent of the normalization unit as it uses a ratio of the document length to the average document length in the collection. The final score of each document determines its place in the ranking and is calculated as:

$$G(q,d) = \sum_{t \in q \cap d} \frac{(k+1) \times tf_{t,d}}{tf_{t,d} + k \times (1 - b + b \times \frac{|d|}{avdl})} \times log\frac{N+1}{df_t}$$

where q is a *FLAIR query* containing one or more linguistic forms, t is a linguistic form, d is a document, $tf_{t,d}$ is the number of occurrences of t in d, $|d|$ is document length, $avdl$ is the average document length in the collection, df_t is the number of documents containing t, and k is a free parameter set to 1.7. The free parameter b specifies the importance of the document length. The functionality of the tool allows the user to adjust the importance of the document length with a slider that assigns a value from 0 to 1 to the parameter b.

2.1 Technical Implementation

FLAIR is written in Java and implemented as a Java EE web application. The core architecture revolves around a client-server implementation that

---

[3]`https://code.google.com/p/boilerpipe/`
[4]`http://nlp.stanford.edu/software/`
`corenlp.shtml`
[5]`http://nlp.stanford.edu/software/`
`srparser.shtml`

uses WebSocket (Fette and Melnikov, 2011) and Ajax (Garrett and others, 2005) technologies for full-duplex, responsive communication. All server operations are performed in parallel, and each operation is divided into subtasks that are executed asynchronously. Operations initiated by the client are dispatched as asynchronous messages to the server. The client then waits for a response from the latter, which are relayed as rudimentary push messages encoded in JSON.[6] By using WebSockets to implement the server endpoint, we were able to reduce most of the overhead associated with HTTP responses.

The sequence of operations performed within the *client* boundary is described as follows:

1. Send search query to server and initiate web search

2. Wait for completion signal from server

3. Initiate text parsing

4. Wait for completion signal from server

5. Request parsed data from server

6. Cache parsed data

7. Re-rank results according to parameters

The sequence of operations performed within the *server* boundary is described as follows:

1. Receive search query from client

2. Begin web search operation:

   (a) Fetch top N valid search results
   (b) For each search result, fetch page text
   (c) Signal completion

3. Wait for request from client

4. Begin text parsing operation:

   (a) For each valid search result, parse text and collate data
   (b) Signal completion

5. Wait for request from client

6. Send parsed data to client

---

3 FLAIR Interface

The main layout consists of four elements – a settings panel, a search field, a list of results, and a reading interface, where the identified target constructions are highlighted. The interactive visualization incorporates the technique of parallel coordinates used for visualizing multivariate data (Inselberg and Dimsdale, 1991).

The visualization provides an overview of the distribution of the selected linguistic characteristics in the set of retrieved documents. Vertical axes represent parameters – linguistic forms, number of sentences, number of words and the readability score, and each polyline stands for a document having certain linguistic characteristics and thus, going through different points on the parameter axes. The interactive design allows for more control over a user-selected set of linguistic characteristics. Users can select a range of values for one or more constructions to precisely identify and retrieve documents.

Figures 2 and 3 demonstrate *FLAIR* in use: The user has entered the query *Germany* and selected *Past Perfect* and *Present Perfect* as target constructions. After reranking the 20 retrieved documents, the interactive visualization was used to select only the documents with a non-zero frequency of both constructions.

4 Detection of Linguistic Forms

We based our choice of the 87 linguistic forms on the official school curriculum for English in the state of Baden-Württemberg, Germany.[7] As most of the linguistic structures listed there do not have a one-to-one mapping to the standard output of NLP tools, we used a rule-based approach to approximate them.

For closed word classes, string matching (e.g., *articles*) or look-up lists (e.g, *prepositions*) can be used to differentiate between their forms. However, detection of some grammatical constructions and syntactic structures requires a deeper syntactic analysis. Identification of the degrees of comparison of *long adjectives* requires keeping track of two consequent tokens and their POS tags, as is the case with the construction *used to* that cannot be simply matched (cf. the passive *"It is used to build rockets"*). More challenging structures, such

---

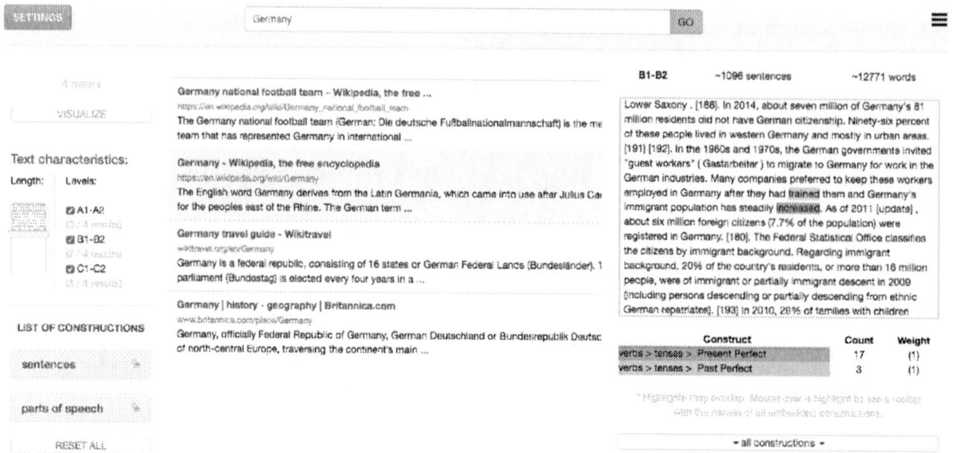

Figure 2: *FLAIR* interface: the settings panel, the list of results and the reading interface.

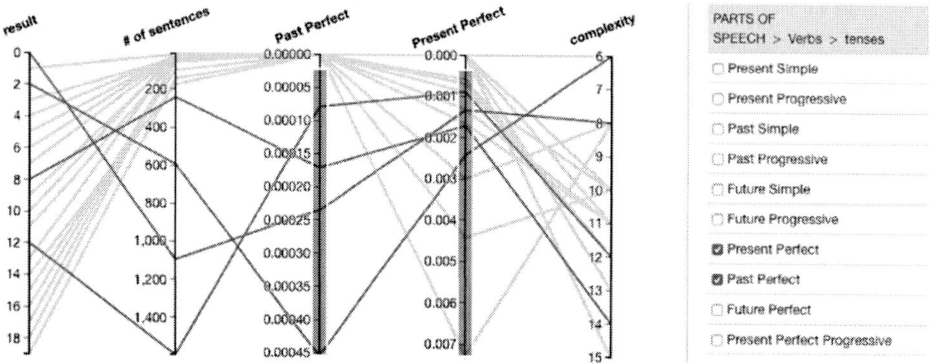

Figure 3: The visualization component of *FLAIR*. Vertical axes correspond to text characteristics and the lines going through the axes represent documents.

as *real* and *unreal conditionals* and different grammatical *tenses*, are identified by means of complex patterns and additional constraints. For a more elaborate discussion of the detection of linguistic forms, the pilot evaluation and the use cases, see Chinkina and Meurers (2016).

5 Performance Evaluation

Parallelization of the tool allowed us to reduce the overall processing time by at least a factor of 25 (e.g., 35 seconds compared to 15 minutes for top 20 results). However, due to the highly parallel nature of the system, its performance is largely dependent on the hardware on which it is deployed. Amongst the different operations performed by the pipeline, web crawling and text annotation prove to be the most time-consuming and resource-intensive tasks. Web crawling is an I/O task that is contingent on external factors such as remote network resources and bandwidth, thereby making it a potential bottleneck and also an unreliable target for profiling. We conducted several searches and calculated the relative time each operation took. It took around 50-65% of the total time (from entering the query till displaying a list of results) to fetch the results and extract the documents and around 20-30% of the total time to parse them.

The Stanford parser is responsible for text annotation operations, and its shift-reduce constituent parser offers best-in-class performance and accuracy.[8] We analyzed the performance of the parser on the constructions that our tool depends on for the detection of linguistic patterns. Among the

---

[8]See `http://nlp.stanford.edu/software/srparser.shtml`

biggest challenges were *gerunds* that got annotated as either nouns (*NN*) or gerunds/present participles (*VBG*). *Phrasal verbs*, such as *settle in*, also appeared to be problematic for the parser and were sometimes not presented as a single entity in the list of dependencies.

The *FLAIR* light-weight algorithm for detecting linguistic forms builds upon the results of the Stanford parser while adding negligible overhead. To evaluate it, we collected nine news articles with the average length of 39 sentences by submitting three search queries and saving the top three results for each of them. We then annotated all sentences for the 87 grammatical constructions and compared the results to the system output. Table 1 provides the precision, recall, and F-measure for selected linguistic forms identified by *FLAIR*[9].

Linguistic target	Prec.	Rec.	F_1
Yes/no questions	1.00	1.00	1.00
Irregular verbs	1.00	0.96	0.98
used to	0.83	1.00	0.91
Phrasal verbs	1.00	0.61	0.76
Tenses (Present Simple, ...)	0.95	0.84	0.88
Conditionals (real, unreal)	0.65	0.83	0.73
Mean (81 targets)	0.94	0.90	0.91
Median (81 targets)	1.00	0.97	0.95

Table 1: Evaluating the FLAIR algorithm

As the numbers show, some constructions are easily detectable (plural irregular noun forms, e.g., *children*) while others cannot be reliably identified by the parser (conditionals). The reasons for a low performance are many-fold: the ambiguity of a construction (*real conditionals*), the unreliable output of the text extractor module (*simple sentences*) or the Stanford Parser (*-ing verb forms*), and the *FLAIR* parser module itself (*unreal conditionals*). Given the decent F-scores and our goal of covering the whole curriculum, we include all constructions into the final system – independent of their F-score. As for the effectiveness of the tool ina real-life setting, full user studies with language teachers and learners are necessary for a proper evaluation of distinctive components of *FLAIR* (see Section 7).

---

6 Related Work

While most of the state-of-the-art IR systems designed for language teachers and learners implement a text complexity module, they differ in how they treat vocabulary and grammar. Vocabulary models are built using either word lists (*LAWSE* by Ott and Meurers, 2011) or the data from learner models (*REAP* by Brown and Eskenazi, 2004). Grammar is given little to no attention: Bennöhr (2005) takes into account the complexity of different conjunctions in her *TextFinder* algorithm.

Distinguishing features of *FLAIR* aimed at making it usable in a real-life setting are that (i) it covers the full range of grammatical forms and categories specified in the official English curriculum for German schools, and (ii) its parallel processing model allows to efficiently retrieve, annotate and rerank 20 web documents in a matter of seconds.

7 Conclusion and Outlook

The paper presented *FLAIR* – an Information Retrieval system that uses state-of-the-art NLP tools and algorithms to maximize the number of specific linguistic forms in the top retrieved texts. It supports language teachers in their search for appropriate reading material in the following way:

- A parsing algorithm detects the 87 linguistic constructions spelled out in the official curriculum for the English language.

- Parallel processing allows to fetch and parse several documents at the same time, making the system efficient for real-life use.

- The responsive design of *FLAIR* ensures a seamless interaction with the system.

The tool offers input enrichment of online materials. In a broader context of computer-assisted language learning, it can be used to support input enhancement (e.g., *WERTi* by Meurers et al., 2010) and exercise generation (e.g., *Language Muse*[SM] by Burstein et al., 2012).

Recent work includes the integration of the Academic Word List (Coxhead, 2000) to estimate the register of documents on-the-fly and rerank them accordingly. The option of searching for and highlighting the occurrences of words from customized vocabulary lists has also been implemented. In addition to the already available length and readability filters, we are working on the options to constrain the search space by including support for i) search restricted to specific web domains and data sets, such as Project Gutenberg[10] or news pages, and ii) search through one's own data set. We also plan to implement and test more sophisticated text readability formulas (Vajjala and Meurers, 2014) and extend our information retrieval algorithm. Finally, a pilot online user study targeting language teachers is the first step we are taking to empirically evaluate the efficacy of the tool.

On the technical side, *FLAIR* was built from the ground up to be easily scalable and extensible. Our implementation taps the parallelizability of text parsing and distributes the task homogenously over any given hardware. While *FLAIR* presently supports the English language exclusively, its architecture enables us to add support for more languages and grammatical constructions with a minimal amount of work.

Acknowledgments

This research was funded by the LEAD Graduate School [GSC1028], a project of the Excellence Initiative of the German federal and state governments. Maria Chinkina is a doctoral student at the LEAD Graduate School.

We would also like to thank the language teachers at Fachsprachzentrum Tübingen for trying out the tool and providing valuable feedback.

References

Jasmine Bennöhr. 2005. A web-based personalised textfinder for language learners. Master's thesis, University of Edinburgh.

Jonathan Brown and Maxine Eskenazi. 2004. Retrieval of authentic documents for reader-specific lexical practice. In *InSTIL/ICALL Symposium 2004*.

Maria Chinkina and Detmar Meurers. 2016. Linguistically-aware information retrieval: Providing input enrichment for second language learners. In *Proceedings of the 11th Workshop on Innovative Use of NLP for Building Educational Applications*, San Diego, CA.

Averil Coxhead. 2000. A new academic word list. *TESOL quarterly*, 34(2):213–238.

Ian Fette and Alexey Melnikov. 2011. The websocket protocol.

Jesse James Garrett et al. 2005. Ajax: A new approach to web applications.

Susan M Gass and Evangeline Marlos Varonis. 1994. Input, interaction, and second language production. *Studies in second language acquisition*, 16(03):283–302.

Alfred Inselberg and Bernard Dimsdale. 1991. Parallel coordinates. In *Human-Machine Interactive Systems*, pages 199–233. Springer.

Christian Kohlschütter, Peter Fankhauser, and Wolfgang Nejdl. 2010. Boilerplate detection using shallow text features. In *Proceedings of the third ACM international conference on Web search and data mining*, pages 441–450. ACM.

Stephen Krashen. 1977. Some issues relating to the monitor model. *On Tesol*, 77(144-158).

Christopher D. Manning, Mihai Surdeanu, John Bauer, Jenny Finkel, Steven J. Bethard, and David McClosky. 2014. The Stanford CoreNLP natural language processing toolkit. In *Proceedings of 52nd Annual Meeting of the Association for Computational Linguistics: System Demonstrations*, pages 55–60.

Niels Ott and Detmar Meurers. 2011. Information retrieval for education: Making search engines language aware. *Themes in Science and Technology Education*, 3(1-2):pp–9.

Kristen Purcell, Lee Rainie, Alan Heaps, Judy Buchanan, Linda Friedrich, Amanda Jacklin, Clara Chen, and Kathryn Zickuhr. 2012. How teens do research in the digital world. *Pew Internet & American Life Project*.

Stephen E Robertson and Steve Walker. 1994. Some simple effective approximations to the 2-poisson model for probabilistic weighted retrieval. In *Proceedings of the 17th annual international ACM SIGIR conference on Research and development in information retrieval*, pages 232–241.

Dan I Slobin. 1985. Crosslinguistic evidence for the language-making capacity. *The crosslinguistic study of language acquisition*, 2:1157–1256.

Merrill Swain. 1985. Communicative competence: Some roles of comprehensible input and comprehensible output in its development. *Input in second language acquisition*, 15:165–179.

Martha Trahey and Lydia White. 1993. Positive evidence and preemption in the second language classroom. *Studies in second language acquisition*, 15(02):181–204.

Sowmya Vajjala and Detmar Meurers. 2014. Assessing the relative reading level of sentence pairs for text simplification. In *Proceedings of the 14th Conference of the European Chapter of the Association for Computational Linguistics (EACL-14)*, Gothenburg, Sweden. Association for Computational Linguistics.

---

[10]http://gutenberg.org

`TermSuite`: Terminology Extraction with Term Variant Detection

Damien Cram
LINA - UMR CNRS 6241
Université de Nantes, France
`damien.cram@univ-nantes.fr`

Béatrice Daille
LINA - UMR CNRS 6241
Université de Nantes, France
`beatrice.daille@univ-nantes.fr`

Abstract

We introduce, `TermSuite`, a JAVA and UIMA-based toolkit to build terminologies from corpora. `TermSuite` follows the classic two steps of terminology extraction tools, the identification of term candidates and their ranking, but implements new features. It is multilingually designed, scalable, and handles term variants. We focus on the main components: UIMA Tokens Regex for defining term and variant patterns over word annotations, and the grouping component for clustering terms and variants that works both at morphological and syntactic levels.

1 Introduction

Terminologies play a central role in any NLP applications such as information retrieval, information extraction, or ontology acquisition. A terminology is a coherent set of terms that constitutes the vocabulary of a domain. It also reflects the conceptual system of that domain. A term could be a single term (SWT), such as *rotor*, or a complex term. Complex terms are either compounds such as *broadband*, or multi-word terms (MWT) such as *frequency band*. Terms are functional classes of lexical items used in discourse, and as such they are subjected to linguistic variations such as modification or coordination.

As specialized domains are poorly covered by general dictionaries, Term Extraction Tools (TET) that extract terminology from corpora have been developed since the early nineties. This first generation of TET (Cabré et al., 2001) was monolingually designed, not scalable, and they were not handling term variants, except for ACABIT (Daille, 2001) and FASTR (Jacquemin, 2001).

This last question has always been a pain in the neck for TET.

The current generation of TET improves on various aspects. As an example, TermoStat[1] deals with several Romance languages, reaches to treat text up to 30 megabytes, and proposes a first structuring based on lexical inclusion. `TermSuite` goes a step forward: it is multilingually designed, scalable, and handles term variants. It is able to perform term extraction from languages that behave differently from the linguistic point of view. Complex terms in languages such as German and Russian are mostly compounds, while in Roman languages they are MWT. `TermSuite` extracts single terms and any kind of complex terms. For some generic domains and some applications, large amounts of data have to be processed. `TermSuite` is scalable and has been applied to corpora of 1.1 gigabytes using a personal computer configuration. Finally, `TermSuite` identifies a broad range of term variants, from spelling to syntactic variants that may be used to structure the extracted terminology with various conceptual relations.

Since the first `TermSuite` release (Rocheteau and Daille, 2011), several enhancements about TET have been made. We developed UIMA Tokens Regex, a tool to define term and variant patterns using word annotations within the UIMA framework (Ferrucci and Lally, 2004) and a grouping tool to cluster terms and variants. Both tools are designed to treat in an uniform way all linguistic kinds of complex terms.

After a brief reminder of `TermSuite` general architecture, we present its term spotting tool UIMA Tokens Regex, its variant grouping tool, and the variant specifications we design for English, French, Spanish, German, and Russian. Fi-

---

[1] `http://termostat.ling.umontreal.ca/`

13

Proceedings of the 54th Annual Meeting of the Association for Computational Linguistics—System Demonstrations, pages 13–18,
Berlin, Germany, August 7-12, 2016. ©2016 Association for Computational Linguistics

nally, we provide some figures and considerations about `TermSuite` resources and behaviour.

2 `TermSuite` architecture

TET are dedicated to compute the termhood and the unithood of a term candidate (Kageura and Umino, 1996). Two steps make up the core of the terminology extraction process (Pazienza et al., 2005):

1. Spotting: Identification and collection of term-like units in the texts, mostly a subset of nominal phrases;

2. Filtering and sorting: Filtering of the extracted term-like units that may not be terms, syntactically or terminologically; Sorting of the term candidates according to their unithood, their terminological degree and their most interest for the target application.

`TermSuite` adopts these two steps. Term-like units are collected with the following NLP pipeline: tokenization, POS tagging, lemmatization, stemming, splitting, and MWT spotting with UIMA Tokens Regex. They are ranked according to the most popular termhood measure. But in order to improve the term extraction process and to provide a first structuring of the term candidates, a component dedicating to term variant recognition has been added. Indeed, term variant recognition improves the outputs of term extraction: the ranking of the term candidates is more accurate and more terms are detected (Daille and Blancafort, 2013).

Figure 2 shows the output of `TermSuite` TET within the graphical interface. The main window shows the terms rank according to termhood. A term candidate may group miscellaneous term variants. When a term is highlighted, the occurrences spot by UIMA Tokens Regex are showed in the bottom window and the term features in the right window.

3 Spotting multiword terms

We design a component in charge of spotting multi-word terms and their variants in text, which is based on UIMA Tokens Regex[2], a concise and expressive language coupled with an efficient rule engine. UIMA Tokens Regex allows the user to

---

[2]`http://github.com/JuleStar/`
`uima-tokens-regex/`

define rules over a sequence of UIMA annotations, *ie.* over tokens of the corpus, each rule being in the form of a regular expression. Compared to RUTA (Kluegl et al., 2016), UIMA Tokens Regex operates only on annotations that appear sequentially, which is the case for word annotations. The occurrence recognition engine has been thus implemented as a finite-state machine with linear complexity.

3.1 Syntax

UIMA Tokens Regex syntax is formally defined by an `ANTLR`[3] grammar and inspired by `Stanford TokensRegex` (Chang and Manning, 2014).

Matchers Before defining regular expressions over annotations, each annotation needs to be atomically matchable. That is why UIMA Tokens Regex defines a syntax for *matchers*. A *matcher* can be of three types:

[*Boolean Exp*]	an expression matching the values of annotation attributes.
/*String RegExp*/	A valid Java regular expression matching against the text covered by the annotation.
The dot "."	matches any annotation.

The *Boolean Exp* within brackets is a combination of *atomic boolean expressions*, boolean operators & and ‖, and parentheses. An *atomic boolean expression* is of the form:

```
property op literal
```

Where `property` is an annotation feature defined in `TermSuite` UIMA type system, `op` is one of `==`, `!=`, `<`, `<=`, `>`, and `>=`, and `literal` is either a string, a boolean (`true` or `false`), or a number (integer or double).

Rules *Rules* are named regular expressions that are defined as follows:

```
term "rule name": TokensRegex;
```

Where *TokensRegex* is a sequence of quantified *matchers*. The quantifiers are:

?	0 or 1
$\star$	0 or several
+	at least 1
{n}	exactly n
{m, n}	between m and n

---

[3]`http://antlr.org/`

3.2 Engine

UIMA Tokens Regex engine parses the list of rules and creates for each of these rules a finite-state automaton. The engine provides automata with the sequence of UIMA annotations of the preprocessed input document. UIMA Tokens Regex engine implements the default behaviour of a regular expression engine: it is *greedy*, *backtracking*, picking out the *first alternative*, and *impatient*.

Every time an automaton (*ie.* a *rule*) matches, `TermSuite` generates a rule *occurrence* and stores the offset indexes of the matched text.

3.3 Application to terminology extraction

Example In `TermSuite` type system, the values of the feature `category` are the part-of-speech (POS) tags. Rule an below extracts MWT composed of one or several adjectives followed by a noun.

```
term "an": [category=="adjective"]+
           [category=="noun"] ;
```

Matcher predefinition For the sake of both readability and reusability, UIMA Tokens Regex allows the user to predefine matchers. Thus, Rule an can be expressed concisely as A+ N using the matchers N and A:

```
matcher N: [category=="noun"];
matcher Vpp: [V & mood=="participle"
             & tense=="past"];
matcher A: [(Vpp | category=="adjective")
            & lemma!="same"
            & lemma!="other"];
matcher C: /^(and|or)$/;
matcher D: [category=="determiner"
          & subCategory != "possessive"];
matcher P: [category=="adposition"
          & subCategory=="preposition"];

term "an": A+ N ;
term "npn": N P D? N ;
term "acan": ~D A C A N ;
```

Rule `acan` extracts coordination variants that match the "adjective conjunction adjective noun" pattern, such as *onshore and offshore locations*. The quantifier ? expresses an optional determiner. Rule npn can extract both MWT: *energy of wind* and *energy of the wind*.

Features The annotation features available in `TermSuite` type system are `category`, `subCategory`, `lemma`, and `stem` and inflectional features such as `mood`, `tense`, or `case`.

Lexical filtering Matcher A above shows an example of lexical filtering that prohibits occurrences of the listed lemma in the pattern. For example, Rule an will not match the term candidate *same energy*.

Contextual filtering Contextual POS are preceded by *tilde* ($\sim$). Rule acan shows an example of contextual filtering. A determinant should occur for the pattern to be matched, but it will be not part of collected MWT.

4 Variant grouping

`TermSuite` is able to gather terms according to syntactic and morphological variant patterns that are defined with YAML syntax (Ben-Kiki et al., 2005).

4.1 Syntax

A variant rule states a set of conditions that two term candidates must fulfil to be paired. It consists of:

a rule name a string expression between double quotes (`"`), ended by a colon (`:`),

a source pattern and **a target pattern**, which are sequences of `matcher` labels.

a boolean expression a logical expression on source and target term features, denoted by rule. The field `rule` is interpreted by a Groovy engine and must be defined in valid Groovy syntax.

Example The example below is the simplest variant grouping rule defined for English.

```
"S-I-NN-(N|A)":
  source: N N
  target: N N N, N A N
  rule: s[0]==t[0] && s[1]==t[2]
```

This rule is named `S-I-NN-(N|A)`. It states that one term candidate (the source) must be of pattern N N, and the second term candidate (the target) of patterns N N N or N A N. The `rule` field states that the `lemma` property of $s[0]$, the first noun of the *source*, has the same lemma as $t[0]$, the first noun of the `target`. Likewise $s[1]$ and $t[2]$ must share the same lemma. For example, this variant grouping rule will be satisfied for the two terms *turbine structure* and *turbine base structure*.

Word features The `rule` field expresses conditions on word features. The two main features used for grouping are `lemma` and `stem`. `lemma` is the default one, that is why stating $s[0] == t[0]$ is equivalent to $s[0].lemma == t[0].lemma$. The rule "S-PI-NN-P" below makes use of the `stem` property. An example of grouping is *effect of rotation* and *rotational effect* where *rotational* is derived from *rotation*.

```
"S-PI-NN-P":
  source: N P N
  target: A N, N N
  rule: s[0]==t[1] && s[2].stem==t[0].stem
```

Morphological variants `TermSuite` implements Compost, a multilingual splitter (Loginova Clouet and Daille, 2014) that makes the decision as to whether the term composed of one graphic unit, is a SWT or a compound, and for compounds, it gives one or several candidate analyses ranked by their scores. We only keep the best split. The compound elements are reachable when `TermSuite` comes to apply the variant grouping rules. The syntax of YAML variant rules allows the user to express morphological variants between two terms:

```
"M-I-EN-N|A":
  source: N [compound]
  target: N N, A N
  rule: s[0][0]==t[0][0] && s[0][1] == t[1]
```

In the rule `M-I-EN-N|A` above, the tag `[compound]` after the source pattern states that the source has to be a morphosyntactic compound. In the `rule` field, we access the component features with the second index of the two-based indexing arrays, the first index referring to the POS position in the source or target patterns. As examples, this rule groups the two term candidates *windfarm* and *windmill farm*, and also *hydropower* and *hydroelectric power*.

4.2 Engine

Term variant grouping applies on term pairs with a complexity of $O(n^2)$, where n is the number of term candidates extracted by UIMA Tokens Regex. `TermSuite` copes with this issue by pre-indexing each term candidate with all its pairs of single-word lemmas. For example, the term of length 3 *offshore wind turbine* has three indexing keys: (`offshore`, `wind`), (`offshore`, `turbine`), and (`turbine`, `wind`). The grouping engine operates over all terms sharing the same indexing key, for all indexing keys. Therefore, the

	MWT	Variants
en	43	41
fr	35	37
de	20	30
es	62	40
ru	18	16

Table 1: Numbers of rules provided in `TermSuite`

$O(n^2)$ complexity applies to small subsets of term candidates, and the weight of variant grouping in the overall terminology extraction process is quite reasonable (see Section 7).

5 Language grammars

We define MWT spotting rules and variant grouping rules for the five languages supported by `TermSuite`: Fr, En, Es, De, and Ru. Table 1 shows the number of rules by languages for MWT spotting and for term variant grouping.

6 Ranking by termhood

Term candidates are ranked according to their termhood that is measured with *weirdness ratio* (WR). WR is the quotient of the relative frequency in both the domain specific corpus $\mathcal{C}$ and a general language corpus $\mathcal{G}$.

$$WR(t, \mathcal{C}) = \frac{f_{norm}(t, \mathcal{C})}{f_{norm}(t, \mathcal{G})} \qquad (1)$$

Where f_{norm} stands for the normalized frequency of a term in a given corpus, *ie.* the average number of its occurrences every 1000 words, and $\mathcal{G}$ is a general language corpus.

6.1 General language corpus

The general language corpora used for computing WR are part of the compilation of newspapers provided by CLEF 2004 (Jones et al., 2005). These corpora cover numerous and miscellaneous topics, which are useful to obtain a corpus representative of the general language. The corpora of the general language that we use to compute the frequencies of term candidates are:

Newspaper	Lang	Size	Nb words
Der Spiegel	De	$382M$	60M
Glasgow Herald	En	$302M$	28M
Agencia EFE	Es	$1.1G$	171M
Le Monde	Fr	$1.1G$	82M
Izvestia	Ru	$66M$	5.8M

6.2 WR behaviour

Figure 1 gives WR distribution on the English part of the domain-specific monolingual comparable corpora for Wind Energy[4] [EOL]. [EOL] is available for seven languages and has a minimum size of $330K$ words by language. The x-axis of Figure 1 is set to WR base-10 logarithm, hence a value of 2 means that the term candidate is a 100 times more frequent in the specific corpus C than in G.

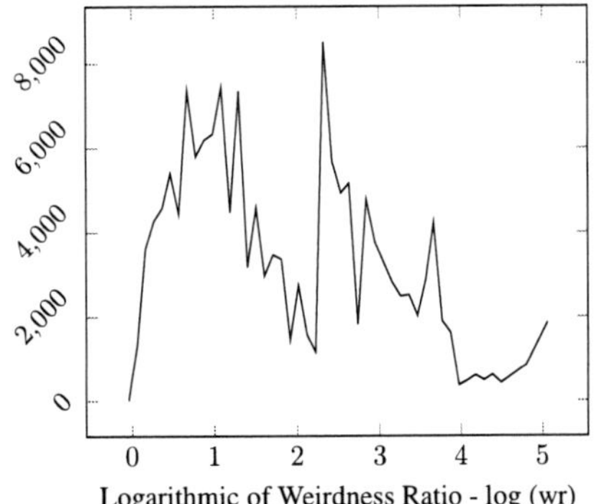

Logarithmic of Weirdness Ratio - log (wr)

Figure 1: Distribution of WR base-10 logarithm over all terms extracted by TermSuite on English [EOL].

We distinguish two sets of terms on Figure 1. The first one, starting around 0 until $log(wr) \simeq 2$, contains the terms that are not domain specific since they occur in both the specialised and the general language corpora. The second set, from the peak at $log(wr) \simeq 2$ to the upper bound, contains both the terms that appear much more frequently in C than in G and the terms that never occur in G. Actually, the first peak at $log(wr) \simeq 2$ refers to terms that occur once in C and never in G, the second lower peak refers to terms that occur twice in C and never in G, and so on.

We did not provide the distributions for other [EOL] languages nor for other corpora, because their WR distributions are similar. For all configurations, the first peak always appears at WR $\simeq 2$ and the upper bound at WR $\simeq 5$. As a result of the analysis of WR distribution, we set 2 as default value of $log(wr)$ threshold for accepting candidates as terms.

7 Performances

TermSuite operates on English [EOL] in 11 seconds with the technical configuration: Ubuntu 14.04, 16Go RAM, Intel(R) Core(TM) i7-4800MQ (4x2, 2.7Ghz). We detail the execution times of each main component with the use of two part-of-speech taggers TreeTagger[5](TT) and Mate[6]:

	TT	Mate
Tokenizer	1.3s	*idem*
POS/Lemmatiser	2.4s	81s
Stemmer	0.67s	*idem*
MWT Spotter	4.8s	*idem*
Morph. Compound Finder	0.14s	*idem*
Syntactic Term Gatherer	0.23s	*idem*
Graphical Term Gatherer	0.27s	*idem*
Total (without UIMA overheads)	9.8s	88.5s

Scalability Time complexity is linear. The processing of Agencia EFE corpus (*cf.* Section 6.1), the biggest tested so far (171 million words), takes 101 minutes to process. This performance proves a very satisfactory vertical scalability in the context of smaller domain-specific corpora. No kind of parallelism has been implemented so far, not even Java multi-threading, which is the best opportunity of optimization if an improvement of performances is required.

8 Release

TermSuite is a Java (7+) program. It can be used in three ways: the Java API, the command line API, or the graphical user interface as shown on Figure 2. Its only third-party dependency is TreeTagger, which needs to be installed separately and referenced by TermSuite configuration.

TermSuite is under licence Apache 2.0. The source code and all its components and linguistic resources are released on Github[7]. The latest released versions, currently 2.1, are available on Maven Central[8]. All links, documentation, resources, and guides about TermSuite are available on its official website:

> http://termsuite.github.io/

Acknowledgements

TermSuite development is supported by IS-TEX, French Excellence Initiative of Scientific

---

[4] http://www.lina.univ-nantes.fr/taln/maven/wind-energy.tgz

[5] http://www.cis.uni-muenchen.de/~schmid/tools/TreeTagger/

[6] https://code.google.com/p/mate-tools/

[7] https://github.com/termsuite/

[8] Maven group id is fr.univ-nantes.termsuite

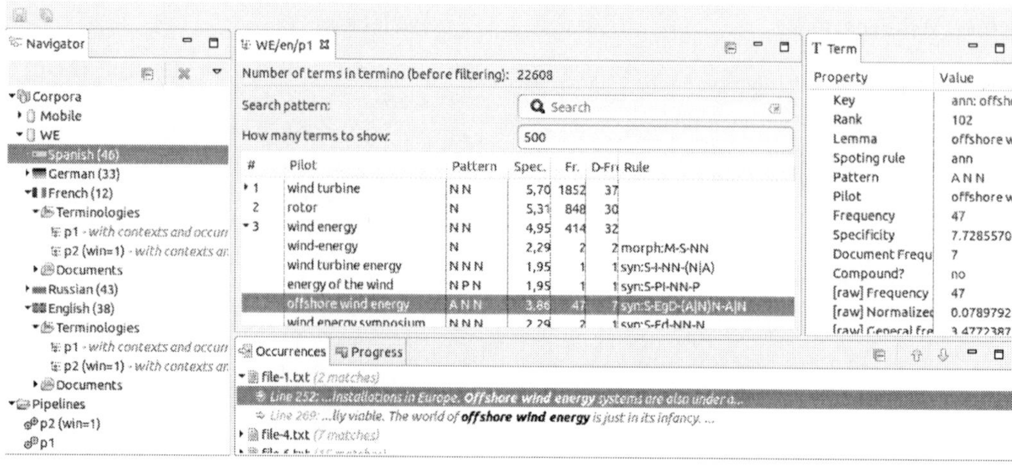

Figure 2: `TermSuite` graphical user interface

and Technical Information.

References

Oren Ben-Kiki, Clark Evans, and Brian Ingerson. 2005. Yaml ain't markup language (yaml[TM]) version 1.1. *yaml. org, Tech. Rep.*

M. Teresa Cabré, Rosa Estopà Bagot, and Jordi Vivaldi Platresi. 2001. Automatic term detection: A review of current systems. In D. Bourigault, C. Jacquemin, and M.-C. L'Homme, editors, *Recent Advances in Computational Terminology*, volume 2 of *Natural Language Processing*, pages 53–88. John Benjamins.

Angel X. Chang and Christopher D. Manning. 2014. TokensRegex: Defining cascaded regular expressions over tokens. Technical Report CSTR 2014-02, Department of Computer Science, Stanford University.

Béatrice Daille and Helena Blancafort. 2013. Knowledge-poor and knowledge-rich approaches for multilingual terminology extraction. In *Proceedings, 13th International Conference on Intelligent Text Processing and Computational Linguistics (CICLing)*, page 14p, Samos, Greece.

Béatrice Daille. 2001. Qualitative terminology extraction. In D. Bourigault, C. Jacquemin, and M.-C. L'Homme, editors, *Recent Advances in Computational Terminology*, volume 2 of *Natural Language Processing*, pages 149–166. John Benjamins.

David Ferrucci and Adam Lally. 2004. UIMA: an architectural approach to unstructured information processing in the corporate research environment. *Natural Language Engineering*, 10:327–348.

Christian Jacquemin. 2001. *Spotting and Discovering Terms through Natural Language Processing*. Cambridge: MIT Press.

Gareth J. F. Jones, Michael Burke, John Judge, Anna Khasin, Adenike Lam-Adesina, and Joachim Wagner, 2005. *Multilingual Information Access for Text, Speech and Images: 5th Workshop of the Cross-Language Evaluation Forum, CLEF 2004, Bath, UK, September 15-17, 2004, Revised Selected Papers*, chapter Dublin City University at CLEF 2004: Experiments in Monolingual, Bilingual and Multilingual Retrieval, pages 207–220. Springer Berlin Heidelberg, Berlin, Heidelberg.

Kyo Kageura and Bin Umino. 1996. Methods of automatic term recognition: a review. *Terminology*, 3(2):259–289.

Peter Kluegl, Martin Toepfer, Philip-Daniel Beck, Georg Fette, and Frank Puppe. 2016. UIMA ruta: Rapid development of rule-based information extraction applications. *Natural Language Engineering*, 22(1):1–40.

Elizaveta Loginova Clouet and Béatrice Daille. 2014. Splitting of Compound Terms in non-Prototypical Compounding Languages. In *Workshop on Computational Approaches to Compound Analysis, COLING 2014*, pages 11 – 19, Dublin, Ireland, August.

Maria Teresa Pazienza, Marco Pennacchiotti, and Fabio Massimo Zanzotto. 2005. Terminology extraction: An analysis of linguistic and statistical approaches. In S. Sirmakessis, editor, *Proceedings of the NEMIS 2004 Final Conference*, volume 185 of *Studies in Fuzziness and Soft Computing*, pages 225–279. Springer Berlin Heidelberg.

J. Rocheteau and B. Daille. 2011. TTC TermSuite - A UIMA Application for Multilingual Terminology Extraction from Comparable Corpora. In *Proceedings of the 5th International Joint Conference on Natural Language Processing (IJCNLP 2011*, Thailand, November. Asian Federation of ACL.

DeepLife: An Entity-aware Search, Analytics and Exploration Platform for Health and Life Sciences

Patrick Ernst, Amy Siu, Dragan Milchevski, Johannes Hoffart, Gerhard Weikum
Max-Planck Institute for Informatics
Campus E1 4
66123 Saarbrücken, Germany
`{pernst, siu, dmilchev, jhoffart, weikum}@mpi-inf.mpg.de`

Abstract

Despite the abundance of biomedical literature and health discussions in online communities, it is often tedious to retrieve informative contents for health-centric information needs. Users can query scholarly work in PubMed by keywords and MeSH terms, and resort to Google for everything else. This demo paper presents the DeepLife system, to overcome the limitations of existing search engines for life science and health topics. DeepLife integrates large knowledge bases and harnesses entity linking methods, to support search and exploration of scientific literature, newspaper feeds, and social media, in terms of keywords and phrases, biomedical entities, and taxonomic categories. It also provides functionality for entity-aware text analytics over health-centric contents.

1 Introduction

There is an ever-growing abundance of biomedical information and health-related contents on the Internet: scientific publications in PubMed, ontologies and knowledge bases on genes, proteins, drugs, etc., health portals like the one by the Mayo Clinic, online communities where patients and doctors discuss diseases, therapies, drug side effects, etc., and more. However, this wealth of information is in contrast to the limited support of finding relevant contents, especially when laymen search for specific topics off the mainstream or when experts want high recall on advanced topics from many sources. A typical user approach is to combine keywords with Medical Subject Headings (MeSH) terms when searching PubMed, and to use Google for everything else.

As an example, consider a user who takes asthma medication and plans to go for a 3-month trip to China including rural areas. Which vaccinations are needed, which asthma drugs are not compatible with these vaccines or other drugs that may be needed and purchased during the trip (e.g. diarrhea, sinusitis, influenza)? What is the experience of other travelers? As an example for an expert user's needs, consider a medical student who is investigating the conditions and risk factors under which Zika spreads and causes health problems.

State of the Art and its Limitations: These kinds of users face the following shortcomings of available search engines:

- *Restricted search functionality:* The search engines for PubMed or health portals like upto-date.com or mayoclinic.org support only keyword queries with some support for MeSH-like annotations, but lack query functionality that can incorporate hierarchical taxonomies and linkage with knowledge bases. Search over social media sites is even more limited.

- *Limited coverage and diversity:* Other than Google, all search engines can tap only into one kind of content: either scholarly publications or user-provided social media, but never both. The same holds for intermediate-style contents like health portals.

- *Restriction to molecular entities:* For contents about genes, proteins, pathways, etc., there are structured-data sites that come with richer query and exploration functionality. However, for entities at the level of diseases, therapies,

Proceedings of the 54th Annual Meeting of the Association for Computational Linguistics—System Demonstrations, pages 19–24,
Berlin, Germany, August 7-12, 2016. ©2016 Association for Computational Linguistics

symptoms, risk factors, etc., there are no services of this kind.

- *Lack of support for interactive exploration:* The only user-friendly support for interactive sessions is auto-completion suggestions for user queries. However, these are solely based on the query-and-click history of previous users. This has no awareness of emerging topics in the underlying contents and entity-level background knowledge.

This state of the art for health-related search is in sharp contrast with the state of the art for general-purpose search, say over daily news or general-purpose social media (e.g., discussing celebrities). Advances in recognizing and disambiguating textual mentions of named entities and the linkage to comprehensive knowledge bases like DBpedia, Freebase, Wikidata and Yago have enabled powerful and user-friendly retrieval systems. Google supports entity-centric search through transparent interlinkage with the Google Knowledge Graph; Microsoft, Facebook, etc. have similar functionalities. Academic systems such as Broccoli (Bast and Buchhold, 2013), STICS (Hoffart et al., 2014) and Semantic Scholar (Valenzuela et al., 2015) are highly expressive in their capabilities for querying and exploration, with entity-centric auto-completion suggestions and other advanced features. However, none of these covers biomedical or health contents.

Our Approach and Contribution: This paper presents a novel system, called *DeepLife*, which provides this kind of user-friendly and expressive support for health-related contents from a wide variety of sources, including scholarly publications, newspaper articles and online communities. Our approach is inspired by the STICS system (Hoffart et al., 2014). However, our content is completely different, and coping with textual mentions of biomedical entities is much harder than recognizing and disambiguating prominent people or places in news articles. This paper presents the system architecture of DeepLife, demonstrates its usefulness for various use cases, and discusses how we overcame the aforementioned limitations of prior work and the challenges regarding coverage, scale and usability.

Salient features of DeepLife include the following novelties:

- integrating large knowledge bases like the Unified Medical Language System (UMLS) and KnowLife (Ernst et al., 2015) into a search engine over a variety of health-related sources and document feeds,

- providing capabilities for search and exploration based on flexible combinations of keywords (and phrases), biomedical entities, facts, and taxonomic categories,

- supporting users by powerful auto-completion suggestions, interactive query sessions, and basic forms of entity-aware text analytics.

DeepLife is available for interactive use at `https://gate.d5.mpi-inf.mpg.de/deeplife/en-health/`.

2 Related Work

In the biomedical domain, the majority of information retrieval systems limit their scopes to PubMed scientific publications. Kim et al. (2008) only uses molecular entities for query expansion. The scopes of Textpresso (Müller et al., 2004), GoPubMed (Doms and Schroeder, 2005), FACTA+ (Tsuruoka et al., 2011), EVEX (Van Landeghem et al., 2012), Bio-TextQuest+ (Papanikolaou et al., 2014) and CRAB (Guo et al., 2014) are restricted to genes, proteins, or chemicals. MEDIE (Miyao et al., 2006) and GeneView (Thomas et al., 2012) annotate PubMed articles with various kinds of biomedical entities and events, but both systems do not offer interactive real-time exploration and analytics. Contrary to the systems aforementioned, PolySearch2 (Liu et al., 2015) goes beyond scientific publications, but its search and exploration interface is not entity-aware.

Besides scientific publications, bio-surveillance systems aggregate and analyze news articles to identify health threats, such as disease outbreaks and food hazards. HealthMap (Freifeld et al., 2008) and EpiSpider (Keller et al., 2009) rely on user created ProMED reports and do not process documents automatically. Contrary to these user-based approaches, Global Health Monitor (Don et al., 2008) and the Medical Information System (MedISys) (Rortais et al., 2010) in combination with PULS (Steinberger et al., 2008) automatically extract entities and events from relevant medical news. However, the amount of entities both systems can distinguish is limited.

Pang et al. (2015) emphasize the need for better exploratory search capabilities for health content,

Genre	Sources	Documents	Entity Occurrences	Distinct Entities
Clinical Trials	2	16,476	49,170	8,962
Encyclopedic Articles	44	11,139	405,795	16,505
News	121	76,534	3,058,111	38,295
Scientific Publications	15	19,884,225	214,531,153	453,647
Social Media	1	9,473	117,421	4,433
Total	**182**	**19,997,847**	**218,161,650**	**454,620**

Table 1: Input corpus snapshot on June 1st, 2016

but they do not consider semantic assets, like entities or a knowledge base.

3 DeepLife's Knowledge Base

Knowledge bases (KBs) store facts about entities, their properties, and the relationships between entities. A fact is a triple consisting of two entities e_1, e_2, which serve as left- and right-hand arguments of a relation R, denoted by $R(e_1, e_2)$. We augment and integrate two large knowledge bases to generate DeepLife's KB covering the entire spectrum of biomedical entities, together with an extensive type system featuring salient facts.

UMLS: As entity dictionary, we rely on the Unified Medical Language System (UMLS). UMLS is the largest collection of biomedical entities and covers 3,221,702 entities with 12,842,558 entity names. It integrates source vocabularies from different biomedical domains into a coherent structure. Due to its broad coverage, we are able to detect all kinds of entities in text, i.e. entities about diseases, anatomy, genes, treatments, etc. However, the UMLS semantic type system is shallow, i.e. it only assigns 127 types to more than 3 million entities. Therefore, we generate our own type system by automatically augmenting UMLS with type hierarchies from its source vocabularies. For each vocabulary, we compute its entity coverage in our text corpus depending on the entities' semantic types. The hierarchy of the vocabulary with the highest coverage for a particular semantic type is then used, i.e. for genes the Gene Ontology (GO) is used, for anatomical entities the Foundational Model of Anatomy (FMA) and for drugs and diseases the Medical Subject Headings (MeSH).

KnowLife: Although UMLS is rich on entities and types, it lacks cross-domain facts, i.e. relationships connecting different biomedical domains. To bridge this gap, we integrate KnowLife, a large knowledge base for health and life sciences, au-

tomatically constructed from Web sources (Ernst et al., 2015). KnowLife contains more than 500,000 of such cross-domain facts at a precision of 96% connecting different biomedical areas such as genes, diseases, anatomic parts, symptoms, treatments, as well as environmental and lifestyle risk factors for diseases. To integrate the facts into our system, we represent them as types. For all facts, $R(e_1, e_2)$, we create a new type by using the relation R and the right-hand argument e_2 as type name. For example, for all left-hand arguments e_1 appearing in facts such as $isRiskFactor(e_1, Asthma)$ we create the type $RiskFactorsforAsthma$.

Altogether, DeepLife's knowledge base covers 3.2 million entities with around 12.8 million entity names and synonyms, 64,568 custom types from source vocabularies and 136,437 fact types.

4 Entity Extraction

DeepLife has currently indexed 19,997,847 documents and extracted 218,161,650 entities from a continuous stream of 182 RSS feeds spanning five text genres. As Table 1 shows, this constantly growing and diverse corpus covers the full spectrum of biomedical information on the web. Clinical trials and scientific publications describe research findings and target professionals. DeepLife thereby includes the entire Pubmed MEDLINE collection. Encyclopaedic articles are educational resources providing insights to laymen. Social media, such as patient discussion forums, are mainly used to share experiences and to receive advice. By including news articles, our system is always up-to-date on the latest health topics, such as disease outbreaks or lifestyle information.

Entity Recognition: To process incoming articles in real-time and to stay up-to-date, our system applies an agile entity recognition method. StanfordCoreNLP is used to split sentences, tokenize words and determine part-of-speech tags. OpenNLP Chunker is used to generate an initial set of noun chunk candidates. We extend this set by applying a rule-based approach, e.g. splitting or merging prepositional phrases, conjunctions, as well as proper and common nouns. Candidates are then matched against the entity names in UMLS using string-similarity, giving preference to the longest possible matching chunk. To efficiently handle the large dictionary and volume of candidates, we use our own method which is based on

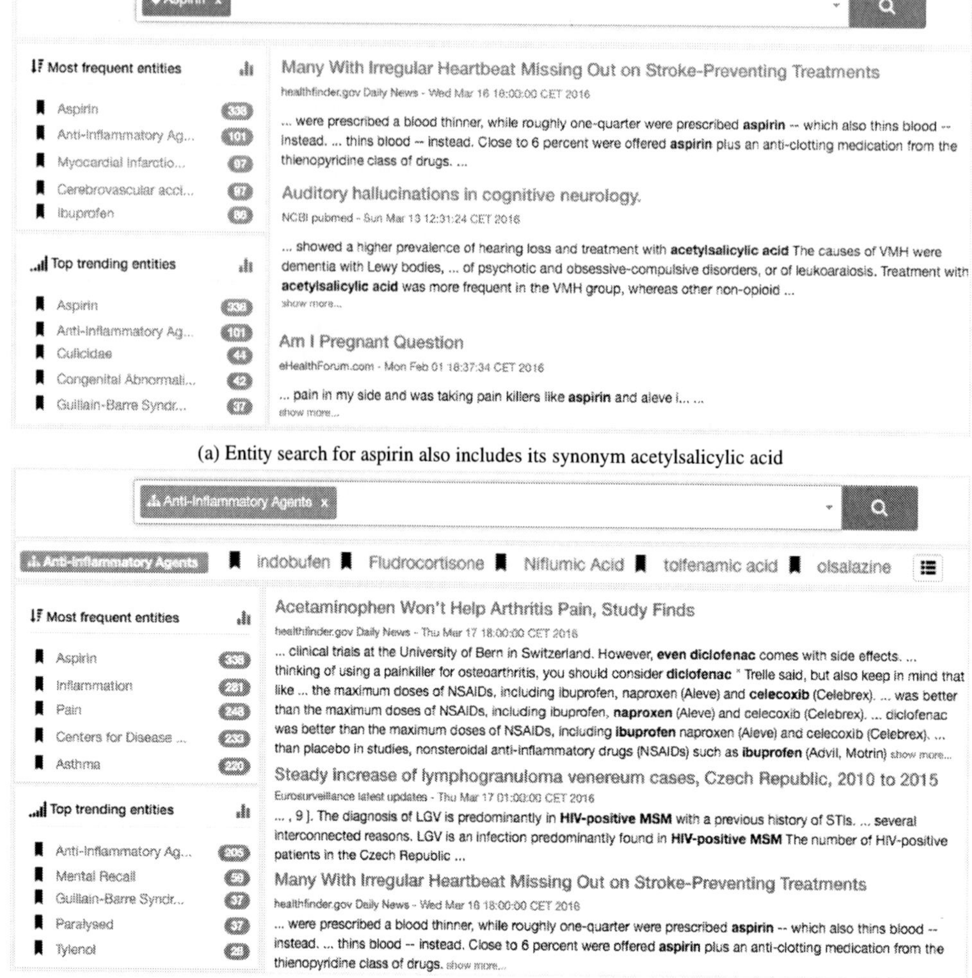

(a) Entity search for aspirin also includes its synonym acetylsalicylic acid

(b) Searching for anti-inflammatory agents expands to all agents in this category

Figure 1: Entity and Category Search

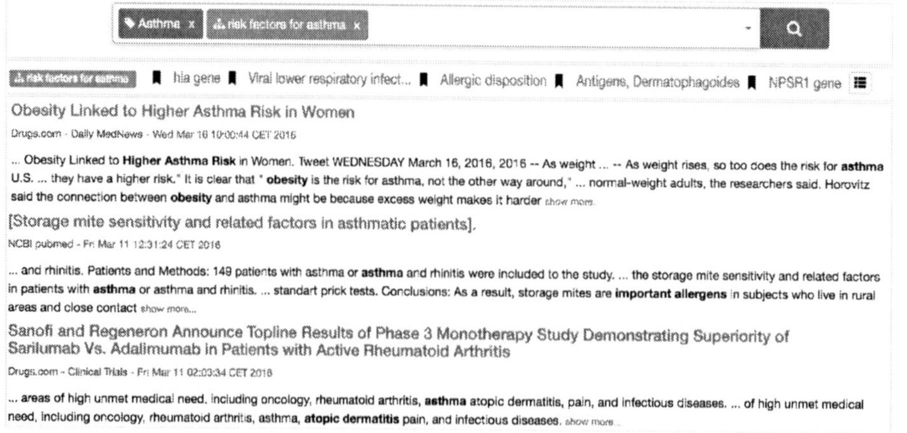

Figure 2: Combined Category and Entity Search for Asthma Risk Factors

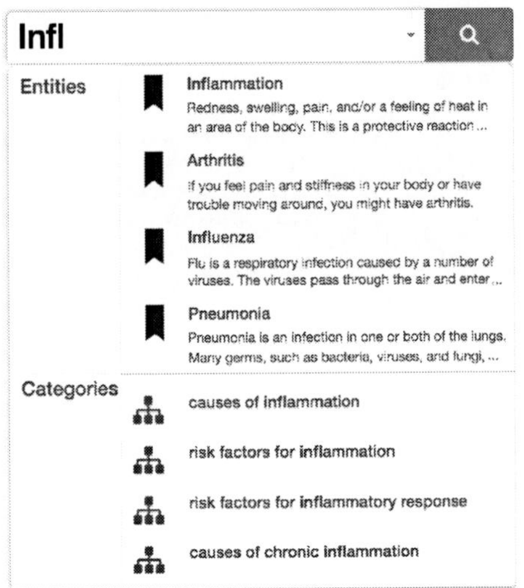

Figure 3: Entity/Category Auto-completion

locality sensitive hashing (LSH) with min-wise independent permutations (MinHash) to quickly find matching candidates (Siu et al., 2013). LSH probabilistically reduces the high-dimensional space of all character-level 3-grams, while MinHash quickly estimates the similarity between two sets of 3-grams. A successful match provides us also with the entity's semantic type.

Entity Disambiguation: The entity type information is used to disambiguate between multiple entity candidates matched to the same noun chunk in the input text. In the first filtering step, we reduce the number of entity candidates by only retaining the most specifically typed entities according to the UMLS semantic type system. Taking into account that UMLS provides a ranked list of entities for every possible name, we further disambiguate between the remaining candidates by determining the highest ranked entities. In case two entities share the same rank, we determine their popularities by the number of occurrences in different UMLS source vocabularies and prefer the more popular entity. As shown in Table 1, our system has currently extracted 218,161,650 mentions of 454,620 distinct entities.

5 Demo Scenarios

Entities are at the core of our system. Combining them with facts and types from DeepLife's knowledge base enables us to realize different use cases showcasing novel features of our system.

Entity-aware Auto-completion: Formulating queries with DeepLife is user-friendly and responsive. Providing an entity auto-completion which combines prefix matching with entity popularity, the system lets users easily explore and navigate through an extensive amount of entities and categories. For a user-provided prefix, the system retrieves entity and category candidates, where any token of their name or synonyms matches the prefix. These candidates are then ranked by corpus statistics which the system constantly updates. For example, Figure 3 depicts *Arthritis* as the second suggestion, because its synonym *Joint Inflammation* matches the prefix, and because of its high prevalence in the corpus.

Entity and Category Search: The entity-based search of our system excels over traditional keyword-based search. It increases recall, since the system automatically includes all synonyms of an entity, as well as precision, since the disambiguation removes unwanted occurrences. For example, as depicted in Figure 1a, if users search for *Aspirin*, documents mentioning its synonym *Acetylsalicylic Acid* are also retrieved. An important feature of our system is the possibility to search for categories of entities. This allows users to broaden their search request to all entities of the same type, i.e. entities which share common attributes or features. For example, to search for all "aspirin like drugs" which share therapeutic properties, one can search for the category *Anti-inflammatory Agents* (see Figure 1b). The system automatically determines all entities within the category via DeepLife's type system to retrieve relevant documents. Figure 1b also highlights DeepLife's diverse set of sources. The search results cover news, publications, as well as discussions. To tap into specific sources, users can easily customize queries with search filters.

Cross-domain Combined Search: DeepLife's knowledge base empowers our system to provide an intuitive method for searching facts by combining category and entity search. This is especially useful for layman users. Consider a user who is suffering from asthma and is interested in finding all risk factors triggering the disease. In this case, using the category *Risk Factors for Asthma* generated from facts together with the entity *Asthma* as search query, the system retrieves all documents mentioning *Asthma* with its risk factors (see Figure 2). Displaying the individual risk factors (e.g. *HLA Gene, Viral Lower Respiratory Infection, etc.*) as an expansion of the category provides immediate insights and facilitates further

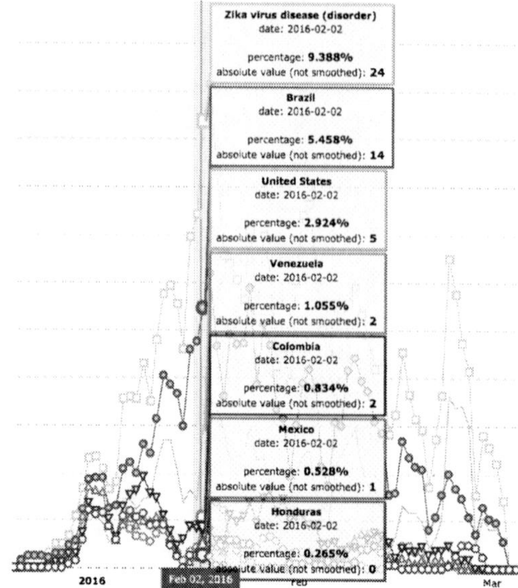

Figure 4: Countries co-occurring with Zika

exploration.

Analytics: Our system offers interactive entity-based analytics to spot trends and topic shifts. Such analyses benefit from the improved recall and precision aspects aforementioned. Statistics, based on entity occurrences in documents over time, are computed and visualized. For example in Figure 4, entity occurrences of *Zika* and related countries in our corpus (Y-Axis) are visualized over time (X-Axis). Users can zoom into specific time frames and explore documents the statistics are based on. Not only can entities be tracked individually, the analytics can also be constrained on one entity of main interest, i.e. only those documents in which this entity appears. In the same example in Figure 4, to gather insights about countries affected by the virus, the user set *Zika virus disease* as the main entity to compute analytics based on documents where Zika and a particular country were mentioned.

References

Hannah Bast and Björn Buchhold. 2013. An index for efficient semantic full-text search. In *Proc. of CIKM*. pages 369–378.

Andreas Doms and Michael Schroeder. 2005. Gopubmed: exploring pubmed with the gene ontology. *Nucleic Acids Res* 33:W783–6.

Son Don, Ai Kawazoe, and Nigel Collier. 2008. Global health monitor - a web-based system for detecting and mapping infectious diseases. In *Proc. of IJCNLP*. pages 951–956.

Patrick Ernst, Amy Siu, and Gerhard Weikum. 2015. Knowlife: a versatile approach for constructing a large knowledge graph for biomedical sciences. *BMC Bioinformatics* 16(1):1–13.

Clark Freifeld, Kenneth Mandl, Ben Reis, and John Brownstein. 2008. Healthmap: Global infectious disease monitoring through automated classification and visualization of internet media reports. *JAMIA* 15(2):150–157.

Yufan Guo, Diarmuid Ó Séaghdha, Ilona Silins, Lin Sun, Johan Högberg, Ulla Stenius, and Anna Korhonen. 2014. Crab 2.0: A text mining tool for supporting literature review in chemical cancer risk assessment. In *Proc. of COLING*. pages 76–80.

Johannes Hoffart, Dragan Milchevski, and Gerhard Weikum. 2014. Stics: Searching with strings, things, and cats. In *Proc. of SIGIR*. pages 1247–1248.

Mikaela Keller, Michael Blench, Herman Tolentino, Clark C. Freifeld, Kenneth D. Mandl, and Abla Mawudeku et al. 2009. Use of unstructured event-based reports for global infectious disease surveillance. *Emerging Infectious Disease Journal* 15(5):689.

Jung-jae Kim, Piotr Pezik, and Dietrich Rebholz-Schuhmann. 2008. Medevi: Retrieving textual evidence of relations between biomedical concepts from medline. *Bioinformatics* 24(11):1410–1412.

Yifeng Liu, Yongjie Liang, and David Wishart. 2015. Polysearch2: a significantly improved text-mining system for discovering associations between human diseases, genes, drugs, metabolites, toxins and more. *Nucleic Acids Research* 43(W1):W535–W542.

Yusuke Miyao, Tomoko Ohta, Katsuya Masuda, Yoshimasa Tsuruoka, Kazuhiro Yoshida, Takashi Ninomiya, and Jun'ichi Tsujii. 2006. Semantic retrieval for the accurate identification of relational concepts in massive textbases. In *Proc. of ACL*. pages 1017–1024.

Hans-Michael Müller, Eimear E Kenny, and Paul W Sternberg. 2004. Textpresso: An ontology-based information retrieval and extraction system for biological literature. *PLoS Biol* 2(11).

Patrick CI Pang, Karin Verspoor, Jon Pearce, and Shanton Chang. 2015. Better health explorer: Designing for health information seekers. In *Proc. of OZCHI*. pages 588–597.

Nikolas Papanikolaou, Georgios A. Pavlopoulos, Evangelos Pafilis, Theodosios Theodosiou, Reinhard Schneider, and Venkata P. et al. Satagopam. 2014. Biotextquest+: a knowledge integration platform for literature mining and concept discovery. *Bioinformatics* 30(22):3249–3256.

Agnès Rortais, Jenya Belyaeva, Monica Gemo, Erik van der Goot, and Jens Linge. 2010. Medisys: An early-warning system for the detection of (re-)emerging food- and feed-borne hazards. *Food Research Internat.* 43(5):1553–1556.

Amy Siu, Dat Ba Nguyen, and Gerhard Weikum. 2013. Fast entity recognition in biomedical text. In *Proc. of Workshop on Data Mining for Healthcare at KDD*.

Ralf Steinberger, Flavio Fuart, Erik van der Goot, Clive Best, Peter von Etter, and Roman Yangarber. 2008. *Text Mining from the Web for Medical Intelligence*, IOS Press, volume 19.

Philippe Thomas, Johannes Starlinger, Alexander Vowinkel, Sebastian Arzt, and Ulf Leser. 2012. Geneview: a comprehensive semantic search engine for pubmed. *Nucleic Acids Research* 40(W1):W585–W591.

Yoshimasa Tsuruoka, Makoto Miwa, Kaisei Hamamoto, Jun'ichi Tsujii, and Sophia Ananiadou. 2011. Discovering and visualizing indirect associations between biomedical concepts. *Bioinformatics* 27(13):i111–i119.

Marco Valenzuela, Vu Ha, and Oren Etzioni. 2015. Identifying meaningful citations. In *Proc. of the Workshop on Scholarly Big Data at AAAI*.

Sofie Van Landeghem, Kai Hakala, Samuel Rönnqvist, Tapio Salakoski, Yves Van de Peer, and Filip Ginter. 2012. Exploring biomolecular literature with evex: Connecting genes through events, homology, and indirect associations. *Advances in Bioinformatics* 2012:12.

Visualizing and Curating Knowledge Graphs
over Time and Space

Tong Ge[1], Yafang Wang[1]*, Gerard de Melo[2], Haofeng Li[1], Baoquan Chen[1]
[1]Shandong University, China; [2]Tsinghua University, China

Abstract

Publicly available knowledge repositories, such as Wikipedia and Freebase, benefit significantly from volunteers, whose contributions ensure that the knowledge keeps expanding and is kept up-to-date and accurate. User interactions are often limited to hypertext, tabular, or graph visualization interfaces. For spatio-temporal information, however, other interaction paradigms may be better-suited. We present an integrated system that combines crowdsourcing, automatic or semi-automatic knowledge harvesting from text, and visual analytics. It enables users to analyze large quantities of structured data and unstructured textual data from a spatio-temporal perspective and gain deep insights that are not easily observed in individual facts.

1 Introduction

There has been an unprecedented growth of publicly available knowledge repositories such as the Open Directory, Wikipedia, Freebase, etc. Many additional knowledge bases and knowledge graphs are built upon these, including DBpedia, YAGO, and Google's Knowledge Graph. Such repositories benefit significantly from human volunteers, whose contributions ensure that the knowledge keeps expanding and is kept up-to-date and accurate.

Despite the massive growth of such structured data, user interactions are often limited to simple browsing interfaces, showing encyclopedic text with hyperlinks, tabular listings, or graph visualizations. Sometimes, however, users may seek a spatio-temporal perspective of such knowledge. Given that the spatio-temporal dimensions are fundamental with respect to both the physical world and human cognition, they constitute more than just a particular facet of human knowledge. Of course, there has been ample previous work on spatio-temporal visualization. However, most previous work either deals with social media (Ardon et al., 2013) rather than knowledge repositories, or focuses on geo-located entities such as buildings, cities, and so on (Hoffart et al., 2011a).

From a data analytics perspective, however, much other knowledge can also be analyzed spatio-temporally. For example, given a person like Napoleon or a disease such as the Bubonic Plague, we may wish to explore relevant geographical distributions. This notion of spatio-temporal analytics goes beyond simple geolocation and time metadata.

In fact, the relevant spatio-temporal cues may need to be extracted from text. Unfortunately, accurate spatio-temporal extraction is also a challenging task (Wang et al., 2011b). Most existing information extraction tools neglect spatio-temporal information and tend to produce very noisy extractions.

It appears that the best strategy is to put the human in the loop by combining knowledge harvesting with methods to refine the extractions, similar to YALI (Wang et al., 2013), a browser plug-in that calls AIDA (Hoffart et al., 2011b) for named entity recognition and disambiguation (NERD) in a real-time manner. That system transparently collects user feedback to gather statistics on name-entity pairs and implicit training data for improving N-ERD accuracy.

Overall, we observe that there is a need for more sophisticated spatio-temporal knowledge analytics frameworks with advanced knowledge harvesting and knowledge visualization support. In this paper, we present an integrated system to achieve these goals, enabling users to analyze large amounts of structured and unstructured textual data and gain deeper insights that are not easily observed in individual facts.

The corresponding author:yafang.wang@sdu.edu.cn

Proceedings of the 54th Annual Meeting of the Association for Computational Linguistics—System Demonstrations, pages 25–30,
Berlin, Germany, August 7-12, 2016. ©2016 Association for Computational Linguistics

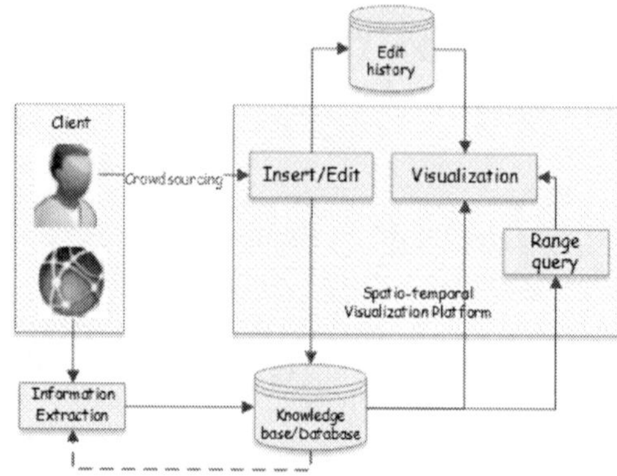

Figure 1: System architecture

2   Architecture

Figure 1 depicts the overall architecture of our system. Spatio-temporal events come from three different sources: crowdsourcing, information extraction, and existing knowledge repositories. Our system provides users with interfaces to enter textual information, videos, and images of events. The crowdsourced events are used as seed facts to extract additional spatio-temporal event information from the Internet. We describe this in more detail in Section 3. The extracted spatio-temporal facts are stored in the knowledge base. Both the crowdsourced facts and the extracted facts are presented visually in the visualization platform. Users can browse as well as edit the event information. Finally, the system comes pre-loaded with events taken from the Web of Data, particularly the YAGO (Suchanek et al., 2007) knowledge base, which contains events from different categories that serve as seed data for the platform.

The system maintains the edit history for every event, allowing users to revert any previous modification. Moreover, users' personal activity logs are also captured and are available for browsing.

Relevant spatio-temporal events are simultaneously visualized with a map and on a timeline. A heat-map is added as the top layer of the map to reflect the distribution and frequency of events. There is also a streaming graph and line chart visualization enabling the user to analyze events based on their frequency. These may allow the user to discover salient correlations.

System Implementation.   Our system is implemented in Java, with Apache Tomcat[1] as the Web server. While parsing text documents, we rely on OpenNLP[2] for part-of-speech tagging, lemmatizing verbs, and stemming nouns. All data are stored in a PostgreSQL[3] database. The maps used in our system are based on OpenStreetMap[4].

3   Spatio-Temporal Knowledge Harvesting

Spatio-Temporal Facts.   Crowdsourcing is just one way to populate the spatio-temporal knowledge in our system. Additional facts are semi-automatically mined from the Web using information extraction techniques. We build on previous work that has developed methods for extracting temporal facts (Wang et al., 2011a), but extend this line of work to also procure spatial facts.

Our aim is to extract spatio-temporal factual knowledge from free text. A fact here consists of a relation and two arguments, as well as optional temporal and spatial attributes. For instance, the spatio-temporal fact

playsForClub(Beckham; Real_Madrid)
@<[2003,2008);Spain>

expresses that Beckham played for Real Madrid from 2003 to 2007 in Spain. Temporal attributes involve either a time interval or a time point, indicating that the fact applies to a specific time period or just a given point in time, respectively. Spatial attributes are described in terms of a disambiguated location name entity. For example, "Georgia" often refers to the country in Europe, but may also refer to the state with the same name in the US. Thus, we use disambiguated entity identifiers.

Pattern Analysis.   The extraction process starts with a set of seed facts for a given relation. For example, *playsForClub*(Beckham; Real_Madrid)@<[2003,2008);Spain> would be a valid seed fact for the *playsForClub* relation. The input text is processed to construct a pattern-fact graph. Named entities are recognized and disambiguated using AIDA (Hoffart et al., 2011b). When a pair of entities matches a seed fact, the surface string between the two entities is lifted to a pattern. This is constructed by replacing the entities with

---

[1] http://tomcat.apache.org/
[2] http://opennlp.apache.org/
[3] http://www.postgresql.org/
[4] https://www.openstreetmap.org/

26

placeholders marked with their types, and keeping only canonical lemmatized forms of nouns and verbs as well as the last preposition. We use n-gram based feature vectors to describe the patterns (Wang et al., 2011a).

For example, given a sentence such as "Ronaldo signed for Milan from Real Madrid.", Milan is disambiguated as A.C._Milan. The corresponding pattern for leaving Real Madrid is "sign for $\langle$club$\rangle$ from". Each pattern is evaluated by investigating how frequent the pattern occurs with seed facts of a particular relation. The normalized value (between 0 and 1) is assigned as the initial value for each pattern, for the *fact extraction* stage.

Fact Candidate Gathering. Entity pairs that match patterns whose strength is above a minimum threshold become fact candidates and are fed into the *fact extraction* stage of label propagation. Temporal and spatial expressions occurring within a window of k words in the sentence are considered as the temporal or spatial attribute of the fact candidate (Wang et al., 2011a). These fact candidates may have both temporal and spatial attributes simultaneously.

Fact Extraction. Building on (Wang et al., 2011a), we utilize Label Propagation (Talukdar and Crammer, 2009) to determine the relation and observation type expressed by each pattern. We create a graph $G = (V_F \cup V_P, E)$ with one vertex $v \in V_F$ for each fact candidate observed in the text and one vertex $v \in V_P$ for each pattern. Edges between V_F and V_P are introduced whenever a fact candidate appeared with a pattern. Their weight is derived from the co-occurrence frequency. Edges among V_P nodes have weights derived from the n-gram overlap of the patterns.

Let $\mathcal{L}$ be the set of labels, consisting of the relation names plus a special dummy label to capture noise. Further, let $\mathbf{Y} \in \mathbb{R}_+^{|\mathcal{V}| \times |\mathcal{L}|}$ denote the graph's initial label assignment, and $\widehat{\mathbf{Y}} \in \mathbb{R}_+^{|\mathcal{V}| \times |\mathcal{L}|}$ stand for the estimated labels of all vertices, $\mathbf{S}_l$ encode the seeds' weights on its diagonal, and $\mathbf{R}_{*l}$ be a matrix of zeroes except for a column for the dummy label. Then, the objective function is:

$$\mathcal{L}(\widehat{\mathbf{Y}}) = \sum_\ell \left[\begin{array}{c} (\mathbf{Y}_{*\ell} - \widehat{\mathbf{Y}}_{*\ell})^T \mathbf{S}_\ell (\mathbf{Y}_{*\ell} - \widehat{\mathbf{Y}}_{*\ell}) \\ + \mu_1 \widehat{\mathbf{Y}}_{*\ell}^T \mathbf{L} \widehat{\mathbf{Y}}_{*\ell} + \mu_2 \|\widehat{\mathbf{Y}}_{*\ell} - \mathbf{R}_{*\ell}\|^2 \end{array} \right] \tag{1}$$

Figure 2 shows an example of a pattern-fact

graph. Existing events in the database serve as seeds in the graph. For instance, *playsForClub*(David_Beckham, LA_Galaxy)@US is a seed fact in the example, which will propagate the label `playsForClub` to other nodes in the graph. After optimizing the objective, the fact candidates which bear a relation's label with weight above a threshold are accepted as new facts (Wang et al., 2011a). These facts, which may include temporal or spatial or both kinds of attributes, are stored in the database with provenance information, and can subsequently be used in several kinds of visualizations.

4 Data Visualization and Analytics

Our system enables several different forms of visual analytics, as illustrated in Figure 3, which combines several different screenshots of the system.

Spatio-Temporal Range Queries. Users may issue range queries for both temporal and spatial knowledge. In Figure 3, Screenshots 1, 3, and 4 show results of temporal range queries, while Screenshot 5 shows the result of a spatial range query. After choosing a particular span on the timeline at the bottom, the events relevant for the selected time interval are displayed both on a temporal axis and on the map. A heat-map visualizes the frequency of events with respect to their geographical distribution. Users may also scroll the timeline to look at different events. The events shown on the map dynamically change when the scrollbar is moved. In Screenshot 1, we see that items on the timeline are shown with different symbols to indicate different categories of events. Screenshots 3 and 4 show results from different time intervals. If users choose a spatial range by drawing on the map, any events relevant to this geographical area during the selected time interval are retrieved. Screenshot 5 shows how the system can visualize the retrieval results using a pie chart. The area highlighted in blue is the bounding box of the polygon, as determined within Algorithm 1. The different colors in the pie chart indicate different event categories and their relative frequency.

Event Browsing and Checking. Users can either consult the events listed on the timeline by clicking on the icons, or browse the streaming graph and line chart, which show the frequency of events. When selecting an event on the timeline, a pop-up

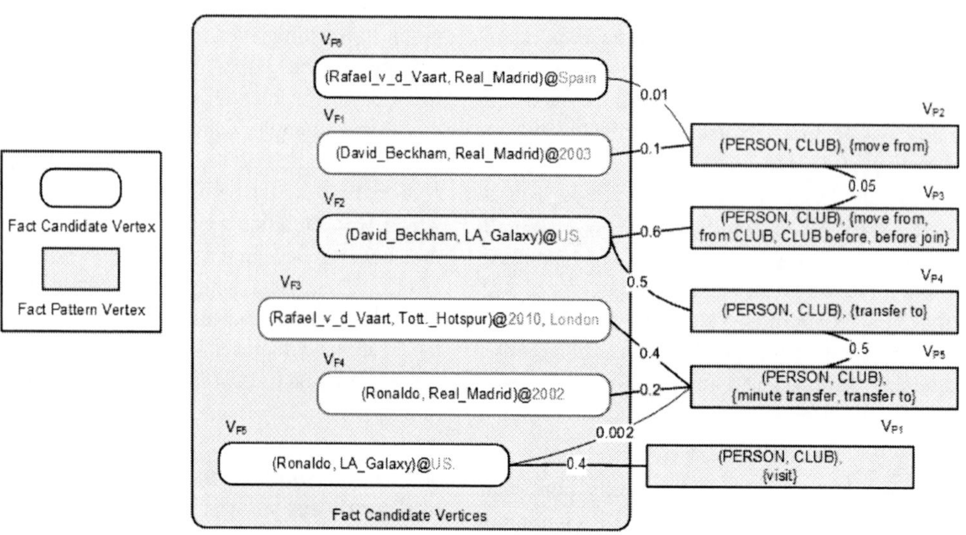

Figure 2: Spatio-temporal pattern-fact graph

Algorithm 1 Spatial range query algorithm

Input: spatial polygon on the map $\mathbf{P}$, event database E
Output: events in the polygon.

1: $min_x \leftarrow$ minimum latitude of all points of $\mathbf{P}$ ▷ Get bounding box of polygon $\mathbf{P}$
2: $max_x \leftarrow$ maximum latitude of all points of $\mathbf{P}$
3: $min_y \leftarrow$ minimum longitude of all points of $\mathbf{P}$
4: $max_y \leftarrow$ maximum longitude of all points of $\mathbf{P}$
5: $EP = \{e \in E \mid min_x \leq e.x \leq max_x \wedge min_y \leq e.y \leq max_y\}$ ▷ Query event database
6: $ED \leftarrow$ edges of polygon $\mathbf{P}$ ▷ Get edges of polygon
7: **for** each $e \in EP$ **do**
8:     $line \leftarrow (x, y; -\infty, y)$
9:     **if** e not located on the edges $\wedge$ $line$ intersects ED with even numbers **then**
10:        $EP \leftarrow EP - e$
11: **return** EP

---

window appears on top of the map near the relevant location. Normally, this window simply provides the entity label, as in Screenshot 4, while detailed information about the event is displayed in the side-bar on the left, as in Screenshot 6. However, when the user moves the cursor over the label, it expands and additional information is displayed. For an example of this, see Screenshot 3, which shows information for the "Battle of Noreia". There are also links for related videos and images. If there is no interaction with a pop-up window for an extended period of time, it is made transparent. When users move the cursor above an event on the timeline, an icon on the map pops up to provide the location and name of that event. At the same time, an icon is displayed in the histogram, which is located be-neath the timeline. With these coupled effects, the user simultaneously obtains information about both the accurate location on the map and the accurate time point within the timeline (see Screenshot 4).

Users can also scroll the map to navigate to places of interest, and observe how frequently relevant events happen in that area, as visualized with the heat-map. When the user double clicks on a location on the map, all the events pertaining to that location are shown on the left of the window. Screenshot 6 shows three events that occurred in Beijing. Further details for each event are displayed if the user clicks on them.

Our system also supports querying related events for a specific person. Screenshot 8 provides the results when querying for Napoleon, where impor-

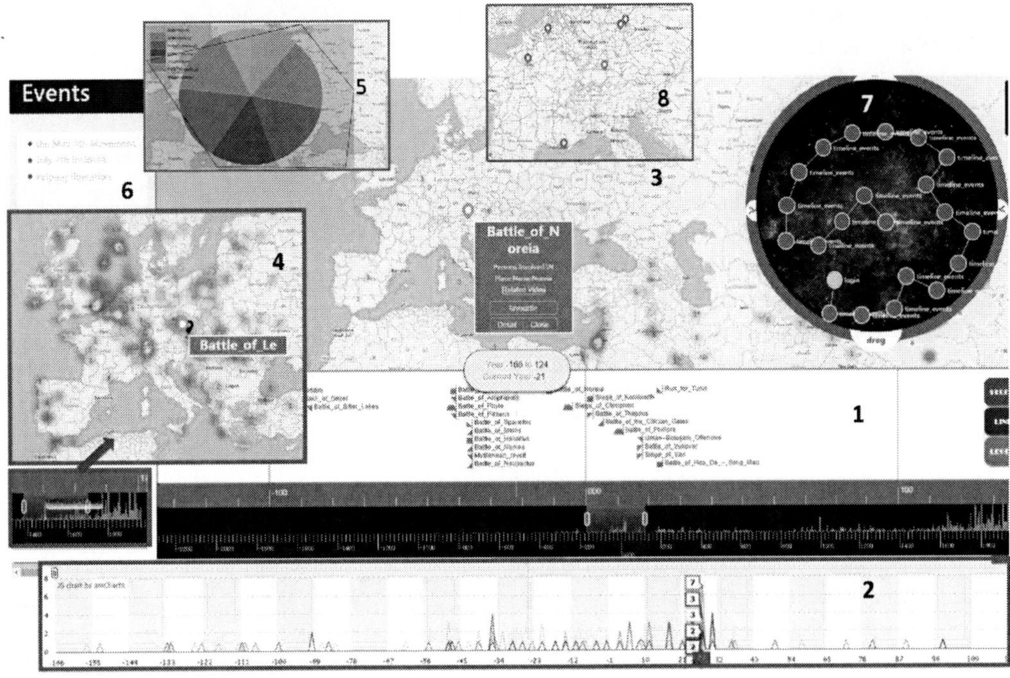

Figure 3: User interface screenshots

tant events related to Napolean are displayed on the map.

Visual Analytics. Users may use the line chart on the timeline and the heat-map to jointly inspect statistics pertaining to the retrieved events. For instance, Screenshot 2 shows the results as displayed in the line chart on the timeline. Different colors here refer to different event categories. As the user moves the time window at the bottom of the timeline, events on the timeline and maps are updated. The histogram at the bottom of the timeline shows the overall event statistics for the current state of the knowledge base. Each column refers to the number of events for a given five year interval. The heat-map changes profoundly when transitioning from Screenshot 3 to Screenshot 4, especially for Europe. The total number of events increases as well. The line chart visualization of events on the timeline[5] supports zooming in and out by adjusting the time interval. Hence, it is not necessary to initiate a new query if one wishes to drill down on particular subsets of events among the query results.

Adding/Editing Event Information. After logging into the system, users can enter or update event information. Our system provides an interface to add or edit textual information, images, and videos for events. This can be used to extend current text-based knowledge bases into multimodal ones (de Melo and Tandon, 2016).

The system further also stores the patterns from the extraction component. Hence, users can track and investigate the provenance of extracted facts in more detail. They can not only edit or remove noisy facts but also engage in a sort of debugging process to correct or remove noisy patterns. Corrected or deleted patterns and facts provide valuable feedback to the system in future extraction rounds.

After logging in, all user activities, including *queries*, *additions*, *edits*, etc. are recorded in order to facilitate navigation as well as providing for potential user analytics. For example, users may arrive at an interesting result using an entire series of operations. Then they may continue to browse the data aiming at further analyses. At some point in time, they may wish to go back to consult previously obtained results. It may be challenging to remember the exact sequence of operations that had led to a particular set of results, especially when there are many different querying conditions. The activity log addresses this by making it easy to go

---

[5]We use the line chart developed by AmCharts `www.amcharts.com/`

back to any earlier step. Screenshot 7 shows the use of a graph visualization to depict all the operations of a user after login. This same data can also be used for studying user behavior.

Furthermore, similarly to Wikipedia, the tool captures the complete edit history for a particular event. The interface for this uses a tabular form, not shown here due to space constraints. Wikipedia's edit history has seen a rich number of uses in previous research. For instance, one can study the evolution of entity types or the time of appearance of entities and their geographical distribution.

Providing Ground-Truth Data for Relation Extraction Evaluation. Our system continuously gathers ground-truth information on factual events (especially spatio-temporal facts) based on user contributions. The knowledge in our system consists of relations of interest: event *happened in* place, event *happened on* date, person *is related to* person, person *is related to* event, etc. This can serve as a growing basis for systematically evaluating and comparing different relation extraction methods and systems, going well beyond currently used benchmarks.

Historical Maps. Geographical boundaries are fluid. For instance, countries have changed and borders have evolved quite substantially during the course of history. Our system allows uploads of historical map data to reflect previous epochs. Subsequently, users can choose to have our system display available historical maps rather than the standard map layer, based on the temporal selection.

5 Conclusion

We have presented a novel integrated system that combines crowdsourcing, semi-automatic knowledge harvesting from text, and visual analytics for spatio-temporal data. Unlike previous work, the system goes beyond just showing geo-located entities on the map by enabling spatio-temporal analytics for a wide range of entities and enabling users to drill down on specific kinds of results. The system combines user contributions with spatio-temporal knowledge harvesting in order to enable large-scale data analytics across large amounts of data. Given the broad appeal of Wikipedia and similar websites, we believe that this sort of platform can serve the needs of a broad range of users, from casually interested people wishing to issue simple queries over the collected knowledge all the way to experts in digital humanities seeking novel insights via the system's advanced knowledge harvesting support.

Acknowledgments

This project was sponsored by National 973 Program (No. 2015CB352500), National Natural Science Foundation of China (No. 61503217), Shandong Provincial Natural Science Foundation of China (No. ZR2014FP002), and The Fundamental Research Funds of Shandong University (No. 2014T-B005, 2014JC001). Gerard de Melo's research is supported by China 973 Program Grants 2011C-BA00300, 2011CBA00301, and NSFC Grants 61033001, 61361136003, 61550110504.

References

Sebastien Ardon, Amitabha Bagchi, Anirban Mahanti, Amit Ruhela, Aaditeshwar Seth, Rudra Mohan Tripathy, and Sipat Triukose. 2013. Spatio-temporal and events based analysis of topic popularity in Twitter. In *CIKM*, pages 219–228.

Gerard de Melo and Niket Tandon. 2016. Seeing is believing: The quest for multimodal knowledge. *ACM SIGWEB Newsletter*, 2016(Spring).

Johannes Hoffart, Fabian M. Suchanek, Klaus Berberich, Edwin Lewis-Kelham, Gerard de Melo, and Gerhard Weikum. 2011a. YAGO2: Exploring and querying world knowledge in time, space, context, and many languages. In *WWW*.

Johannes Hoffart, Mohamed Amir Yosef, Ilaria Bordino, Hagen Fürstenau, Manfred Pinkal, Marc Spaniol, Bilyana Taneva, Stefan Thater, and Gerhard Weikum. 2011b. Robust disambiguation of named entities in text. In *EMNLP*.

Fabian M. Suchanek, Gjergji Kasneci, and Gerhard Weikum. 2007. Yago: A Core of Semantic Knowledge. In *WWW*.

Partha Pratim Talukdar and Koby Crammer. 2009. New regularized algorithms for transductive learning. In *ECML PKDD*, pages 442–457.

Yafang Wang, Bin Yang, Lizhen Qu, Marc Spaniol, and Gerhard Weikum. 2011a. Harvesting facts from textual web sources by constrained label propagation. In *CIKM*, pages 837–846.

Yafang Wang, Bin Yang, Spyros Zoupanos, Marc Spaniol, and Gerhard Weikum. 2011b. Scalable spatio-temporal knowledge harvesting. In *WWW*, pages 143–144.

Yafang Wang, Lili Jiang, Johannes Hoffart, and Gerhard Weikum. 2013. Yali: a crowdsourcing plug-in for NERD. In *SIGIR*, pages 1111–1112.

A Web-framework for ODIN Annotation

Ryan Georgi   Michael Wayne Goodman   Fei Xia

University of Washington
Seattle, WA, USA
{rgeorgi,goodmami,fxia}@uw.edu

Abstract

The current release of the ODIN (Online Database of Interlinear Text) database contains over 150,000 linguistic examples, from nearly 1,500 languages, extracted from PDFs found on the web, representing a significant source of data for language research, particularly for low-resource languages. Errors introduced during PDF-to-text conversion or poorly formatted examples can make the task of automatically analyzing the data more difficult, so we aim to clean and normalize the examples in order to maximize accuracy during analysis. In this paper we describe a system that allows users to automatically and manually correct errors in the source data in order to get the best possible analysis of the data. We also describe a RESTful service for managing collections of linguistic examples on the web. All software is distributed under an open-source license.

1   Introduction

The current release of the ODIN (Online Database of INterlinear Text) database contains over 150,000 linguistic examples in the form of interlinear glossed text (IGT), an example of which is shown in Fig. 1. These IGT instances are extracted from PDFs found on the web, representing a significant source of data for computational typology, as well as providing information for resource-poor languages (RPLs). These instances are additionally useful for inducing annotation on RPLs, as demonstrated by Georgi et al. (2014, 2015), in which the relationships between words and glosses are identified and encoded for the purpose of enriching the data with annotations not present in the original examples. However,

```
keené     ʔaksí dónq-ine-m
DEM.PLUR dog   five-DEF-ACC
'these five dogs'
```

Figure 1: An IGT instance of Aari [aiw], an Omotic language of Ethiopia. Extracted from Dryer (2007)

the PDF-to-text conversion process can introduce noise into the data, and some examples are not formatted well in the original document. These and other issues can decrease the efficacy of the automatic structural analysis.

To address these issues, we have created a web interface that combines automatic cleaning and normalization procedures with a user-friendly browser-based GUI to enable human annotators to review and improve the data quality of the available IGT instances. Additionally, as editing is meant as one of multiple capabilities of the final system, this browser interface is driven by a RESTful (Fielding, 2000) backend system that will support future interface extensions.

2   Related Work

The system we describe is not the first web-based editor of IGT, but none of the existing systems (for IGT or annotation in general) that we're aware of fit our use case. TYPECRAFT[1] (Beermann and Mihaylov, 2014) is a wiki-based collaborative IGT editor. As it directly targets IGT, the editor is designed to support tabular annotations and is a useful tool for users creating new IGT. However, it limits the kinds of annotations (morphemes, POS tags, glosses, etc.) and it is not obvious how the ODIN model (see Section 3) would fit, nor how our automated transformation scripts (see Section 4) would be integrated. The *brat*

---

[1] http://typecraft.org

Proceedings of the 54th Annual Meeting of the Association for Computational Linguistics—System Demonstrations, pages 31–36,
Berlin, Germany, August 7-12, 2016. ©2016 Association for Computational Linguistics

rapid annotation tool[2] (BRAT; Stenetorp et al., 2012), with its RESTful web API, is somewhat similar in implementation to our system, but does not seem to support tabular visualization of hierarchical annotations. The current annotation task for our users is primarily correcting errors in text extracted from PDFs, which is similar in some ways to how RECAPTCHA (Von Ahn et al., 2008) lets users provide clean transcriptions of text in images. But, unlike RECAPTCHA, our task requires some knowledge of IGT structure.

3 ODIN Data

The data that we are seeking to annotate in this paper comes from the ODIN 2.1 data release,[3] which provides the data in two formats: the plain text format, and in Xigt, an extensible format for encoding IGT (Goodman et al., 2014).

3.1 Building ODIN

The ODIN database was constructed in several steps. First, documents were retrieved using a meta-crawling approach, where queries with IGT-like search terms such as {3SG, ACC} were directed to online search engines. The resulting documents were converted to text format using an off-the-shelf PDF-to-text conversion tool. This text output was subsequently used to extract features to detect the IGT instances within the text, as well as build a language identification system. The full details of the construction of the ODIN database can be found in Lewis and Xia (2010).

3.2 Extracted Textual IGTs

The first format for representing IGT is intended to be human-readable while maintaining the appropriate metadata for processing. An example of this format can be seen in Fig. 2. This format includes the textual content of the IGT, as well as whether a line belongs to the language line (L), gloss line (G) or translation line (T) of the instance, or whether it is metadata (M). In addition, secondary tags exist for more fine-grained categorization, such as for corrupted instances (CR), language name metadata (LN), etc. Furthermore, a `doc_id` is provided for reference to the original source document, as well as line numbers referring to the lines from the `pdftotext`[4] output of the PDF document.

3.3 Xigt-encoded IGTs

The Xigt format (Goodman et al., 2014) encodes all of this information in a model that is better suited for computational work. The Xigt package provides codes for either XML or JSON, and enables standoff annotation that is capable of preserving the original text format while adding multiple annotation layers (Xia et al., 2016). This is the format used for storing additional annotation, including the syntactic enrichment found in Xia et al. (2016), as well as metadata such as annotator comments. This standoff annotation is implemented as XML elements we call *tiers* that refer back to the elements they annotate.

4 Automatic Processing

The data in ODIN was assembled using an approach that combined metacrawling for IGT-containing documents with a classifier trained to detect IGT-formatted instances (Lewis and Xia, 2010). The resulting data can look like that in Fig. 2; with a variety of corruption and non-linguistically relevant data. To speed up annotation, we run several automated cleaning and normalization steps before handing the instance off to human annotators.

4.1 Cleaning

In the first step, we attempt to clean any artifacts introduced by the PDF-to-text conversion process. First, invalid characters for XML data, such as the form feed control character U+000C, are automatically replaced with the Unicode replacement character U+FFFD. Line and character corruption are addressed next. The instance in Fig. 2 exhibits both line corruption and character corruption. For line corruption, we merge two lines of the same type (e.g., L) if they are adjacent, one or both has the corruption tag CR, and any characters in the lines line up with whitespace in the other. In this example, the 'ak' on line 875 would be combined with the rest of the text on 876 as the two lines are merged into one. The output of the cleaning process is output to a new *cleaned* Xigt tier. The cleaning process also removes blank lines (if any) and superfluous initial columns of whitespace (consistently across lines to avoid altering column alignments). Currently we do not attempt to automatically fix character corruption (e.g., when a character's diacritics are erroneously extracted as a separate character), but instead allow users to cor-

---

[2]`http://brat.nlplab.org`
[3]`http://depts.washington.edu/uwcl/odin`
[4]`http://www.foolabs.com/xpdf`

```
doc_id=1482 874 878 M+AC+LN L+CR L+SY+CR G T+DB
language: Haitian (hat)
line=874 tag=M+AC+LN:  (25) Haitian CF (Lefebvre      1998:165)
line=875 tag=L+CR    :                         ak
line=876 tag=L+SY+CR:        Jani     pale            lii/j
line=877 tag=G       :        (John speak with        he)
line=878 tag=T+DB    :        (a) 'John speaks with   him', (b) 'John speaks with    himself'
```

Figure 2: A text-format ODIN IGT instance exhibiting line corruption, character corruption, and language names and parentheticals, extracted from Heine (2001).

rect the corrupted characters (including Unicode), and we make the original PDF available to the user for consultation, if it is necessary. We are also investigating an alternative PDF extractor that more accurately extracts Unicode characters, diacritics, combined ligatures, etc.

4.2 Normalization

The second automated step we perform relates to information that is either non-linguistic or meta-linguistic in nature. In Fig. 2, such information includes the instance numbering (25), the language name (Haitian), author citation (Lefebvre), and quotation marks (on line 878). In the instance in Fig. 2, these elements have been placed on a line above the language line, which the IGT detection algorithm has tagged as non-IGT data (tag=M). Other times, this data occurs on the language line and thus instance numbering on the language line are removed with regular expressions. Other information, such as the language name or linguistic construction, are detected and placed on a separate M line. However, not all data can be reliably automatically extracted, such as the co-indexation variables i and j in line 876 which could be interpreted as being part of the word.

4.3 Enrichment

In addition to cleaning and normalizing, through the use of the INterlinear Text ENrichment Toolkit (INTENT) (Georgi, 2016; Xia et al., 2016), we automatically generate word alignments and part-of-speech tags for the different lines of IGT. Currently, this is visualized in the editor, as seen in Fig. 5, and will be able to be corrected by the annotators for subsequent tasks.

5 A RESTful IGT Server

While our immediate needs for the editor are fairly simple, we anticipate expansion for future tasks that may be required by the RiPLes (information engineering and synthesis for Resource-Poor Languages) project (Xia et al., 2016). In order to fa-

cilitate such expansion, we created the backend for the editor as a general-purpose RESTful IGT server with the HTTP methods listed in Fig. 4.

The data is stored in a custom JSON-based filesystem database so that individual IGTs can be updated without having to reserialize an entire corpus, but the database abstraction layer makes it straightforward to later add support for other databases. Through the `Accept` request header, a user may ask for either the XML or JSON serialization of the data. More information on this interface can be found at the project page at: https://github.com/xigt/sleipnir

6 Online Editing Environment

The main interface that end-users will experience at this point is the online editing environment, a screenshot of which is provided in Fig. 3. This browser-based interface allows us to invite annotators around the world to participate without needing to install Python or any of the supporting packages required to work with the Xigt-formatted ODIN data.

The interface is contained in three main panes; in Fig. 3, labels (1) and (2) mark the corpus and instance browsers, respectively, while the rest of the window is dedicated to the instance editor.

Loading an Instance   To start working on an instance, an annotator first selects the corpus from the corpus browser (1) and then the particular instance from (2). Instances that have been previously annotated are highlighted with the color of their rating, while the currently displayed instance is highlighted in cyan.

Validating an Instance as IGT   Once an instance is loaded in the editor, the annotator is presented with an interface showing only the raw text of the instance (not shown), and the rating buttons (4). Since instances in ODIN have been automatically identified, some instances may not, in fact, be IGT, or may be too corrupted to derive what the original content might have been. At this point,

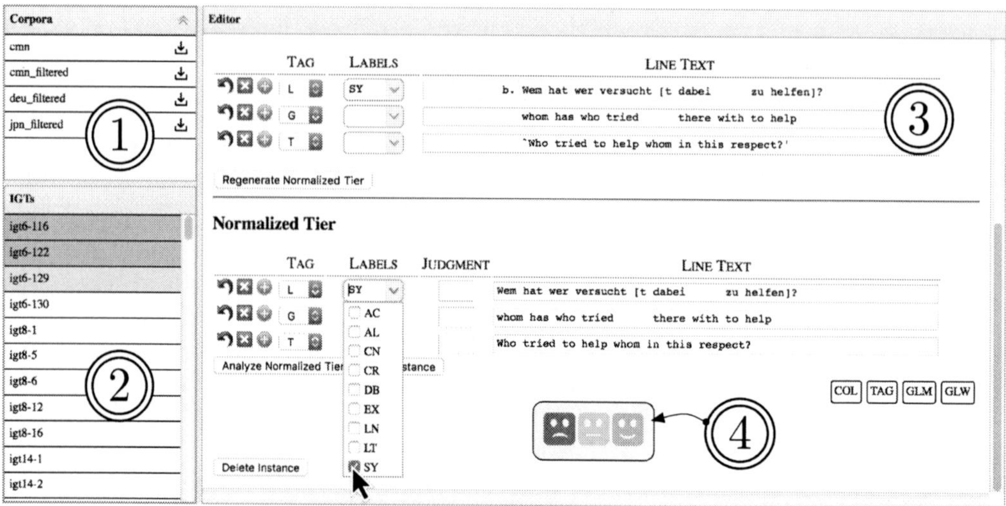

Figure 3: Screenshot of the browser-based editor being used to edit a sentence. (1) and (2) show the corpus and instance browsers, respectively, while (3) labels the instance editing area, and (4) shows the rating system.

```
GET /corpora
     retrieve list of available corpora

GET /corpora/<CID>
     retrieve a corpus by its identifier <CID>

GET /corpora/<CID>/summary
     retrieve a summary of the contents of corpus <CID>

GET /corpora/<CID>/igts
     retrieve the list of IGTs for corpus <CID> (parameters
     exist for filtering this list)

GET /corpora/<CID>/igts/<IID>
     retrieve a single IGT by its identifier <IID> from cor-
     pus <CID>

POST /corpora
     add a new corpus

POST /corpora/<CID>/igts
     add a new IGT to corpus <CID>

PUT /corpora/<CID>/igts/<IID>
     assign or replace IGT <IID> in corpus <CID>

DELETE /corpora/<CID>
     delete corpus <CID>

DELETE /corpora/<CID>/igts/<IID>
     delete IGT <IID> in corpus <CID>
```

Figure 4: HTTP methods for the IGT server, where <CID> refers to the corpus identifier and <IID> the single IGT identifier.

the annotator may click the red "bad quality" rating button to flag that instance. If the instance is IGT and of acceptable quality they may continue onto the next task.

Cleaning After the annotator has verified that an instance is valid, they may click the *Generate Cleaned Tier* button to trigger the automatic cleaning procedure described in Section 4.1. The annotator is then given an opportunity to manually correct any errors made by the automatic corruption removal. The cleaning stage only corrects errors introduced by the PDF-to-text conversion process, so for clean instances there is little to be done here. If the annotator has made a mistake or wishes to start over, they may restore the content of an item to the state after automatically cleaning, or they may regenerate the clean tier entirely by re-invoking the cleaning procedure on the raw data. The raw tier cannot be edited, so the annotator can always get back to the original representation. Once satisfied, the annotator may continue to the normalization step.

Normalization By clicking the *Generate Normalized Tier* button, the annotator triggers the normalization procedure described in Section 4.2. In addition to placing non-IGT information on M lines, annotators are also asked to correct spurious or missing whitespace, ensure that there are an equal number of language-line and gloss-line tokens, and, when possible, an equal number of morpheme or clitic boundaries denoted by '-' or '=', following the Leipzig Glossing Rules (Comrie et al., 2015). Just as with the cleaning step,

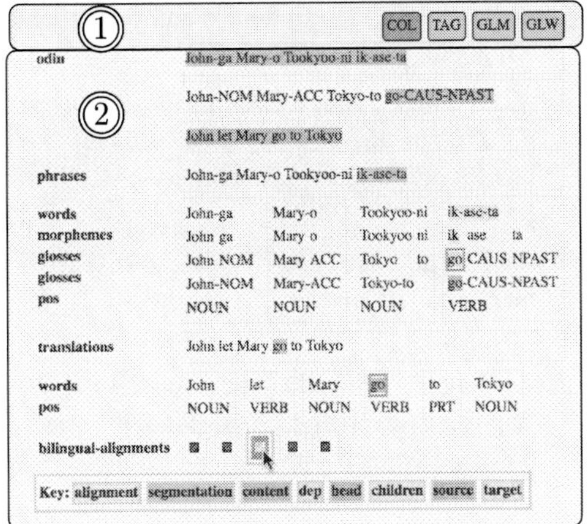

Figure 5: Normalized tier analysis, with the section labeled (1) showing the annotation indicator labels and (2) showing the enrichment and alignment information. The colors highlighted in (2) are to indicate which elements of the IGT instance are referenced by another element. Here, the alignment between the English *go* and the Japanese *ikaseta*s visualized. The titles on the left refer to the tier type represented in the Xigt representation.[6]

the annotator may restore the original normalized content of an item or regenerate the normalized tier entirely. At this point, if the annotator believes they have satisfactorily met the normalization guidelines, they are done editing and continue to the analysis step to ensure the system is able to accurately infer the IGT structure.

Analysis   When the annotator clicks the *Analyze Normalized Tier* button, the editor will present an analysis of the IGT such as the one shown in Fig. 5. This analysis includes both a series of indicators (1) to alert the annotator to the aforementioned guidelines, and a visualization of the automatic alignment and enrichment (2) performed by INTENT (see Section 4.3). The enrichment includes both the automatic word, morpheme, and gloss segmentation (**words, morphemes, glosses**, respectively), as well as word alignment between gloss and translation and part-of-speech tags for each line (**bilingual-alignments, pos**). There are currently four indicators:

COL   language and gloss tokens are aligned with whitespace into columns

TAG   language, gloss, and translation lines all ex-

ist and have no extraneous metadata on them

GLM   language and gloss lines have the same number of morphological units

GLW   language and gloss lines have the same number of whitespace-separated tokens

When an indicator shows red, the annotator should go back to the normalization (or possibly, the cleaning) step and make more corrections, then reanalyze. Occasionally an indicator shows red when there is no error; e.g., a word in the language line might have a hyphen that is not a morphological boundary and is thus glossed with a non-hyphenated token. The visualization of the automatically aligned and enriched IGT illustrates to the annotator how well the system was able to infer the structure of the IGT. Some problems that could not be detected with the indicators may become obvious by the presence of incorrect alignments, and the annotator can use this information to adjust the textual representation until proper alignments are obtained. These two facets of the analysis—indicators and visualization—help the annotator see how usable the instance will be for further processing.

Rating and Saving the Instance   Finally, if the annotator has proceeded to the normalization or analysis steps, they may choose to rate the instance as bad (red), unclean (yellow) or clean (green), depending on the level of corruption of the instance. A field is provided to add further comments that will be saved into the IGT file.

User Management   Currently, users are identified by a unique 8-character userid string, that also serves as the login. Annotator accounts are created and a backend corpus management script is used to initialize copies of corpus subsections that are assigned to the annotators. Annotators' ratings and comments are saved in these files along with their userid, so that inter-annotator agreement can be quickly and efficiently calculated across selected overlapping corpus segments.

Availability   A fully functioning demonstration of the interface containing Chinese, German, and Japanese instances may be accessed at:
`http://editor.xigt.org/user/demo`
The source code is released under the MIT license

---

[6]See Goodman et al. (2014) for more.

and is available at:
`https://github.com/xigt/yggdrasil`

7 Conclusion and Future Improvements

The system we have presented here greatly streamlines the process of refining and displaying IGT data. Such clean, electronically available IGT data can be of great use to linguists searching for examples of particular phenomena, typologists looking to compare linguistic information over the thousands of languages for which IGT data is available, and computational linguists looking to build NLP tools for resource-poor languages.

In the future, we hope to further expand the editing capabilities of the system to include giving annotators the ability to edit word alignment and POS tag data. Such annotation would provide a high-quality set of data for typological research, as well as evaluation data for the automatic enrichment methods used.

Finally, while the current system is used only for display and editing, we hope to include the ability to search over IGT corpora in a subsequent version of the tool, replacing the current ODIN search capability[7].

Acknowledgments

This work is supported by the National Science Foundation under Grant No. BCS-0748919. Any opinions, findings, and conclusions or recommendations expressed in this material are those of the authors and do not necessarily reflect the views of the NSF.

References

Dorothee Beermann and Pavel Mihaylov. 2014. TypeCraft collaborative databasing and resource sharing for linguists. *Language resources and evaluation* 48(2):203–225.

Bernard Comrie, Martin Haspelmath, and Balthasar Bickel. 2015. Leipzig glossing rules. `https://www.eva.mpg.de/lingua/pdf/Glossing-Rules.pdf`.

Matthew S Dryer. 2007. Noun phrase structure. In Timothy Shopen, editor, *Language Typology and Syntactic Description*, Language typology and syntactic description, Cambridge, United Kingdom, pages 151–205.

Roy Fielding. 2000. *Architectural Styles and the Design of Network-based Software Architecture*. Ph.D. thesis, University of California, Irvine.

Ryan Georgi. 2016. the INterlinear Text ENrichment Toolkit. `http://intent-project.info/`.

Ryan Georgi, William D Lewis, and Fei Xia. 2014. Capturing divergence in dependency trees to improve syntactic projection. *Language Resources and Evaluation* 48(4):709–739.

Ryan Georgi, Fei Xia, and William D Lewis. 2015. Enriching interlinear text using automatically constructed annotators. *LaTeCH 2015* page 58.

Michael Wayne Goodman, Joshua Crowgey, Fei Xia, and Emily M Bender. 2014. Xigt: extensible interlinear glossed text for natural language processing. *Language Resources and Evaluation* 49(2):455–485.

Bernd Heine. 2001. Accounting for creole reflexive forms. *Pidgins and Creoles Archive* (8).

William D Lewis and Fei Xia. 2010. Developing ODIN: A Multilingual Repository of Annotated Language Data for Hundreds of the World's Languages. *Literary and Linguistic Computing* 25(3):303–319.

Pontus Stenetorp, Sampo Pyysalo, Goran Topić, Tomoko Ohta, Sophia Ananiadou, and Jun'ichi Tsujii. 2012. BRAT: a web-based tool for NLP-assisted text annotation. In *Proceedings of the Demonstrations at the 13th Conference of the European Chapter of the Association for Computational Linguistics*. Association for Computational Linguistics, pages 102–107.

Luis Von Ahn, Benjamin Maurer, Colin McMillen, David Abraham, and Manuel Blum. 2008. recaptcha: Human-based character recognition via web security measures. *Science* 321(5895):1465–1468.

Fei Xia, William D Lewis, Michael Wayne Goodman, Glenn Slayden, Ryan Georgi, Joshua Crowgey, and Emily M Bender. 2016. Enriching a massively multilingual database of interlinear glossed text. *Language Resources and Evaluation* pages 1–29.

---

[7] http://odin.linguistlist.org/

Real-Time Discovery and Geospatial Visualization of Mobility and Industry Events from Large-Scale, Heterogeneous Data Streams

Leonhard Hennig*, Philippe Thomas*, Renlong Ai*, Johannes Kirschnick*, He Wang*,
Jakob Pannier†, Nora Zimmermann,† Sven Schmeier*, Feiyu Xu*, Jan Ostwald†,
Hans Uszkoreit*
*DFKI, Berlin, `firstname.lastname@dfki.de`
†DB Systel, Berlin, `firstname.lastname@deutschebahn.com`

Abstract

Monitoring mobility- and industry-relevant events is important in areas such as personal travel planning and supply chain management, but extracting events pertaining to specific companies, transit routes and locations from heterogeneous, high-volume text streams remains a significant challenge. We present *Spree*, a scalable system for real-time, automatic event extraction from social media, news and domain-specific RSS feeds. Our system is tailored to a range of mobility- and industry-related events, and processes German texts within a distributed linguistic analysis pipeline implemented in Apache Flink. The pipeline detects and disambiguates highly ambiguous domain-relevant entities, such as street names, and extracts various events with their geo-locations. Event streams are visualized on a dynamic, interactive map for monitoring and analysis.

1 Introduction

Monitoring relevant news and events is of central importance in many economic and personal decision processes, such as supplier/supply chain management, market research, and personal travel planning. Social media, news sites, but also more specialized information systems such as on-line traffic and public transport information sources, provide valuable streams of text messages that can be used to improve decision making processes. For example, a sourcing department of a company may wish to monitor world-wide news for disruptive or risk-related events pertaining to their suppliers (e.g. natural disasters, strikes, liquidity risks), while a traveler wants to be informed about traffic events related to her itinerary (e.g. delays, cancellations). We thus want to extract and recognize events from message streams that mention very specific entities, such as companies, locations, or routes. For example, from the sentence "On Friday, Amazon employees once more went on strike in the company's shipping center in Leipzig.", we would like to extract a *strike* event with arguments *time=Friday*, *organization=Amazon*, and *location=Leipzig*.

Detecting such events in textual message streams raises a number of challenges. Social media streams, such as Twitter, are of very high volume and often contain duplicated, imprecise and potentially non-trustworthy information. They are written in a very informal, not always grammatically well-formed style (Osborne et al., 2014), which cannot easily be processed with standard linguistic tools. News sites provide well-formed texts, but their content is very heterogeneous and often hard to separate from non-relevant web page elements. Both types of sources relate information about an unbounded number of topics, which means that relevant messages need to be distinguished from irrelevant data. Domain-specific information sources, on the other hand, are topic-focused, but employ a wide variety of formats, from telegraph style texts to table entries. Processing such sources hence often requires customized analysis pipelines as well as domain adaptation of existing linguistic tools. We also typically require that documents are processed in (near) real-time in order to enable timely responses to important events. Finally, utilizing domain-specific, large entity datasets raises additional challenges for named entity recognition and linking, including significantly more cross-type ambiguities (e.g. synonymous street and transport stop names) and a higher rate of ambiguous, long-tail entities (e.g., there is a "main street" or "bus route #1" in many

Proceedings of the 54th Annual Meeting of the Association for Computational Linguistics—System Demonstrations, pages 37–42,
Berlin, Germany, August 7-12, 2016. ©2016 Association for Computational Linguistics

towns).

We introduce *Spree*, a scalable platform for real-time, fine-grained event extraction and geospatial visualization (Section 2). It is designed to process German texts from social media, news, web sites and traffic information sources in a distributed, scalable, and fault-tolerant manner (Section 3). These features are realized by implementing the system's main components within the Apache Flink framework (Alexandrov et al., 2014), a big data analytics platform which provides a high through-put, streaming computing environment. Events are automatically detected and geo-located within a linguistic analysis pipeline (Section 4), and visualized for the end user in a web-based application (Section 5). The system in its current version is tailored to the mobility and supply chain domains, and allows users to monitor and analyze messages for a range of events.

2   System Overview and Architecture

The system was designed based on the following requirements:

- Combine mobility and industry data from structured knowledge resources with information from highly dynamic, unstructured or semi-structured document streams

- Identify and extract mobility and industry-related entities and events from dynamic data streams

- Enable large-scale, fault-tolerant processing of data streams in (near) real-time

- Visualize identified events on a dynamic, interactive map

Figure 1 gives an overview of the system architecture. The system separates data ingestion (crawling) from the actual processing, which facilitates the integration of new data sources. Data ingestion and processing are loosely coupled via a message queue (MQ). The streaming processing of documents encompasses three major tasks: Preprocessing of documents (including HTML-to-text conversion, boilerplating, and linguistic preprocessing), entity discovery and linking, and event extraction. Components are coupled with a shared document schema which stores annotation results. Annotated documents are persisted to a distributed index. Additional structured knowledge is stored in relational databases, and served

via REST interfaces. The user interface is implemented as a light-weight web application.

3   Data Sources

This section describes the data streams and knowledge resources that are implemented in the *Spree* system. Table 1 shows summary statistics of the data streams, and Table 2 shows summary statistics of the knowledge resources.

Data	Size
Tweets	11.5 M
News	1.2 M
RSS items	12.4 M

Table 1: Data statistics, Jan 1st – Mar 31st, 2016

Type	# Concepts	Resource
Company	112,347	Internal Dataset
City	27,075	OpenStreetMap
Street	104,598	OpenStreetMap
Station	9,860	Deutsche Bahn
Route	25,907	Deutsche Bahn

Table 2: Data statistics for knowledge resources

3.1   Data Streams

All source data streams are handled with individual crawlers, which push documents to Kafka MQ[1] for further processing by the analysis pipeline (see Section 4).

Twitter We use the Twitter Search API[2] to obtain a topically focused streaming sample of tweets. For our current system, we define the search filter using a list of approximately 150 domain-relevant users/channels and 300 search terms. Channels include e.g. airline companies, traffic information sources, and railway companies. Search terms comprise event-related keywords such as "traffic jam" or "roadworks", but also major highway names, railway route identifiers, and airport codes. This limits the number of tweets to approximately 50.000 per day, at a rate of about 35 tweets a minute.

News We retrieve news pages and general web

---

[1] kafka.apache.org
[2] dev.twitter.com/rest/public/search

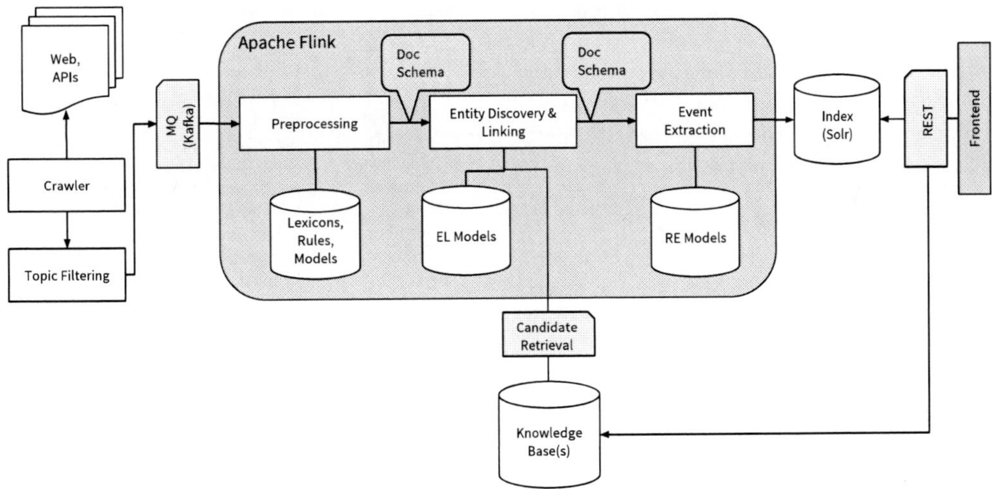

Figure 1: System architecture

sites using the uberMetrics Search API[3], which provides an interface to more than 400 million web sources that are crawled on a regular basis. The API allows us to define complex boolean search queries to filter the set of web pages that our system needs to process. We employ the same search terms as for Twitter, and limit the language to German. This provides approximately 13.200 documents per day (9/min).

RSS Feeds We implemented custom crawlers for a representative set of approximately 100 RSS feeds that provide traffic and transportation information. Feed sources include federal and state police, radio stations, and air travel sources. The feeds are fetched at regular intervals, yielding approximately 136.000 feed items per day (95/min).

3.2 Knowledge Bases

We integrate several types of knowledge resources for domain-specific named entity recognition, entity linking and event extraction. All resources are stored in a PostgreSQL relational database.

Companies We maintain a list of approx. 800K German companies, which includes many small and medium enterprises. From this list we selected a subset of 112,347 companies with ≥ 20 employees. Company entries comprise information about the company's name, judicial form, number of employees, and industry sector, and are associated with one or more postal addresses which were

geocoded using Nominatim[4]. If applicable, entries are linked to DBpedia[5] and Freebase[6].

OpenStreetMap OpenStreetMap provides data dumps[7] that we use as a knowledge resource for location names. In particular, we utilize city, town, village, highway and road data for Germany, including names and geo-shape information.

GTFS Our final resource consists of transportation data of the German railway company Deutsche Bahn AG. This dataset contains railway and public transport stops, timetables, and transit routes, and includes geographical information for each entity. The data is provided in the commonly used General Transit Feed Specification (GTFS) format[8].

4 Document Processing Pipeline

This section describes the implementation of the streaming pipeline to process documents in the *Spree* system.

4.1 Data Schema

We store analysis results of individual pipeline components in a shared document schema that is inspired by the Common Analysis Structure (CAS) approach implemented in UIMA (Ferrucci and Lally, 2004). The schema defines elements,

---

[3]`doc.ubermetrics-technologies.com/`
`api-reference/`

[4]`nominatim.openstreetmap.org`
[5]`dbpedia.org`
[6]`freebase.com`
[7]`planet.openstreetmap.org`
[8]`developers.google.com/transit/gtfs`

such as documents, sentences, tokens, concepts and relations. Annotations are either realized as attributes of these classes, or in a generic fashion using a labeled span scheme. We use Avro[9], a compact binary data format, to serialize documents between pipeline processing steps.

4.2 Stream Processing

Document processing is implemented in an analysis pipeline that is realized within the Apache Flink framework (Alexandrov et al., 2014)[10]. Flink's core is a streaming data flow engine that provides data distribution, communication, and fault tolerance for distributed computations over data streams. All document processors ingest messages (documents) from the MQ system. This architecture ensures data durability via Kafka's replication and disk persistence features, and consistent data movement and computation with Apache Flink. Together, these frameworks guarantee exactly-once delivery of events, can handle back pressure in case of data stream peaks, and provide high throughput. Our system thus can easily scale to larger and faster data streams than those we currently handle, for example when extending the system to monitor more data streams, other languages, or a wider range of events.

Our document processing implementation reads messages from Kafka and converts them to the internal document schema. For news and web sites, we extract text from the HTML and remove boilerplate code[11]. We perform language detection, and discard any non-German documents. All remaining documents are then passed to the linguistic analysis components, described next.

4.3 Linguistic Analysis

The linguistic analysis components process documents to detect and geo-locate mobility- and industry-related entities and events.

Documents are first segmented into sentences and tokens. We use the Mate Tools suite (Bohnet, 2010) to part-of-speech tag words, and for dependency parsing of sentences. For named entity recognition, we utilize SProUT (Drozdzynski et al., 2004), which implements a regular expression-like formalism and gazetteers for detecting concepts in text. SProUT uses rule sets to

Name	Arguments
Accident	Road, route, loc, time
Delay	Road, route, flight, cause, loc, time
Disaster	Type, trigger, casualties, loc, time
Traffic Jam	Road, loc, time
Rail Replacem.	Route, loc, time
Road Closure	Road, cause, loc, time
Acquisition	Buyer, acquired, loc, time
Merger	Old, new, trigger, loc, time
Spin-off	Parent, child, loc, time
Layoffs	Company, trigger, number, loc, time
Strike	Company, trigger, loc, time
Insolvency	Company, trigger, cause, loc, time

Table 3: Event types recognized by our pipeline, and their arguments.

deal with frequent morphologic variations and abbreviations, e.g. "strasse" and "straße" ("street"), or "Pl." for "Platz" ("place"). We construct gazetteers for companies, cities and towns, streets, transport stops, and transit routes, from the knowledge resources described in Section 3.2. All gazetteers store name variants, database identifier information, as well as geo-locations.

We perform an entity linking step next to disambiguate the candidate entities of a recognized concept. Since our system is based on a very extensive set of company and geo-location entities, entity linking is particularly challenging. For example, many public transit route names are identical across German cities (e.g. "S1" for "train line #1"), and street names are also very often re-used in different cities. We implement a straight-forward, geo-location-based disambiguation algorithm. For ambiguous entities, such as streets, transit stops, or small villages, the algorithm chooses the candidate whose coordinates are contained in the geo-shape of "larger" entities co-occurring in the text. In turn, unambiguous stop or street entities can also be used to resolve "larger" ambiguous entities, e.g. transit routes, using a similar strategy. Additionally, Twitter allows users to tag locations in a message. This can either be a precise location (longitude, latitude) or a general location label (e.g., a city name with geo-shape). For tweets with a location label, we retain only candidate entities located within the user-tagged geo-shape, and then apply our disambiguation algorithm.

Finally, our pipeline detects events and event arguments by matching dependency parse trees of sentences to a set of automatically learned dependency patterns, as proposed by Xu et al. (2007).

---

[9]avro.apache.org
[10]flink.apache.org
[11]github.com/kohlschutter/boilerpipe

We define an event in the spirit of the ACE / ERE guidelines (Linguistic Data Consortium, 2015) as a n-ary relation with a set of required and optional arguments, which include location and time. The dependency patterns we use for event detection are extracted from a manually curated set of event-specific training sentences, which were annotated with event type, argument types, and argument roles. For Twitter texts, where we typically cannot expect high-quality dependency parses, we complement our approach with a key phrase-based event detection strategy. By carefully selecting the trigger key phrase set, we can identify event types with high precision. Table 3 summarizes the events and arguments recognized by our system.

5 Web Application

Annotated documents are persisted to a distributed Solr index[12]. The index stores basic document information, such as URL, title and text, and additionally information about extracted entities and events. It serves as a back-end for the visualization component of the system, which is realized as a light-weight web application. The front-end is available at `http://ta.dfki.de`.

Figure 2a shows the main view of the front-end. The view displays the most recent events on an interactive map. Each icon represents a single event. Events co-located in a particular area are clustered to avoid cluttering. The clusters split into individual event icons when zooming in on the location. The map is updated frequently to refresh the event set, giving a dynamic view of ongoing developments. The user interface provides various filtering options for event types, data sources, and transport modes, as well as a company search.

Events can be selected, which opens an overlay with detailed information about the event and its source document. Details include the event type, time, and location, as well as an explanatory text snippet from the source document. The detail view also shows a set of illustrative supply chains between companies that may potentially be affected by the event, see Figure 2b. Since data about suppliers is typically non-public information, we dynamically generate example supply chains by randomly selecting a pair of companies in the vicinity of the event's location, and computing a route between them using Mapbox [13].

---

[12]`lucene.apache.org/solr`
[13]`mapbox.com/api-documentation`

Selecting a "supply chain problem" involving a particular company opens another detail view. This detail view displays information about the affected company, and includes infobox-style facts from background knowledge bases, but also recent events and news referencing the company.

6 Evaluation

We conducted a preliminary evaluation of our system's event extraction performance on the dataset described in Table 1. Figure 3 shows the distribution of recognized events. The largest proportion of events is extracted from Twitter messages. Company-related events are mostly found in news articles, while mobility-related events are mainly reported in Twitter and RSS feeds.

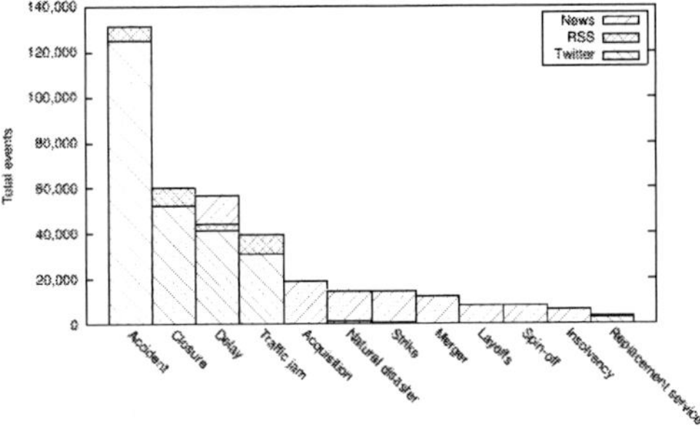

Figure 3: Event distribution for RSS, Twitter and News.

To evaluate event extraction accuracy, we manually judge a random sample of 150 documents (50 per source) for each event. A document is considered to correctly state an event if it explicitly reports a past, current or future event. All other documents are labeled as incorrect.

Table 4 lists the precision scores per source and micro-averaged across sources for selected event types. On average, 64% of the identified events are judged to be correct. Best results are observed for RSS feeds. This is an expected result, since traffic information RSS feeds are often well structured and employ very formalized wording. Some events types are more reliably observed in specific sources, e.g. *Strike* and *Layoffs* in news. The overall precision on Twitter is surprisingly high, with the exception of *Traffic Jam* events. This can be attributed to the fact that our key phrase-based approach used the German word "Stau" ("jam"), which often appears in non-traffic contexts to denote slow or halting progress.

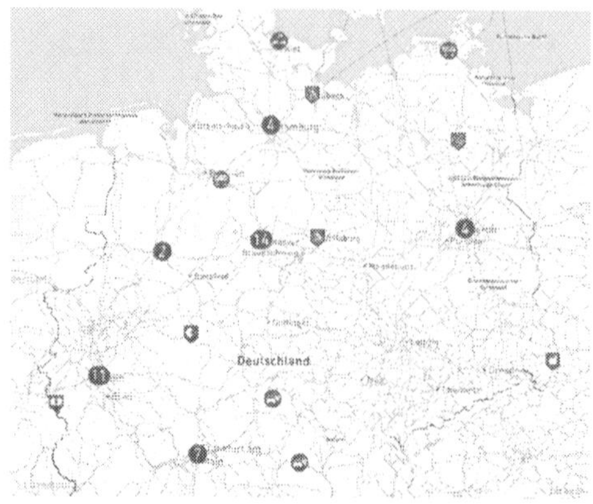
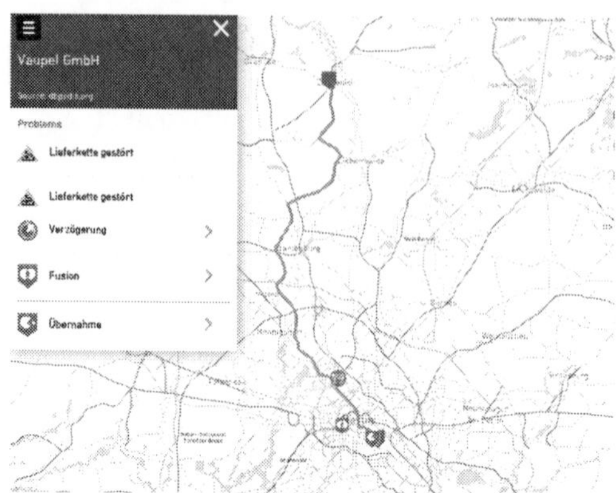

(a) Event visualization UI   (b) Company view with supply chain route

Figure 2: User interface of the *Spree* system

Event type	Twitter	RSS	News	Avg
Traffic jam	0.28	1.0	–	0.64
Strike	0.58	–	0.66	0.62
Delays	0.74	0.94	0.26	0.65
Disaster	0.52	0.94	0.48	0.57
Layoffs	0.66	–	0.76	0.71

Table 4: Precision of event recognition for selected event types. Empty cells indicate that the corresponding event did not occur in the given document type.

7 Conclusion

We have presented *Spree*, a scalable, real-time event extraction system for mobility and industry events. Our system discovers and visualizes events from heterogeneous data streams, including Twitter, RSS feeds and news documents, on an interactive map. Data streams are automatically filtered for relevant events, and geo-located using information from the extracted entities. Our system recognizes an extensive set of fine-grained entities of different types, including companies, streets, routes and transport stops, and extracts ACE/ERE-style events, together with their argument fillers, using a dependency pattern-based approach. Implemented in Apache Flink, it is highly scalable and allows both batch and streaming processing.

Acknowledgments

This research was partially supported by the German Federal Ministry of Economics and Energy (BMWi) through the projects SDW (01MD15010A) and SD4M (01MD15007B), and by the German Federal Ministry of Education and Research (BMBF) through the project BBDC (01IS14013E).

References

A. Alexandrov, R. Bergmann, S. Ewen, J. Freytag, F. Hueske, A. Heise, O. Kao, M. Leich, U. Leser, V. Markl, F. Naumann, M. Peters, A. Rheinländer, M. Sax, S. Schelter, Ma. Höger, K. Tzoumas, and D. Warneke. 2014. The Stratosphere Platform for Big Data Analytics. *The VLDB Journal*, 23(6):939–964.

B. Bohnet. 2010. Top accuracy and fast dependency parsing is not a contradiction. In *Proc. of COLING*, pages 89–97.

W. Drozdzynski, H. Krieger, J. Piskorski, U. Schäfer, and F. Xu. 2004. Shallow processing with unification and typed feature structures — foundations and applications. *Künstliche Intelligenz*, 1:17–23.

D. Ferrucci and A. Lally. 2004. UIMA: An architectural approach to unstructured information processing in the corporate research environment. *Nat. Lang. Eng.*, 10(3–4):327–348.

Linguistic Data Consortium. 2015. Rich ERE annotation guidelines overview. `http://cairo.lti.cs.cmu.edu/kbp/2015/event/summary_rich_ere_v4.1.pdf`.

M. Osborne, S. Moran, R. McCreadie, A. Von Lunen, M. Sykora, E. Cano, N. Ireson, C. Macdonald, I. Ounis, Y. He, T. Jackson, F. Ciravegna, and A. O'Brien. 2014. Real-time detection, tracking, and monitoring of automatically discovered events in social media. In *Proc. of ACL: System Demonstrations*, pages 37–42.

Feiyu Xu, Hans Uszkoreit, and Hong Li. 2007. A Seed-driven Bottom-up Machine Learning Framework for Extracting Relations of Various Complexity. In *Proc. of ACL*, pages 584–591.

TranscRater:
a Tool for Automatic Speech Recognition Quality Estimation

Shahab Jalalvand[1,2]**, Matteo Negri**[1]**, Marco Turchi**[1]**,
José G. C. de Souza**[1,2]**, Daniele Falavigna**[1]**, Mohammed R. H. Qwaider**[1]

[1] Fondazione Bruno Kessler, Trento, Italy
[2] University of Trento, Italy
{jalalvand,negri,turchi,desouza,falavi,qwaider}@fbk.eu

Abstract

We present TranscRater, an open-source tool for automatic speech recognition (ASR) quality estimation (QE). The tool allows users to perform ASR evaluation bypassing the need of reference transcripts and confidence information, which is common to current assessment protocols. TranscRater includes: *i)* methods to extract a variety of quality indicators from *(signal, transcription)* pairs and *ii)* machine learning algorithms which make possible to build ASR QE models exploiting the extracted features. Confirming the positive results of previous evaluations, new experiments with TranscRater indicate its effectiveness both in WER prediction and transcription ranking tasks.

1 Introduction

How to determine the quality of an automatic transcription without reference transcripts and without confidence information? This is the key problem addressed by research on ASR quality estimation (Negri et al., 2014; C. de Souza et al., 2015; Jalalvand et al., 2015b), and the task for which TranscRater, the tool described in this paper, has been designed.

The work on ASR quality estimation (ASR QE) has several motivations. First, the steady increase of applications involving automatic speech recognition (e.g. video/TV programs subtitling, voice search engines, voice question answering, spoken dialog systems, meeting and broadcast news transcriptions) calls for **an accurate method to estimate ASR output quality at run-time**. Often, indeed, the nature of such applications (consider for instance spoken dialog systems) requires quick re-

sponse capabilities that are incompatible with traditional reference-based protocols.

Second, even when real-time processing is not a priority, standard evaluation based on computing word-error rate (WER) against gold references is not always a viable solution. In many situations (as in the case of languages for which even the ASR training data is scarce), the bottleneck represented by the limited availability of reference transcripts and the costs of their manual creation calls for **a method to predict ASR output quality that is reference-independent**.

Third, even when designed to bypass the need of references, current quality prediction methods heavily depend on confidence information about the inner workings of the ASR system that produced the transcriptions (Evermann and Woodland, 2000; Wessel et al., 2001). Such information, describing how the system is certain about the quality of its own hypotheses, often reflects a biased perspective influenced by individual decoder features. More importantly, it is not always accessible and, in this frequent case, the sole elements available for quality prediction are the signal and its transcription (consider, for instance, the increasing amount of captioned Youtube videos generated by a "black-box" ASR system[1]). These issues call for **a method to predict ASR output quality that is also confidence-independent**.

TranscRater (Transcription Rater) provides a unified ASR QE framework designed to meet the three aforementioned requirements. Its development was inspired by software previously released for the machine translation (MT) (Specia et al., 2013; Shah et al., 2014; Servan et al., 2015) equivalent of ASR QE, in which MT quality has to be estimated at run-time and without reference trans-

---

[1]More than 157 millions in 10 languages, as announced by Google already in 2012 (source: `http://goo.gl/5Wlkjl`).

Proceedings of the 54th Annual Meeting of the Association for Computational Linguistics—System Demonstrations, pages 43–48,
Berlin, Germany, August 7-12, 2016. ©2016 Association for Computational Linguistics

lations (Mehdad et al., 2012; Camargo de Souza et al., 2013; C. de Souza et al., 2014). Indeed, the two tasks deal with similar issues. In both cases, we have an input "source" (a written sentence and a recorded signal) and an output text (a translation and a transcription) that has to be assessed without any pre-created term of comparison. They can also be approached with similar supervised classification (C. de Souza et al., 2015) or regression strategies (Negri et al., 2014; C. de Souza et al., 2015). Finally, they have similar applications like:

- Deciding if an input source has been correctly processed;

- Ranking the output of multiple independent systems (Jalalvand et al., 2015b);

- Estimating the human effort required to manually revise an output segment;

- Performing data selection for system improvement based on active learning.

To support these applications, TranscRater provides an extensible ASR QE framework consisting of a variety of feature extractors and machine learning algorithms. The implemented feature extraction methods allow capturing predictive quality indicators both from the input signal and from the output transcription. This basic set of "black box" indicators has been successfully evaluated in a number of experiments, both on regression and on classification tasks, showing that ASR QE predictions can closely approximate the quality scores obtained with standard reference-based methods. The existing feature extractors can be easily extended to integrate new features, either capturing additional system-independent aspects, or relying on confidence information about the ASR system that produced the transcriptions, if available. Experimental results demonstrate that, also in the "glass-box" scenario in which the ASR system is known, the available features are able to improve the performance obtained with confidence information.

The integration of different machine learning algorithms makes TranscRater a powerful framework to quickly set up an ASR QE model given some training data, tune it by choosing among the possible feature configurations and process new, unseen test data to predict their quality. As a standalone environment, with few documented external dependencies, TranscRater provides the first off-the-shelf solution to approach ASR QE and extend its application to new scenarios.

2 ASR QE

The basic ASR QE task consists in training a model from (*signal, transcription, label*) triplets, and using it to return quality predictions for a test set of unseen (*signal, transcription*) instances. In this supervised learning setting, the training labels can be either numeric scores (Negri et al., 2014) or class identifiers (binary or multi-class) (C. de Souza et al., 2015). Class assignments can be manually done according to some criteria, or inferred by thresholding numeric scores. Numeric quality indicators can be easily obtained by measuring the similarity (or the distance) between the transcription and its manually-created reference. For instance, the models described in previous works on ASR QE learn from training data labelled with real values obtained by computing the transcription word error rate (WER[2]).

According to the type of training labels, the problem can be approached either as a regression or as a classification task. As a consequence, also the evaluation metrics will change. Precision/recall/F1 (or other metrics, such as balanced accuracy, in case of very unbalanced distributions) will be used for classification while, similar to MT QE, the mean absolute error (MAE) or similar metrics will be used for regression.

A variant of the basic ASR QE task is to consider it as a QE-based ranking problem (Jalalvand et al., 2015b), in which each utterance is captured by multiple microphones or transcribed by multiple ASR systems. In this case, the capability to rank transcriptions from the best to the worst can be evaluated in terms of normalized discounted cumulative gain (NDCG) or similar metrics.

3 The TranscRater tool

TranscRater combines in a single open-source framework: *i)* a set of *features* capturing different aspects of transcription quality and *ii)* different learning *algorithms* suitable to address the challenges posed by different application scenarios.

TranscRater internally consists of two main

---

[2]WER is the minimum edit distance between the transcription and the reference. Edit distance is calculated as the number of edits (word insertions, deletions, substitutions) divided by the number of words in the reference.

modules: feature extraction and machine learning. At training stage, the tool receives as input a set of signal recordings, their transcriptions and the corresponding reference transcripts. The speech signals are provided as separate files in the RIFF Microsoft PCM format with 16K sampling rate. Their transcriptions and the corresponding references are provided in single separate text files (one transcription per row). References are used to compute the WER label of each training instance, thus connecting the problem to the task formulation provided in §2. The features extracted from each training instance are passed to the learning module, together with the corresponding label. The label is a WER score which, depending on the type of problem addressed, can be used either to directly train a regressor or to infer a ranking for multiple hypotheses. In either case, the learning module will train the corresponding model with the proper learning algorithm, and tune it using k-fold cross-validation.

At test stage, the model is used to predict the label of new, unseen (*signal, transcription*) instances. For each test point, the output is either a WER prediction or a rank, whose reliability can be respectively evaluated in terms of MAE or NDCG (as discussed in §2). Output predictions are provided in a single file (one WER prediction per row for regression and one rank prediction per row for ranking). MAE or NDCG scores are provided as the standard output of the test functions.

Internally, TranscRater stores the extracted features in the SVM-light[3] format. This makes possible to use the tool as a feature extractor and to embed it in applications different from the ones described in this paper. The features to be used, the type of learning algorithm, the input files and the links to resources and libraries can be easily set through a configuration file.

3.1 Feature sets

The feature extraction module of TranscRater allows the user to extract 72 features that can be categorized in the following four groups:

- Signal (SIG) features, designed to capture the difficulty of transcribing the input signal given the general recording conditions in which it was acquired;

- Lexical (LEX) features, designed to capture

the difficulty to transcribe the input signal given the pronunciation difficulty and the ambiguity of the terms it contains;

- Language model (LM) features, designed to capture the plausibility of the transcription from the fluency point of view;

- Part-of-speech (POS) features, designed to capture the plausibility of the transcription from the syntax point of view.

SIG (44). Signal features are extracted using the OpenSmile[4] toolkit (Eyben et al., 2013). Each speech signal is broken down into 25ms length frames with 10ms overlap. For each frame, we compute 13 Mel Frequency Cepstral Coefficients (MFCC), their delta, acceleration and log-energy as well as the prosody features like fundamental frequency (F0), voicing probability, loudness contours and pitch. The final SIG feature vector for the entire input signal is obtained by averaging the values of each feature computed on all the frames.

LEX (7). Lexicon-based features are extracted using a lexical feature dictionary (optionally provided by the user). In this dictionary each individual word is assigned to a feature vector containing the frequency of fricatives, liquids, nasals, stops and vowels in its pronunciation. Other elements of the vector are the number of homophones (words with the same pronunciation) and quasi-homophones (words with similar pronunciation).

LM (12). Language model features include the mean of word probabilities, the sum of the log probabilities and the perplexity score for each transcription. In previous experiments (Jalalvand et al., 2015b; Jalalvand and Falavigna, 2015) we showed that, instead of only one LM, using a combination of neural network and n-gram LMs trained on task-specific and generic data can significantly improve the accuracy of quality prediction. For this reason, TranscRater allows using up to four different language models: two RNNLM (Mikolov et al., 2010) trained on generic and specific data and two n-gramLM trained on generic and specific data. To work with neural network LMs, the tool makes use of RNNLM,[5] while for n-gram LMs it uses SRILM[6] (Stolcke et al., 2000).

POS (9). Part-of-speech features are extracted using the TreeTagger.[7] For each word in the transcription, they consider the score assigned to the predicted POS of the word itself, the previous and the following one. This sliding window is used to compute the average value for the entire transcription and obtain the sentence-level POS feature vector. The intuition is that a low confidence of the POS tagger in labeling a sentence is an indicator of possible syntax issues and, in turn, of poor transcription quality. POS features also include the number and the percentage of content words (numbers, nouns, verbs, adjectives, adverbs).

These feature groups were successfully tested in various conditions including clean/noisy data, single/multiple microphones and ASR systems (Jalalvand et al., 2015b; Jalalvand et al., 2015a). In such conditions, they proved to be a reliable predictor when confidence information about the ASR system inner workings is not accessible.

3.2 Learning algorithms

For regression-based tasks (WER prediction), TranscRater includes an interface to the Scikit-learn package (Pedregosa et al., 2011), a Python machine learning library that contains a large set of classification and regression algorithms. Based on the empirical results reported in (Negri et al., 2014; C. de Souza et al., 2015; Jalalvand et al., 2015b), which indicate that Extremely Randomized Trees (XRT (Geurts et al., 2006)) is a very competitive algorithm in several WER prediction tasks, the current version of the tool exploits XRT. However, adapting the interface to apply other algorithms is an easy task and one of the future extension directions. The main hyper-parameters of the model, such as the number of tree bags, the number of trees per bag, the number of features per tree and the number of instances in the leaves, are tuned using grid search with k-fold cross-validation on the training set to minimize the mean absolute error (MAE) between the true WERs and the predicted ones.

As mentioned before, TranscRater provides the possibility to evaluate multiple transcriptions (e.g. obtained from different microphones or ASR systems) and rank them based on their quality. This can be done either *indirectly*, by exploiting the predicted WER labels in a "ranking by regression"

approach (RR) or *directly*, by exploiting machine-learned ranking methods (MLR). To train and test MLR models, TranscRater exploits RankLib[8], a library of learning-to-rank algorithms. The current version of the tool includes an interface to the Random Forest algorithm (RF (Breiman, 2001)), the same used in (Jalalvand et al., 2015b).

MLR predicts ranks through pairwise comparison between the transcriptions. The main parameters such as the number of bags, the number of trees per bag and the number of leaves per tree are tuned on training set using k-fold cross-validation to maximize the NDCG measure.

3.3 Implementation

TranscRater is written in Python and is made of several parts linked together using bash scripts. In order to run the toolkit on Linux, the following libraries are required: *i*) Java 8 (JDK-1.8); *ii*) Python 2.7 (or above) and *iii*) Scikit-learn (version 0.15.2). Moreover, the user has to download and compile the following libraries: OpenSmile, RNNLM, SRILM and TreeTagger for the feature extraction module as well as RankLib for using machine-learned ranking option.

4 Benchmarking

The features and algorithms contained in TranscRater have been successfully used in previous works (Negri et al., 2014; C. de Souza et al., 2015; Jalalvand et al., 2015b; Jalalvand et al., 2015a). To further investigate their effectiveness, in this section we provide new results, both in WER prediction (MAE) and transcription ranking (NDCG), together with some efficiency analysis (Time in seconds[9]). To this aim, we use data from the 3rd CHiME challenge,[10] which were collected for multiple distant microphone speech recognition in noisy environments (Barker et al., 2015). CHiME-3 data consists of sentences of the Wall Street Journal corpus, uttered by four speakers in four noisy environments, and recorded by five microphones placed on the frame of a tablet PC (a sixth one, placed on the back, mainly records background noise). Training and test respectively contain 1,640 and 1,320 sentences. Transcriptions are

---

[7]http://www.cis.uni-muenchen.de/~schmid/tools/TreeTagger/data/tree-tagger-linux-3.2.tar.gz

[8]https://people.cs.umass.edu/~vdang/data/RankLib-v2.1.tar.gz

[9]Experiments were run with a PC with 8 Intel Xeon processors 3.4 GHz and 8 GB RAM.

[10]http://spandh.dcs.shef.ac.uk/chime_challenge/chime2015/data.html

produced by a baseline ASR system, provided by the task organizers, which uses the deep neural network recipe of Kaldi (Povey et al., 2011).

In WER prediction, different models built with TranscRater are compared with a baseline commonly used for regression tasks, which labels all the test instances with the average WER value computed on the training set. In ranking mode, baseline results are computed by averaging the NDCG scores obtained in one hundred iterations in which test instances are randomly ranked.

Features	Train&Test Time	Total Time	MAE↓
Baseline	—	—	28.7
SIG	00m18s	09m32s	27.3
LEX+LM+POS	00m19s	01m19s	22.2
SIG+LEX+LM+POS	00m26s	10m22s	23.5

Table 1: Time and MAE results in regression mode.

Table 1 shows the results of models trained with different feature groups for **WER prediction** with a single microphone. In terms of time, in this as in the following experiments, the total time (feature extraction + training + test) is mostly determined by feature extraction and the bottleneck is clearly represented by the extraction of signal (SIG) features. In terms of MAE, SIG features are also those achieving the worst result. Although they significantly improve over the baseline, they are outperformed by LEX+LM+POS and, even in combination with them, they do not help. However, as suggested by previous works like (Negri et al., 2014) in which some of the SIG features are among the most predictive ones, the usefulness of signal features highly depends on data and, in specific conditions, they definitely improve results. Their ineffectiveness in the experiments of this paper likely depends on the lack of word-level time boundaries, which prevented us to compute more discriminative features like word log-energies, noise log-energies and signal-to-noise ratio (the best indicator of the acoustic quality of an input utterance).

Features	Train&Test Time	Total Time	NDCG↑
Baseline	—	—	73.6
SIG	02m03s	15m11s	73.5
LEX+LM+POS	01m10s	03m13s	80.4
SIG+LEX+LM+POS	05m53s	19m23s	79.4

Table 2: Time and NDCG results in ranking by regression.

Table 2 shows the results achieved by the same feature groups when **ranking by regression** (RR) the transcriptions from five microphones. In terms

of computation time, the higher costs of SIG features are still evident (the significant increase for all groups is due to the higher number of audio files to be processed). Also in this case, SIG features do not help, neither alone nor in combination with the other groups. Indeed, the highest results are achieved by the combination of LEX+LM+POS. Their large NDCG improvement over the baseline (+6.8), combined with the significantly lower computation time, seems to make this combination particularly suitable for the ranking by regression strategy.

Features	Train&Test Time	Total Time	NDCG↑
Baseline	—	—	73.6
SIG	01m14s	13m00s	78.1
LEX+LM+POS	00m59s	03m05s	81.3
SIG+LEX+LM+POS	01m41s	15m10s	83.1

Table 3: Time and NDCG with machine-learned ranking.

Table 3 shows the results achieved, in the same multi-microphone scenario, by the **machine-learned ranking** approach (MLR). In terms of time, MLR is slightly more efficient than RR, at least on this dataset. Though surprising (MLR performs lots of pairwise comparisons, which are in principle more demanding), such difference is not very informative as it might depend on hyper-parameter settings (e.g. the number of iterations for XRT, manually set to 20), whose optimization was out of the scope of our analysis. In terms of NDCG, the results are higher compared to RR but the differences between feature groups are confirmed. Interestingly, with MLR even the SIG features in isolation significantly improve over the baseline (+4.5 points). The NDCG improvement with the combined feature groups is up to 9.5 points, confirming the effectiveness of the combined features shown in previous works.

5 Conclusion

We presented TranscRater, an open-source tool for ASR quality estimation. TranscRater provides an extensible framework including feature extractors, machine learning algorithms (for WER prediction and transcription ranking), optimization and evaluation functions. Its source code can be downloaded from `https://github.com/hlt-mt/TranscRater`. Its license is FreeBSD, a lax permissive non-copyleft license, compatible with the GNU GPL and with any use, including commercial.

References

J. Barker, R. Marxer, E. Vincent, and S. Watanabe. 2015. The third 'CHiME' Speech Separation and Recognition Challenge: Dataset, Task and Baselines. In *Proc. of the 15th IEEE Automatic Speech Recognition and Understanding Workshop (ASRU)*, pages 1–9, Scottsdale, Arizona, USA.

L. Breiman. 2001. Random Forests. *Machine Learning*, 45(1):5–32.

J. G. C. de Souza, J. González-Rubio, C. Buck, M. Turchi, and M. Negri. 2014. FBK-UPV-UEdin participation in the WMT14 Quality Estimation shared-task. In *Proc. of the Ninth Workshop on Statistical Machine Translation*, pages 322–328, Baltimore, Maryland, USA.

J. G. C. de Souza, H. Zamani, M. Negri, M. Turchi, and D. Falavigna. 2015. Multitask Learning for Adaptive Quality Estimation of Automatically Transcribed Utterances. In *Proc. of the 2015 Conference of the North American Chapter of the Association for Computational Linguistics - Human Language Technologies (NAACL-HLT)*, pages 714–724, Denver, Colorado, USA.

J. G. Camargo de Souza, C. Buck, M. Turchi, and M. Negri. 2013. FBK-UEdin Participation to the WMT13 Quality Estimation Shared Task. In *Proc. of the Eighth Workshop on Statistical Machine Translation*, pages 352–358, Sofia, Bulgaria.

G. Evermann and P. Woodland. 2000. Large Vocabulary Decoding and Confidence Estimation using Word Posterior Probabilities. In *Proc. of the IEEE International Conference on Acoustics, Speech, and Signal Processing (ICASSP)*, pages 1655–1658, Istanbul, Turkey.

F. Eyben, F. Weninger, and B. Schuller. 2013. Recent developments in opensmile, the munich open-source multimedia feature extractor. In *Proc. of ACM Multimedia*, pages 835–838, Barcelona, Spain. ACM.

P. Geurts, D. Ernst, and L. Wehenkel. 2006. Extremely Randomized Trees. *Machine Learning*, 63(1):3–42.

S. Jalalvand and D. Falavigna. 2015. Stacked Auto-Encoder for ASR Error Detection and Word Error Rate Prediction. In *Proc. of the 16th Annual Conference of the International Speech Communication Association (INTERPSEECH)*, pages 2142–2146, Dresden, Germany.

S. Jalalvand, D. Falavigna, M. Matassoni, P. Svaizer, and M. Omologo. 2015a. Boosted Acoustic Model Learning and Hypotheses Rescoring on the CHiME-3 Task. In *Proc. of the IEEE Automatic Speech Recognition and Understanding Workshop (ASRU)*, pages 409–415, Scottsdale, Arizona, USA.

S. Jalalvand, M. Negri, D. Falavigna, and M. Turchi. 2015b. Driving ROVER With Segment-based ASR Quality Estimation. In *Proc. of the 53rd Annual Meeting of the Association for Computational Linguistics (ACL)*, pages 1095–1105, Beijing, China.

Y. Mehdad, M. Negri, and M. Federico. 2012. Match without a Referee: Evaluating MT Adequacy without Reference Translations. In *Proc. of the Machine Translation Workshop (WMT2012)*, pages 171–180, Montréal, Canada.

T. Mikolov, M. Karafiát, L. Burget, J. Cernocký, and S. Khudanpur. 2010. Recurrent Neural Network Based Language Model. In *Proc. of INTERSPEECH*, pages 1045–1048, Makuhari, Chiba, Japan.

M. Negri, M. Turchi, J. G. C. de Souza, and F. Daniele. 2014. Quality Estimation for Automatic Speech Recognition. In *Proc. of the 25th International Conference on Computational Linguistics: Technical Papers (COLING)*, pages 1813–1823, Dublin, Ireland.

F. Pedregosa, G. Varoquaux, A. Gramfort, V. Michel, B. Thirion, O. Grisel, M. Blondel, P. Prettenhofer, R. Weiss, V. Dubourg, et al. 2011. Scikit-learn: Machine Learning in Python. *Machine Learning Research*, 12:2825–2830.

D. Povey, A. Ghoshal, G. Boulianne, L. Burget, O. Glembek, N. Goel, M. Hannemann, P. Motlicek, Y. Qian, P. Schwarz, J. Silovsky, G. Stemmer, and K. Vesely. 2011. The Kaldi Speech Recognition Toolkit. In *Proc. of the IEEE Workshop on Automatic Speech Recognition and Understanding (ASRU)*, Hawaii, USA.

C. Servan, N.-T. Le, N. Q. Luong, B. Lecouteux, and L. Besacier. 2015. An open source toolkit for word-level confidence estimation in machine translation. In *Proc. of the 12th International Workshop on Spoken Language Translation (IWSLT)*, Vietnam.

K. Shah, M. Turchi, and L. Specia. 2014. An Efficient and User-friendly Tool for Machine Translation Quality Estimation. In *Proc. of the Ninth International Conference on Language Resources and Evaluation (LREC'14)*, Reykjavik, Iceland.

L. Specia, K. Shah, J. G. de Souza, and T. Cohn. 2013. Quest - a translation quality estimation framework. In *Proc. of the 51st Annual Meeting of the Association for Computational Linguistics: System Demonstrations*, pages 79–84, Sofia, Bulgaria. Association for Computational Linguistics.

A. Stolcke, H. Bratt, J. Butzberger, H. Franco, V. R. Gadde, M. Plauche, C. Richey, E. Shriberg, K. Sonmez, F. Weng, and J. Zheng. 2000. The SRI March 2000 HUBS Conversational Speech Transcription System. In *Proc. of the NIST Speech Transcription Workshop*.

F. Wessel, R. Schluter, K. Macherey, and H. Ney. 2001. Confidence Measures for Large Vocabulary Continuous Speech Recognition. *IEEE Transactions on Audio, Speech and Language Processing*, 9(3):288–298.

TMop: a Tool for Unsupervised Translation Memory Cleaning

Masoud Jalili Sabet[1], **Matteo Negri**[2], **Marco Turchi**[2],
José G. C. de Souza[2], **Marcello Federico**[2]

[1] School of Electrical and Computer Engineering, University of Tehran, Iran
[2] Fondazione Bruno Kessler, Trento, Italy
`jalili.masoud@ut.ac.ir`
`{negri,turchi,desouza,federico}@fbk.eu`

Abstract

We present TMop, the first open-source tool for automatic Translation Memory (TM) cleaning. The tool implements a fully unsupervised approach to the task, which allows spotting unreliable translation units (sentence pairs in different languages, which are supposed to be translations of each other) without requiring labeled training data. TMop includes a highly configurable and extensible set of filters capturing different aspects of translation quality. It has been evaluated on a test set composed of 1,000 translation units (TUs) randomly extracted from the English-Italian version of MyMemory, a large-scale public TM. Results indicate its effectiveness in automatic removing "bad" TUs, with comparable performance to a state-of-the-art supervised method (76.3 vs. 77.7 balanced accuracy).

1 Introduction

Computer-assisted translation (CAT) refers to a framework in which the work of human translators is supported by machines. Its advantages, especially in terms of productivity and translation consistency, have motivated huge investments both economic (by the translation industry) and intellectual (by the research community). Indeed, the high market potential of solutions geared to speed up the translation process and reduce its costs has attracted increasing interest from both sides.

Advanced CAT tools currently integrate the strengths of two complementary technologies: translation memories (TM - a high-precision mechanism for storing and retrieving previously translated segments) and machine translation (MT - a high-recall technology for translating unseen segments). The success of the integration has determined the quick growth of market shares that are held by CAT, as opposed to fully manual translation that became a niche of the global translation market. However, differently from MT that is constantly improving and reducing the distance from human translation, core TM technology has slightly changed over the years. This is in contrast with the fact that TMs are still more widely used than MT, especially in domains featuring high text repetitiveness (e.g. software manuals).

Translation memories have a long tradition in CAT, with a first proposal dating back to (Arthern, 1979). They consist of databases that store previously translated segments, together with the corresponding source text. Such (*source, target*) pairs, whose granularity can range from the phrase level to the sentence or even the paragraph level, are called translation units (TUs). When working with a CAT tool, each time a segment of a document to be translated matches with the *source* side of a TU, the corresponding *target* is proposed as a suggestion to the user. The user can also store each translated (*source, target*) pair in the TM for future use, thus increasing the size and the coverage of the TM. Due to such constant growth, in which they evolve over time incorporating users style and terminology, the so-called private TMs represent an invaluable asset for individual translators and translation companies. Collaboratively-created public TMs grow in a less controlled way but still remain a practical resource for the translators' community at large.

The usefulness of TM suggestions mainly depends on two factors: the matching process and the quality of the TU. To increase recall, the retrieval is based on computing a "fuzzy match" score. Depending on how the matching is performed, its output can be a mix of perfect and partial matches requiring variable amounts of correc-

Proceedings of the 54th Annual Meeting of the Association for Computational Linguistics—System Demonstrations, pages 49–54,
Berlin, Germany, August 7-12, 2016. ©2016 Association for Computational Linguistics

tions by the user. For this reason, most prior works on TM technology focused on improving this aspect (Gupta et al., 2014; Bloodgood and Strauss, 2014; Vanallemeersch and Vandeghinste, 2015; Chatzitheodoroou, 2015; Gupta et al., 2015).

The other relevant factor, TU quality, relates to the reliability of the *target* translations. Indeed, a perfectly matching *source* text associated to a wrong translation would make the corresponding suggestion useless or, even worse, an obstacle to productivity. On this aspect, prior research is limited to the work proposed in (Barbu, 2015), which so far represents the only attempt to automatically spot false translations in the bi-segments of a TM. However, casting the problem as a supervised binary classification task, this approach highly depends on the availability of labelled training data.

Our work goes beyond the initial effort of Barbu (2015) in two ways. First, **we propose a configurable and extensible open source framework for TM cleaning**. In this way, we address the demand of easy-to-use TM management tools whose development is out of the reach of individual translators and translation companies. Such demand is not only justified by productivity reasons (remove bad suggestions as a cause of slow production), but also for usability reasons. Loading, searching and editing a TM are indeed time-consuming and resource-demanding operations. In case of very large databases (up to millions of TUs) the accurate removal of useless units can significantly increase usability. Though paid, the few existing tools that incorporate some data cleaning methods (e.g. Apsic X-Bench[1]) only implement very simple syntactic checks (e.g. repetitions, opening/closing tags consistency). These are insufficient to capture the variety of errors that can be encountered in a TM (especially in the public ones).

Second, **our approach to TM cleaning is fully unsupervised**. This is to cope with the lack of labelled training data which, due to the high acquisition costs, represents a bottleneck rendering supervised solutions unpractical. It is worth remarking that also current approaches to tasks closely related to TM cleaning (e.g. MT quality estimation (Mehdad et al., 2012; C. de Souza et al., 2014)) suffer from the same problem. Besides not being customised for the specificities of the TM cleaning scenario (their usefulness for the task should be demonstrated), their dependence on labelled

training data is a strong requirement from the TM cleaning application perspective.

2 The TM cleaning task

The identification of "bad" TUs is a multifaceted problem. First, it deals with the recognition of *a variety of errors*. These include:

- Surface errors, such as opening/closing tags inconsistencies and empty or suspiciously long/short translations;

- Language inconsistencies, for instance due to the inversion between the *source* and *target* languages;

- Translation fluency issues, such as typos and grammatical errors (e.g. morpho-syntactic disagreements, wrong word ordering);

- Translation adequacy issues, such as the presence of untranslated terms, wrong lexical choices or more complex phenomena (e.g. negation and quantification errors) for which a syntactically correct *target* can be a semantically poor translation of the *source* segment.

The *severity* of the errors is another aspect to take into account. Deciding if a given error makes a TU useless is often difficult even for humans. For instance, judging about the usefulness of a TU whose *target* side has missing/extra words would be a highly subjective task.[2] For this reason, identifying "bad" TUs with an automatic approach opens a number of problems related to: *i)* defining when a given issue becomes a real error (e.g. the ratio of acceptable missing words), *ii)* combining potentially contradictory evidence (e.g. syntactic and semantic issues), and *iii)* making these actions easily customisable by different users having different needs, experience and quality standards.

What *action* to take when one or more errors are identified in a TU is also important. Ideally, a TM cleaning tool should allow users either to simply flag problematic TUs (leaving the final decision to a human judgment), or to automatically remove them without further human intervention.

Finally, two critical aspects are the external *knowledge* and *resources* required by the TM-cleaning process. On one side, collecting evidence

---

[2] Likely, the perceived severity of a missing word out of n perfectly translated terms will be inversely proportional to n.

for each TU can involve processing steps that access external data and tools. On the other side, decision making can require variable amounts of labelled training data (i.e. positive/negative examples of "good"/"bad" TUs). For both tasks, the recourse to external support can be an advantage in terms of performance due to the possibility to get informed judgments taken from models trained in a supervised fashion. At the same time, it can be a limitation in terms of usability and portability across languages. When available, external resources and tools (e.g. syntactic/semantic parsers) can indeed be too slow to process huge amounts of data. Most importantly, labelled training data are usually difficult to acquire. In case of need, a TM cleaning tool should hence minimise the dependence of its performance from the availability of external resources.

All these aspects were considered in the design of TMop, whose capability to cope with a variety of errors, customise its actions based on their severity and avoid the recourse to external knowledge/resources are described in the next section.

3 The TMop framework

TMop (Translation Memory open-source purifier) is an open-source TM cleaning software written in Python. It consists of three parts: core, filters and policy managers. The core, the main part of the software, manages the workflow between filters, policy managers and input/output files. The filters (§3.2) are responsible for detecting "bad" TUs. Each of them can detect a specific type of problems (e.g. formatting, fluency, adequacy) and will emit an *accept* or *reject* judgment for each TU. Policy managers (§3.3) collect the individual results from each filter and take a final decision for each TM entry based on different possible strategies. Filters, policies and basic parameters can be set by means of a configuration file, which was structured by keeping ease of use and flexibility as the main design criteria.

TMop implements a fully unsupervised approach to TM cleaning. The *accept/reject* criteria are learned from the TM itself and no training data are required to inform the process.[3] Nevertheless, the filters' output could be also used to instantiate feature vectors in any supervised learning scenario supported by training data.

---

[3] The tool has been recently used also in the unsupervised approach by Jalili Sabet et al. (2016).

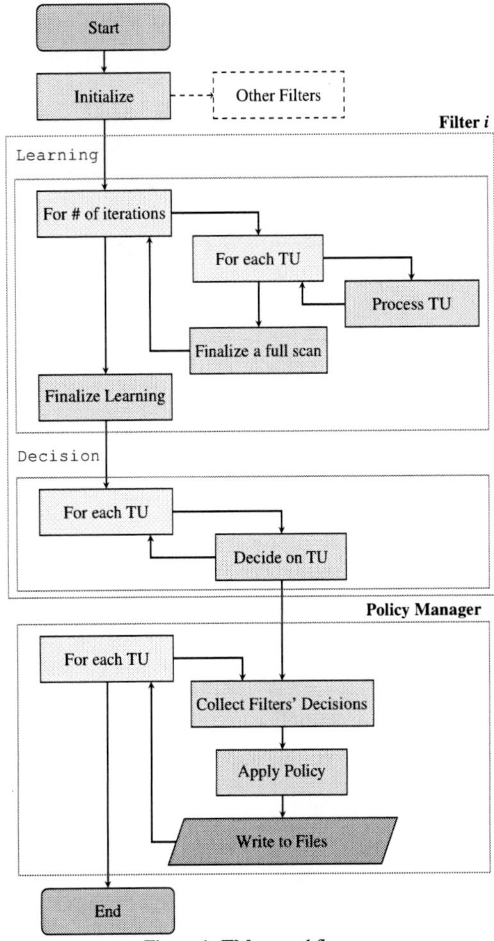

Figure 1: TMop workflow

3.1 Workflow

The input file of TMop is a TM represented as a text file containing one TU per line in the form (*ID*, *source*, *target*). The output consists of several files, the most important of which are the *accept* and *reject* files containing the TUs identified as "good"/"bad", in the same format of the input. As depicted in Figure 1, TMop **filters** operate in two steps. In the first one, the `learning` step, each filter i iterates over the TM or a subset of it to gather the basic statistics needed to define its *accept/reject* criteria. For instance, by computing mean and standard deviation values for a given indicator (e.g. sentence length ratio, proportion of aligned words), quantiles or std counts in case of normal value distributions will be used as decision boundaries. Then, in the `decision` step, each filter uses the gathered information to decide about each TU. At the end of this process, for each

TU the **policy manager** collects all the decisions taken by the filters and applies the policy set by the user in the configuration file to assign an *accept* or *reject* judgment. The final labels, the TUs and the filters outputs are saved in different files.

3.2 Filters

Our filters capture different aspects of the similarity between the source and the target of a TU. The full set consists of 23 filters, which are organized in four groups.

Basic filters (8 in total). This group (**B**) extends the filters proposed by Barbu (2015) and substantially covers those offered by commercial TM cleaning tools. They capture translation quality by looking at surface aspects, such as the possible mismatches in the number of dates, numbers, URLs, XML tags, ref and image tags present in the source and target segments. Other filters model the similarity between source and target by computing the direct and inverse ratio between the number of characters and words, as well as the average word length in the two segments. Finally, two filters look for uncommon character or word repetitions.

Language identification filter (1). This filter (**LI**) exploits the Langid tool (Lui and Baldwin, 2012) to verify the consistency between the source and target languages of a TU and those indicated in the TM. Though simple, it is quite effective since often the two languages are inverted or even completely different from the expected ones.

QE-derived filters (9). This group (**QE**) contains filters borrowed from the closely-related task of MT quality estimation, in which the complexity of the source, the fluency of the target and the adequacy between source and target are modeled as quality indicators. Focusing on the adequacy aspect, we exploit a subset of the features proposed by C. de Souza et al. (2013). They use word alignment information to link source and target words and capture the quantity of meaning preserved by the translation. For each segment of a TU, word alignment information is used to calculate: *i)* the proportion of aligned and unaligned word n-grams (n=1,2), *ii)* the ratio between the longest aligned/unaligned word sequence and the length of the segment, *iii)* the average length of the aligned/unaligned word sequences, and *iv)* the position of the first/last unaligned word, normalized by the length of the segment. Word alignment

models can be trained on the whole TM with one of the many existing word aligners. For instance, the results of WE filters reported in §4 were obtained using MGIZA++ (Gao and Vogel, 2008).

Word embedding filters (5). Cross-lingual word embeddings provide a common vector representation for words in different languages and allow looking at the source and target segments at the same time. In TMop, they are computed using the method proposed in (Søgaard et al., 2015) but, instead of considering bilingual documents as atomic concepts to bridge the two languages, they exploit the TUs contained in the TM itself. Given a TU and a 100-dimensional vector representation of each word in the source and target segments, this group of filters (**WE**) includes: *i)* the cosine similarity between the source and target segment vectors obtained by averaging (or using the median) the source and target word vectors; *ii)* the average embedding alignment score obtained by computing the cosine similarity between each source word and all the target words and averaging over the largest cosine score of each source word; *iii)* the average cosine similarity between source/target word alignments; *iv)* a score that merges features *(ii)* and *(iii)* by complementing word alignments (also in this case obtained using MGIZA++) with the alignments obtained from word embedding and averaging all the alignment weights.

3.3 Policies

Decision policies allow TMop combining the output of the active filters into a final decision for each TU. Simple decision-making strategies can consider the number of *accept* and *reject* judgments, but more complex methods can be easily implemented by the user (both filters and policy managers can be easily modified and extended by exploiting well-documented abstract base classes).

TMop currently implements three policies: *OneNo*, *20%No* and *MajorityVoting*. The first one copies a TU in the *reject* file if at least one filter rejects it. The second and the third policy take this decision only if at least twenty or fifty percent of the filters reject the TU respectively.

These three policies reflect different TM cleaning strategies. The first one is a very aggressive (recall-oriented) solution that tends to flag more TUs as "bad". The third one is a more conservative (precision-oriented) solution, as it requires at least half of the judgments to be negative for pushing a TU in the *reject* file. Depending on the user needs and the overall quality of the TM, the choice of the policy will allow keeping under control the number of false positives ("bad" TUs accepted) and false negatives ("good" TUs rejected).

4 Benchmarking

We test TMop on the English-Italian version of MyMemory,[4] one of the world's largest collaborative public TMs. This dump contains about 11M TUs coming from heterogeneous sources: aggregated private TMs, either provided by translators or automatically extracted from the web/corpora, as well as anonymous contributions of (*source, target*) bi-segments. Its uncontrolled sources call for accurate cleaning methods (e.g. to make it more accurate, smaller and manageable).

From the TM we randomly extracted a subset of 1M TUs to compute the statistics of each filter and a collection of 2,500 TUs manually annotated with binary labels. Data annotation was done by two Italian native speakers properly trained with the same guidelines prepared by the TM owner for periodic manual revisions. After agreement computation (Cohen's kappa is 0.78), a reconciliation ended up with about 65% positive and 35% negative examples. This pool is randomly split in two parts. One (1,000 instances) is used as test set for our evaluation. The other (1,500 instances) is used to replicate the supervised approach of Barbu (2015), which leverages human-labelled data to train an SVM binary classifier. We use it as a term of comparison to assess the performance of the different groups of filters.

To handle the imbalanced (65%-35%) data distribution, and equally reward the correct classification on both classes, we evaluate performance in terms of balanced accuracy (BA), computed as the average of the accuracies on the two classes (Brodersen et al., 2010).

In Table 1, different combinations of the four groups of filters are shown with results aggregated with the *20%No* policy, which, on this data, results to be the best performing policy among the ones implemented in TMop. Based on the statistics collected in the `learning` phase of each filter, the *accept/reject* criterion applied in these experiments considers as "good" all the TUs for

[4]http://mymemory.translated.net

Filters	BA↑
(Barbu, 2015)	77.7
B	52.8
LI	69.0
QE	71.2
WE	65.0
B + LI	55.4
B + QE	70.1
B + WE	68.7
QE + LI	71.7
QE + WE	67.9
LI + WE	68.1
B + QE + LI	72.9
B + WE + LI	70.3
B + QE + WE	73.3
B + QE + LI + WE	76.3

Table 1: Balanced accuracy of different filter combinations on a 1,000 TU, EN-IT test set. B=Basic, LI=language identification, QE=quality estimation, WE=word embedding.

which the filter value is below one standard deviation from the mean and "bad" otherwise.

Looking at the results, it is worth noting that the LI, QE and WE groups, both alone and in combination, outperform the basic filters (B), which substantially represent those implemented by commercial tools. Although relying on an external component (the word aligner), QE filters produce the best performance in isolation, showing that word alignment information is a good indicator of translation quality. The results obtained by combining the different groups confirm their complementarity. In particular, when using all the groups, the performance is close to the results achieved by the supervised method by Barbu (2015), which relies on human-labelled data (76.3 vs. 77.7).

The choice of which filter combination to use strongly depends on the application scenario and it is often a trade-off. A first important aspect concerns the type of user. When the expertise to train a word aligner is not available, combining B, WE and LI is the best solution, though it comes at the cost of lower accuracy. Another aspect is the processing time that the user can afford. TM cleaning is an operation conceived to be performed once in a while (possibly overnight), once the TM has grown enough to justify a new sanity check. However, although it does not require real-time processing, the size of the TM can motivate the selection of faster filter combinations. An analysis of the efficiency of the four groups, made by counting the number of processed TUs per second,[5] indicates that B and QE are the fastest filters (processing on average ~2,000 TUs/sec.). The LI filter is slower, processing ~300 TUs per second, while the large number of times the cosine similarity score is computed does not allow the WE filter to process more than 50 TUs per second.

5 Conclusion

We presented TMop, the first open-source tool for automatic Translation Memory (TM) cleaning. We summarised its design criteria, workflow and main components, also reporting some efficiency and performance indicators. TMop is implemented in Python and can be downloaded, together with complete documentation, from `https://github.com/hlt-mt/TMOP`. Its license is FreeBSD, a very open permissive noncopyleft license, compatible with the GNU GPL and with any use, including commercial.

Acknowledgments

This work has been partially supported by the EC-funded project ModernMT (H2020 grant agreement no. 645487). The work carried out at FBK by Masoud Jalili Sabet was sponsored by the EAMT summer internships 2015 program and supported by Prof. Heshaam Faili (University of Tehran). The authors would also like to thank Translated for providing a dump of MyMemory.

References

Peter Arthern. 1979. Machine Translation and Computerized Terminology Systems: a Translator's Viewpoint. In *Translating and the computer. Proc. of a seminar*, pages 77–108, London, UK.

Eduard Barbu. 2015. Spotting False Translation Segments in Translation Memories. In *Proc. of the Workshop Natural Language Processing for Translation Memories*, pages 9–16, Hissar, Bulgaria.

Michael Bloodgood and Benjamin Strauss. 2014. Translation Memory Retrieval Methods. In *Proc. of the 14th Conference of the EACL*, pages 202–210, Gothenburg, Sweden.

Kay Henning Brodersen, Cheng Soon Ong, Klaas Enno Stephan, and Joachim M. Buhmann. 2010. The Balanced Accuracy and Its Posterior Distribution. In *Proc. of the 2010 20th International Conference on Pattern Recognition*, ICPR '10, pages 3121–3124.

José G. C. de Souza, Christian Buck, Marco Turchi, and Matteo Negri. 2013. FBK-UEdin Participation to the WMT13 Quality Estimation Shared Task. In *Proc. of the Eighth Workshop on Statistical Machine Translation*, pages 352–358, Sofia, Bulgaria. Association for Computational Linguistics.

José G. C. de Souza, Jesús González-Rubio, Christian Buck, Marco Turchi, and Matteo Negri. 2014. FBK-UPV-UEdin Participation in the WMT14 Quality Estimation Shared-task. In *Proc. of the Ninth Workshop on Statistical Machine Translation*, pages 322–328, Baltimore, Maryland, USA.

Konstantinos Chatzitheodoroou. 2015. Improving Translation Memory Fuzzy Matching by Paraphrasing. In *Proc. of the Workshop Natural Language Processing for Translation Memories*, pages 24–30, Hissar, Bulgaria.

Qin Gao and Stephan Vogel. 2008. Parallel Implementations of Word Alignment Tool. In *In Proc. of the ACL 2008 Software Engineering, Testing, and Quality Assurance Workshop*.

Rohit Gupta, Hanna Bechara, and Constantin Orasan. 2014. Intelligent Translation Memory Matching and Retrieval Metric Exploiting Linguistic Technology. In *Proc. of Translating and the Computer: Vol. 36.*, pages 86–89.

Rohit Gupta, Constantin Orasan, Marcos Zampieri, Mihaela Vela, and Josef Van Genabith. 2015. Can Translation Memories afford not to use paraphrasing? In *Proc. of the 18th Annual Conference of the European Association for Machine Translation*, pages 35–42, Antalya, Turkey.

Masoud Jalili Sabet, Matteo Negri, Marco Turchi, and Eduard Barbu. 2016. An Unsupervised Method for Automatic Translation Memory Cleaning. In *Proc. of the 54th Annual Meeting of the Association for Computational Linguistics*, Berlin, Germany.

Marco Lui and Timothy Baldwin. 2012. langid.py: An Off-the-shelf Language Identification Tool. In *Proc. of the ACL 2012 system demonstrations*, pages 25–30. Association for Computational Linguistics.

Yashar Mehdad, Matteo Negri, and Marcello Federico. 2012. Match without a Referee: Evaluating MT Adequacy without Reference Translations. In *Proc. of the Machine Translation Workshop (WMT2012)*, pages 171–180, Montréal, Canada.

Anders Søgaard, Željko Agić, Héctor Martínez Alonso, Barbara Plank, Bernd Bohnet, and Anders Johannsen. 2015. Inverted indexing for cross-lingual NLP. In *The 53rd Annual Meeting of the Association for Computational Linguistics (ACL 2015)*.

Tom Vanallemeersch and Vincent Vandeghinste. 2015. Assessing Linguistically Aware Fuzzy Matching in Translation Memories. In *Proc. of the 18th Annual Conference of the European Association for Machine Translation*, pages 153–160, Antalya, Turkey.

---

[5]Experiments were run with a PC with an Intel Core i5 M540 @ 2.53GHz and 6 GB RAM.

MMFEAT: A Toolkit for Extracting Multi-Modal Features

Douwe Kiela
Computer Laboratory
University of Cambridge
`douwe.kiela@cl.cam.ac.uk`

Abstract

Research at the intersection of language and other modalities, most notably vision, is becoming increasingly important in natural language processing. We introduce a toolkit that can be used to obtain feature representations for visual and auditory information. MMFEAT is an easy-to-use Python toolkit, which has been developed with the purpose of making non-linguistic modalities more accessible to natural language processing researchers.

1 Introduction

Distributional models are built on the assumption that the meaning of a word is represented as a distribution over others (Turney and Pantel, 2010; Clark, 2015), which implies that they suffer from the grounding problem (Harnad, 1990). That is, they do not account for the fact that human semantic knowledge is grounded in the perceptual system (Louwerse, 2008). There has been a lot of interest within the Natural Language Processing community for making use of extra-linguistic perceptual information, much of it in a subfield called multi-modal semantics. Such multi-modal models outperform language-only models on a range of tasks, including modelling semantic similarity and relatedness (Bruni et al., 2014; Silberer and Lapata, 2014), improving lexical entailment (Kiela et al., 2015b), predicting compositionality (Roller and Schulte im Walde, 2013), bilingual lexicon induction (Bergsma and Van Durme, 2011) and metaphor identification (Shutova et al., 2016). Although most of this work has relied on vision for the perceptual input, recent approaches have also used auditory (Lopopolo and van Miltenburg, 2015; Kiela and Clark, 2015) and even olfactory (Kiela et al., 2015a) information.

In this demonstration paper, we describe MM-FEAT, a Python toolkit that makes it easy to obtain images and sound files and extract visual or auditory features from them. The toolkit includes two standalone command-line tools that do not require any knowledge of the Python programming language: one that can be used for automatically obtaining files from a variety of sources, including Google, Bing and FreeSound (*miner.py*); and one that can be used for extracting different types of features from directories of data files (*extract.py*). In addition, the package comes with code for manipulating multi-modal spaces and several demos to illustrate the wide range of applications. The toolkit is open source under the BSD license and available at `https://github.com/douwekiela/mmfeat`.

2 Background

2.1 Bag of multi-modal words

Although it is possible to ground distributional semantics in perception using e.g. co-occurrence patterns of image tags (Baroni and Lenci, 2008) or surrogates of human semantic knowledge such as feature norms (Andrews et al., 2009), the *de facto* method for grounding representations in perception has relied on processing raw image data (Baroni, 2016). The traditional method for obtaining visual representations (Feng and Lapata, 2010; Leong and Mihalcea, 2011; Bruni et al., 2011) has been to apply the bag-of-visual-words (BoVW) approach (Sivic and Zisserman, 2003). The method can be described as follows:

1. obtain relevant images for a word or set of words;

2. for each image, get local feature descriptors;

3. cluster feature descriptors with k-means to find the centroids, a.k.a. the "visual words";

Proceedings of the 54th Annual Meeting of the Association for Computational Linguistics—System Demonstrations, pages 55–60,
Berlin, Germany, August 7-12, 2016. ©2016 Association for Computational Linguistics

4. quantize the local descriptors by comparing them to the cluster centroids; and

5. combine relevant image representations into an overall visual representation for a word.

The local feature descriptors in step (2) tend to be variants of the dense scale-invariant feature transform (SIFT) algorithm (Lowe, 2004), where an image is laid out as a dense grid and feature descriptors are computed for each keypoint.

A similar method has recently been applied to the auditory modality (Lopopolo and van Miltenburg, 2015; Kiela and Clark, 2015), using sound files from FreeSound (Font et al., 2013). Bag-of-audio-words (BoAW) uses mel-frequency cepstral coefficients (MFCCs) (O'Shaughnessy, 1987) for the local descriptors, although other local frame representations may also be used. In MFCC, frequency bands are spaced along the mel scale (Stevens et al., 1937), which has the advantage that it approximates human auditory perception more closely than e.g. linearly-spaced frequency bands.

2.2 Convolutional neural networks

In computer vision, the BoVW method has been superseded by deep convolutional neural networks (CNNs) (LeCun et al., 1998; Krizhevsky et al., 2012). Kiela and Bottou (2014) showed that such networks learn high-quality representations that can successfully be transferred to natural language processing tasks. Their method works as follows:

1. obtain relevant images for a word or set of words;

2. for each image, do a forward pass through a CNN trained on an image recognition task and extract the pre-softmax layer;

3. combine relevant image representations into an overall visual representation for a word.

They used the pre-softmax layer (referred to as FC7) from a CNN trained by Oquab et al. (2014), which was an adaptation of the well-known CNN by Krizhevsky et al. (2012) that played a key role in the deep learning revolution in computer vision (Razavian et al., 2014; LeCun et al., 2015). Such CNN-derived representations perform much better than BoVW features and have since been used in a variety of NLP applications (Kiela et al., 2015c; Lazaridou et al., 2015; Shutova et al., 2016; Bulat et al., 2016).

2.3 Related work

The process for obtaining perceptual representations thus involves three distinct steps: obtaining files relevant to words or phrases, obtaining representations for the files, and aggregating these into visual or auditory representations. To our knowledge, this is the first toolkit that spans this entire process. There are libraries that cover some of these steps. Notably, VSEM (Bruni et al., 2013) is a Matlab library for visual semantics representation that implements BoVW and useful functionality for manipulating visual representations. DISSECT (Dinu et al., 2013) is a toolkit for distributional compositional semantics that makes it easy to work with (textual) distributional spaces. Lopopolo and van Miltenburg (2015) have also released their code for obtaining BoAW representations[1].

3 MMFeat Overview

The MMFeat toolkit is written in Python. There are two command-line tools (described below) for obtaining files and extracting representations that do not require any knowledge of Python. The Python interface maintains a modular structure and contains the following modules:

- mmfeat.miner
- mmfeat.bow
- mmfeat.cnn
- mmfeat.space

Source files (images or sounds) can be obtained with the *miner* module, although this is not a requirement: it is straightforward to build an index of a data directory that matches words or phrases with relevant files. The miner module automatically generates this index, a Python dictionary mapping labels to lists of filenames, which is stored as a Python pickle file *index.pkl* in the data directory. The index is used by the *bow* and *cnn* modules, which together form the core of the package for obtaining perceptual representations. The *space* package allows for the manipulation and combination of multi-modal spaces.

miner Three data sources are currently supported: Google Images[2] (GoogleMiner), Bing Images[3] (BingMiner) and FreeSound[4] (FreeSound-Miner). All three of them require API keys,

[1]https://github.com/evanmiltenburg/soundmodels-iwcs
[2]https://images.google.com
[3]https://www.bing.com/images
[4]https://www.freesound.org

which can be obtained online and are stored in the *miner.yaml* settings file in the root folder.

bow The bag-of-words methods are contained in this module. BoVW and BoAW are accessible through the mmfeat.bow.vw and mmfeat.bow.aw modules respectively, through the BoVW and BoAW classes. These classes obtain feature descriptors and perform clustering and quantization through a standard set of methods. BoVW uses dense SIFT for its local feature descriptors; BoAW uses MFCC. The modules also contain an interface for loading local feature descriptors from Matlab, allowing for simple integraton with e.g. VLFeat[5]. The centroids obtained by the clustering (sometimes also called the "codebook") are stored in the data directory for re-use at a later stage.

cnn The CNN module uses Python bindings to the Caffe deep learning framework (Jia et al., 2014). It supports the pre-trained reference adaptation of AlexNet (Krizhevsky et al., 2012), GoogLeNet (Szegedy et al., 2015) and VGGNet (Simonyan and Zisserman, 2015). The interface is identical to the *bow* interface.

space An additional module is provided for making it easy to manipulate perceptual representations. The module contains methods for aggregating image or sound file representations into visual or auditory representations; combining perceptual representations with textual representations into multi-modal ones; computing nearest neighbors and similarity scores; and calculating Spearman ρ_s correlation scores relative to human similarity and relatedness judgments.

3.1 Dependencies

MMFeat has the following dependencies: *scipy*, *scikit-learn* and *numpy*. These are standard Python libraries that are easy to install using your favorite package manager. The BoAW module additionally requires *librosa*[6] to obtain MFCC descriptors. The CNN module requires Caffe[7]. It is recommended to make use of Caffe's GPU support, if available, for increased processing speeds. More detailed installation instructions are provided in the readme file online and in the documentation of the respective projects.

---

[5] http://www.vlfeat.org
[6] https://github.com/bmcfee/librosa
[7] http://caffe.berkeleyvision.org

4 Tools

MMFeat comes with two easy-to-use command-line tools for those unfamiliar with the Python programming language.

4.1 Mining: *miner.py*

The *miner.py* tool takes three arguments: the data source (bing, google or freesound), a query file that contains a line-by-line list of queries, and a data directory to store the mined image or sound files in. Its usage is as follows:

```
miner.py {bing,google,freesound} \
    query_file data_dir [-n int]
```

The -n option can be used to specify the number of images to download per query. The following examples show how to use the tool to get 10 images from Bing and 100 sound files from FreeSound for the queries "dog" and "cat":

```
$ echo -e "dog\ncat" > queries.txt
$ python miner.py -n 10 bing \
    queries.txt ./img_data_dir
$ python miner.py -n 100 freesound \
    queries.txt ./sound_data_dir
```

4.2 Feature extraction: *extract.py*

The *extract.py* tool takes three arguments: the type of model to apply (boaw, bovw or cnn), the data directory where relevant files and the index are stored, and the output file where the representations are written to. Its usage is as follows:

```
extract.py [-k int] [-c string] \
    [-o {pickle,json,csv}] [-s float] \
    [-m {vgg,alexnet,googlenet}] \
    {boaw,bovw,cnn} data_dir out_file
```

The -k option sets the number of clusters to use in the bag of words methods (the k in k-means). The -c option allows for pointing to an existing codebook, if available. The -s option allows for subsampling the number of files to use for the clustering process (which can require significant amounts of memory) and is in the range 0-1. The tool can output representation in Python pickle, JSON and CSV formats. The following examples show how the three models can easily be applied:

```
python extract.py -k 100 -s 0.1 bovw \
    ./img_data_dir ./output_vectors.pkl
python extract.py -gpu -o json cnn \
    ./img_data_dir ./output_vectors.json
python extract.py -k 300 -s 0.5 -o csv \
    boaw ./sound_data_dir ./out_vecs.csv
```

5 Getting Started

The command-line tools mirror the Python interface, which allows for more fine-grained control over the process. In what follows, we walk through an example illustrating the process. The code should be self-explanatory.

Mining The first step is to mine some images from Google Images:

```
datadir = '/path/to/data'
words = ['dog', 'cat']
n_images = 10

from mmfeat.miner import *

miner = GoogleMiner(datadir, \
        '/path/to/miner.yaml')
miner.getResults(words, n_images)
miner.save()
```

Applying models We then apply both the BoVW and CNN models, in a manner familiar to scikit-learn users, by calling the fit() method:

```
from mmfeat.bow import *
from mmfeat.cnn import *

b = BoVW(k=100, subsample=0.1)
c = CNN(modelType='alexnet', gpu=True)
b.load(data_dir)
b.fit()
c.load(data_dir)
c.fit()
```

Building the space We subsequently construct the aggregated space of visual representations and print these to the screen:

```
from mmfeat.space import *

for lkp in [b.toLookup(), c.toLookup()]:
    vs = AggSpace(lkp, 'mean')
    print vs.space
```

These short examples are meant to show how one can straightforwardly obtain perceptual representations that can be applied in a wide variety of experiments.

6 Demos

To illustrate the range of possible applications, the toolkit comes with a set of demonstrations of its usage. The following demos are available:

1-Similarity and relatedness The demo downloads images for the concepts in the well-known MEN (Bruni et al., 2012) and SimLex-999 (Hill et al., 2014) datasets, obtains CNN-derived visual representations and calculates the Spearman ρ_s correlations for textual, visual and multi-modal representations.

2-ESP game To illustrate that it is not necessary to mine images or sound files and that an existing data directory can be used, this demo builds an index for the ESP Game dataset (Von Ahn and Dabbish, 2004) and obtains and stores CNN representations for future use in other applications.

3-Matlab interface To show that local feature descriptors from Matlab can be used, this demo contains Matlab code (*run_dsift.m*) that uses VLFeat to obtain descriptors, which are then used in the BoVW model to obtain visual representations.

4-Instrument clustering The demo downloads sound files from FreeSound for a set of instruments and applies BoAW. The mean auditory representations are clustered and the cluster assignments are reported to the screen, showing similar instruments in similar clusters.

5-Image dispersion This demo obtains images for the concepts of *elephant* and *happiness* and applies BoVW. It then shows that the former has a lower image dispersion score and is consequently more concrete than the latter, as described in Kiela et al. (2014).

7 Conclusions

The field of natural language processing has broadened in scope to address increasingly challenging tasks. While the core NLP tasks will remain predominantly focused on linguistic input, it is important to address the fact that humans acquire and apply language in perceptually rich environments. Moving towards human-level AI will require the integration and modeling of multiple modalities beyond language.

Advances in multi-modal semantics show how textual information can fruitfully be combined with other modalities, opening up many avenues for further exploration. Some NLP researchers may consider non-textual modalities challenging or outside of their area of expertise. We hope that this toolkit enables them in carrying out research that uses extra-linguistic input.

Acknowledgments

The author was supported by EPSRC grant EP/I037512/1 and would like to thank Anita Verö, Stephen Clark and the reviewers for helpful suggestions.

References

Mark Andrews, Gabriella Vigliocco, and David Vinson. 2009. Integrating experiential and distributional data to learn semantic representations. *Psychological review*, 116(3):463.

Marco Baroni and Alessandro Lenci. 2008. Concepts and properties in word spaces. *Italian Journal of Linguistics*, 20(1):55–88.

Marco Baroni. 2016. Grounding distributional semantics in the visual world. *Language and Linguistics Compass*, 10(1):3–13.

Shane Bergsma and Benjamin Van Durme. 2011. Learning bilingual lexicons using the visual similarity of labeled web images. In *IJCAI*, pages 1764–1769.

Elia Bruni, Giang Binh Tran, and Marco Baroni. 2011. Distributional semantics from text and images. In *Proceedings of the GEMS 2011 workshop on geometrical models of natural language semantics*, pages 22–32. Association for Computational Linguistics.

Elia Bruni, Gemma Boleda, Marco Baroni, and Nam-Khanh Tran. 2012. Distributional semantics in technicolor. In *ACL*, pages 136–145.

Elia Bruni, Ulisse Bordignon, Adam Liska, Jasper Uijlings, and Irina Sergienya. 2013. Vsem: An open library for visual semantics representation. In *Proceedings of the 51st Annual Meeting of the Association for Computational Linguistics*, pages 187–192, Sofia, Bulgaria.

Elia Bruni, Nam-Khanh Tran, and Marco Baroni. 2014. Multimodal distributional semantics. *Journal of Artifical Intelligence Research*, 49:1–47.

Luana Bulat, Douwe Kiela, and Stephen Clark. 2016. Vision and Feature Norms: Improving automatic feature norm learning through cross-modal maps. In *Proceedings of NAACL-HLT 2016*, San Diego, CA.

Stephen Clark. 2015. Vector Space Models of Lexical Meaning. In Shalom Lappin and Chris Fox, editors, *Handbook of Contemporary Semantics*, chapter 16. Wiley-Blackwell, Oxford.

Georgiana Dinu, Nghia The Pham, and Marco Baroni. 2013. DISSECT - DIStributional SEmantics Composition Toolkit. In *Proceedings of the 51st Annual Meeting of the Association for Computational Linguistics*, pages 31—36, Sofia, Bulgaria.

Yansong Feng and Mirella Lapata. 2010. Visual information in semantic representation. In *Proceedings of NAACL*, pages 91–99.

Frederic Font, Gerard Roma, and Xavier Serra. 2013. Freesound technical demo. In *Proceedings of the 21st acm international conference on multimedia*, pages 411–412. ACM.

Stevan Harnad. 1990. The symbol grounding problem. *Physica D*, 42:335–346.

Felix Hill, Roi Reichart, and Anna Korhonen. 2014. SimLex-999: Evaluating semantic models with (genuine) similarity estimation. *CoRR*, abs/1408.3456.

Yangqing Jia, Evan Shelhamer, Jeff Donahue, Sergey Karayev, Jonathan Long, Ross B. Girshick, Sergio Guadarrama, and Trevor Darrell. 2014. Caffe: Convolutional architecture for fast feature embedding. In *ACM Multimedia*, pages 675–678.

Douwe Kiela and Léon Bottou. 2014. Learning image embeddings using convolutional neural networks for improved multi-modal semantics. In *Proceedings of EMNLP*, pages 36–45.

Douwe Kiela and Stephen Clark. 2015. Multi- and cross-modal semantics beyond vision: Grounding in auditory perception. In *Proceedings of the 2015 Conference on Empirical Methods in Natural Language Processing*, pages 2461–2470, Lisbon, Portugal, September. Association for Computational Linguistics.

Douwe Kiela, Felix Hill, Anna Korhonen, and Stephen Clark. 2014. Improving multi-modal representations using image dispersion: Why less is sometimes more. In *Proceedings of ACL*, pages 835–841.

Douwe Kiela, Luana Bulat, and Stephen Clark. 2015a. Grounding semantics in olfactory perception. In *Proceedings of ACL*, pages 231–236, Beijing, China, July.

Douwe Kiela, Laura Rimell, Ivan Vulić, and Stephen Clark. 2015b. Exploiting image generality for lexical entailment detection. In *Proceedings of the 53rd Annual Meeting of the Association for Computational Linguistics and the 7th International Joint Conference on Natural Language Processing (Volume 2: Short Papers)*, pages 119–124, Beijing, China, July. Association for Computational Linguistics.

Douwe Kiela, Ivan Vulić, and Stephen Clark. 2015c. Visual bilingual lexicon induction with transferred convnet features. In *Proceedings of the 2015 Conference on Empirical Methods in Natural Language Processing*, pages 148–158, Lisbon, Portugal, September. Association for Computational Linguistics.

Alex Krizhevsky, Ilya Sutskever, and Geoffrey E. Hinton. 2012. ImageNet classification with deep convolutional neural networks. In *Proceedings of NIPS*, pages 1106–1114.

Angeliki Lazaridou, Dat Tien Nguyen, Raffaella Bernardi, and Marco Baroni. 2015. Unveiling the dreams of word embeddings: Towards language-driven image generation. *CoRR*, abs/1506.03500.

Yann LeCun, Léon Bottou, Yoshua Bengio, and Patrick Haffner. 1998. Gradient-based learning applied to document recognition. *Proceedings of the IEEE*, 86(11):2278–2324.

Yann LeCun, Yoshua Bengio, and Geoffrey Hinton. 2015. Deep learning. *Nature*, 521(7553):436—444.

Chee Wee Leong and Rada Mihalcea. 2011. Going beyond text: A hybrid image-text approach for measuring word relatedness. In *Proceedings of IJCNLP*, pages 1403–1407.

A. Lopopolo and E. van Miltenburg. 2015. Sound-based distributional models. In *Proceedings of the 11th International Conference on Computational Semantics (IWCS 2015)*.

Max M. Louwerse. 2008. Symbol interdependency in symbolic and embodied cognition. *Topics in Cognitive Science*, 59(1):617–645.

David G. Lowe. 2004. Distinctive image features from scale-invariant keypoints. *International Journal of Computer Vision*, 60(2):91–110.

Maxime Oquab, Léon Bottou, Ivan Laptev, and Josef Sivic. 2014. Learning and transferring mid-level image representations using convolutional neural networks. In *Proceedings of CVPR*, pages 1717–1724.

D. O'Shaughnessy. 1987. *Speech communication: human and machine*. Addison-Wesley series in electrical engineering: digital signal processing. Universities Press (India) Pvt. Limited.

Ali Razavian, Hossein Azizpour, Josephine Sullivan, and Stefan Carlsson. 2014. CNN features off-the-shelf: an astounding baseline for recognition. In *Proceedings of the IEEE Conference on Computer Vision and Pattern Recognition Workshops*, pages 806–813.

Stephen Roller and Sabine Schulte im Walde. 2013. A multimodal LDA model integrating textual, cognitive and visual modalities. In *Proceedings of EMNLP*, pages 1146–1157.

Ekaterina Shutova, Douwe Kiela, and Jean Maillard. 2016. Black holes and white rabbits: Metaphor identification with visual features. In *Proceedings of NAACL-HTL 2016*, San Diego. Association for Computational Linguistics.

Carina Silberer and Mirella Lapata. 2014. Learning grounded meaning representations with autoencoders. In *Proceedings of ACL*, pages 721–732.

Karen Simonyan and Andrew Zisserman. 2015. Very deep convolutional networks for large-scale image recognition. In *Proceedings of ICLR*.

Josef Sivic and Andrew Zisserman. 2003. Video google: A text retrieval approach to object matching in videos. In *Proceedings of ICCV*, pages 1470–1477.

Stanley Smith Stevens, John Volkmann, and Edwin B. Newman. 1937. A scale for the measurement of the psychological magnitude pitch. *Journal of the Acoustical Society of America*, 8(3):185—190.

Christian Szegedy, Wei Liu, Yangqing Jia, Pierre Sermanet, Scott Reed, Dragomir Anguelov, Dumitru Erhan, Vincent Vanhoucke, and Andrew Rabinovich. 2015. Going deeper with convolutions. In *Proceedings of the IEEE Conference on Computer Vision and Pattern Recognition*, pages 1–9.

Peter D. Turney and Patrick Pantel. 2010. From Frequency to Meaning: vector space models of semantics. *Journal of Artifical Intelligence Research*, 37(1):141–188, January.

Luis Von Ahn and Laura Dabbish. 2004. Labeling images with a computer game. In *Proceedings of the SIGCHI conference on human factors in computing systems*, pages 319–326. ACM.

JEDI: Joint Entity and Relation Detection using Type Inference

Johannes Kirschnick[1], Holmer Hemsen[1], Volker Markl[1,2]
[1]DFKI Project Office Berlin, Alt-Moabit 91c, Berlin
`firstname.lastname@dfki.de`
[2]Technische Univeristät Berlin
Database Systems and Information Management Group
Einsteinufer 17, 10587 Berlin, Germany
`firstname.lastname@tu-berlin.de`

Abstract

FREEBASE contains entities and relation information but is highly incomplete. Relevant information is ubiquitous in web text, but extraction deems challenging. We present JEDI, an automated system to jointly extract typed named entities and FREEBASE relations using dependency pattern from text. An innovative method for constraint solving on entity types of multiple relations is used to disambiguate pattern. The high precision in the evaluation supports our claim that we can detect entities and relations together, alleviating the need to train a custom classifier for an entity type[1].

1 Introduction

Finding, tagging and extracting relations in web text is one of the more challenging tasks in Information Extraction (IE). It consists of correctly labeling entities as instances of a particular type (such as Person, Organization or Location) and detecting relations between them, such as *worksIn*, *bornIn* or even more fine grained ones such as *receiveDegree*. These relations are stored for further analysis in knowledge bases, but often existing ones are highly incomplete. Min et al. (2013) report that in the collaborative-edited FREEBASE[2] knowledge base 93.8% of the person entities are missing a *place of birth* entry. To close the cap automated methods are needed that can detect these relations, by analyzing the abundance of web text.

A typical process to detect relations uses the linking words (pattern) between two entities to label a relation, but this poses the challenge of dealing with ambiguous pattern.

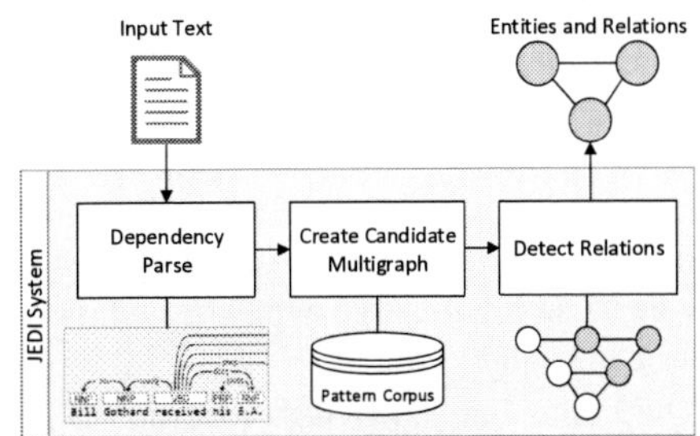

Figure 1: JEDI System Overview. Text is annotated with dependency information. Candidate entities connecting shortest path pattern are scored against a corpus. Constraint solving on the relation types resolves ambiguities and determines the final relations.

Consider the following sentences that both contain the pattern *receive* indicating completely different relations: *"<u>Bill</u> received his <u>B.A.</u> in Biblical Studies from Wheaton College."*, and *"<u>Leo</u> received an <u>Oscar</u> for Revenant."*.

The first sentence contains the binary relation *receiveDegree*, linking a person to a degree, but in the second, the same pattern indicates the *personAward* relation. To correctly disambiguate, we need to incorporate context. This paper proposes the novel method of using the entity types of multiple binary relations to solve the disambiguation.

Motivation Typically labeling relations and entities is done in sequence, leading to a pipeline architecture which first detects entities and subsequently tries to link them to extract relations. As detection errors can easily propagate, there is potential in executing these steps jointly. It is driven by the motivation that instead of focusing on individual binary assignments, multiple entities found in the text can be used to constraint and restrict each other's entity and relation types.

Figure 1 shows an overview of the entire solution. Entity mentions and potential relations indi-

---

[1]Demonstrator is available at jedi.textmining.tu-berlin.de
[2]Freebase is available at www.freebase.com

61

Proceedings of the 54th Annual Meeting of the Association for Computational Linguistics—System Demonstrations, pages 61–66,
Berlin, Germany, August 7-12, 2016. ©2016 Association for Computational Linguistics

cated by a pattern form a multi graph. Selecting a particular type for an entity prunes the number of potential relations that this entity can participate in. Furthermore, having established a relation between a pair of entities further restricts the potential relations that can hold between any other entity and one of the pair's members due to inferred type restrictions. Thus all candidate entities in a sentence are considered together to support or restrict any contained relations.

Contributions This paper presents and evaluates JEDI a system to translate the relation detection problem into a constraint satisfaction problem. The graph of entities and potential relations forms a resolution graph, where each entity is constrained on the potential types it can hold. Solving this problem jointly resolves entity and relation types without training an entity classifier, allowing to detect the large number of relation and types defined in FREEBASE.

The evaluation shows high precision across a variety of texts and relations. We furthermore release the implementation as open source and provide a web demonstrator to showcase the system.

2   Related Work

Most prominent for relation extraction is the idea that entities that co-occur with a similar context have similar meanings, driven by the distributional hypothesis (Harris, 1954). The shortest path kernel is a good estimator for approximating the distribution and has been used by Bunescu and Mooney (2005). Culotta and Sorensen (2004) showed that it is possible to train a relation classifier on the extracted pattern to predict a small number of relations.

Kate and Mooney (2010) proposed a card style resolution algorithm, which infers recursively the most probable relation assignment for a given entity pair, but still requires an entity classifier and only works for a small number of relations.

Mintz et al. (2009) proposed to use clustering to group together entity co-occurrences based on their shortest path, to extract relation types. This eliminates the need for a classifier for relation detection, but requires one for entity extraction. Pattern can only be assigned to one relation and thus capture only the most dominating meaning. The problem of relation extraction can also be solved using matrix decomposition, as shown by Riedel et al. (2013). Their work targets FREEBASE rela-

tions, but demands a complex training step which decomposes the co-occurrence matrix and is dependent on the text domain as well.

The SOFIE system (Suchanek et al., 2009) uses logical reasoning to find instances of a relation in text. It does not require any pre-training as it learns the extraction rules alongside the relation detection, but is limited in the amount of data it can process, because of the costly resolution step. Similar to our approach Singh et al. (2013) proposed to model the entity tagging and relation extraction problem jointly, using belief propagation to find relation instances, but targeting a much smaller number of relations. The idea to incorporate types into the relation extraction process was explored by Koch et al. (2014) improving the relation detection performance.

Contrary to existing systems JEDI does not need a pre-trained entity classifier. We leverage a very large corpus of shortest path patterns as reference and use constraint propagation to solve ambiguities. Our system also maps into the large number of predefined FREEBASE relations, alleviating the need to manually specify any relations. The system can be easily incorporated into a more complex IE pipeline that uses the results for example for entity linking.

3   Pattern Corpus

To detect meaningful patterns we use FREEPAL (Kirschnick et al., 2014). A dataset of 10 million lexico-syntactic pattern-relation assignments built using distant supervision (Mintz et al., 2009). Each pattern was generated from a shortest dependency path between two known FREEBASE entities in a sentence that participate in a known relation. The corpus uses CLUEWEB09 as text basis and the FACC1 entity annotations (Gabrilovich et al., 2013) to generate a distribution of relations over pattern. An entropy score indicates the degree of ambiguity, which we use for scoring the relation assignments. Overall more than 75% of the contained pattern were observed with more than one relation, requiring a disambiguation method.

4   Jointly Detecting Entities and Relations

The process of detecting relations is described in Figure 2 and consists of the following steps, described in the following:

- Pre-process input text

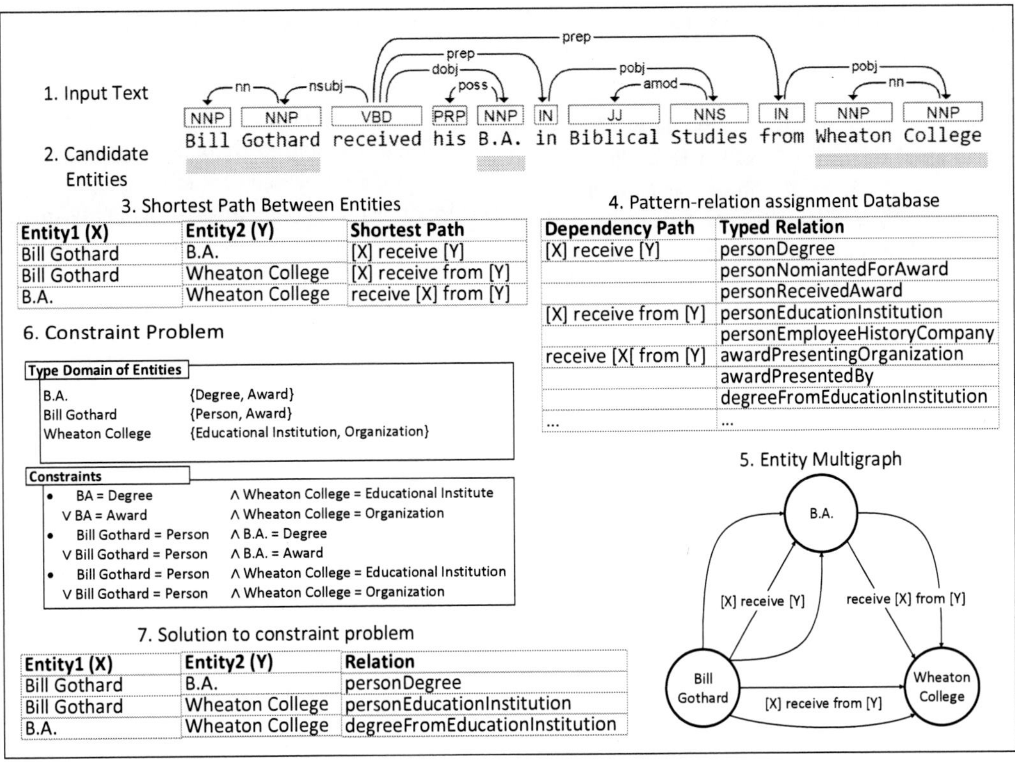

Figure 2: Solution overview: Candidate Entities (2) are selected from the source text (1). Shortest path in the dependency tree is extracted (3), pruned against pattern-relation assignment database (4), type information is translated into a multi graph (5) which defines the constraint satisfaction problem (6). The solution yields an assignment of entity types and relations (7). (Types are omitted for readability)

- Selection of candidate entities
- Extract shortest dependency path (pattern) between all pairwise candidate entities
- Match the pattern using the FREEPAL corpus to determine candidate relations
- Translate the relation detection into a constraint satisfaction problem which determines the potential types of all entities and thus the connecting relations

4.1 Pre-Processing

The target text is annotated with part-of-speech tags and dependency information using the Stanford CoreNLP Toolkit (Manning et al., 2014). Coreference resolution is applied to further link entity mentions across sentence boundaries providing more link targets between entities.

4.2 Selecting Candidate Entities

Instead of trying to find any of the 10 million pattern from the pattern corpus in a given text, where every match would provide a candidate subject and object pair for a relation, we reverse the problem and produce a set of candidate entities and try to match the connecting pattern with the corpus.

JEDI works with any candidate entities, produced for example by an existing entity tagger or just based on simple heuristics. One such simple heuristic is to use nouns, with the extension to join together adjacent nouns to effectively form noun phrases. Nouns are grouped, if they are directly adjacent and connected through a dependency link of the type *poss* or *nsubj*, while also allowing the connecting word "of". This captures entities of the form "University of Illinois" and "Wheaton College", but fails to separate appositions such as "Bishop Oldham" or "Professor Smith", but this can be later rectified. This heuristic can be easily changed as the remaining processing does not depend on the text form or type of the entities. Using nouns also helps in finding entities generally not covered by specific NER systems, such as "biblical studies" as a field of study, without specifically training a tagger for this target type.

4.3 Extracting the Shortest Path

Finding the shortest path between two entities equals finding a path in the dependency graph between the head words of each entity. We use a simplified instance of Collins Head finding rule (Collins, 2003) to determine the head in multiword entities. The pattern is derived by picking up all tokens in their lemmatized form on the path, substituting the start with X and the end with the label Y. To make the pattern more readable, all tokens are sorted based on their appearance in the source text.

This produces pattern of the form **[X] receive [Y] [1-dobj-2,1-nsubj-0]**. The pattern is further enriched with the individual dependency annotations to differentiate similar textual pattern[3].

Conjunctions We apply a simple normalization to conjunctions inspired by CLAUSIE (Corro and Gemulla, 2013). Removing the last token in patterns containing a conjunction dependency.

Coreference Resolution Coreference information expands mentions across sentence boundaries. Mentions that are connected through a chain are treated as if they are the same entity, if the source of the chain is marked as a candidate entity. Thus we substitute the coreference target with the source in the extraction process.

4.4 Pattern-Relation Assignments

The shortest path generation process generates a large number of pattern. To reduce the search space, all extracted pattern are matched against the FREEPAL corpus. This produces for each match a list of potential relations that this pattern has been observed with. Only pattern with an entropy smaller than 3.7[4] and that have been observed at least five times are considered. This reduces the noise by filtering out very unspecific pattern such as *[X] be [Y]*, but at the same time still allows for a lot of ambiguous pattern.

Each pattern is associated with a list of FREEBASE relations, for which the argument types are retrieved. This is used to restrict the X and Y entity types of the pattern respectively. We use the FREEBASE type normalization presented in FIGER (Ling and Weld, 2012) to reduce the number of entity types down to 112.

To address the problem of arbitrary granularity, we broaden the accepted argument types using a simple type hierarchy. For example, the *diedIn* relation, which indicates that a person died in a particular location, restricts the subject argument to be of type deceased person. While this is very specific it prevents linking to this entity in other relations, which only accept the more generic person type. The type hierarchy is generated by retrieving the *type hints* category for each type, using the FREEBASE API. While this does not produce a complete type hierarchy, it adds the most commonly used sub types for a given type.

4.5 Constraint Solving using Type Inference

The extracted pattern for each pair of entities form a multi-graph, where edges are assigned a confidence score based on the FREEPAL entropy. The resolution process tries to eagerly generate a type assignment for each entity, so that at least one edge between connected vertices, a particular relation, holds according to the type requirements. The choco library (Prud'homme et al., 2015) is used for constraint solving. Each edge is transformed into a constraint, using logical conjunctions between all connected vertex pairs and disjunction for each edge between two vertices and their types. This emits for each relation a constraint with all possible type and subtype combinations.

Scoring Constraint solving produces more than one potential solution. We use a scoring mechanism to rank the different solutions, taking into account the number of matched entities, the entropy score taken from the FREEPAL dataset, as well as the type hierarchy. This ensures that if possible, the most specific type assignment for a large number of entities is favored in the resolution process.

Backtracking If there is no assignment possible - there is a conflict in the graph. Conflicts can arise when detecting relations that are not part of the corpus for a given pattern or wrong pattern as a result of erroneously linking entities in a co-reference chain. Backtracking is used to repeatedly remove vertices and all associated edges from the graph until either a solution is found or all nodes are removed in which case there is no solution. To find the highest scoring assignment backtracking is used to evaluate multiple different graphs, even when a solution is found.

---

[3]Dependency information for all pattern is omitted in the paper for readability, but used during the resolution process.

[4]This entropy cutoff was derived empirically.

Relation	P	R	F
Education Degree	0	0	0
Place of Birth	0.76	0.60	0.68
Place of Death	0.89	0.27	0.41
Student Graduate	0.78	0.41	0.53

Table 1: Baseline performance. Precision, Recall and F-measure without Coreference Resolution and type inference using the Noun strategy.

Relation	P	R	F
Education Degree	0.94	0.61	0.74
Place of Birth	0.77	0.60	0.67
Place of Death	0.88	0.35	0.50
Student Graduate	0.76	0.37	0.50

Table 2: Type inference performance without Coreference Resolution using the Noun strategy.

Relation	Resolution Strategies and Comparison Results								
	Named Entities			Nouns			Akbik (2014)		
	P	R	F	P	R	F	P	R	F
Education Degree	**0.96**	0.03	0.05	**0.96**	0.74	0.83	0.87	0.29	0.44
Place of Birth	0.77	0.52	0.62	**0.83**	0.58	0.68	0.82	0.19	0.31
Place of Death	**0.92**	0.48	0.63	**0.92**	0.48	0.63	0.82	0.13	0.22
Student Graduate	0.78	0.51	0.62	0.77	0.51	0.61	**0.92**	0.17	0.29

Table 3: Performance with type inference and Coreference Resolution using Named Entities and Nouns as entity markers, comparing to Akbik (2014), reporting Precision, Recall and F-measures.

Stopping The search is terminated early when an adjustable time limit is hit, to ensure that the most probable solution is found early. This trade-off guarantees that the algorithm finishes in finite time, at the expense of not always finding the global optimal solution.

Result Once a solution is found, all vertices of the graph are bound to a type. The qualifying relation between any two connected vertices is selected as the one which has the highest score associated with it. This produces triples of the form **<entity, entity, relation>**.

5 Evaluation

The "Relation Extraction Corpus"[5] is used for evaluation – comparing precision, recall and F-measure. The corpus contains text snippets for four separate relations: person holding an education degree *educationDegree* (1580 triples), **place of death** (1955 triples), **place of birth** (8703 triples) and person graduated from education institute *studentGraduate* (32653 triples). Each excerpt is annotated by humans as to whether it supports a particular binary relation.

5.1 Results

Baseline Table 1 shows the baseline performance of the noun strategy without constraint solving, using the most likely relation for an identified pattern based on the FREEPAL entropy score.

The results show high precision for all relations except for education degree. This supports the use of the FREEPAL dataset for relation extraction, as it covers already a large variety of pattern instances. No instances of the education degree relation were found as almost all pattern for this relation are dominated by the received award relation.

Type Inference The effect of type inference can be seen in Table 2. Instances of the degree relation are found with high precision, while the other relations are still found, highlighting that the resolution process is not introducing errors.

Table 3 shows the performance of the entity candidate selection strategy (See section 4.2), including Coreference Resolution. The Noun strategy is compared with Named Entities obtained with the Stanford NER classifier (Finkel et al., 2005). For reference we present the results from Akbik et al. (2014), where the authors used a manual process to find a set of extraction pattern for a given relation.

Using the simple NOUNS strategy for selecting candidate entities performs on par or better to the NER strategy. Coreferences further improve the F-measure by up to .11 points. This supports our claim that we can detect entities and relations together, alleviating the need to train a custom classifier for an entity type - nouns are sufficient. The education degree relation (not part of the results) is a good example for an entity type, where the standard NER tagger almost always fails to identify the degree entity.

6 Conclusion

We present JEDI a system to extract typed named entities and FREEBASE relations together. Shortest dependency pattern are used to link entities, and constraint solving on the relation argument

---

[5] https://code.google.com/p/relation-extraction-corpus/

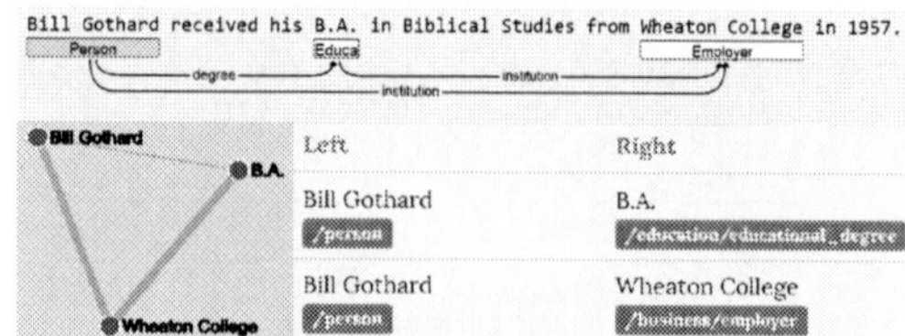

Figure 3: Demo system showing output of the relation detection process with found entity types and connecting FREEBASE relations.

types is used to disambiguate pattern with multiple meanings.

The evaluation shows that the method increases the precision and recall scores for ambiguous relations significantly. As the resolution takes advantage of entities that are connected in chains, it is further possible to detect n-ary relations using only binary pattern. The method proves to work well without any pre-training of NER classifiers and validates that pattern learned using distant supervision are effective. This makes it possible to expand existing knowledge bases with information found in web text.

A web demonstrator of the complete system as shown in Figure 3 is available at jedi.textmining.tu-berlin.de. The system is implemented as an UIMA module such that it can be easily incorporated into existing IE pipelines, the source code is hosted at github.com/jkirsch/jedi.

Acknowledgments

We would like to thank the anonymous reviewers for their helpful comments. Johannes Kirschnick received funding from the German Federal Ministry of Economics and Energy (BMWi) under grant agreement 01MD15007B (SD4M) and Holmer Hemsen under 01MD15010A (SDW).

References

Alan Akbik, Thilo Michael, and Christoph Boden. 2014. Exploratory Relation Extraction in Large Text Corpora. In *COLING*, pages 2087–2096.

Razvan C Bunescu and Raymond J Mooney. 2005. A shortest path dependency kernel for relation extraction. In *HLT/EMNLP*, pages 724–731.

Michael Collins. 2003. Head-driven statistical models for natural language parsing. *Computational linguistics*, 29(4):589–637.

Luciano Del Corro and Rainer Gemulla. 2013. ClausIE : Clause-Based Open Information Extraction. In *WWW*, pages 355–365.

Aron Culotta and Jeffrey Sorensen. 2004. Dependency tree kernels for relation extraction. *ACL*, pages 423–429.

Jenny Rose Finkel, Trond Grenager, and Christopher Manning. 2005. Incorporating non-local information into information extraction systems by Gibbs sampling. ACL, pages 363–370.

Evgeniy Gabrilovich, Michael Ringgaard, and Amarnag Subramanya. 2013. FACC1: Freebase annotation of ClueWeb corpora, Version 1 (Release date 2013-06-26, Format version 1, Correction level 0).

ZS Harris. 1954. Distributional structure. *Word*, pages 775–794.

Rohit J. Kate and Raymond J. Mooney. 2010. Joint entity and relation extraction using card-pyramid parsing. *CoNLL*, pages 203–212.

Johannes Kirschnick, Alan Akbik, and Holmer Hemsen. 2014. Freepal: A Large Collection of Deep Lexico-Syntactic Patterns for Relation Extraction. In *LREC*, pages 2071–2075.

Mitchell Koch, John Gilmer, Stephen Soderland, and Daniel S Weld. 2014. Type-Aware Distantly Supervised Relation Extraction with Linked Arguments. In *EMNLP*, pages 1891–1901.

Xiao Ling and DS Weld. 2012. Fine-Grained Entity Recognition. *AAAI*, pages 94–100.

Christopher D Manning, Mihai Surdeanu, John Bauer, Jenny Finkel, Steven J Bethard, and David McClosky. 2014. The Stanford CoreNLP Natural Language Processing Toolkit. In *ACL (System Demonstrations)*, pages 55–60.

Bonan Min, Ralph Grishman, Li Wan, Chang Wang, and David Gondek. 2013. Distant supervision for relation extraction with an incomplete knowledge base. In *HLT-NAACL*, pages 777–782.

Mike Mintz, Steven Bills, Rion Snow, and Dan Jurafsky. 2009. Distant supervision for relation extraction without labeled data. ACL, pages 1003–1011.

Charles Prud'homme, Jean-Guillaume Fages, and Xavier Lorca, 2015. *Choco Documentation*. Available at http://www.choco-solver.org.

Sebastian Riedel, Limin Yao, Andrew McCallum, and Benjamin M Marlin. 2013. Relation Extraction with Matrix Factorization and Universal Schemas. In *HLT-NAACL*, pages 74–84.

Sameer Singh, Sebastian Riedel, Brian Martin, Jiaping Zheng, and Andrew McCallum. 2013. Joint inference of entities, relations, and coreference. In *AKBC*, pages 1–6.

Fabian M. Suchanek, Mauro Sozio, and Gerhard Weikum. 2009. SOFIE: A Self-Organizing Framework for Information Extraction. In *WWW 2009*.

OpenDial: A Toolkit for Developing Spoken Dialogue Systems with Probabilistic Rules

Pierre Lison
Language Technology Group
University of Oslo (Norway)
`plison@ifi.uio.no`

Casey Kennington[*]
Department of Computer Science
Boise State University (USA)
`casey.kennington@cs.boisestate.edu`

Abstract

We present a new release of OpenDial, an open-source toolkit for building and evaluating spoken dialogue systems. The toolkit relies on an information-state architecture where the dialogue state is represented as a Bayesian network and acts as a shared memory for all system modules. The domain models are specified via probabilistic rules encoded in XML. OpenDial has been deployed in several application domains such as human–robot interaction, intelligent tutoring systems and multi-modal in-car driver assistants.

1 Introduction

The recent advent of voice-controlled personal assistants (such as Siri, Cortana or Alexa) has popularised the use of speech as a means for interfacing with everyday devices. These dialogue systems are built on complex architectures that include components such as speech recognition, language understanding, dialogue management, generation, speech synthesis, situation awareness and multi-modal inputs/outputs. To allow developers to abstract from implementation details and focus on high-level domain modelling, a number of software frameworks have been developed to glue together these components, such as Olympus/Ravenclaw (Bohus and Rudnicky, 2009), the AT&T Statistical Dialog toolkit (Williams et al., 2010), InproTK (Baumann and Schlangen, 2012) or IrisTK (Skantze and Al Moubayed, 2012).

Existing frameworks can be grouped in two categories. On the one hand, symbolic frameworks rely on finite-state automata or logical methods to represent and reason over the current dialogue state. While they provide fine-grained control over the dialogue, these approaches are often poor at handling errors and uncertainty. On the other hand, statistical frameworks capture the interaction dynamics in a probabilistic manner and seek to optimise the dialogue behaviour from data. However, these methods typically require large amounts of data, making them difficult to apply in domains for which dialogue data is scarce.

In this paper, we present a new release of Open-Dial[1], a Java-based, open-source software toolkit designed to facilitate the development of spoken dialogue systems in domains such as personal assistants, in-car driving interfaces, intelligent tutoring systems, or even autonomous robots. OpenDial adopts a hybrid approach that combines the benefits of logical and statistical methods to dialogue modelling into a single framework. The toolkit relies on *probabilistic rules* to represent the internal models of the domain (i.e. the probability and utility models employed to update the dialogue state and make decisions) in a compact and human-readable format. Crucially, the probabilistic rules can contain unknown parameters that can be efficiently estimated from dialogue data using supervised or reinforcement learning.

This paper is structured as follows. Section 2 presents the toolkit architecture and Section 3 explains how to specify dialogue domains with probabilistic rules. Section 4 reviews the toolkit's implementation and Section 5 its deployment in several application domains. Finally, Sections 6 and 7 relate OpenDial with other frameworks and summarise the key contributions of the toolkit.

2 Architecture

OpenDial relies on a information-state architecture (Larsson and Traum, 2000) in which all com-

---

[*]The present work was conducted while the author was affiliated to CITEC, Bielefeld University (Germany).

[1]http://www.opendial-toolkit.net

Proceedings of the 54th Annual Meeting of the Association for Computational Linguistics—System Demonstrations, pages 67–72,
Berlin, Germany, August 7-12, 2016. ©2016 Association for Computational Linguistics

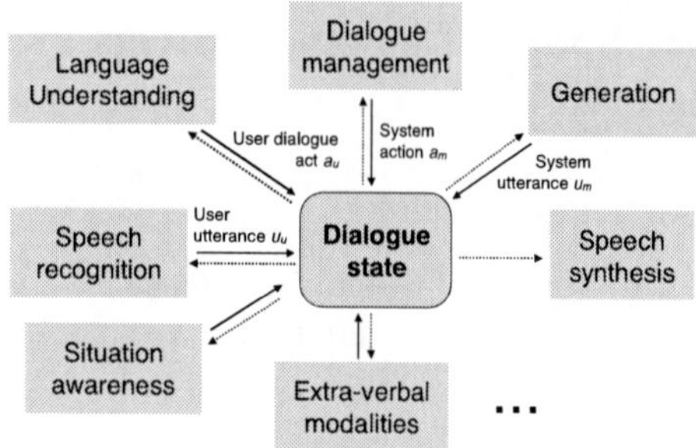

Figure 1: Information-state architecture for the toolkit, with the dialogue state acting as a central shared memory for all system components.

ponents work together on a shared memory that represents the current dialogue state. This dialogue state is factored into distinct variables, each representing a particular aspect of the interaction (e.g. the user intention, the dialogue history or the external context). The dialogue state is encoded as a Bayesian network, which is a directed graphical model where the nodes represent the state variables and the edges are conditional dependencies. The key benefit of this probabilistic representation of the dialogue state is the ability to capture uncertainties and partially observable variables, which are commonplace in most dialogue domains.

Figure 1 illustrates the general architecture. The dialogue system is composed of a set of components which are continuously monitoring the dialogue state for relevant changes. When such a change occurs, the corresponding modules can react to such events and further modify the dialogue state, thereby generating new updates. A typical information flow starts with the speech recogniser, which periodically outputs recognition hypotheses u_u.[2] Language understanding maps these hypotheses into representations of the dialogue act a_u expressed by the user. Dialogue management then selects the system action a_m to perform. If the selected action is a communicative act, language generation is triggered to find its linguistic realisation, denoted u_m. Finally, the constructed utterance is sent to the speech synthesiser.

OpenDial provides two ways to integrate new components into a dialogue system. The first is to specify a *model*, which is a collection of probabilistic rules (see next section). Each model is

associated with one or more *trigger variables*, i.e. variables that trigger the instantiation of the rules upon their update. Alternatively, one can also implement an external module from scratch and connect it to the dialogue state. OpenDial provides a Java API to easily integrate such external modules, which may either wait for update events from the dialogue state or run asynchronously.

3 Dialogue domains

OpenDial is fully domain-independent. To apply it to a particular domain, the system developer provides a specification of the dialogue domain encoded in XML. This XML file contains the following information:

1. The initial dialogue state;

2. A collection of domain models, which are themselves composed of probabilistic rules;

3. Prior distributions for unknown parameters in the probabilistic rules (if any);

4. Optional configuration settings.

3.1 Probabilistic rules

The probabilistic rules in the domain models are expressed as *if...then...else* constructions that map logical conditions on some state variables to probabilistic effects on some other state variables. Due to space constraints, we only provide here a brief overview of the formalism, the reader is invited to consult Lison (2015) for more details.

The rule conditions are expressed as logical formulae, using the usual logic operators (conjunctions, disjunctions, and negations) and various binary relations (equality, inequalities, string matching, etc.). The conditions may also include underspecified (i.e. free) variables which are universally quantified on the top of the rule. Each condition is associated with a distribution over mutually exclusive effects, where each effect is an assignment of values to some state variable(s). Here is a simple example of probabilistic rule:

$$\forall x, \textbf{if } (a_u = Request(x) \wedge a_m = Verify(x)) \textbf{ then}$$
$$\left\{ P(a_u{}' = Confirm(x)) = 0.9 \right.$$

The rule expresses a prediction on the future user dialogue act a_u' based on the last user dialogue act a_u and system's action a_m. The rule stipulates that if the user requested some x and the system replied

---

[2] We denote user-specific variables with the subscript u and machine-specific variables with the subscript m.

by asking whether the request is indeed x, the user is expected to comply and confirm their request with probability 0.9. A void effect with no prediction is implicitly associated with the remaining probability mass (0.1 here). The universal quantification on x indicates that this probability is independent of the type of user request.

The *if...then...else* structure of the probabilistic rules partitions the state space into groups of similar states (corresponding to the logical conditions). In particular, the sequential ordering of the conditions enable dialogue developers to write rules with "backoff strategies", starting from the most specific conditions and then gradually moving to more generic cases if the top conditions do not apply. Such partitioning of the state space is important to ensure the probabilistic rules are able to generalise to new, unseen situations.

Probabilistic rules can express both conditional probability distributions and utility functions. At runtime, the rules are instantiated as latent nodes in the Bayesian network representing the dialogue state. The rules can therefore be seen as high-level templates for the construction of directed graphical models (Lison, 2015). The latest release of OpenDial offers several new functionalities such as the support for custom functions and the ability to directly manipulate relational structures – such as dependency trees, semantic graphs or hierarchical task networks – in the probabilistic rules.

3.2 Example

Listing 1 provides a simple example of dialogue domain in XML. The domain specifies the behaviour of a elevator that can move between three floors through a voice-controlled interface. The interaction starts with a system prompt (*"Which floor do you want?"*) followed by the user request (e.g. *"third floor, please"*). If the request is uncertain, the elevator should ask the user to confirm (e.g. *"Do you want the third floor?"*).

The domain contains an initial state with one variable (the initial prompt) and three models: an intent recognition model mapping the user utterance u_u to the corresponding dialogue act a_u, an action selection model encoding the utility of the system actions a_m, and a third model responsible for generating the system responses u_m and predicting the next user act a'_u. Each model is associated with a trigger variable and is composed of a set of probabilistic rules. The rules are writ-

```xml
<domain>
  <initialstate>
    <variable id="u_m">
      <value prob="1">Which floor do you want?</value>
    </variable>
  </initialstate>

  <!-- Intent recognition -->
  <model trigger="u_u">
    <rule>
      <case>
        <condition operator="and">
          <if var="X" relation="in" value="[first,second,third]"/>
          <if var="u_u" relation="contains" value="{X} (floor)?"/>
        </condition>
        <effect prob="1">
          <set var="a_u" value="Request({X})"/>
        </effect>
      </case>
      <case>
        <condition operator="and">
          <if var="u_u" relation="contains" value="(yes|exactly)"/>
          <if var="a_m" relation="=" value="Verify({X})"/>
        </condition>
        <effect prob="1">
          <set var="a_u" value="Confirm({X})"/>
        </effect>
      </case>
    </rule>
  </model>

  <!-- Action selection model -->
  <model trigger="a_u">
    <rule>
      <case>
        <condition operator="or">
          <if var="a_u" relation="=" value="Request({X})"/>
          <if var="a_u" relation="=" value="Confirm({X})"/>
        </condition>
        <effect util="1">
          <set var="a_m" value="GoTo({X})"/>
        </effect>
        <effect util="0.5">
          <set var="a_m" value="Verify({X})"/>
        </effect>
      </case>
      <case>
        <effect util="-2">
          <set var="a_m" value="GoTo({X})"/>
        </effect>
      </case>
    </rule>
  </model>

  <!-- Generation and user action models -->
  <model trigger="a_m">
    <rule>
      <case>
        <condition>
          <if var="a_m" relation="=" value="GoTo({X})"/>
        </condition>
        <effect util="1">
          <set var="u_m" value="Ok, going to the {X} floor"/>
        </effect>
      </case>
      <case>
        <condition>
          <if var="a_m" relation="=" value="Verify({X})"/>
        </condition>
        <effect util="1">
          <set var="u_m" value="Do you want the {X} floor?"/>
        </effect>
      </case>
    </rule>

    <rule>
      <case>
        <condition operator="and">
          <if var="a_m" relation="=" value="Verify({X})"/>
          <if var="a_u" relation="=" value="Request({X})"/>
        </condition>
        <effect prob="0.9">
          <set var="a_u'" value="Confirm({X})"/>
        </effect>
      </case>
    </rule>
  </model>

</domain>
```

Listing 1: Dialogue domain example in XML.

ten as sequences of *if-then-else* cases, where each case has a (possibly void) condition and a set of corresponding effects. Curly brackets such as {X} denote underspecified variables.

Intent recognition contains one single rule which maps utterances matching the pattern "x *(floor)?*" where $x \in$ ["first", "second","third"] to the dialogue act Request(x), and maps the responses "*yes*" or "*exactly*" following the system action Verify(x) to the dialogue act Confirm(x). This rule is deterministic, since all its effects have a probability 1 if their condition is met. A default value is assigned to a_u if no condition applies.

The action selection model expresses the utility of two system actions: GoTo(x), representing the action of moving to the floor x, and the clarification Verify(x). The two actions respectively have a utility of 1 and 0.5 if the last user act is Request(x) or Confirm(x). Otherwise, the action GoTo(x) has a negative utility of -2. The action GoTo(x) will therefore be selected if the probability of the user act Request(x) is higher than 0.8, while Verify(x) will be chosen if this probability is lower.

The generation model simply maps the system actions to their corresponding surface realisations.[3] Finally, the prediction model (corresponding to the example in the previous section) states that the probability of the user confirming their request when asked to do so is set to 0.9.

The example could of course be extended in many ways – for instance by explicitly specifying the current floor as state variable, and providing prior distributions on the floor requested by the user, conditioned on the current one. The user guide on the OpenDial website provides several additional examples of dialogue domains.

3.3 Parameter Estimation

The probabilistic rules in the example were associated with fixed probabilities or utilities. However, in most domains, these values are difficult to determine in advance and are best learned from empirical data. The toolkit allows dialogue developers to estimate unknown parameters via Bayesian learning. In practice, this is done by replacing the probability or utility values in the rules by parameters associated with prior distributions. For instance, the utilities 1, 0.5 and -2 in the action selection model can be replaced by three Gaussians representing the spread of possible utility values, and the probability 0.9 in the prediction rule can be replaced by a Dirichlet expressing the prior belief about the user response. System developers can then exploit dialogue data to automatically learn the posterior distributions for these parameters. Two methods have been developed: supervised learning from Wizard-of-Oz data (Lison, 2015) and reinforcement learning from real or simulated experience (Lison, 2013). Both learning methods assume that the rule structure – the mapping between conditions and effects – is provided by the developer, while the numerical parameters are determined via statistical estimation. Indeed, system developers often have a good grasp of the general structure of the dialogue domain but are typically unable to quantify the precise probability of a prediction or utility of an action.

4   Implementation

OpenDial is implemented in Java and is released under an open-source MIT license. The software comes along with a graphical user interface which allows developers to run a given dialogue domain and test its behaviour in an interactive manner. Three views are available in the interface. The "chat window" view, shown in Figure 2(a), displays the dialogue history and let the user enter new (text or speech) inputs. In the "dialogue monitor" view, shown in Figure 2(b), the user can inspect the Bayesian network representing the current dialogue state, perform various inference queries (e.g. calculating marginal distributions), and look at previous state updates. This last feature is particularly useful for debugging. Finally, the "domain editor" view provides an interactive editor for the XML domain file.

To ensure the system can quickly react to new events, most processes operate in anytime mode, which implies they can be gracefully interrupted and deliver their outputs at any time. Both exact and approximate inference are employed to update the dialogue state and plan system actions.

A collection of plugins extends the toolkit with additional modules. Plugins are notably available to connect OpenDial to Nuance and AT&T cloud-based speech APIs, to the MaltParser for data-driven dependency parsing, the Sphinx speech recogniser and the MARY speech synthesiser.[4]

---

[3]In a real elevator, an external module will of course need to convert the actions GoTo(x) into a physical motion.

[4]See http://developer.nuance.com, http://developer.att.com/ apis/speech (to be closed), http://cmusphinx.sourceforge.net,

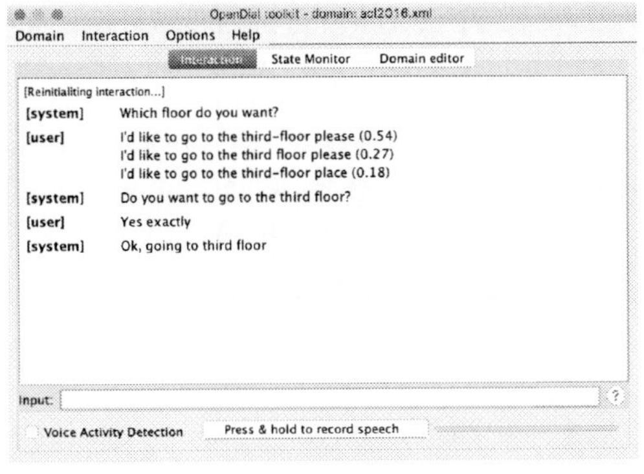

(a) Chat window

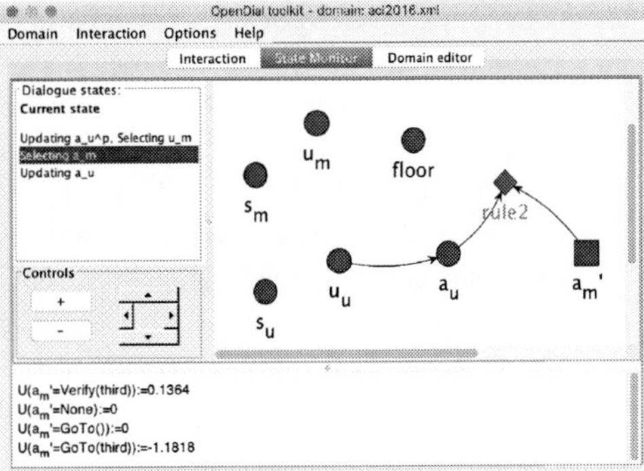

(b) Dialogue state monitor

Figure 2: Graphical user interface for OpenDial.

5 Application Domains

OpenDial has been deployed in several application domains, either directly as an end-to-end dialogue system, or as a specific component in a larger software architecture, typically to handle dialogue state tracking and management tasks.

An important application domain is human–robot interaction. Lison (2015) illustrates how OpenDial is used in a human–robot interaction domain where a humanoid robot is instructed to navigate through a simple environment, fetch an object and bring it to a particular landmark. The experiment shows in particular how the parameters of probabilistic rules can be efficiently learned from limited amounts of Wizard-of-Oz data.

OpenDial was used in another human–robot interaction domain with multiple human participants. Kennington et al. (2014) describe how OpenDial was employed as the primary dialogue manager in a twenty-questions game scenario between a robot and up to three human participants. Using Wizard-of-Oz data, the parameters were estimated with the toolkit's training regime. During evaluation, multiple instantiations of OpenDial were used to model the interaction with each participant. Even though the instantiations were mutually independent, all shared the same modules, allowing communication between them when turn-taking decisions needed to be made.

OpenDial was also deployed as a dialogue manager in an in-car dialogue scenario (Kousidis et al., 2014). The objective was to deliver upcoming calendar entries to the driver (e.g. *"on Tuesday you have lunch with John at the cafeteria"*)

Figure 3: Driver's view from the OpenDS driving simulator [http://www.opends.eu].

via speech and the toolkit was employed to determine when the speech should be interrupted. The driver could also indicate to the system via speech or a head nod that the interrupted speech should continue. Information from the simulated driving environment (see Figure 3) was used to make the system "situationally aware" and able to react to dangerous events by interrupting speech, allowing the driver to focus on the primary task of driving. OpenDial was employed to dynamically track the state of the dialogue system over time.

6 Discussion

The purpose of OpenDial is to combine the expressivity of logic-based frameworks with the robustness and adaptivity of statistical systems. In line with logic-based frameworks (Larsson and Traum, 2000; Bohus and Rudnicky, 2009), the toolkit provides system developers with powerful abstractions to structure the domain models, since probabilistic rules can make use of complex logical formulae and universal quantification. And in line with statistical approaches (Young et al., 2013),

---

http://www.maltparser.org and http://mary.dfki.de.

OpenDial is also able to explicitly handle uncertain knowledge and stochastic relations between variables thanks to its probabilistic representation of the dialogue state and its ability to estimate unknown parameters from data.

The presented framework is very general and can be employed to design a wide spectrum of models, from traditional handcrafted models (such as finite-state automata) on one extreme to probabilistic models fully estimated from data on the other extreme. The choice of model within this spectrum boils down to a design decision based on the relative availabilities of training data and domain knowledge. Furthermore, OpenDial enables users to quickly develop a working system with little or no data, then gradually extend and refine their models as more data becomes available.

The primary focus of OpenDial is on high-level processes such as language understanding, dialogue management and generation. Compared to frameworks such as IrisTK (Skantze and Al Moubayed, 2012) or InproTK (Baumann and Schlangen, 2012), OpenDial offers more limited support for lower-level interaction control such as attentional behaviours or turn-taking strategies. How to reconcile the "low-level" and "high-level" aspects of dialogue modelling in a principled manner is an important question for future work.

7 Conclusion

We presented a new release of OpenDial, a Java-based toolkit for developing and evaluating spoken dialogue systems. The toolkit rests on a hybrid modelling framework that seeks to combine the benefits of logical and probabilistic approaches to dialogue. The dialogue state is represented as a Bayesian network, and the domain models are specified using probabilistic rules. Unknown rule parameters can be automatically estimated from dialogue data using Bayesian learning.

OpenDial is in our view particularly well-suited to handle dialogue domains that exhibits both a complex state-action space and high levels of noise and uncertainty. Typical examples of such dialogue domains are human-robot interaction, virtual assistants and tutoring systems. These domains must often deal with state-action spaces that include multiple tasks to perform in rich interaction contexts. They are also confronted with substantial levels of uncertainty, arising from speech recognition errors and partially observable environments. Due its hybrid modelling approach, the toolkit is able to capture such dialogue domains in a relatively small set of probabilistic rules and associated parameters, allowing them to be tuned from modest amounts of training data, which is a critical requirement in many applications.

Source code and documentation

The www.opendial-toolkit.net website presents the release along with the source code and a step-by-step user guide. A screencast is also available at https://www.youtube.com/watch?v=X8x8Qj5Z7Ag.

References

T. Baumann and D. Schlangen. 2012. The InproTK 2012 release. In *NAACL-HLT Workshop on Future Directions and Needs in the Spoken Dialog Community*, pages 29–32, Montréal, Canada.

D. Bohus and A. Rudnicky. 2009. The RavenClaw dialog management framework: Architecture and systems. *Computer Speech & Language*, 23(3):332–361.

C. Kennington, K. Funakoshi, Y. Takahashi, and M. Nakano. 2014. Probabilistic multiparty dialogue management for a game master robot. In *Proceedings of the ACM/IEEE international conference on Human-robot interaction*, pages 200–201.

S. Kousidis, C. Kennington, T. Baumann, H. Buschmeier, S. Kopp, and D. Schlangen. 2014. A Multimodal In-Car Dialogue System That Tracks The Driver's Attention. In *Proceedings of ICMI*, Istanbul, Turkey.

S. Larsson and D. R. Traum. 2000. Information state and dialogue management in the TRINDI dialogue move engine toolkit. *Natural Language Engineering*, 6(3-4):323–340.

P. Lison. 2013. Model-based Bayesian reinforcement learning for dialogue management. In *Proceedings of the 14th Annual Conference of the International Speech Communication Association*, Lyon, France.

P. Lison. 2015. A hybrid approach to dialogue management based on probabilistic rules. *Computer Speech & Language*, 34(1):232 – 255.

G. Skantze and S. Al Moubayed. 2012. IrisTK: A statechart-based toolkit for multi-party face-to-face interaction. In *Proceedings of the 14th International Conference on Multimodal Interaction (ICMI 2012)*, pages 69–76, New York, USA.

J. Williams, I. Arizmendi, and A. Conkie. 2010. Demonstration of AT&T Let's Go: A production-grade statistical spoken dialog system. In *Proceedings of the the IEEE Spoken Language Technology Workshop*, pages 157–158.

S. Young, M. Gasic, B. Thomson, and J. Williams. 2013. POMDP-based statistical spoken dialogue systems: A review. *Proceedings of the IEEE*, PP(99):1–20.

MUSEEC: A Multilingual Text Summarization Tool

Marina Litvak[1], Natalia Vanetik[1], Mark Last[2], and Elena Churkin[1]

[1]Department of Software Engineering
Shamoon College of Engineering, Beer Sheva, Israel
{marinal,natalyav}@sce.ac.il, elenach@ac.sce.ac.il
[2]Department of Information Systems Engineering
Ben Gurion University of the Negev, Beer Sheva, Israel
mlast@bgu.ac.il

Abstract

The MUSEEC (MUltilingual SEntence Extraction and Compression) summarization tool implements several extractive summarization techniques – at the level of complete and compressed sentences – that can be applied, with some minor adaptations, to documents in multiple languages.

The current version of MUSEEC provides the following summarization methods: (1) MUSE – a supervised summarizer, based on a genetic algorithm (GA), that ranks document sentences and extracts top–ranking sentences into a summary, (2) POLY – an unsupervised summarizer, based on linear programming (LP), that selects the best extract of document sentences, and (3) WECOM – an unsupervised extension of POLY that compiles a document summary from compressed sentences. In this paper, we provide an overview of MUSEEC methods and its architecture in general.

1 Introduction

High quality summaries can significantly reduce the information overload of many professionals in a variety of fields. Moreover, the publication of information on the Internet in an ever–increasing variety of languages dictates the importance of developing *multi–lingual* summarization tools that can be readily applied to documents in multiple languages.

There is a distinction between *extractive* summarization that is aimed at the selection of a subset of the most relevant fragments – mostly complete sentences – from a source text, and *abstractive* summarization that generates a summary as a reformulated synopsis expressing the main idea of the input documents.

Unlike the abstractive summarization methods, which require natural language processing operations, language-independent summarizers work in an extractive manner, usually via ranking fragments of a summarized text by a relevance score and selecting the top-ranked fragments (e.g., sentences) into a summary. Because sentence scoring methods, like MUSE (MUltilingual Sentence Extractor) (Last and Litvak, 2012), use a greedy approach, they cannot necessarily find the best extract out of all possible combinations of sentences.

Another approach, based on the maximum coverage principle (McDonald, 2007; Gillick and Favre, 2009), tries to find the best subset of extracted sentences. This problem is known as NP-hard (Khuller et al., 1999), but an approximate solution can be found by the POLY algorithm (Litvak and Vanetik, 2013) in polynomial time.

Given the tight length constraints, extractive systems that select entire sentences are quite limited in the quality of summaries they can produce. Compressive summarization seeks to overcome this limitation by compiling summaries from compressed sentences that are composed of strictly relevant information(Knight and Marcu, 2002). WECOM (Weighted COMpression) summarization approach (Vanetik et al., 2016) combines methods for term weighting and sentence compression into a *weighted compression* model. WECOM extends POLY by utilizing the choice of POLY's objective functions for the term-weighting model.

In this paper, we present MUSEEC, a multilingual text summarization platform, which currently implements three single-document summarization algorithms: MUSE (Last and Litvak, 2012), POLY algorithm (Litvak and Vanetik, 2013), and WECOM (Vanetik et al., 2016).

73

Proceedings of the 54th Annual Meeting of the Association for Computational Linguistics—System Demonstrations, pages 73–78,
Berlin, Germany, August 7-12, 2016. ©2016 Association for Computational Linguistics

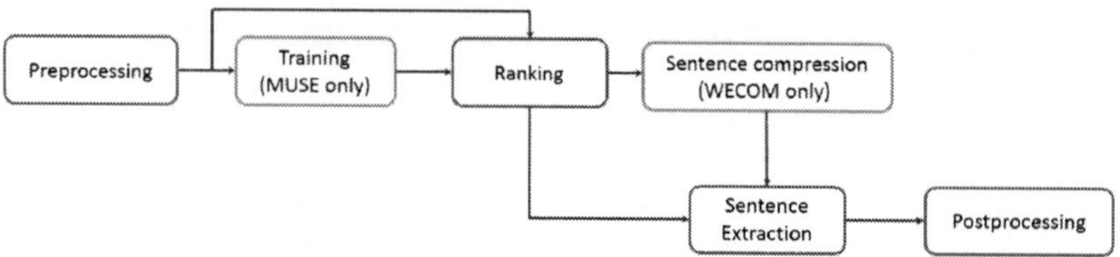

Figure 1: MUSEEC pipeline

2 MUSEEC: Overview

MUSEEC can be applied to documents in multiple languages. The current version was tested on nine languages: English, Hebrew, Arabic, Persian, Russian, Chinese, German, French, and Spanish, and its summarization quality was evaluated on three languages: English, Hebrew and Arabic.[1] The sections below provide brief descriptions of the system architecture and its main components.

2.1 MUSEEC Architecture

As shown in Figure 1, MUSEEC runs a pipeline that is composed of the following components:

1. **Preprocessing**. MUSEEC can work with documents written in any language by treating the text as a sequence of UTF-8 characters. It performs the following pre-processing operations: (1) sentence segmentation, (2) word segmentation, (3) stemming, and (4) stop-word removal. The last two operations are skipped if they are unavailable for a given language. Some optional, linguistic features require Part-of Speech (POS) tagging as a pre-processing step as well.

2. **Training**. This stage is optional and it is relevant only for the supervised MUSE algorithm. Given a set of training parameters, MUSE finds the best vector of weights for a linear combination of chosen sentence features. The resulting vector (trained model) can be saved and used for future summarization of documents in the same or any other language.

3. **Ranking**. At this stage, entire sentences or their parts (in case of compressive summarization) are ranked.

4. **Sentence Compression**. This stage is also optional and it is relevant only for compressive summarization performed by WECOM. Given ranked sentence parts, new, shorter sentences are compiled and ranked.

5. **Extraction**. Complete sentences are selected in the case of MUSE and POLY, and compressed sentences in the case of WECOM.

6. **Postprocessing**. The generated summaries can be post-processed by anaphora resolution (AR) and named entity (NE) tagging operations, if the corresponding tools are provided for a given language. MUSEEC utilizes Stanford CoreNLP package for English.

7. **Results Presentation**. Summaries are presented in two formats: sentences highlighted in the original document, selected by the user from a list of input documents, and a list of extracted sentences shown in their original order. The user can also sort sentences by their rank and see their scores.

MUSEEC allows the user to setup various summarization parameters, general and specific for a chosen algorithm, which are listed in Table 1. The table does not contain explicit WECOM settings because running WECOM equivalent to running POLY with "compressive" choice for the summary type.

2.2 MUltilingual Sentence Extractor (MUSE)

MUSE implements a supervised learning approach to extractive summarization, where the best set of weights for a linear combination of sentence scoring metrics is found by a GA trained on a collection of documents and their gold standard summaries. MUSE training can be performed from the MUSEEC tool. The obtained weighting vector is used for sentence scoring in future summarizations. Since most sentence scoring methods have a linear computational complexity, only the training phase of MUSE, which may be applied in advance, is time-consuming. In MUSEEC, one can use ROUGE-1 and ROUGE-2, Recall (Lin and Hovy, 2003) [2] as fitness functions for measuring summarization quality—similarity with gold stan-

---

[1]MUSEEC also participated in MultiLing 2011, 2013, and 2015 contests on English, Hebrew and Arabic, and demonstrated excellent results.

[2]We utilized the language-independent implementation of ROUGE that operates Unicode characters (Krapivin, 2014)

Parameter name	Description	Possible values	Default value
General			
Input path	Documents folder	Path name	
Output path	Summaries folder	Path name	
Summary type	Summarization approach	Compressive, Extractive	Extractive
Method	Summarization method	MUSE, POLY	MUSE (extr.), WECOM (comp.)
Limit by	Summary length unit	Words, Sentences, Ratio, Characters	Words
Limit	Summary length limit	Numeric value	Depends on unit
AR	Anaphora resolution	Check box	unchecked
NER	Named Entity tagging	Check box	unchecked
MUSE			
Mode	Train a new model, summarize documents evaluate summarizer	Train, Summarize, Evaluate	Summarize
Model	Model to save (training mode), or model to use (summarize mode)	Path name	
Sent. features	Sentence scoring features	31 basic metrics, 75 linguistic features	31 basic metrics
GA training			
Ratio split	Ratio of training data	[0..1]	1
Population	GA settings		500
Size	GA settings		100
Elite count	GA settings		5
Rouge	Rouge type as a fitness func.	1, 2	Rouge-1
POLY			
Objective function	Optimization function	8 functions, described in Section 2.3	Function 2 in Section 2.3

Table 1: MUSEEC general and method-specific parameters.

dard summaries, which should be *maximized* during the training. The reader is referred to (Litvak et al., 2010) for a detailed description of the optimization procedure implemented by MUSE.

The user can choose a subset of sentence metrics that will be included by MUSE in the linear combination. By default, MUSEEC will use the 31 language-independent metrics presented in (Last and Litvak, 2012). MUSEEC also allows the user to employ additional, linguistic features, which are currently available only for the English language. These features are based on lemmatization, multi-word expressions (MWE), NE recognition (NER), and POS tagging, all performed with Stanford CoreNLP package. The list of linguistic features is available in (Dlikman, 2015).

The training time of the GA is proportional to the number of GA iterations[3] multiplied by the number of individuals in a population, times the fitness (ROUGE) evaluation time. The summarization time (given a model) is linear in number of terms for all basic features.

---

[3]On average, in our experiments the GA performed $5 - 6$ iterations of selection and reproduction before reaching convergence.

2.3 POLYnomial summarization with POLYtopes (POLY)

Following the maximum coverage principle, the goal of POLY, which is an unsupervised summarizer, is to find the best subset of sentences that, under length constraints, can be presented as a summary. POLY uses an efficient text representation model with the purpose of representing all possible extracts[4] without computing them explicitly, that saves a great portion of computation time. Each sentence is represented by a hyperplane, and all sentences derived from a document form hyperplane intersections (polytope). Then, all possible extracts can be represented by subplanes of hyperplane intersections that are not located far from the boundary of the polytope. POLY is aimed at finding the extract that optimizes the chosen objective function.

MUSEEC provides the following categories of objective functions, described in detail in (Litvak and Vanetik, 2013).

1. **Maximal weighted term sum**, that maximizes the information coverage as a weighted term sum with following weight options supported:

1. Term sum: all terms get weight 1;

2. POS_F: terms appearing earlier in the text get higher weight;

3. POS_L: terms appearing close to the end of the text get higher weight;

4. POS_B: terms appearing closer to text boundaries (beginning or end) get higher weight;

5. TF: weight of a term is set to its frequency in the document;

6. TF_IDF: weight of a term is set to its tf*idf value;

2. **McDonald – maximal sentence coverage and minimal sentence overlap**, that maximizes the summary similarity to the text and minimizes the similarity between sentences in a summary, based on the Jaccard similarity measure (based on (McDonald, 2007));

3. **Gillick – maximal bigram sum and minimal sentence overlap**, that maximizes the information coverage as a bigram sum while minimizing the similarity between sentences (based on (Gillick

---

[4]exponential in the number of sentences

and Favre, 2009)).

All functions produce term weights in $[0, 1]$ that are then used for calculating the importance scores of each sentence.

Like in MUSE, the sentences with the highest score are added to the summary in a greedy manner. The overall complexity of POLY is polynomial in number of sentences. Further details about the POLY algorithm can be found in (Litvak and Vanetik, 2013).

2.4 WEighted Compression (WECOM)

In WECOM (Vanetik et al., 2016), we shorten sentences by iteratively removing Elementary Discourse Units (EDUs), which were defined as *grammatically independent parts of a sentence* in (Marcu, 1997). We preserve the important content by optimizing the weighting function that measures cumulative importance and preserve a valid syntax by following the syntactic structure of a sentence. The implemented approach consists of the following steps:

Term weight assignment. We apply a weighting model (using one of the options available for POLY) that assigns a non-negative weight to each occurrence of every term in all sentences of the document.

EDU selection and ranking. At this stage, we prepare a list of candidate EDUs for removal. First, we generate the list of EDUs from constituency-based syntax trees (Manning and Schütze, 1999) of sentences. Then, we omit from the list those EDUs that may create a grammatically incorrect sentence if they were to be removed. Finally, we compute weights for all remaining EDU candidates from term weights obtained in the first stage and sort them by increasing weight.

Budgeted sentence compression and selection. We define a summary cost as its length measured in words or characters[5]. We are given a *budget* for the summary cost, for example, the maximal number of words in a summary. The compressive part of WECOM is responsible for selecting EDUs in all sentences such that

(1) the weight to cost ratio of the summary is maximal; and

(2) the summary length does not exceed a given budget.

---

[5]depends on the user's choice of a summary maximal length

The compressed sentences are expected to be *more succinct* than the originals, to contain the important content from the originals, and to be grammatically correct. The compressed sentences are selected to a summary by the greedy manner. The overall complexity of WECOM is bound by $Nlog(N)$, where N is a number of terms in all sentences.

3 Experimental Results

Tables 2, 3, and 4 contain the summarized results of automated evaluations for the MultiLing 2015, single-document summarization (MSS) task. The quality of the summaries is measured by ROUGE-1 (Recall, Precision, and F-measure), (C.-Y, 2004). We also demonstrate the absolute ranks of each submission–P-Rank, R-Rank, and F-Rank–with their scores sorted by Precision, Recall, and F-measure, respectively. Only the best submissions (in terms of F-measure) for each participating system are presented and sorted in descending order of their F-measure scores. Two systems–Oracles and Lead–were used as top-line and baseline summarizers, respectively. Oracles compute summaries for each article using the combinatorial covering algorithm in (Davis et al., 2012)–sentences were selected from a text to maximally cover the tokens in the human summary. Since the Oracles system can actually "see" the human summaries, it is considered as the optimal algorithm and its scores are the best scores that extractive approaches can achieve. The Lead system simply extracts the leading substring of the body text of the articles having the same length as the human summary of the article.

system	P score	R score	F score	P-Rank	R-Rank	F-Rank
Oracles	0.601	0.619	0.610	1	1	1
MUSE	**0.488**	**0.500**	**0.494**	**2**	**3**	**2**
CCS	0.477	0.495	0.485	4	6	3
POLY	0.475	0.494	0.484	5	8	5
EXB	0.467	0.495	0.480	9	13	4
NTNU	0.470	0.456	0.462	13	12	17
LCS-IESI	0.461	0.456	0.458	15	15	18
UA-DLSI	0.457	0.456	0.456	17	18	16
Lead	0.425	0.434	0.429	20	24	20

Table 2: MSS task. English.

As can be seen, MUSE outperformed all other participating systems except for CCS in Hebrew. CCS (the CCS-5 submission, to be precise) uses the document tree structure of sections, subsections, paragraphs, and sentences, and compiles a summary from the leading sentences of recursive

system	P score	R score	F score	P-Rank	R-Rank	F-Rank
CCS	0.202	0.213	0.207	1	1	1
MUSE	**0.196**	**0.210**	**0.203**	**2**	**2**	**2**
POLY	**0.189**	0.203	0.196	4	4	6
EXB	0.186	0.205	0.195	5	5	4
Oracles	0.182	0.204	0.192	6	6	5
Lead	0.168	0.178	0.173	12	13	12
LCS-IESI	0.181	0.170	0.172	13	7	14

Table 3: MSS task. Hebrew.

system	P score	R score	F score	P-Rank	R-Rank	F-Rank
Oracles	0.630	0.658	0.644	1	1	1
MUSE	**0.562**	**0.569**	**0.565**	**2**	**4**	**2**
CCS	0.554	0.571	0.562	4	3	3
EXB	0.546	0.571	0.558	8	2	7
POLY	**0.545**	0.560	0.552	10	9	9
LCS-IESI	0.540	0.527	0.531	11	13	12
Lead	0.524	0.535	0.529	13	12	13

Table 4: MSS task. Arabic.

bottom-up interweaving of the node leading sentences, starting from leaves (usually, paragraphs in a section). POLY got very close scores, though it is an unsupervised approach and its comparison to a supervised summarizer is not fair.

MUSEEC also participated in the multi-document summarization (MMS) task, on English, Hebrew and Arabic. MUSE got first place on Hebrew, and 2nd places on English and Arabic languages, out of 9 participants. POLY got third place on Hebrew, 4th place on English, and 5th place on Arabic, out of 9 participants. We explain the differences between scores in Hebrew and other languages by the lack of NLP tools for this language. For example, none of the competing systems performed stemming for Hebrew. Also, it is possible that the quality of the gold standard summaries or the level of agreement between annotators in Hebrew was lower than in other languages.

WECOM was evaluated in (Vanetik et al., 2016) on three different datasets (DUC 2002, DUC 2004, and DUC 2007) using automated and human experiments. Both automated and human scores have shown that compression significantly improves the quality of generated summaries. Table 5 contains results for POLY and WECOM summarizers on the DUC 2002 dataset. Statistical testing (using a paired T-test) showed that there is a significant improvement in ROUGE-1 recall between ILP concept-based extraction method of Gillick and Favre (2009) and WECOM with weights generated by Gillick and Favre's method. Another significant improvement is between ILP extraction method of McDonald (2007) and WECOM with weights generated by McDonald's method.

System	R-1 R	R-1 P	R-1 F	R-2 R	R-2 P	R-2 F
POLY + Gillick	0.401	0.407	0.401	0.160	0.162	0.160
WECOM + Gillick	**0.410***	0.413	0.409	0.166	0.166	0.165
POLY + McDonald	0.393	0.407	0.396	0.156	0.159	0.156
WECOM + McDonald	**0.401***	0.403	0.399	0.158	0.158	0.157
POLY + POS_F	0.448	0.453	0.447	0.213	0.214	0.212
WECOM + POS_F	0.450	0.450	0.447	0.211	0.210	0.210

Table 5: ROUGE-1 and -2 scores. DUC 2002.

Practical running times for MUSE (summarization) and POLY are tens of milliseconds per a text document of a few thousand words. WECOM running time is strictly dependent on the running time of dependency parsing performed by Stanford CoreNLP package, which takes $2 - 3$ seconds per sentence. Given pre-saved pre-processing results, WECOM takes tens of milliseconds per document as well.

4   Possible Extensions

MUSEEC functionality can be easily extended using its API. New algorithms can be added by implementing new ranking and/or compression modules of the pipeline. The pipeline is dynamically built before running a summarization algorithm, and it can be configured by a programmer[6]. The currently implemented algorithms can also be extended. For example, a new sentence feature for MUSE can be implemented by preparing one concrete class implementing a predefined interface. Using Java reflection, it does not require changes in any other code. New objective functions can be provided for POLY by implementation of one concrete class implementing the predefined interface and adding a few rows in the objective functions factory for creation instances of a new class (using factory method design pattern). Using dependency injections design pattern, MUSEEC can switch from Stanford CoreNLP package to any other tool for text preprocessing. MUSEEC is totally language-independent and works for any language with input texts provided in UTF-8 encoding. If no text processing tools for a given language are provided, MUSEEC skips the relevant stages in its pipeline (for example, it does not perform stemming for Chinese). Providing new NLP tools can improve MUSEEC summarization quality on additional languages. The subsequent stages in the MUSEEC pipeline (sentence

---

[6]Because building pipeline requires programming skills, this option cannot be applied from GUI.

ranking and compression) are totally language-independent and work with structured data generated during pre-processing. The optional capabilities of NE tagging and AR in the post-processing stage may be also extended with additional NLP tools for specific languages.

The programmer and user guidelines for extending and using MUSEEC can be provided upon request.

5   Final Remarks

In this paper, we present MUSEEC - a platform for summarizing documents in multiple languages. MUSEEC implements several variations of three single-document summarization methods: MUSE, POLY, and WECOM. The big advantage of MUSEEC is its multilinguality. The system has been successfully evaluated on benchmark document collections in three languages (English, Arabic, and Hebrew) and tested on six more languages. Also, MUSEEC has a flexible architecture and API, and it can be extended to other algorithms and languages.

However, MUSEEC has the following limitations: all its methods, especially compressive, are dependent on the pre-processing tools, in terms of summarization quality and performance. In order to improve coherency of the generated summaries, the MUSEEC user can apply AR as well as NE tagging to the generated summaries. More sophisticated post-processing operations performed on the extracted text in MUSEEC can further improve the user experience.

The MUSEEC tool, along with its code, is available under a BSD license on `https://bitbucket.org/elenach/onr_gui/wiki/Home`. In the future, we intend to prepare a Web application allowing users to apply MUSEEC online.

Acknowledgments

This work was partially funded by the U.S. Department of the Navy, Office of Naval Research.

References

Lin C.-Y. 2004. ROUGE: A Package for Automatic Evaluation of summaries. In *Proceedings of the Workshop on Text Summarization Branches Out (WAS 2004)*, pages 25–26.

S.T. Davis, J.M. Conroy, and J.D. Schlesinger. 2012. OCCAMS – An Optimal Combinatorial Covering Algorithm for Multi-document Summarization. In *Proceedings of the IEEE 12th International Conference on Data Mining Workshops*, pages 454–463.

A. Dlikman. 2015. Linguistic features and machine learning methods in single-document extractive summarization. Master's thesis, Ben-Gurion University of the Negev, Beer-Sheva, Israel. http://www.ise.bgu.ac.il/faculty/mlast/papers/Thesis-ver7.pdf.

D. Gillick and B. Favre. 2009. A scalable global model for summarization. In *Proceedings of the NAACL HLT Workshop on Integer Linear Programming for Natural Language Processing*.

S. Khuller, A. Moss, and J. Naor. 1999. The budgeted maximum coverage problem. *Information Precessing Letters*, 70(1):39–45.

K. Knight and D. Marcu. 2002. Summarization beyond sentence extraction: A probabilistic approach to sentence compression. *Artificial Intelligence*, 139:91–107.

E. Krapivin. 2014. JRouge—Java ROUGE Implementation. https://bitbucket.org/nocgod/jrouge/wiki/Home.

M. Last and M. Litvak. 2012. Cross-lingual training of summarization systems using annotated corpora in a foreign language. *Information Retrieval*, pages 1–28, September.

C.-Y. Lin and E. Hovy. 2003. Automatic evaluation of summaries using N-gram co-occurrence statistics. In *NAACL '03: Proceedings of the 2003 Conference of the North American Chapter of the Association for Computational Linguistics on Human Language Technology*, pages 71–78.

M. Litvak and N. Vanetik. 2013. Mining the gaps: Towards polynomial summarization. In *Proceedings of the International Joint Conference on Natural Language Processing*, pages 655–660.

M. Litvak, M. Last, and M. Friedman. 2010. A new approach to improving multilingual summarization using a Genetic Algorithm. In *ACL '10: Proceedings of the 48th Annual Meeting of the Association for Computational Linguistics*, pages 927–936.

C. D. Manning and H. Schütze. 1999. *Foundations of statistical natural language processing*, volume 999. MIT Press.

D. Marcu. 1997. From discourse structures to text summaries. In *Proceedings of the ACL*, volume 97, pages 82–88.

R. McDonald. 2007. A study of global inference algorithms in multi-document summarization. In *Advances in Information Retrieval*, pages 557–564.

N. Vanetik, M. Litvak, M. Last, and E. Churkin. 2016. An unsupervised constrained optimization approach to compressive summarization. Manuscript submitted for publication.

Language Muse: Automated Linguistic Activity Generation
for English Language Learners

Nitin Madnani   Jill Burstein   John Sabatini   Kietha Biggers   Slava Andreyev
{nmadnani, jburstein, jsabatini, kbiggers, sandreyev}@ets.org

Educational Testing Service
Princeton, NJ 08541

Abstract

Current education standards in the U.S. require school students to read and understand complex texts from different subject areas (e.g., social studies). However, such texts usually contain figurative language, complex phrases and sentences, as well as unfamiliar discourse relations. This may present an obstacle to students whose native language is not English — a growing sub-population in the US. [1] One way to help such students is to create classroom activities centered around linguistic elements found in subject area texts (DelliCarpini, 2008). We present a web-based tool that uses NLP algorithms to automatically generate customizable linguistic activities that are grounded in language learning research.

1 Introduction

Recent educational standards adopted by several states in the U.S. (CCSSO, 2010) explicitly emphasize the need for students to read progressively more complex texts in different subject areas, to prepare for college and careers. However, to accomplish this, learners need to have a grasp of linguistic features related to vocabulary, word senses, figurative language, English conventions, and discourse structures.

English language learners (ELLs) generally struggle to acquire English language skills: reading, writing, speaking, and listening. These learners could be disadvantaged further if there were simply an increase in the complexity of texts without concurrent scaffolding to help them with the demands likely to enter the curriculum as a result of the new Standards (Coleman and Goldenberg, 2012).

This suggests the need for subject area teachers to incorporate a more linguistically-based approach to support content comprehension (Christie, 1989; Christie, 1999). Yet, teachers often lack the training necessary to identify English language features that may challenge diverse groups of ELLs (Slavin and Cheung, 2004; Walqui and Heritage, 2012).

In this paper, we present *Language Muse*, an open-access, web-based tool that can address these needs.[2] Specifically, *Language Muse* can help subject area teachers support ELLs by automatically generating customizable activities derived from actual texts used in their classrooms. The activities are generated using several existing NLP algorithms and are designed to help ELLs with multiple aspects of language learning needed to support content comprehension: vocabulary, grammatical structures, and discourse & text organization.

Although *Language Muse* is related to existing work in the NLP literature on automatic question generation (Mitkov and Ha, 2003; Brown et al., 2005; Heilman and Smith, 2010), it can generate multiple activities for teachers' own texts, cover a significantly larger set of language constructs, and offer teachers much more customizability.

In subsequent sections, we first provide a description of the *Language Muse* NLP. Next, we describe how teachers interact with the backend and create activities. Finally, we present the results of a survey conducted with actual ELL teachers, and conclude with future work.

2 NLP Backend

Language Muse relies on a backend that uses NLP techniques and resources to identify a variety of linguistic features contained in an input text. The features being identified can be categorized as: (a) lexical entities (single word and multi-word expressions), (b) syntactic structure, and (c) rhetorical

---

[1] See `http://www.ncela.us/files/uploads/9/growingLEP_0809.pdf`

[2] `http://languagemuse.10clouds.com`

Proceedings of the 54th Annual Meeting of the Association for Computational Linguistics—System Demonstrations, pages 79–84,
Berlin, Germany, August 7-12, 2016. ©2016 Association for Computational Linguistics

(a) Lexical Entities	
Cognates	Identified using a manually-created dictionary that was verified by a native Spanish speaker (most U.S. ELLs speak Spanish as their native language).
Academic Words & Definitions	Words that describe complex and abstract concepts, and are used across disciplines, e.g., *analyze, benefit*. Identified using a manually-created list and definitions extracted using the Wordnik API (`http://developer.wordnik.com`).
Frequent Concepts	Words that appear repeatedly across the text. Identified using a heuristic that measures repetitions across paragraphs.
Multiword Expressions	Idioms, Phrasal Verbs, etc. Identified using a rank-ratio based collocation detection algorithm trained on the Google Web1T n-gram corpus (Futagi et al., 2008)
Contractions	Identified using regular expressions defined on constituency parses.
Complex Words	Morphologically complex or irregular verbs. Identified using a rule-based morphological analyzer (Leacock and Chodorow, 2003).
Morphological Variants	Generated using an algorithm that first over-generates variants using rules and then filters using co-occurrence statistics computed over Gigaword.
Synonyms	Generated using a thresholded combination of WordNet (Fellbaum, 1998), a distributional thesaurus (Lin, 1998), and SMT-based paraphrases (Bannard and Callison-Burch, 2005).
Antonyms	Generated using WordNet.
Homonyms	Generated using a manually-created list (Burstein et al., 2004).
(b) Syntactic Structure	
Note: All modules below use regular expressions on constituency parses.	
Relative Clauses	Sentences containing an explicit relative clause.
1+ Clauses	Sentences containing 1 independent clause and $>=$ 1 one dependent clause. Note that this can also include sentences with relative clauses.
Complex NPs	Noun phrases with a hyphenated adjective or a prepositional phrase modifier.
Complex Verbs	Verb phrases with $>=$ 2 verb forms, e.g., *will have gone, plans to leave*
(c) Rhetorical and Discourse Relations	
Note: All modules below use an adapted rule-based discourse analyzer (Burstein et al., 1998).	
Cause-Effect	Terms indicating a cause-effect relation between text segments, e.g., "The discovery of fossils of tropical plants in Antarctica *led to the hypothesis* that ..."
Compare-Contrast	Terms indicating a comparison or contrast between text segments, e.g., "He was a wise and patient leader; *however*, his son ..."
Evidence & Details	Terms indicating specific evidence or details between text segments, e.g., "Recent theories, *such as the influence of plate tectonics on the movement of continents*, have ..."

Table 1: The inventory of features provided by the backend NLP engine in Language Muse.

and discourse relations. Before we describe each category in detail, it is important to note that since the primary use case for *Language Muse* is to help teachers plan appropriate classroom activities for ELLs, it is important for the automatically generated activities to be as accurate as possible. Therefore, for many of the features, we rely on manually crafted resources, either directly or indirectly as a filter for a noisier statistical approach.

Table 1 shows the linguistic features that our system can identify in the three aforementioned categories and provides a brief description of the backend module is used to generate it.

3 Activity Generation

In this section, we describe how users interact with *Language Muse*, i.e., how they can automatically generate linguistic activities for any text and customize them to their own liking. *Language Muse* is completely free to use for all teachers. Teachers request an account using the form on the web site and receive their login information via email.

Once a teacher logs into *Language Muse*, she can get started either by choosing one of the 33 texts that we provide across three different content areas (English Language Arts, Science, and Social Studies), or by uploading her own classroom text (in plain text/.doc/.docx formats). The system currently limits the texts to 5000 words. All texts uploaded by a teacher are saved into her personal library for later re-use.

The text is then sent to the NLP backend for processing, which returns a JSON object containing all identified (or generated) linguistic features. At that point, the teacher can generate any of the available linguistic activities, each of which is based on one of the linguistic features. All activities were designed based on input from ELL content-area teachers. There are a total of 24 activities, grouped according to whether an activity is word-based, sentence-based, or paragraph-based. This form of hierarchical grouping is based on ELL literature which suggests that each level in the hierarchy presents distinct challenges and opportunities for language learning. Table 2 shows a few of the available activities and provides a brief description.

3.1 Recommended Activities

Based on the number of feature instances detected by the backend, *Language Muse* may recommend certain activities over others to the teacher. For example, if there were more words with synonyms but only a few cause-effect terms, it might recommend the *Synonyms in Paragraphs* activity but not the *Cause/Effect Relationships* activity. Some activities may also be unavailable since no instances of the corresponding linguistic feature could be detected by the backend. *Language Muse* makes a visual distinction between recommended activities, possible activities, and unavailable activities as shown in Figure 1. Clicking on an activity shows its description and a sample question.

3.2 Same Feature, Multiple Activities

Some activities are based on the same underlying linguistic feature but use it differently, depending on their level. For example, a word-level activity asks students to match words in one list to words in another list based on how similar they are in meaning. That activity uses automatically generated synonyms for the words in the text and then automatically populates the two lists – one with the original words and the other with the generated synonyms. There is a similar paragraph-level cloze activity that shows students a paragraph from the text and asks them to replace pre-identified words with their synonyms such that the meaning is unchanged. This activity uses the same underlying feature — automatically generated synonyms — but presents it differently. This exposes ELLs to a different part of the language construct.

3.3 Automatically-generated Answers

The questions for all activities are automatically generated based on linguistic features in the text. However, for 15 of those activities, *Language Muse* also automatically populates an answer key for the teacher. For example, for the word-based synonym activity described in §3.2, we know which pairs of words in the two lists match each other since the synonyms were automatically generated. Automatically-generated answers reduce the time that a teacher needs to edit an activity for her classroom. See Table 2 for additional examples.

3.4 Customizability

It is impossible for *Language Muse* to always provide exactly what every teacher is looking for. Therefore, almost all aspects of the activities it generates can be customized to suit a teacher's needs. Among other things, the teacher can choose to:

- edit the instructions shown to the students,
- hide any or all automatically chosen words/sentences/paragraphs,

Sentence activities
Multiple Clause Sentences. Shows multi-clause sentences and asks students to break them up into two or more shorter sentences. Although the sentences for the activity are identified automatically in the text, the answers are not generated automatically. Example: *Organelles are structures visible within a cell that have their own structure.* ⇒ (1) *Organelles are structures visible within a cell.* (2) *Organelles have their own structure.*
Cause/Effect Relationships. Shows sentences containing causal relationships and asks students to identify the cause, the effect, and the connector word that denotes the causal relationship. The sentences with causal relationships in the text are identified automatically but only the connector word part of the answer is automatically generated. Example: Off the coast of Canada, commercial cod fishing had to stop because the population of cod collapsed. ⇒ *The population of cod collapsed off the coast of Canada* (cause), *Commercial cod fishing had to stop* (effect), *because* (connector).
Homonyms in Sentences. Shows sentences with blanks and asks students to fill in the right word from a list that contains homonyms as distractors. Examples can be seen in Figure 2.
Paragraph activities
Variant Word Forms in Paragraphs. Uses inflectional and derivational word variants generated by the backend. Shows students a paragraph of text with blanks and asks them to fill in the right morphological variant. Answers and distractors are automatically generated. Example: *Scientists suspect that there are more than 10 million _______ (different/difference) types of life forms on Earth.*
Phrasal Verbs. Asks students to pick the correct preposition to complete the phrasal verbs found in the paragraph. Answers and distractors are automatically generated. Example: *People usually think _______ (at/on/of) the heart, lungs and brain as vital organs.*

Table 2: A subset of the linguistic activities available to teachers in *Language Muse*.

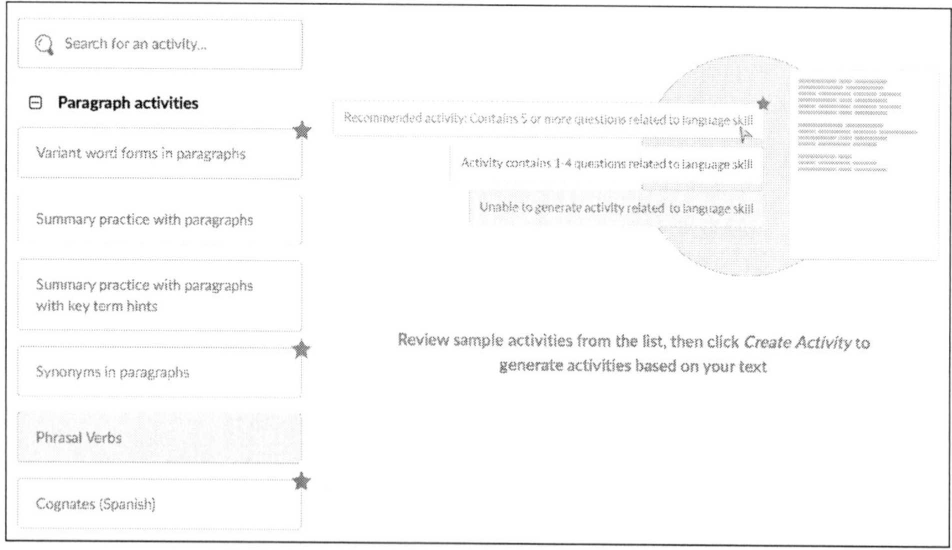

Figure 1: Activities where 5 or more questions can be generated are recommended by *Language Muse* and marked with a star. Activities with fewer than 5 questions are not marked but can still be chosen by the teacher. Activities with no available questions are greyed out and cannot be chosen.

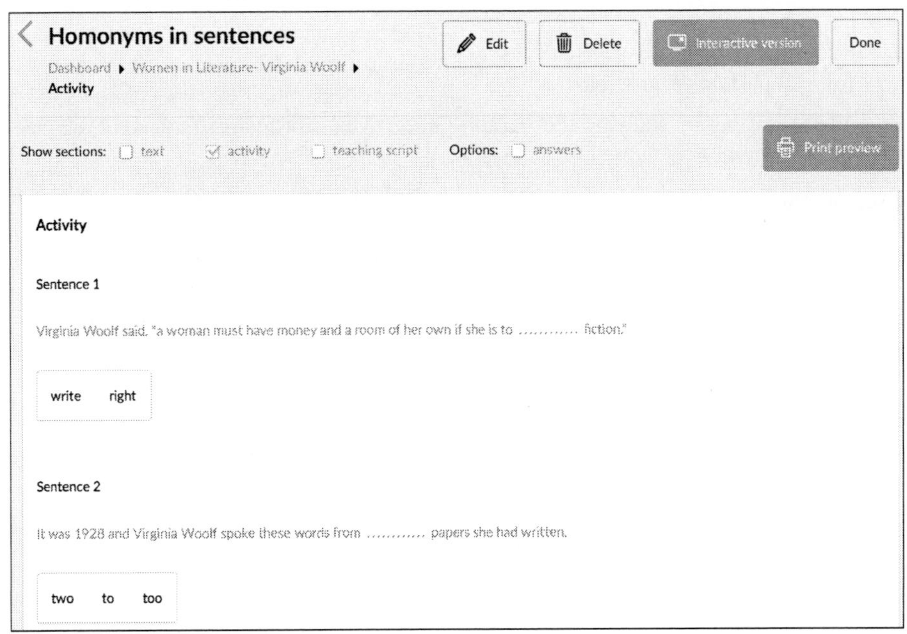

Figure 2: The Homonyms in Sentences activity generated from a Language Arts text on Virginia Woolf. The questions, answers, and distractors are all automatically generated.

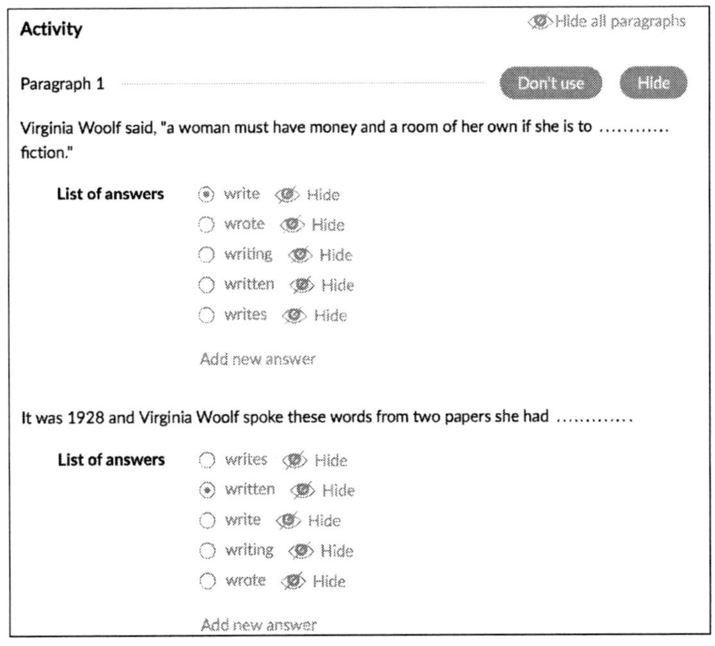

Figure 3: An example of a customizable multiple choice activity (*Variant Word Forms in Paragraphs*). Teachers can (a) change the generated correct answer, (b) hide any generated distractors, (c) add their own answers, and (d) hide a paragraph entirely or use it only as context without generating questions.

- edit the automatically generated answers or add her own, and
- edit the list of automatically generated distractors for multiple choice questions.

Figure 3 illustrates this by showing the *Variant Word Forms in Paragraphs* activity in edit mode.

4   Teacher Survey

We wanted to evaluate whether activities generated by *Language Muse* are useful to teachers. To do this, we worked with seventeen 6th-8th grade teachers who taught English language arts, science, and social studies. Four teachers had been teaching for two years or less, five for 3-9 years, and the rest for > 10 years. All but two currently had responsibility for teaching ELLs and eight had been teaching ELLs for > 5 years. We asked them to examine 9 different activities from *Language Muse* and tell us whether they would consider using them in their classrooms. Figure 4 shows the results of our survey which are encouraging for a first version.

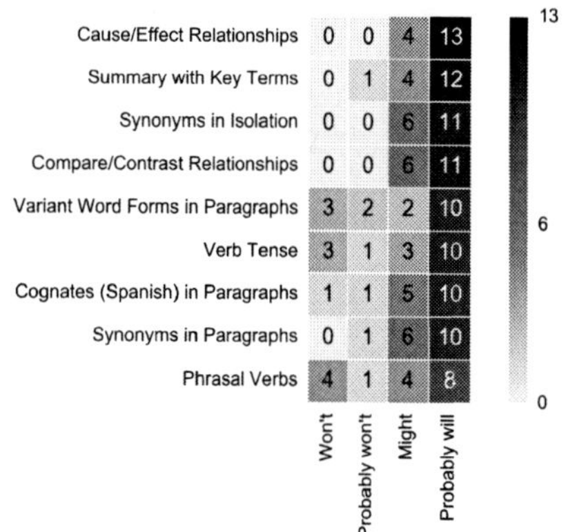

Figure 4: A heatmap showing the results of our teacher survey. Each cell shows the number of middle school teachers responding to whether they would use the corresponding activity in classrooms.

5   Conclusions & Future Work

We presented *Language Muse*, an open-access, web-based tool that can help content-area teachers support ELL students with content comprehension. We are currently working on the next version which will allow students to log into Language Muse to complete any activities assigned to them by their teachers and also receive feedback. All development on Language Muse continues to be informed by frequent and detailed interactions with teachers.

Acknowledgments

Research presented in this paper was supported by the Institute of Education Science, U.S. Department of Education, Award Number R305A140472, and by the 10Clouds front-end development team.

References

Colin Bannard and Chris Callison-Burch. 2005. Paraphrasing with Bilingual Parallel Corpora. In *Proceedings of ACL.*

Jonathan C Brown, Gwen A Frishkoff, and Maxine Eskenazi. 2005. Automatic Question Generation for Vocabulary Assessment. In *Proceedings of EMNLP.*

Jill Burstein, Karen Kukich, Susanne Wolff, Chi Lu, and Martin Chodorow. 1998. Enriching Automated Scoring using Discourse Marking. In *Proceedings of the ACL Workshop on Discourse Relations and Discourse Marking.*

Jill Burstein, Martin Chodorow, and Claudia Leacock. 2004. Automated Essay Evaluation: The Criterion Online Writing Service. *AI Magazine*, 25(3):27.

CCSSO. 2010. *Common Core State Standards for English language Arts & Literacy in History/Social Studies, Science, and Technical Subjects. Appendix A: Research supporting key elements of the Standards.* Washington, DC.

Frances Christie. 1989. *Language Education.* Oxford University Press, Oxford, UK.

Frances Christie. 1999. *Pedagogy and the Shaping of Consciousness: Linguistics and Social Processes.* Continuum, London, UK.

Rhonda Coleman and Claude Goldenberg. 2012. The Common Core Challenge for English Language Learners. *Principal Leadership*, pages 46–51.

Margo DelliCarpini. 2008. Success with ELLs. *English Journal*, 98(2):98–101.

Christiane Fellbaum. 1998. *WordNet.* Blackwell Publishing Ltd.

Yoko Futagi, Paul Deane, Martin Chodorow, and Joel Tetreault. 2008. A Computational Approach to Detecting Collocation Errors in the Writing of Non-native Speakers of English. *Computer Assisted Language Learning*, 21(4).

Michael Heilman and Noah A Smith. 2010. Good question! Statistical Ranking for Question Generation. In *Proceedings of NAACL.*

Claudia Leacock and Martin Chodorow. 2003. C-rater: Automated scoring of Short-answer Questions. *Computers and the Humanities*, 37(4).

Dekang Lin. 1998. Automatic Retrieval and Clustering of Similar Words. In *Proceedings of COLING.*

Ruslan Mitkov and Le An Ha. 2003. Computer-aided Generation of Multiple-choice Tests. In *Proceedings of the Workshop on Building Educational Applications.*

R. E. Slavin and A. Cheung. 2004. How do English language Learners Learn to Read? *Educational Leadership*, 61.

A. Walqui and M. Heritage. 2012. Instruction for Diverse Groups of ELLs. In *Understanding Language Conference*, Stanford, CA.

ccg2lambda: A Compositional Semantics System

Pascual Martínez-Gómez[4]
pascual.mg@aist.go.jp

Koji Mineshima[1]
mineshima.koji@ocha.ac.jp

Yusuke Miyao[2]
yusuke@nii.ac.jp

Daisuke Bekki[1,2]
bekki@is.ocha.ac.jp

[1]Ochanomizu University
Tokyo, Japan

[2]NII
Tokyo, Japan

[4]AIRC, AIST
Tokyo, Japan

Abstract

We demonstrate a simple and easy-to-use system to produce logical semantic representations of sentences. Our software operates by composing semantic formulas bottom-up given a CCG parse tree. It uses flexible semantic templates to specify semantic patterns. Templates for English and Japanese accompany our software, and they are easy to understand, use and extend to cover other linguistic phenomena or languages. We also provide scripts to use our semantic representations in a textual entailment task, and a visualization tool to display semantically augmented CCG trees in HTML.

1 Introduction

We are motivated by NLP problems that benefit from any degree of computer language understanding or semantic parsing. Two prominent examples are Textual Entailment and Question-Answering, where the most successful approaches (Abzianidze, 2015; Berant et al., 2013) require symbolic representations of the semantics of sentences. We are inspired by the theoretical developments in the formal semantics literature, where higher-order logical (HOL) formulas are used to derive meaning representations (MR); despite what is typically believed in the NLP community, Mineshima et al. (2015) demonstrated that HOL can be used effectively at a reasonable speed.

In this paper, we describe ccg2lambda, our system to obtain MRs given derivations (trees) of a Combinatory Categorial Grammar (CCG) (Steedman, 2000). In order to obtain the MRs, our system is guided by the combinatory characteristics of CCG derivations and a list of manually designed semantic templates. The linguistic intuitions behind the design of those semantic templates and the evaluation of the MRs that they produce is detailed in Mineshima et al. (2015), and is not repeated here. In that paper, we tackled a Textual Entailment task, where the meanings of premises and conclusions were represented symbolically, and their entailment relation was judged with a theorem prover of higher-order logics. With this system, we obtained a state-of-the-art performance on the FraCaS dataset (Cooper et al., 1994).

ccg2lambda and the accompanying semantic templates are open source[1]. Semantic templates are already available for English and Japanese, and they are easily extensible to other linguistic phenomena and other languages for which CCG parsers are available. Here we describe how to use ccg2lambda and how to specify semantic templates for other researchers to extend our work.

2 Related Work

The most similar system to ours is Boxer (Bos et al., 2004), which outputs first order formulas given CCG trees. Our system can additionally produce higher-order formulas, which are more expressive and potentially accurate (Mineshima et al., 2015).

There are three prominent textbook systems for computational semantics, that of Bird et al. (2009), Blackburn and Bos (2005) and van Eijck and Unger (2010). These three systems, together with the Lambda Calculator[2] (Champollion et al., 2007) are excellent educational resources that are very accessible to beginner linguists in general, and semanticists in particular. The development of ccg2lambda is inspired by these systems, in that we aimed to produce a software that is easy to understand, use and extend with only basic knowledge of formal semantics and lambda calcu-

---

[1]https://github.com/mynlp/ccg2lambda
[2]http://lambdacalculator.com/

Proceedings of the 54th Annual Meeting of the Association for Computational Linguistics—System Demonstrations, pages 85–90,
Berlin, Germany, August 7-12, 2016. ©2016 Association for Computational Linguistics

lus. However, these systems are mainly developed for educational purposes and are not connected to fully fledged parsers, hence not immediately usable as a component of larger NLP systems.

We have developed `ccg2lambda` to process trees that are produced by wide-coverage CCG parsers (e.g. C&C and Jigg[3]). Other semantic parsers such as those developed by Bos et al. (2004), Abzianidze (2015) and Lewis and Steedman (2013) also connect to wide-coverage CCG parsers, but they do not emphasize easy accessibility or extensibility. NL2KR (Vo et al., 2015) is an interactive system with powerful generalization capabilities, but it does not allow fine-grained lexicon specifications (only CCG categories) and does not output machine readable semantics. Instead, `ccg2lambda` produces XML machine-readable MRs, which make our system easy to integrate in larger logic or statistical NLP systems.

3   System Overview

Although our main system contribution is a semantic parser, we use the problem of textual entailment as an end-to-end task. Figure 1 schematically shows the several components of our system.

The first stage is to *parse sentences into CCG trees* (see Figure 2 for an example). Our system currently supports the C&C parser (Clark and Curran, 2004) for English, and Jigg (Noji and Miyao, 2016) for Japanese.

The second stage is the *semantic composition*, where MRs are constructed compositionally over CCG trees using lambda calculus, thus allowing higher-order logics if necessary. To this end, our system is guided by the compositional rules of the CCG tree and the semantic templates provided by the user. In Section 4 we describe in detail how these semantic templates are specified and how they control the semantic outputs. The output of this stage is a Stanford CoreNLP-style XML file (Manning et al., 2014) where each sentence has three XML nodes: `<tokens>`, `<ccg>` and `<semantics>`. Thus, sentence semantics can simply be read off the root node of the CCG tree.

In the case of recognizing textual entailment, the third stage is the *theorem construction*, definition of predicate types, and execution with a logic prover. This stage is not essential to our system, but it is added to this paper to show the usefulness of our semantic representations in an NLP task.

4   Semantic Composition

`ccg2lambda` receives CCG trees and outputs (possibly higher-order) logic formulas. To that end, we use i) the combinatory characteristics of CCG trees to guide the semantic compositions, and ii) a list of semantic templates to assign a precise meaning to CCG constituents.

See Figure 2 for an example of CCG derivation for the sentence "Some woman ordered tea", augmented with its semantics. Nodes have CCG syntactic categories (e.g. N or $S\backslash NP$), which is what our system receives as input. On the same figure, we have added the logical semantic representations (e.g. $\lambda x.\text{woman}(x)$) below the syntactic categories. Our system outputs these logical formulas. For clarity, leaves also display the token base forms. The symbols $<, >$ and lex stand for left and right function application rules, and the type-shift rule in C&C, respectively. These rules and the syntactic categories guide the semantic composition, provided with semantic templates that describe the specific semantics.

4.1   Semantic templates

Semantic templates are defined declaratively in a YAML[4] file, typically by a formal semanticist after an appropriate linguistic analysis. A template applies to a node of the CCG derivation tree if certain conditions are met. Each template has two required attributes: `semantics` and (syntactic) `category`. The attribute `semantics` is a lambda term in NLTK semantics format (Garrette and Klein, 2009). In case a template applies on a CCG leaf (that is, a word), the lambda term in the template is applied on the base form of the word, and β-reduction is performed. For example, the semantic template

- $\text{semantics} : \backslash E.\backslash x.E(x)$

  $\text{category} : N$

applying on a leaf whose base word is "woman" and its syntactic category is N, would produce the expression $(\lambda E.\lambda x.E(x))(\text{woman})$ which is β-reduced to $\lambda x.\text{woman}(x)$. Here, the base form "woman" substitutes all occurrences of the variable E in the `semantics` expression.

In case a template applies on a CCG inner node (a node with children), the lambda abstraction is applied on the semantics of the children, in order.

---

[3]`https://github.com/mynlp/jigg`

[4]`http://www.yaml.org/spec/`

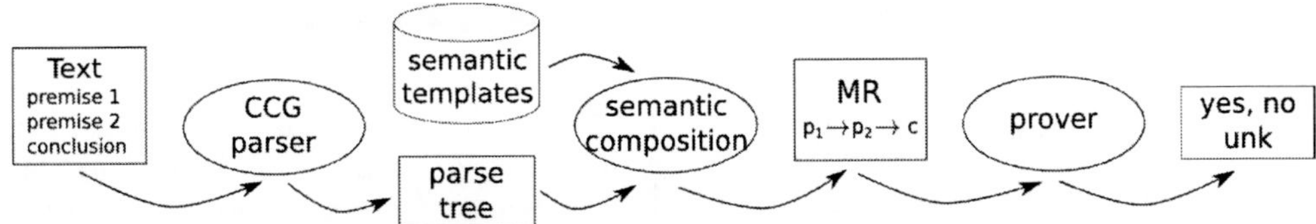

Figure 1: System pipeline for recognizing textual entailment. Syntactic structures of sentences are obtained with a CCG parser. Then, we perform the semantic composition using semantic templates. The resulting meaning representations are used to perform various logical inferences with a theorem prover.

$$
\begin{array}{c}
\text{Some} \\
NP/N \\
\lambda F \lambda G.\exists x.(Fx \wedge Gx)
\end{array}
\quad
\begin{array}{c}
\text{woman} \\
N \\
\lambda x.\text{woman}(x)
\end{array}
\quad
\begin{array}{c}
\text{ordered} \\
(S \backslash NP)/NP \\
\lambda Q_1 \lambda Q_2.Q_2(\lambda x.Q_1(\lambda y.\text{order}(x,y)))
\end{array}
\quad
\begin{array}{c}
\dfrac{\begin{array}{c}\text{tea}\\ N \\ \lambda y.\text{tea}(y)\end{array}}{\begin{array}{c}NP \\ \lambda F.\exists y.(\text{tea}(y) \wedge F(y))\end{array}} \text{ lex}
\end{array}
$$

Figure 2: CCG derivation tree of the sentence "Some woman ordered tea", with its semantics (simplified for illustrative purposes). The actual output of `ccg2lambda` with our provided templates is in Figure 6.

For example, in Figure 2, the template

- semantics : $\backslash E.\backslash F.\exists y.(E(y) \wedge F(y))$

  category : NP

  rule : lex

produces a type-raise from N to NP, and when applied to the CCG node whose child's semantics are $\lambda y.\text{tea}(y)$, it will produce, after β-reduction, the formula $\lambda F.\exists y.(\text{tea}(y) \wedge F(y))$. Here, the child's semantics $\lambda y.\text{tea}(y)$ substitute all occurrences of the variable E. The newly composed semantic representation $\lambda F.\exists y.(\text{tea}(y) \wedge F(y))$ now expects another predicate (a verb) as an argument F (i.e. "order"), which will be filled in the next step of the composition.

The `category` attribute of a semantic template may also specify conditions on the feature structures of CCG nodes (which are provided by the CCG parser), in which case templates apply if the syntactic category *matches* and the feature structure *subsumes* that of the CCG node. For example, if the semantic template specifies a syntactic category NP[dcl = true], it matches a CCG node with a category NP[dcl = true] or a category NP[dcl = true, adj = true].

Other conditions for matching templates to CCG nodes can be specified by adding more attributes to the semantic template. In the example above, the attribute `rule` : lex is used to specify the combination rule of that inner CCG node. In practice, any XML attribute of a CCG node can be used to specify matching conditions, which means that users of `ccg2lambda` can enrich CCG trees with arbitrary annotations such as Named Entities or Events and use them as matching conditions when defining semantic templates without modifying the software. It is also possible to specify attributes of the children of the target CCG node. These conditions are always prefixed by the string `child`, followed by the branch index 0 or 1. For example, a semantic template with the attribute `child1_child0_pos` : NN matches a node whose right child's (`child1`) left child's (`child0`) POS tag is an NN. Moreover, paths to child nodes can be left unspecified, by using the keyword `child_any_X` : Y; in this case, *any* child whose attribute X has value Y will be matched by the template. If more than one template matches a CCG node, the first appearing template is selected.

4.2 System Usage and Output

The command for the semantic composition is:

```
# python semparse.py ccgtrees.xml
templates.yaml semantics.xml
```

where `ccgtrees.xml` is a Jigg's XML style CCG tree, `templates.yaml` contains the semantic templates, and `semantics.xml` is the XML output of the system. We also provide a script to convert C&C XML trees into Jigg's XML style. The output of `semparse.py` follows the conventions of Stanford coreNLP (see Figure 3). However, we follow Jigg's style to represent

```
1  <root>
2    <sentences>
3      <sentence>
4        <tokens>
5          <token base="tea" surf="tea" pos="NN"/>
6          <token .../>
7        </tokens>
8        <ccg>
9          <span id="s1" child="s2" category="N"
                 rule="lex"/>
10          <span .../>
11        </ccg>
12        <semantics>
13          <span id="s1" child="s2" sem="\y._tea(y)"
                 type="_tea : Entity -> Prop"/>
14          <span .../>
15        </semantics>
16      </sentence>
17    </sentences>
18  </root>
```

Figure 3: XML output of the semantic composition. Span nodes of the semantics tag contain logical semantic representations of that constituent.

element characteristics as XML node attributes. For example, the base and surface forms, and the POS tag of a token are all represented as XML attributes in a `<token>` tag.

Our semantic composition produces the `<semantics>` tag, which has as many children nodes (`<span>`) as the CCG tree, the same span identifiers and structure. However, semantic spans also have a "sem" attribute encoding the semantics (using NLTK's semantics format) that have been composed for that constituent. An example of a resulting semantic logic formula in NLTK semantics format is:

$$\backslash\text{F.exists } y. \ (\_\text{tea}(y) \ \& \ F(y))$$

Note that predicates are prefixed with an underscore to avoid collisions with reserved predicates in NLTK semantics format or in a potential prover.

Semantic spans also provide the type of single predicates (attribute "type"). For instance, the type of the predicate _tea is a function that receives an entity as an argument, and produces a proposition:

$$\_\text{tea} : \text{Entity} \rightarrow \text{Prop}$$

Types are automatically inferred using NLTK semantics functionality. However, it is possible to force arbitrary types in a semantic template by adding the attribute "coq_type". For example, we can specify the type for a transitive verb as:

− semantics : ...

category : $(S\backslash NP)/NP$

coq_type : $\text{Entity} \rightarrow \text{Entity} \rightarrow \text{Prop}$

We can activate these types with the flag `--arbi-types` in the call to `semparse.py`.

5 Textual Entailment

The logical formulas that `ccg2lambda` outputs can be used in a variety of applications. In this demonstration, we use them to recognize textual entailment, an NLP problem that often requires precise language understanding. We assume that the user inputs a file with one sentence per line. All sentences are assumed to be premises, except the last sentence, which is assumed to be the conclusion. An entailment problem example is:

premise$_1$: All women ordered coffee or tea.
premise$_2$: Some woman did not order coffee.
conclusion: Some woman ordered tea.

Contrarily to other textual entailment systems based on logics (Angeli and Manning, 2014; MacCartney and Manning, 2007), we do not assume single-premise problems, which makes our system more general. The MRs of the problem above are:

$$p_1 : \forall x.(\text{woman}(x) \rightarrow \exists y.((\text{tea}(y) \lor \text{coffee}(y)) \land \text{order}(x, y)))$$

$$p_2 : \exists x.(\text{woman}(x) \land \neg\exists y.(\text{coffee}(y) \land \text{order}(x, y)))$$

$$c : \exists x.(\text{woman}(x) \land \exists y.(\text{tea}(y) \land \text{order}(x, y)))$$

We build a theorem by concatenating meaning representations of the premises $\{p_1, \ldots, p_n\}$ and the conclusion c with the implication operator, which is a convenience in theorem proving:

$$\text{Theorem} : p_1 \rightarrow \ldots \rightarrow p_n \rightarrow c. \qquad (1)$$

And then, we define predicate types as:

Parameter _tea : Entity $\rightarrow$ Prop.
Parameter _order : Entity $\rightarrow$ Entity $\rightarrow$ Prop.

Finally, we pipe the theorem and type definitions to Coq (Castéran and Bertot, 2004), an interactive higher-order prover that we run fully automated with the use of some tactics (including arithmetics and equational reasoning), as described in Mineshima et al. (2015). We return the label *yes* (entailment) if the conclusion can be logically proved from the premises, *no* if the negated conclusion can be proved, and *unknown* otherwise.

The recognition of textual entailment can be performed with the following command:

`# python prove.py semantics.xml`

where the entailment judgment (*yes*, *no*, *unknown*) is printed to standard output. Moreover, the flag `--graph_out` allows to specify an HTML file to print a graphical visualization of the CCG tree structure of sentences, their semantic composition (every constituent annotated with a component of the formula), and the prover script. An excerpt of the visualization is shown in Section 6.

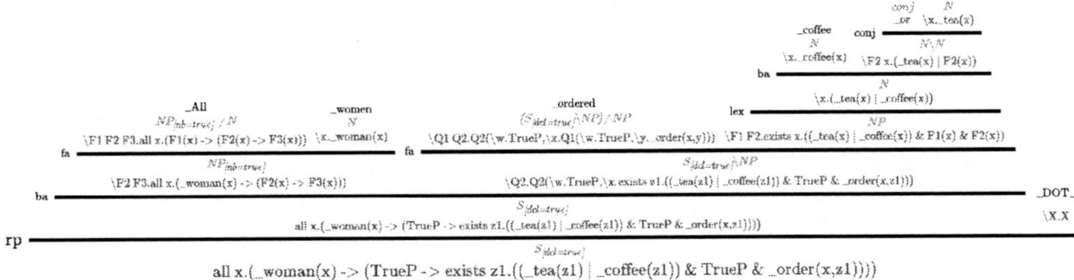

Figure 4: Visualization of the semantic output of `ccg2lambda` for the sentence "All women ordered coffee or tea." where logical semantic representations appear below their respective CCG nodes.

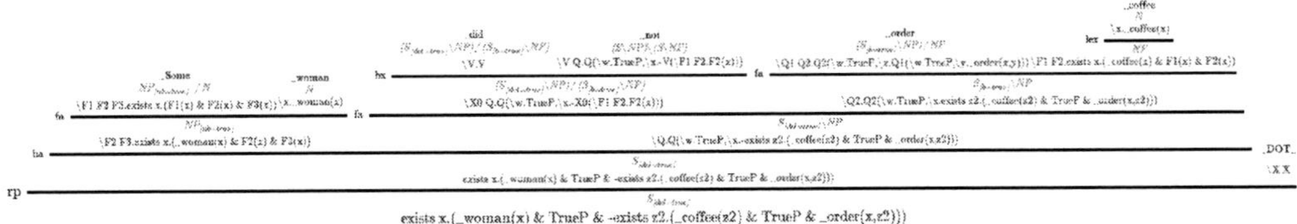

Figure 5: Visualization of the semantic output of `ccg2lambda` for the sentence "Some woman did not order coffee." where logical semantic representations appear below their respective CCG nodes.

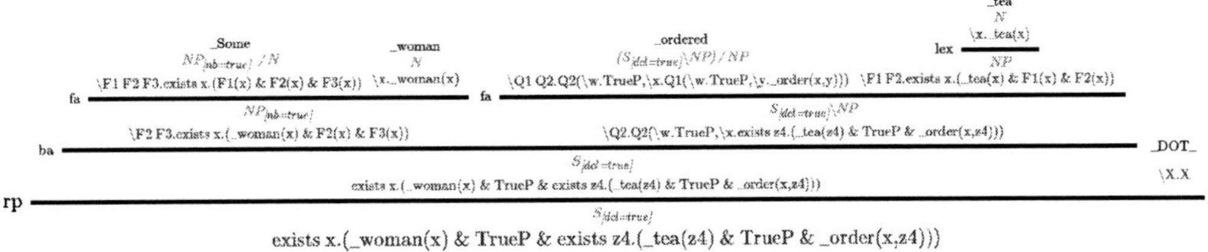

Figure 6: Visualization of the semantic output of `ccg2lambda` for the sentence "Some woman ordered tea." where logical semantic representations appear below their respective CCG nodes.

6   Visualization

For visualization purposes, we provide a separate script that can be called as:

```
# python visualize.py semantics.xml
> semantics.html
```

which produces a file `semantics.html` with an HTML graphical representation of the CCG tree, augmented at every node with the semantics composed up to that node (see Figures 4, 5 and 6 for an excerpt). These semantic representations are obtained with the semantic templates that accompany our software and that were developed and evaluated in Mineshima et al. (2015). The trivial propositions "TrueP" have no effect and appear in the formulas in place of potential modifiers (such as adjectives or adverbs) of more complex sentences. The visualization can be configured to display the root on top, change colors and sizes of the syntactic categories, feature structures, logical formulas and base forms at the leaves.

7   Future Work and Conclusion

As an extension to `ccg2lambda`, it would be valuable to produce (possibly scored) N-best lists of logical formulas, instead of the current single 1-best. Moreover, our current semantic templates do not cover all syntactic categories that C&C or Jigg produce, and we need a good default combination mechanism. Other minor enhancements are to produce logical formulas for each CCG derivation in an N-best list, and to allow features other than the base form to become predicates.

In this paper we have demonstrated our system to convert CCG trees to logic MRs. It operates by composing semantics bottom-up, guided by the combinatory characteristics of the CCG derivation and semantic templates provided by the user. In this release, semantic templates for English and Japanese are also included. As Mineshima et al. (2015) has shown, the MRs obtained by `ccg2lambda` are useful to recognize textual entailment. We believe that these easy-to-produce MRs can be useful to NLP tasks that require precise language understanding or that benefit from using MRs as features in their statistical systems.

Acknowledgments

This work was supported by CREST, JST.

References

Lasha Abzianidze. 2015. A tableau prover for natural logic and language. In *Proceedings of the 2015 Conference on Empirical Methods in Natural Language Processing*, pages 2492–2502, Lisbon, Portugal, September. Association for Computational Linguistics.

Gabor Angeli and Christopher D. Manning. 2014. NaturalLI: Natural logic inference for common sense reasoning. In *Proceedings of the 2014 Conference on Empirical Methods in Natural Language Processing (EMNLP)*, pages 534–545, Doha, Qatar, October. Association for Computational Linguistics.

Jonathan Berant, Andrew Chou, Roy Frostig, and Percy Liang. 2013. Semantic parsing on Freebase from question-answer pairs. In *Proceedings of the 2013 Conference on Empirical Methods in Natural Language Processing*, pages 1533–1544, Seattle, Washington, USA, October. Association for Computational Linguistics.

Steven Bird, Ewan Klein, and Edward Loper. 2009. *Natural Language Processing with Python*. O'Reilly Media, Inc.

Patrick Blackburn and Johan Bos. 2005. *Representation and Inference for Natural Language: A First Course in Computational Semantics*. CSLI.

Johan Bos, Stephen Clark, Mark Steedman, James R Curran, and Julia Hockenmaier. 2004. Wide-coverage semantic representations from a CCG parser. In *Proceedings of the 20th international conference on Computational Linguistics*, pages 1240–1246. Association for Computational Linguistics.

Pierre Castéran and Yves Bertot. 2004. *Interactive Theorem Proving and Program Development. Coq'Art: The Calculus of Inductive Constructions*. Springer Verlag.

Lucas Champollion, Joshua Tauberer, and Maribel Romero. 2007. The Penn Lambda Calculator: Pedagogical software for natural language semantics. In Tracy Holloway King, editor, *Proceedings of the Grammar Engineering Across Frameworks (GEAF0 7) Workshop*, pages 106–127, Stanford. CSLI Publications.

Stephen Clark and James R Curran. 2004. Parsing the WSJ using CCG and log-linear models. In *Proceedings of the 42nd Annual Meeting on Association for Computational Linguistics*, pages 104–111. Association for Computational Linguistics.

Robin Cooper, Richard Crouch, Jan van Eijck, Chris Fox, Josef van Genabith, Jan Jaspers, Hans Kamp, Manfred Pinkal, Massimo Poesio, Stephen Pulman, et al. 1994. FraCaS–a framework for computational semantics. *deliverable*, D6.

Dan Garrette and Ewan Klein. 2009. An extensible toolkit for computational semantics. In *Proceedings of the Eighth International Conference on Computational Semantics*, IWCS-8 '09, pages 116–127, Stroudsburg, PA, USA. Association for Computational Linguistics.

Mike Lewis and Mark Steedman. 2013. Combining distributional and logical semantics. *Transactions of the Association for Computational Linguistics*, 1:179–192.

Bill MacCartney and Christopher D Manning. 2007. Natural logic for textual inference. In *Proceedings of the ACL-PASCAL Workshop on Textual Entailment and Paraphrasing*, pages 193–200. Association for Computational Linguistics.

Christopher Manning, Mihai Surdeanu, John Bauer, Jenny Finkel, Steven Bethard, and David McClosky. 2014. The Stanford CoreNLP natural language processing toolkit. In *Proceedings of 52nd Annual Meeting of the Association for Computational Linguistics: System Demonstrations*, pages 55–60, Baltimore, Maryland, June. Association for Computational Linguistics.

Koji Mineshima, Pascual Martínez-Gómez, Yusuke Miyao, and Daisuke Bekki. 2015. Higher-order logical inference with compositional semantics. In *Proceedings of the 2015 Conference on Empirical Methods in Natural Language Processing*, pages 2055–2061, Lisbon, Portugal, September. Association for Computational Linguistics.

Hiroshi Noji and Yusuke Miyao. 2016. Jigg: A framework for an easy natural language processing pipeline. In *Proceedings of ACL 2016 System Demonstrations*, Berlin, Germany, August. Association for Computational Linguistics.

Mark Steedman. 2000. *The Syntactic Process*. MIT Press.

Jan van Eijck and Christina Unger. 2010. *Computational Semantics with Functional Programming*. Cambridge University Press.

Nguyen Vo, Arindam Mitra, and Chitta Baral. 2015. The NL2KR platform for building natural language translation systems. In *Proceedings of the 53rd Annual Meeting of the Association for Computational Linguistics and the 7th International Joint Conference on Natural Language Processing (Volume 1: Long Papers)*, pages 899–908, Beijing, China, July. Association for Computational Linguistics.

META: A Unified Toolkit for Text Retrieval and Analysis

Sean Massung, Chase Geigle and **ChengXiang Zhai**
Computer Science Department, College of Engineering
University of Illinois at Urbana-Champaign
{massung1,geigle1,czhai}@illinois.edu

Abstract

META is developed to unite machine learning, information retrieval, and natural language processing in one easy-to-use toolkit. Its focus on indexing allows it to perform well on large datasets, supporting online classification and other out-of-core algorithms. META's liberal open source license encourages contributions, and its extensive online documentation, forum, and tutorials make this process straightforward. We run experiments and show META's performance is competitive with or better than existing software.

1 A Unified Framework

As NLP techniques become more and more mature, we have great opportunities to use them to develop and support many applications, such as search engines, classifiers, and integrative applications that involve multiple components. It's possible to develop each application from scratch, but it's much more efficient to have a general toolkit that supports multiple application types.

Existing tools tend to specialize on one particular area, and as such there is a wide variety of tools one must sample when performing different data science tasks. For text-mining tasks, this is even more apparent; it is extremely difficult (if not impossible) to find tools that support both traditional information retrieval tasks (like tokenization, indexing, and search) alongside traditional machine learning tasks (like document classification, regression, and topic modeling).

Table 1 compares META's many features across various dimensions. Note that only META satisfies all the areas while other toolkits focus on a particular area. In the case where the desired functionality is scattered, data science students, researchers, and practitioners must find the appropriate software packages for their needs and compile and configure each appropriate tool. Then, there is the problem of data formatting—it is unlikely that the tools all have standardized upon a single input format, so a certain amount of "data munging" is required. All of this detracts from the actual task at hand, which has a marked impact on productivity.

The goal of the META project is to address these issues. In particular, we provide a unifying framework for existing machine learning and natural language processing algorithms, allowing researchers to quickly run controlled experiments. We have modularized the feature generation, instance representation, data storage formats, and algorithm implementations; this allows users to make seamless transitions along any of these dimensions with minimal effort. Finally, META is dual-licensed under the University of Illinois/NCSA Open Source Licence and the MIT License to reach the broadest audience possible.

Due to space constraints, in this paper, we only delve into META's natural language processing (NLP), information retrieval (IR), and machine learning (ML) components in section 3. However, we briefly outline all of its components here:

Feature generation. META has a collection of tokenizers, filters, and analyzers that convert raw text into a feature representation. Basic features are n-gram words, but other analyzers make use of different parts of the toolkit, such as POS tag n-grams and parse tree features. An arbitrary number of feature representations may be combined; for example, a document could be represented as unigram words, bigram POS tags, and parse tree rewrite rules. Users can easily add their own feature types as well, such as sentence length distribution in a document.

Search. The META search engine can store

Proceedings of the 54th Annual Meeting of the Association for Computational Linguistics—System Demonstrations, pages 91–96,
Berlin, Germany, August 7-12, 2016. ©2016 Association for Computational Linguistics

	Indri *IR*	Lucene *IR*	**MALLET** *ML/NLP*	**LIBLINEAR** *ML*	**SVM**^{MULT} *ML*	scikit *ML/NLP*	**CoreNLP** *ML/NLP*	**META** *all*
Feature generation	✓	✓	✓			✓	✓	✓
Search	✓	✓						✓
Classification			✓	✓	✓	✓	✓	✓
Regression			✓	✓	✓	✓	✓	✓
POS tagging			✓				✓	✓
Parsing							✓	✓
Topic models			✓			✓		✓
n-gram LM								✓
Word embeddings			✓				✓	✓
Graph algorithms								✓
Multithreading		✓	✓			✓	✓	✓

Table 1: Toolkit feature comparison. Citations for all toolkits may be found in their respective comparison sections.

document feature vectors in an inverted index and score them with respect to a query. Rankers include vector space models such as Okapi BM25 (Robertson et al., 1994) and probabilistic models like Dirichlet prior smoothing (Zhai and Lafferty, 2004). A search demo is online[1].

Classification. META includes a normalized adaptive stochastic gradient descent (SGD) implementation (Ross et al., 2013) with pluggable loss functions, allowing creation of an SVM classifier (among others). Both ℓ_1 (Tsuruoka et al., 2009) and ℓ_2 regularization are supported. Ensemble methods for binary classifiers allow multiclass classification. Other classifiers like naïve Bayes and k-nearest neighbors also exist. A confusion matrix class and significance testing framework allow evaluation and comparison of different methods and feature representations.

Regression. Regression via SGD predicts real-valued responses from featurized documents. Evaluation metrics such as mean squared error and R^2 score allow model comparison.

POS tagging. META contains a linear-chain conditional random field for POS tagging and chunking applications, learned using ℓ_2 regularized SGD (Sutton and McCallum, 2012). It also contains an efficient greedy averaged perceptron tagger (Collins, 2002).

Parsing. A fast shift-reduce constituency parser using generalized averaged perceptron (Zhu et al., 2013) is META's grammatical parser. Parse tree featurizers implement different types of structural tree representations (Massung et al., 2013). An NLP demo online presents tokenization, POS-tagging, and parsing[2].

Topic models. META can learn topic models over any feature representation using collapsed variational Bayes (Asuncion et al., 2009), collapsed Gibbs sampling (Griffiths and Steyvers, 2004), stochastic collapsed variational Bayes (Foulds et al., 2013), or approximate distributed LDA (Newman et al., 2009).

n-gram language models (LMs). META takes an ARPA-formatted input[3] and creates a language model that can be queried for token sequence probabilities or used in downstream applications like SyntacticDiff (Massung and Zhai, 2015).

Word embeddings. The GloVe algorithm (Pennington et al., 2014) is implemented in a streaming framework and also features an interactive semantic relationship demo. Word vectors can be used in other applications as part of the META API.

Graph algorithms. Directed and undirected graph implementations exist and various algorithms such as betweenness centrality, PageRank, and myopic search are available. Random graph generation models like Watts-Strogatz and preferential attachment exist. For these algorithms see Easley and Kleinberg (2010).

Multithreading. When possible, META algorithms and applications are parallelized using C++ threads to make full use of available resources.

2 Usability

Consistency across components is a key feature that allows META to work well with large datasets. This is accomplished via a three-layer architecture. On the first layer, we have tokenizers, analyzers, and all the text processing that accompanies them. Once a document representation is determined, this tool chain is run on a corpus. The indexes are the second layer; they pro-

---

[1] https://meta-toolkit.org/search-demo.html
[2] https://meta-toolkit.org/nlp-demo.html
[3] http://www.speech.sri.com/projects/srilm/manpages/ngram-format.5.html

vide an efficient format for storing processed data. The third layer—the application layer—interfaces solely with indexes. This means that we may use the same index for running an SVM as we do to evaluate a ranking function, *without processing the data again.*

Since all applications use these indexes, META supports out-of-core classification with some classifiers. We ran our large classification dataset that doesn't fit in memory—Webspam (Webb et al., 2006)—using the `sgd` classifier. Where LIBLINEAR failed to run, META was able to finish the classification in a few minutes.

Besides using META's rich built-in feature generation, it is possible to directly use LIBSVM-formatted data. This allows preprocessed datasets to be run under META's algorithms. Additionally, META's `forward_index` (used for classification), is easily convertible to LIBSVM format. The reverse is also true: you may do feature generation with META, and use it to generate input for any other program that supports LIBSVM format.

META is hosted publicly on GitHub[4], which provides the project with community involvement through its bug/issue tracker and fork/pull request model. Its API is heavily documented[5], allowing the creation of Web-based applications (listed in section 1). The project website contains several tutorials that cover the major aspects of the toolkit[6] to enable users to get started as fast as possible with little friction. Additionally, a public forum[7] is accessible for all users to view and participate in user support topics, community-written documentation, and developer discussions.

A major design point in META is to allow for most of the functionality to be configured via a configuration file. This enables minimal effort exploratory data analysis without having to write (or recompile) any code. Designing the code in this way also encourages the components of the system to be pluggable: the entire indexing process, for example, consists of several modular layers which can be controlled by the configuration file.

An example snippet of a config file is given below; this creates a bigram part-of-speech analyzer. Multiple `[[analyzers]]` sections may be added, which META automatically combines while processing input.

```
[[analyzers]]
method = "ngram-pos"
ngram = 2
filter = [{type = "icu-tokenizer"},
          {type = "ptb-normalizer"}]
crf-prefix = "crf/model/folder"
```

A simple class hierarchy allows users to add filters, analyzers, ranking functions, and classifiers with full integration to the toolkit (*e.g.* one may specify user-defined classes in the config file). The process for adding these is detailed in the META online tutorials.

This low barrier of entry experiment setup ease led to META's use in text mining and analysis MOOCs reaching over 40,000 students[8,9].

Multi-language support is hard to do correctly. Many toolkits sidestep this issue by only supporting ASCII text or the OS language; META supports multiple (non-romance) languages by default, using the industry standard ICU library[10]. This allows META to tokenize arbitrarily-encoded text in many languages.

Unit tests ensure that contributors are confident that their modifications do not break the toolkit. Unit tests are automatically run after each commit and pull request, so developers immediately know if there is an issue (of course, unit tests may be run manually before committing). The unit tests are run in a continuous integration setup where META is compiled and run on Linux, Mac OS X[11], and Windows[12] under a variety of compilers and software development configurations.

3 Experiments

We evaluate META's performance in NLP, IR, and ML tasks. All experiments were performed on a workstation with an Intel(R) Core(TM) i7-5820K CPU, 16 GB of RAM, and a 4 TB 5900 RPM disk.

3.1 Natural Language Processing

META's part-of-speech taggers for English provide quite reasonable performance. It provides a linear-chain CRF tagger (CRF) as well as an averaged perceptron based greedy tagger (AP). We report the token level accuracy on sections 22–24 of the Penn Treebank, with a few prior model results trained on sections 0–18 in Table 3. "Human annotators" is an estimate based on a 3% error rate reported in the Penn Treebank README

---

[4]https://github.com/meta-toolkit/meta/
[5]https://meta-toolkit.org/doxygen/namespaces.html
[6]https://meta-toolkit.org/
[7]https://forum.meta-toolkit.org/

[8]https://www.coursera.org/course/textretrieval
[9]https://www.coursera.org/course/textanalytics
[10]http://site.icu-project.org/
[11]https://travis-ci.org/meta-toolkit/meta
[12]https://ci.appveyor.com/project/skystrife/meta

	CoreNLP			META		
	Training	Testing	F_1	Training	Testing	F_1
Greedy	7m 27s 8.85 GB	18.6s 1.53 GB	86.7	17m 31s 0.79 GB	12.9s 0.29 GB	86.9
Beam (4)	6h 10m 43s 10.84 GB	46.8s 3.83 GB	89.9	2h 17m 25s 2.29 GB	59.2s 0.94 GB	88.1

Table 2: (NLP) Training/testing performance for the shift-reduce constituency parsers. All models were trained for 40 iterations on the standard training split of the Penn Treebank. Accuracy is reported as labeled F_1 from `evalb` on section 23.

	Extra Data	Accuracy
Human annotators		97.0%
CoreNLP	✓	97.3%
LTag-Spinal		97.3%
SCCN	✓	97.5%
META (CRF)		97.0%
META (AP)		96.9%

Table 3: (NLP) Part-of-speech tagging token-level accuracies. "Extra data" implies the use of large amounts of extra unlabeled data (*e.g.* for distributional similarity features).

	Docs	Size	$|D|_{avg}$	$|V|$
Blog06	3,215,171	26 GB	782.3	10,971,746
Gov2	25,205,179	147 GB	515.5	21,203,125

Table 4: (IR) The two TREC datasets used. Uncleaned versions of blog06 and gov2 were 89 GB and 426 GB respectively.

	Indri	Lucene	MeTA
Blog06	55m 40s	20m 23s	11m 23s
Gov2	8h 13m 43s	1h 59m 42s	1h 12m 10s

Table 5: (IR) Indexing speed.

	Indri	Lucene	MeTA
Blog06	31.02 GB	2.06 GB	2.84 GB
Gov2	170.50 GB	11.02 GB	10.24 GB

Table 6: (IR) Index size.

and is likely overly optimistic (Manning, 2011). CoreNLP's model is the result of Manning (2011), LTag-Spinal is from Shen et al. (2007), and SCCN is from Søgaard (2011). Both of META's taggers are within 0.6% of the existing literature.

META and CoreNLP both provide implementations of shift-reduce constituency parsers, following the framework of Zhu et al. (2013). These can be trained greedily or via beam search. We compared the parser implementations in META and CoreNLP along two dimensions—speed, measured in wall time, and memory consumption, measured as maximum resident set size—for both training and testing a greedy and beam search parser (with a beam size of 4). Training was performed on the standard training split of sections 2–21 of the Penn Treebank, with section 22 used as a development set (only used by CoreNLP). Section 23 was held out for evaluation. The results are summarized in Table 2.

META consistently uses less RAM than CoreNLP, both at training time and testing time. Its training time is slower than CoreNLP for the greedy parser, but less than half of CoreNLP's training time for the beam parser. META's beam parser has worse labeled F_1 score, likely the result

of its simpler model averaging strategy[13]. Overall, however, META's shift-reduce parser is competitive and particularly lightweight.

3.2 Information Retrieval

META's IR performance is compared with two well-known search engine toolkits: LUCENE's latest version 5.5.0[14] and INDRI's version 5.9 (Strohman et al., 2005)[15].

We use the TREC blog06 (Ounis et al., 2006) permalink documents and TREC gov2 corpus (Clarke et al., 2004). To ensure a more uniform indexing environment, all HTML is cleaned before indexing. In addition, each corpus is converted into a single file with one document per line to reduce the effects of many file operations.

During indexing, terms are lower-cased, stop words are removed from a common list of 431 stop words, Porter2 (META) or Porter (Indri, Lucene) stemming is performed, a maximum word length of 32 characters is set, original documents are not stored in the index, and term position information is not stored[16].

We compare the following: indexing speed (Table 5), index size (Table 6), query speed (Table 7), and query accuracy (Table 8) with BM25 using $k_1 = 0.9$ and $b = 0.4$. We use the standard TREC queries associated with each dataset and

---

[13] At training time, both CoreNLP and META perform model averaging, but META computes the average over all updates and CoreNLP performs cross-validation over a default of the best 8 models on the development set.

[14] http://lucene.apache.org/

[15] Indri 5.10 does not provide source code packages and thus could not be used. It is also known as LEMUR.

[16] For Indri, we are unable to disable positions information storage.

	Indri	**Lucene**	**MeTA**
Blog06	55.0s	1.60s	3.67s
Gov2	24m 6.73s	57.53s	1m 3.98s

Table 7: (IR) Query speed.

	Indri		**Lucene**		**MeTA**	
	MAP	P@10	MAP	P@10	MAP	P@10
Blog06	29.13	63.20	29.10	63.60	32.34	64.70
Gov2	25.96	53.69	30.23	59.26	29.97	57.43

Table 8: (IR) Query performance via Mean Average Precision and Precision at 10 documents.

	Docs	**Size**	k	**Features**
20news	18,846	86 MB	20	112,377
Blog	19,320	778 MB	3	548,812
rcv1	804,414	1.1 GB	2	47,152
Webspam	350,000	24 GB	2	16,609,143

Table 9: (ML) Datasets used for k-class categorization.

	liblinear	**scikit**	**SVM**[mult]	**MeTA**
20news	79.4%	74.3%	67.1%	80.1%
	2.58s	0.326s	2.54s	0.648s
Blog	75.8%	76.2%	72.2%	72.2%
	61.3s	0.801s	17.5s	1.11s
rcv1	94.7%	94.0%	83.6%	94.8%
	17.6s	1.66s	2.01s	3.44s
Webspam	✗	97.4%	✗	99.4%
		11m 52s		1m 16s

Table 10: (ML) Accuracy and speed classification results. Reported time is to both train and test the model. For all except Webspam, this excludes IO.

score each system's search results with the usual `trec_eval` program[17].

MeTA leads in indexing speed, though we note that MeTA's default indexer is multithreaded and Lucene does not provide a parallel one[18]. MeTA creates the smallest index for gov2 while Lucene creates the smallest index for blog06; Indri greatly lags behind both. MeTA follows Lucene closely in retrieval speed, with Indri again lagging. As expected, query performance between the three systems is relatively even, and we attribute any small difference in MAP or precision to idiosyncrasies during tokenization.

3.3 Machine Learning

MeTA's ML performance is compared with Li-blinear (Fan et al., 2008), scikit-learn (Pedregosa et al., 2011), and SVMMulticlass[19]. We focus on linear classification with SVM across these tools (MALLET (McCallum, 2002) does not provide an SVM, so it is excluded from the comparisons). Statistics for the four ML datasets can be found in Table 9.

The 20news dataset (Lang, 1995)[20] is split into its standard 60% training and 40% testing sets by post date. The Blog dataset (Schler et al., 2006) is split into 80% training and 20% testing randomly. Both of these two textual datasets were preprocessed using MeTA using the same settings from the IR experiments.

The rcv1 dataset (Lewis et al., 2004) was processed into a training and testing set using the `prep_rcv1` tool provided with Leon Bottou's SGD tool[21]. The resulting training set has 781,265 documents and the testing set has 23,149. The Webspam corpus (Webb et al., 2006) consists of the subset of the Webb Spam Corpus used in the Pascal Large Scale Learning Challenge[22]. The corpus was processed using the provided `convert.py` into byte trigrams. The first 80% of the resulting file is used for training and the last 20% for testing.

In Table 10, we can see that MeTA performs well both in terms of speed and accuracy. Both liblinear and SVMMulticlass were unable to produce models on the Webspam dataset due to memory limitations and lack of a minibatch framework. For scikit-learn and MeTA, we broke the training data into 4 equal sized batches and ran one iteration of SGD per batch. The timing result includes the time to load each chunk into memory; for MeTA this is from its forward-index format[23] and for scikit-learn this is from lib-svm-formatted text files.

4 Conclusion

MeTA is a valuable resource for text mining applications; it is a viable and competitive alternative to existing toolkits that unifies algorithms from NLP, IR, and ML. MeTA is an extensible, consistent framework that enables quick development of complex application systems.

Acknowledgements

This material is based upon work supported by the NSF GRFP under Grant Number DGE-1144245.

---

[17] http://trec.nist.gov/trec_eval/

[18] Additionally, we did not feel that writing a correct and threadsafe indexer as a user is something to be reasonably expected.

[19] http://www.cs.cornell.edu/people/tj/svm_light/svm_multiclass.html

[20] http://qwone.com/~jason/20Newsgroups/

[21] http://leon.bottou.org/projects/sgd

[22] ftp://largescale.ml.tu-berlin.de/largescale/

[23] It took 12m 24s to generate the index.

References

Arthur Asuncion, Max Welling, Padhraic Smyth, and Yee Whye Teh. 2009. On Smoothing and Inference for Topic Models. In *UAI*.

Charles L. A. Clarke, Nick Craswell, and Ian Soboroff. 2004. Overview of the TREC 2004 Terabyte Track. In *TREC*.

Michael Collins. 2002. Discriminative Training Methods for Hidden Markov Models: Theory and Experiments with Perceptron Algorithms. In *EMNLP*.

David Easley and Jon Kleinberg. 2010. *Networks, Crowds, and Markets: Reasoning About a Highly Connected World*. Cambridge University Press, New York, NY, USA.

R. Fan, K. Chang, C. Hsieh, X. Wang, and C. Lin. 2008. LIBLINEAR: A Library for Large Linear Classification. *JMLR* pages 1871–1874.

J. Foulds, L. Boyles, C. DuBois, P. Smyth, and M. Welling. 2013. Stochastic Collapsed Variational Bayesian Inference for Latent Dirichlet Allocation. In *KDD*.

T. L. Griffiths and M. Steyvers. 2004. Finding Scientific Topics. *PNAS* 101.

Ken Lang. 1995. Newsweeder: Learning to filter netnews. In *ICML*.

D. D. Lewis, Y. Yang, T. G. Rose, and F. Li. 2004. RCV1: A New Benchmark Collection for Text Categorization Research. *JMLR* 5.

Christopher D. Manning. 2011. Part-of-speech tagging from 97% to 100%: Is it time for some linguistics? In *Proc. CICLing*.

Sean Massung and ChengXiang Zhai. 2015. SyntacticDiff: Operator-based Transformation for Comparative Text Mining. In *IEEE International Conference on Big Data*.

Sean Massung, ChengXiang Zhai, and Julia Hockenmaier. 2013. Structural Parse Tree Features for Text Representation. In *Proc. IEEE ICSC*.

Andrew Kachites McCallum. 2002. MALLET: A Machine Learning for Language Toolkit. http://mallet.cs.umass.edu/.

David Newman, Arthur Asuncion, Padhraic Smyth, and Max Welling. 2009. Distributed Algorithms for Topic Models. *JMLR* 10.

I. Ounis, C. Macdonald, M. de Rijke, G. Mishne, and I. Soboroff. 2006. Overview of the TREC 2006 Blog Track. In *TREC*.

F. Pedregosa, G. Varoquaux, A. Gramfort, V. Michel, B. Thirion, O. Grisel, M. Blondel, P. Prettenhofer, R. Weiss, V. Dubourg, J. VanderPlas, A. Passos, D. Cournapeau, M. Brucher, M. Perrot, and E. Duchesnay. 2011. Scikit-learn: Machine Learning in Python. *JMLR* 12.

Jeffrey Pennington, Richard Socher, and Christopher D. Manning. 2014. GloVe: Global Vectors for Word Representation. In *EMNLP*.

Stephen E. Robertson, Steve Walker, Susan Jones, Micheline Hancock-Beaulieu, and Mike Gatford. 1994. Okapi at TREC-3. In *TREC*.

Stéphane Ross, Paul Mineiro, and John Langford. 2013. Normalized online learning. In *UAI*.

Jonathan Schler, Moshe Koppel, Shlomo Argamon, and James W. Pennebaker. 2006. Effects of Age and Gender on Blogging. In *AAAI Spring Symposium: Computational Approaches to Analyzing Weblogs*.

Libin Shen, Giorgio Satta, and Aravind Joshi. 2007. Guided learning for bidirectional sequence classification. In *ACL*.

Anders Søgaard. 2011. Semi-supervised condensed nearest neighbor for part-of-speech tagging. In *ACL-HLT*.

Trevor Strohman, Donald Metzler, Howard Turtle, and W. Bruce Croft. 2005. Indri: A language-model based search engine for complex queries (extended version). IR 407, University of Massachusetts.

Charles Sutton and Andrew McCallum. 2012. An Introduction to Conditional Random Fields. In *Foundations and Trends in Machine Learning*.

Yoshimasa Tsuruoka, Jun'ichi Tsujii, and Sophia Ananiadou. 2009. Stochastic gradient descent training for l1-regularized log-linear models with cumulative penalty. In *ACLIJCNLP*.

Steve Webb, James Caverlee, and Carlton Pu. 2006. Introducing the webb spam corpus: Using email spam to identify web spam automatically. In *CEAS*.

ChengXiang Zhai and John Lafferty. 2004. A Study of Smoothing Methods for Language Models Applied to Information Retrieval. *ACM Trans. Inf. Syst.* 22(2).

Muhua Zhu, Yue Zhang, Wenliang Chen, Min Zhang, and Jingbo Zhu. 2013. Fast and Accurate Shift-Reduce Constituent Parsing. In *ACL*.

MDS*Writer*: Annotation tool for creating high-quality multi-document summarization corpora

Christian M. Meyer,[†‡] **Darina Benikova,**[†‡] **Margot Mieskes,**[†¶] **and Iryna Gurevych**[†‡]

[†] Research Training Group AIPHES
[‡] Ubiquitous Knowledge Processing (UKP) Lab,
Technische Universität Darmstadt, Germany
[¶] University of Applied Sciences, Darmstadt, Germany

http://www.aiphes.tu-darmstadt.de

Abstract

In this paper, we present MDS*Writer*, a novel open-source annotation tool for creating multi-document summarization corpora. A major innovation of our tool is that we divide the complex summarization task into multiple steps which enables us to efficiently guide the annotators, to store all their intermediate results, and to record user–system interaction data. This allows for evaluating the individual components of a complex summarization system and learning from the human writing process. MDS*Writer* is highly flexible and can be adapted to various other tasks.

1 Introduction

Motivation. The need for automatic summarization systems has been rapidly increasing since the amount of textual information in the web and at large data centers became intractable for human readers. While single-document summarization systems can merely compress the information of *one* given text, multi-document summaries are even more important, because they can reduce the actual *number* of documents that require attention by a human. In fact, they enable users to acquire the most salient information about a topic without having to deal with the redundancy typically contained in a set of documents. Given that most search engine users only access the documents linked on the first result pages (cf. Jansen and Pooch, 2001), multi-document summaries even have the potential to radically influence our information access strategies to such textual data that remains unseen by most current search practices.

At the same time, automatic summarization is one of the most challenging natural language processing tasks. Successful approaches need to per-

form several subtasks in a complex setup, including content selection, redundancy removal, and coherent writing. Training and evaluating such systems is extremely difficult and requires high-quality reference corpora covering each subtask.

Currently available corpora are, however, still severely limited in terms of domains, genres, and languages covered. Most of them are additionally focused on the results of only one subtask, most often the final summaries, which prevents the training and evaluation of intermediate steps (e.g., redundancy detection). A major corpus creation issue is the lack of tool support for complex annotation setups. Existing annotation tools do not meet our demands, as they are limited to creating final summaries without storing intermediate results and user interactions or are not freely available or support only single document summarization.

Contribution. In this paper, we present MDS-*Writer*, a software for manually creating multi-document summarization corpora. The core innovation of our tool with regard to previous work is that we allow dividing the complex summarization task into multiple steps. This has two major advantages: (i) By linking each step to detailed annotation guidelines, we support the human annotators in creating high-quality summarization corpora in an efficient and reproducible way. (ii) We separately store the results of each intermediate step. This is necessary to properly evaluate the individual components of a complex automatic summarization system, but was largely neglected previously. Storing the intermediate results enables us to improve the evaluation setup beyond measuring inter-annotator agreement for the content selection and ROUGE for the final summaries.

Furthermore, we put a particular focus on recording the interactions between the users and the annotation tool. Our goal is to learn summa-

97

Proceedings of the 54th Annual Meeting of the Association for Computational Linguistics—System Demonstrations, pages 97–102,
Berlin, Germany, August 7-12, 2016. ©2016 Association for Computational Linguistics

rization writing strategies from the recorded user–system interactions and the intermediate results of the individual steps. Thus, we envision next-generation summarization systems that learn the human summarization *process* rather than trying to only replicate its *result*.

To the best of our knowledge, MDS*Writer* is the first attempt to support the complex annotation task of creating multi-document summaries with flexible and reusable software providing access to process data and intermediate results. We designed an initial, multi-step workflow implemented in MDS*Writer*. However, our tool is flexible to deviate from this initial setup allowing a wide range of summary creation workflows, including single-document summarization, and even other complex annotation tasks. We make MDS*Writer* available as open-source software, including our exemplary annotation guidelines and a video tutorial.[1]

2   Related work

There is a vast number of general-purpose tools for annotating corpora, for example, WebAnno (Yimam et al., 2013), Anafora (Chen and Styler, 2013), CSNIPER (Eckart de Castilho et al., 2012), and the UAM CorpusTool (O'Donnell, 2008). However, neither of these tools is suitable for tasks that require access to multiple documents at the same time, as they are focused on annotating linguistic phenomena within single documents or search results with limited contexts.

Tools for cross-document annotation tasks are so far limited to event and entity co-reference, e.g., CROMER (Girardi et al., 2014). These tools are, however, not directly applicable to the task of multi-document summarization. In fact, all tools discussed so far lack a definition of complex annotation workflows spanning multiple steps, which we consider necessary for obtaining intermediate results and systematically guiding the annotators.

With regard to the user–system interactions, the work on the Webis text reuse corpus (Potthast et al., 2013) is similar to ours. They ask crowdsource workers to retrieve sources for a given topic and record their search and text reuse actions. However, they approach a plagiarism detection task and therefore focus on writing essays rather than summaries and they do not provide detailed guidelines which is necessary to create high-quality corpora.

Summarization-specific software tools address the assessment of written summaries, computer-assisted summarization, or the manual construction of summarization corpora. The Pyramid annotation tool (Nenkova and Passonneau, 2004) and the tool[2] used for the MultiLing shared tasks (Giannakopoulos et al., 2015) are limited to comparing and scoring summaries, but do not provide any writing functionality. Orăsan et al.'s (2003) CAST tool assists users with summarizing a document based on the output of an automatic summarization algorithm. However, their tool is restricted to single-document summarization.

The works by Ulrich et al. (2008) and Nakano et al. (2010) are most closely related to ours, since they discuss the creation of multi-document summarization corpora. Unfortunately, their proposed annotation tools are not available as open-source software and thus cannot be reused. In addition to that, they do not record user–system interactions, which we consider important for next-generation automatic summarization methods.

3   MDS*Writer*

MDS*Writer* is a web-based tool implemented in Java/JSP and JavaScript. The user interface consists of a dashboard providing access to all annotation projects and their steps. Each step communicates with a server application that is responsible for recording the user–system interactions and the intermediate results. Below, we describe our proposed setup with seven subsequent steps motivated by our initial annotation guidelines.

Dashboard.   Our tool supports multiple users and topics (i.e., the document sets that are to be summarized). After logging in, a user receives a list of all topics assigned to her or him, the number of documents per topic, and the status of the summarization process. That is, for each annotation step, the tool shows either a green checkmark (if completed), a red cross (if not started), or a yellow circle (if this step comes next) to indicate the user's progress. By clicking on the yellow circle of a topic, the user can continue his or her work. Figure 2 (a) shows an example with ten topics.

Step 1: Nugget identification.   The first step aims at the selection of salient information within the multiple source documents, which is the most important and most time-consuming annotation step. Figure 1 shows the overall setup. Two thirds

---

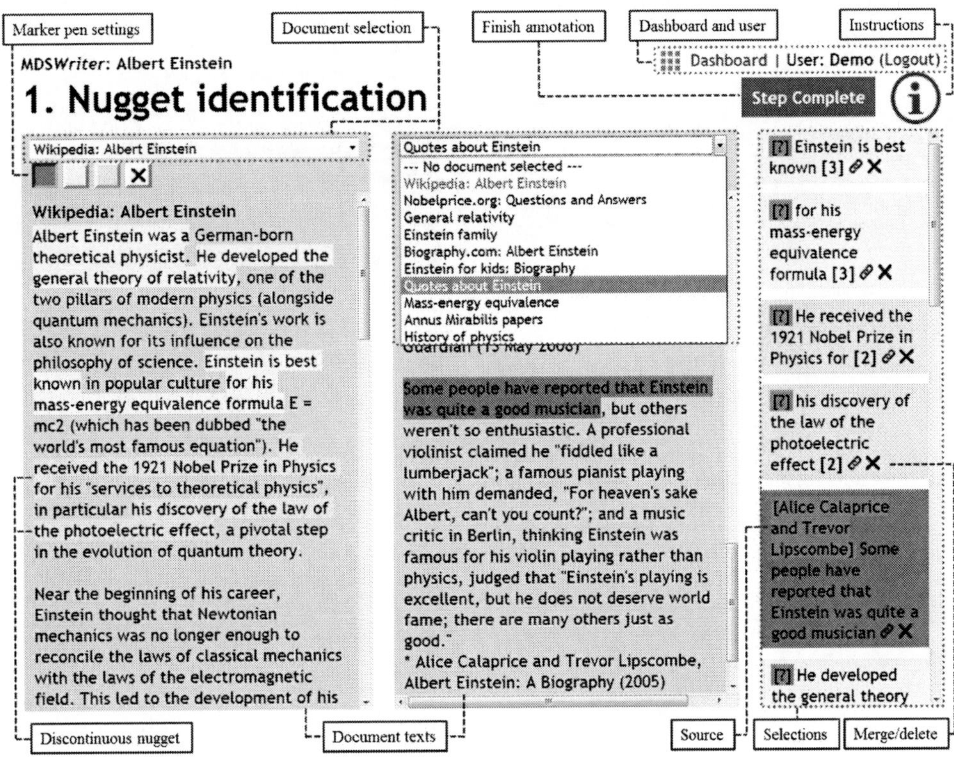

Figure 1: Nugget identification step with explanations of the most important components

of the screen are reserved for displaying the source documents. In the current setup, a user can choose to view a single source document over the full width or display two different source documents next to each other. The latter is useful for comparison and for ensuring consistent annotation.

Analogous to a marker pen, users can select salient parts of the text with the mouse. When releasing the mouse button, the selected text part receives a different background color and the selected text is included in the list of all selections shown on the right-hand side. The users may use three different colors to organize their selections. Existing selections can be modified and deleted.

To systematize the selection process, we define the term *important information nugget* in our annotation guidelines. Each nugget should consist of at least one verb with at least one of its arguments. It should be important, topic-related, and coherent, but not cross sentence boundaries. Typically, each selection in the source document corresponds to one nugget. But nuggets might also be discontinuous in order to support the exclusion of parenthetical phrases and other information of minor importance. Our tool models these cases by defining two distinct selections and merging them by means of a dedicated merge button.

Two special cases are nuggets referring to a certain source (e.g., a book) and nuggets within direct or indirect speech, which indicate a speaker's opinion. In figure 1, the 2005 biography is the source for the music-related selection. If a user would select only the subordinate clause, *some people* would be the speaker. As information about the source or speaker is highly important for both automatic methods and human writers, we provide a method to select this information within the text. The selection list shows the source/speaker in gray color at the beginning of a selection (default: [?]).

Having finished the nugget identification for all source documents, a user can return to the dashboard by clicking on "step complete".

Step 2: Redundancy detection. Redundancy is a key characteristic of multiple documents about a given topic. Automatic summarization methods aim at removing this redundancy. But, at the same time, most methods rely on the redundancy signal when estimating the importance of a phrase or sentence. Therefore, our annotation guidelines for

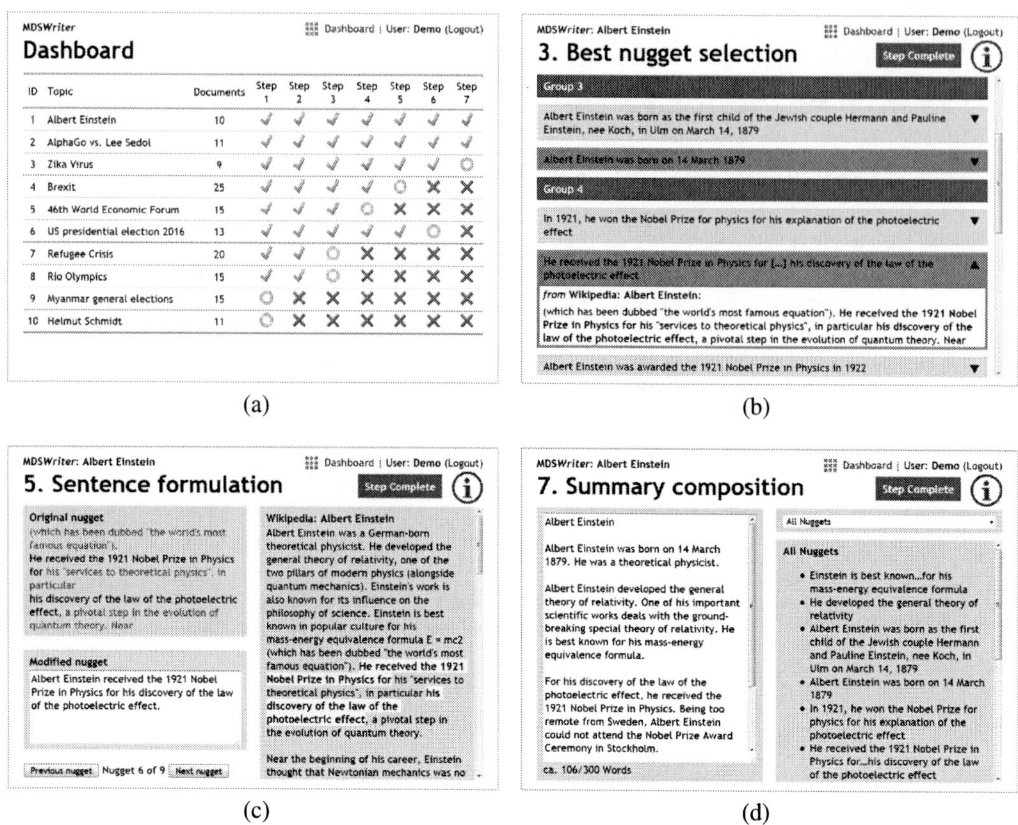

Figure 2: Screenshots of the dashboard (a) and the steps 3 (b), 5 (c), and 7 (d)

step 1 suggest to identify *all* important nuggets, including redundant ones. This type of intermediate result will allow us to create a better setup for evaluating content selection algorithms than comparing their outcome to redundancy-free summaries.

As our ultimate goal is, however, to compose an actual summary, we still need to remove the redundancy, which motivates our second annotation step. Each user receives a list of his or her extracted information nuggets and may now reorder them using drag and drop. As a result, nuggets with the same or a highly similar content will yield a single group. To allow for an informed decision, users may expand each nugget to view a context box showing the title of the source document and a ± 10 words window around the nugget text.

Step 3: Best nugget selection. In the third step, users select a representative nugget from each group, which we call the *best nugget*. We guide their decision by suggesting to prefer declarative and objective statements and to minimize context dependence (e.g., by avoiding deixis or anaphora).

To select the best nugget, users can click on one of the nuggets within a group, which then turns red. Users may change their decisions and open a context box similar to step 2. Figure 2 (b) shows an example with two groups and a context box.

Step 4: Co-reference resolution. Although the users should avoid nuggets with co-references in step 3, there is often no other choice. Therefore, we aim at resolving the remaining co-references as part of a fourth annotation step. Even though human writers make vast use of co-references in a final summary, they usually change them with regard to the source documents. For example, it is uncommon to use a personal pronoun in the very first sentence of a summary, even if this cataphor would be resolved in the following sentences. Therefore, our approach is to first resolve *all* co-references in the best nuggets during step 4 and establish a meaningful discourse structure later when composing the actual summary in step 7.

To achieve this, MDS*Writer* displays one best nugget at a time and allows the user to navigate through them. For each best nugget, we show its direct context, but also provide the entire source document in case the referring expression is not included in the surrounding ten words.

Step 5: Sentence formulation. Since our notion of information nuggets is on sub-sentence level, we ask our users to formulate each best nugget as a complete, grammatical sentence. This type of data will be useful for evaluating sentence compression algorithms, which start with an entire sentence extracted from one of the source documents and aim at compressing it to the most salient information. In our guidelines, we suggest that the changes to the nugget text should be minimal and that both the statement's source (step 1) and the resolved co-references (step 4) should be part of the reformulated sentence. We use the same user interface as in the previous step. That is, we display a single best nugget in its context and ask for the reformulated version. Figure 2 (c) shows a screenshot of a reformulated discontinuous nugget.

Step 6: Summary organization. While important nuggets often keep their original order in single-document summaries, there is no obvious predefined order for multi-document summaries. Therefore, we provide a user interface for organizing the sentences (step 5) in a meaningful way to formulate a coherent summary. A user receives a list of her or his sentences and may change the order using drag and drop. Additionally, it is possible to insert subheadings (e.g., "conclusion").

We consider this step important as previous approaches, for example, by Nakano et al. (2010, p. 3127) "did not instruct summarizers about how to connect parts" and thus do not control for coherence. By explicitly defining the order, we get in a position to learn from the human summarization process and improve the coherence of automatically generated extracts.

The user interface for step 6 is similar to the steps 2 and 3. It shows a sentence list and allows opening a context box with the original nugget.

Step 7: Summary composition. Our final step aims at formulating a coherent summary based on the structure defined in step 6. MDS*Writer* provides a text area that is initialized with the reformulated (step 5) and ordered (step 6) best nuggets, which can be arbitrarily changed. In our setup, we ask the users to make only minimal changes, such as introducing anaphors, discourse connec-

tives, and conjunctions. This will yield summaries that are very close to the source documents, which is especially useful for evaluating extractive summarization methods. However, MDS*Writer* is not limited to this procedure and future uses may strive for abstractive summaries that require substantial revisions.

While writing the summary, the users have access to all source documents, to their original nuggets (step 1) and to their selection of best nuggets (step 3). By means of a word counter, the users can easily produce summaries with a certain word limit. Figure 2 (d) shows the corresponding user interface. Having finished their summary, users complete the entire annotation process for the current topic and return to the dashboard.

Server application. Each user action, ranging from the selection of a new nugget (step 1) to modifications of the final summary (step 7), is automatically sent to our server application. We use a WebSocket connection to ensure efficient bidirectional communication. The user–system interactions and all intermediate results are stored in an SQL database. Conversely, the server loads previously stored inputs, such that the users can interrupt their work at any time without losing data.

The client–server communication is based on a simple text-based protocol. Each message consists of a four character operation code (e.g., 7DNE indicating that step 7 is now complete) and an arbitrary number of tab-separated parameters. The message 1NGN 1 25 100 2 indicates, for example, that the current user added a new nugget of length 100 characters to document 1 at offset 25, which will be displayed in color 2 (yellow).

4   Extensibility

The annotation workflow discussed so far is one example of dividing the complex setup of multi-document summarization into clear-cut steps. We argue that this division is important to ensure consistent and reliable annotations and to record intermediate results and process data. Despite this exemplary setup, MDS*Writer* provides an ideal basis for many other summarization workflows, such as creating structured or aspect-oriented summaries. This can be achieved by rearranging already existing steps and/or adding new steps. To this end, we designed the bidirectional and easy-to-extend message protocol described in the previous section as well as a brief developer guide on GitHub.

Of particular interest is that MDS*Writer* features cross-document annotations, the recording of user–system interactions and intermediate results, which is also highly relevant beyond the summarization scenario. Therefore, we consider MDS*Writer* as an ideal starting point for a wide-range of other complex multi-step annotation tasks, including but not limited to information extraction (combined entity, event, and relation identification), terminology mining (selection of candidates, filtering, describing, and organizing them), and cross-document discourse structure annotation.

5 Conclusion and future work

We introduced MDS*Writer*, a tool for constructing multi-document summaries. Our software fills an important gap as high-quality summarization corpora are urgently needed to train and evaluate automatic summarization systems. Previously available tools are not well-suited for this task, as they do not support cross-document annotations, the modeling of complex tasks with a number of distinct steps, and reusing the tools under free licenses. As a key property of our tool, we store all intermediate annotation results and record the user–system interaction data. We argued that this enables next-generation summarization methods by learning from human summarization strategies and evaluating individual components of a system.

In future work, we plan to create and evaluate an actual corpus for multi-document summarization using our tool. We also plan to provide monitoring components in MDS*Writer*, such as computing inter-annotator agreement in real-time.

Acknowledgements. This work has been supported by the DFG-funded research training group "Adaptive Preparation of Information form Heterogeneous Sources" (AIPHES, GRK 1994/1) and by the Lichtenberg-Professorship Program of the Volkswagen Foundation under grant № I/82806.

References

Wei-Te Chen and Will Styler. 2013. Anafora: A Web-based General Purpose Annotation Tool. In *Proceedings of the 2013 NAACL/HLT Demonstration Session*, pages 14–19, Atlanta, GA, USA.

Richard Eckart de Castilho, Sabine Bartsch, and Iryna Gurevych. 2012. CSniper – Annotation-by-query for Non-canonical Constructions in Large Corpora. In *Proceedings of the 50th Annual Meeting of the ACL: System Demonstrations*, pages 85–90, Jeju Island, Korea.

George Giannakopoulos, Jeff Kubina, John Conroy, Josef Steinberger, Benoit Favre, Mijail Kabadjov, Udo Kruschwitz, and Massimo Poesio. 2015. MultiLing 2015: Multilingual Summarization of Single and Multi-Documents, On-line Fora, and Call-center Conversations. In *Proceedings of the 16th Annual Meeting of the SIGDIAL*, pages 270–274, Prague, Czech Republic.

Christian Girardi, Manuela Speranza, Rachele Sprugnoli, and Sara Tonelli. 2014. CROMER: a Tool for Cross-Document Event and Entity Coreference. In *Proceedings of the Ninth International Conference on Language Resources and Evaluation*, pages 3204–3208, Reykjavik, Iceland.

Bernard J. Jansen and Udo Pooch. 2001. A review of Web searching studies and a framework for future research. *Journal of the American Society for Information Science and Technology*, 52(3):235–246.

Masahiro Nakano, Hideyuki Shibuki, Rintaro Miyazaki, Madoka Ishioroshi, Koichi Kaneko, and Tatsunori Mori. 2010. Construction of Text Summarization Corpus for the Credibility of Information on the Web. In *Proceedings of the Seventh International Conference on Language Resources and Evaluation*, pages 3125–3131, Valletta, Malta.

Ani Nenkova and Rebecca Passonneau. 2004. Evaluating Content Selection in Summarization: The Pyramid Method. In *Proceedings of the Human Language Technology Conference of the North American Chapter of the ACL*, pages 145–152, Boston, MA, USA.

Mick O'Donnell. 2008. Demonstration of the UAM CorpusTool for Text and Image Annotation. In *Proceedings of the 46th Annual Meeting of the ACL: Demo Session*, pages 13–16, Columbus, OH, USA.

Constantin Orăsan, Ruslan Mitkov, and Laura Hasler. 2003. CAST: A computer-aided summarisation tool. In *Proceedings of the 10th Conference of the European Chapter of the ACL*, pages 135–138, Budapest, Hungary.

Martin Potthast, Matthias Hagen, Michael Völske, and Benno Stein. 2013. Crowdsourcing Interaction Logs to Understand Text Reuse from the Web. In *Proceedings of the 51st Annual Meeting of the ACL*, pages 1212–1221, Sofia, Bulgaria.

Jan Ulrich, Gabriel Murray, and Giuseppe Carenini. 2008. A Publicly Available Annotated Corpus for Supervised Email Summarization. In *Enhanced Messaging: Papers from the 2008 AAAI Workshop*, Technical Report WS-08-04, pages 77–82. Menlo Park, CA: AAAI Press.

Seid Muhie Yimam, Iryna Gurevych, Richard Eckart de Castilho, and Chris Biemann. 2013. WebAnno: A Flexible, Web-based and Visually Supported System for Distributed Annotations. In *Proceedings of the 51st Annual Meeting of the ACL: System Demonstrations*, pages 1–6, Sofia, Bulgaria.

Jigg: A Framework for an Easy Natural Language Processing Pipeline

Hiroshi Noji
Graduate School of Information Science
Nara Institute of Science and Technology
8916-5 Takayama, Ikoma, Nara, Japan
`noji@is.naist.jp`

Yusuke Miyao
National Institute of Informatics
2-1-2 Hitotsubashi, Chiyoda-ku,
Tokyo, Japan
`yusuke@nii.ac.jp`

Abstract

We present Jigg, a Scala (or JVM-based) NLP annotation pipeline framework, which is easy to use and is extensible. Jigg supports a very simple interface similar to Stanford CoreNLP, the most successful NLP pipeline toolkit, but has more flexibility to adapt to new types of annotation. On this framework, system developers can easily integrate their downstream system into a NLP pipeline from a raw text by just preparing a wrapper of it.

1 Introduction

A common natural language processing system works as a component in a pipeline. For example, a syntactic parser typically requires that an input sentence is correctly tokenized or assigned part-of-speech (POS) tags. The syntactic trees given by the parser may be required in further downstream tasks such as coreference resolution and semantic role labelling. While this pipeline-based approach has been quite successful due to its modularity, it suffers from several drawbacks from a viewpoint of software use and development:

- For a *user*, building a pipeline connecting existing tools and aggregating the outputs are painful, since often each system outputs the results in a different format;

- For researchers or tool developers of downstream tasks, supporting the full pipeline from an input text in their software is boring and time consuming.

For example, two famous dependency parsing systems, MaltParser (Nivre et al., 2006) and MSTParser (McDonald et al., 2005), both assume that an input sentence is already tokenized and assigned POS tags, and encoded in a specific format, such as the CoNLL format.

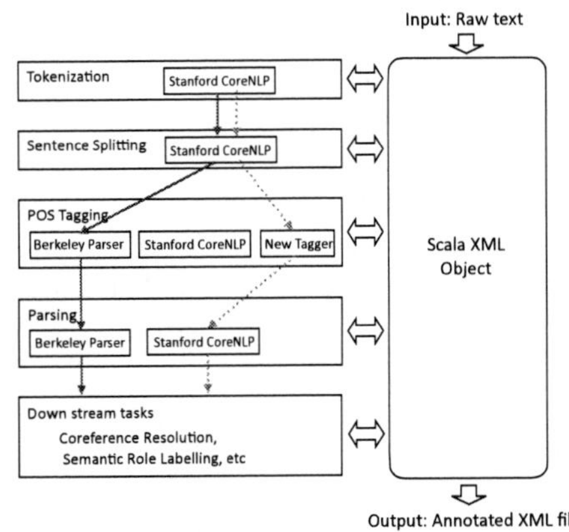

Figure 1: In a pipeline, annotations are performed on a Scala XML object. A pipeline is built by choosing annotator tools at each step, e.g., the bold or dotted lines in the figure. Each component is implemented as a wrapper, which manipulates the XML object. If we prepare a new wrapper of some component, one can integrate it in a pipeline (e.g., the POS tagger in the dotted lines).

In this paper, we present Jigg, which aims to make it easy to incorporate an existing or new tool (component) in an NLP pipeline. Figure 1 describes the overview. Using Jigg, a user can easily construct a pipeline by choosing a tool at each step on a command-line interface. Jigg is written in Scala, and can easily be extended with JVM languages including Java. A new tool can be incorporated into this framework by writing a wrapper of that to follow the common API of Jigg (Scala XML object), which requires typically several dozes of lines of code.

The software design of Jigg is highly inspired by the success of Stanford CoreNLP (Manning et al., 2014), which is now the most widely used NLP toolkit supporting pipeline processing from raw texts. One characteristic of Stanford CoreNLP is

103

Proceedings of the 54th Annual Meeting of the Association for Computational Linguistics—System Demonstrations, pages 103–108,
Berlin, Germany, August 7-12, 2016. ©2016 Association for Computational Linguistics

its simplicity of API, which allows wider users to easily get linguistic annotations for a text. Following this strategy, Jigg is also quite simple to use; all the basic components are included into one jar file, so a user need not install the external dependencies. The basic usage of Jigg is command-line interface, and the behavior can be customized with a Java properties file. On the other hand, it focuses just on processing of a single document on a single machine, and does not provide the solution to more complex scenarios such as distributed processing or visualization, which UIMA and related projects (Ferrucci and Lally, 2004; Kano et al., 2011) may provide.

The largest difference between Jigg and Stanford CoreNLP is the focused NLP components. Stanford CoreNLP is basically a collection of NLP tools developed by the Stanford NLP group, e.g., Stanford POS tagger (Toutanova et al., 2003) and Stanford parser (Socher et al., 2013). Jigg, on the other hand, is an integration framework of various NLP tools developed by various groups. This means that adding a new component in Jigg is easier than Stanford CoreNLP. Also as indicated in Figure 1, Jigg provides a wrapper to Stanford CoreNLP itself, so a user can enjoy combination of Stanford CoreNLP and other tools, e.g., Berkeley parser (Petrov and Klein, 2007) (see Section 2). This difference essentially comes from the underlying object annotated on each step, which is CoreMap object in Stanford CoreNLP, and Scala XML object in Jigg, which gives more flexibility as we describe later (Section 5). Before that, in the following, we first describes the concrete usage (Section 2), the core software design (Section 3), and a way to add a new component (Section 4).

The code is open-source under the Apache License Version 2.0. Followings are the pointers to the related websites:

- Github: `https://github.com/mynlp/jigg`

- Maven: `http://mvnrepository.com/artifact/com.github.mynlp/jigg`

Jigg is also available from Maven, so it can easily be incorporated into another JVM project. See REAME on the project Github for this usage.

2 Basic Usages

As an example, let us consider the scenario to run the Berkeley parser on a raw text. This parser is state-of-the-art but it requires that the input is cor-

```
$ cat sample.txt
This is a cat. That is a dog.
$ echo sample.txt | java -cp "*" \
  jigg.pipeline.Pipeline\
  -annotators "corenlp[tokenize,ssplit],berkeleyparser"\
  -berkeleyparser.grFileName ./eng_sm6.gr > sample.xml
```

Figure 2: A command-line usage to run the Berkeley parser on sentences tokenized and splitted by Stanford CoreNLP.

```
<?xml version='1.0' encoding='UTF-8'?>
<root>
  <document id="d0">
    <sentences>
      <sentence characterOffsetEnd="14" characterOffsetBegin="0" id="s0">
        This is a cat.
        <tokens annotators="corenlp berkeleyparser">
          <token form="This" id="t0" characterOffsetBegin="0" characterOffsetEnd="4" pos="DT"
          <token form="is" id="t1" characterOffsetBegin="5" characterOffsetEnd="7" pos="VBZ"/
          <token form="a" id="t2" characterOffsetBegin="8" characterOffsetEnd="9" pos="DT"/>
          <token form="cat" id="t3" characterOffsetBegin="10" characterOffsetEnd="13" pos="NN
          <token form="." id="t4" characterOffsetBegin="13" characterOffsetEnd="14" pos="."/>
        </tokens>
        <parse root="s0_berksp0" annotators="berkeleyparser">
          <span children="s0_berksp1 s0_berksp2 t4" symbol="S" id="s0_berksp0"/>
          <span children="t0" symbol="NP" id="s0_berksp1"/>
          <span children="t1 s0_berksp3" symbol="VP" id="s0_berksp2"/>
          <span children="t2 t3" symbol="NP" id="s0_berksp3"/>
        </parse>
      </sentence>
      <sentence characterOffsetEnd="29" characterOffsetBegin="15" id="s1">
        That is a dog.
        <tokens annotators="corenlp berkeleyparser">
```

Figure 3: The output of the command in Figure 2 (sample.xml).

rectly tokenized and splitted on sentences. Figure 2 shows a concrete command-line to build a pipeline, on which tokenization and sentence splitting are performed using the components in Stanford CoreNLP. This pipeline corresponds to the bold lines in Figure 1. jigg.pipeline.Pipeline is the path to the main class. −annotators argument is essential, and specifies which components (tools) one wishes to apply. In the command-line, corenlp[tokenize, ssplit] is an abbreviation of two components, corenlp[tokenize] (tokenization) and corenlp[ssplit] (sentence splitting by CoreNLP).[1] The last argument −berkeleyparser.grFileName is necessary and specifies the path to the parser model (learned grammar).

XML output In the current implementation, the output format of annotations is always XML. Figure 3 shows the output for this example. In this output, parse element specifies a (constituent) parse tree with a collection of spans, each of which consists of a root symbol (e.g., S) and child nodes (ids). This format is intended to be easily processed with a computer, and differs in several points from the outputs of Stanford CoreNLP, which we describe more in Section 5.

---

[1]Precisely, the two commands have different meanings and the former abbreviated form is recommended. In the latter separated form, transformation between CoreMap object and Scala XML is performed at each step (twice), while it occurs once in the former one after ssplit.

```scala
import jigg.pipeline.Pipeline
import scala.xml.Node
import java.util.Properties

object ScalaExample {
  def main(args: Array[String]): Unit = {
    val props = new Properties()
    props.setProperty("annotators",
      "corenlp[tokenize,ssplit],berkeleyparser")
    props.setProperty("berkeleyparser.grFileName",
      "eng_sm6.gr")
    val pipeline = new Pipeline(props)
    val annotation: Node = pipeline.annotate(
      "This is a cat. That is a dog")

    // Find all sentence elements recursively,
    // and get the first one.
    val firstSentence = (annotation \\ "sentence")(0)

    // All tokens on the sentence
    val tokens = firstSentence \\ "token"

    println("POS tags on the first sentence: " +
      (tokens map (_ \@ "pos") mkString " "))
    // Output "DT VBZ DT NN ."
  }
}
```

Figure 4: A programmatic usage from Scala.

Properties   As in Stanford CoreNLP, these arguments can be customized through a Java properties file. For example, the following properties file customizes the behavior of corenlp besides the parser:

```
$ cat sample.properties
annotators: corenlp[tokenize,ssplit],berkeleyparser
berkeleyparser.grFileName: ./eng_sm6.gr
corenlp.tokenize.whitespace: true
corenlp.ssplit.eolonly: true
```

This file can be used as follows:

```
jigg.pipeline.Pipeline -props sample.properties
```

Each annotator-specific argument has the form annotator_name.key. In the case of corenlp, all keys of the arguments prefixed with that are directly transferred to the CoreNLP object, so the all arguments defined in Stanford CoreNLP can be used to customize the behavior. The setting above yields tokenization on white spaces, and sentence splitting on new lines only (i.e., the input text is assumed to be properly preprocessed beforehand).

Programmatic usage   Jigg can also be used as a Scala library, which can be called on JVM languages. Figure 4 shows an example on a Scala code. The annotate method of Pipeline object performs annotations on the given input, and returns the annotated XML object (Node class). The example also shows how we can manipulate the Scala XML object, which can be searched with methods similar to XPath, e.g., \\. \@ key returns the attribute value for the key if exists. Figure 5 shows that Jigg can also be used via a Java code.

Another example   Jigg is a growing project, and the supported tools are now increasing. Histori-

```java
Properties props = new Properties();
props.setProperty("annotators",
  "corenlp[tokenize,ssplit],berkeleyparser");
props.setProperty("berkeleyparser.grFileName",
  "eng_sm6.gr");
Pipeline pipeline = new Pipeline(props);
Node annotation = pipeline.annotate(
  "This is a cat. That is a dog");

// Though the search methods such as \\ cannot be
// used on Java, we provide utilities to support
// Java programming.
List<Node> sentences = jigg.util.XMLUtil.findAllSub(
    annotation, "sentence");
Node firstSentence = sentences.get(0);
List<Node> tokens = jigg.util.XMLUtil.findAllSub(
    firstSentence, "token");
System.out.print("POS tags on the first sentence: ");
for (Node token: tokens) {
  String pos = XMLUtil.find(token, "@pos").toString();
  System.out.print(pos + " ");
}
```

Figure 5: Jigg also supports Java programming.

cally, Jigg has been started as a pipeline framework focusing on Japanese language processing. Jigg thus supports many Japanese processing tools such as MeCab (Kudo et al., 2004), a famous morphological analyzer, as well as a Japanese CCG parser based on the Japanese CCGBank (Uematsu et al., 2013). For English, currently the core tool is Stanford CoreNLP. Here we present an interesting application to integrate Berkeley parser into the full pipeline of Stanford CoreNLP:

```
-annotators "corenlp[tokenize,ssplit],berkeleyparser,
  corenlp[lemma,ner,dcoref]"
```

where dcoref is a coreference resolution system relying on constituent parse trees (Recasens et al., 2013). This performs annotation of coreference resolution based on the parse trees given by the Berkeley parser instead of the Stanford parser. Using Jigg, a user can enjoy these combinations of existing tools quite intuitively. Also if a user has her own (higher-performance) system on the pipeline, one can replace the existing component with that in a minimal effort, by writing a wrapper of that tool in JVM languages (see Section 4).

3   Design

We now describe the internal mechanisms of Jigg, which comprise of two steps: the first is a check for correctness of the given pipeline, and the second is annotations on a raw text with the constructed pipeline. We describe the second annotation step first (Section 3.1), and then discuss the first pipeline check phase (Section 3.2).

3.1   Annotation on Scala XML

As shown in Figure 1, each annotator (e.g., the tokenizer in Stanford CoreNLP) communicates with the Scala XML object. Basically, each annotator only adds new elements or attributes into the received XML.[2] For example, the Berkeley parser receives an XML, on which each sentence element is annotated with tokens elements lacking pos attribute on each token. Then, the parser (i.e., the wrapper of the parser) adds the predicted syntactic tree and POS tags on each sentence XML (see Figure 3). Scala XML (Node object) is an immutable data structure, but it is implemented as an immutable tree, so a modification can be performed efficiently (in terms of memory and speed).

3.2 Requirement-based Pipeline Check

On this process, the essential point for the pipeline to correctly work is to guarantee that all the required annotations for an annotator are provided at each step. For example, the berkeleyparser annotator assumes each sentence element in the XML has the following structure:

```
<sentence id="...">
  sentence text
  <tokens>
    <token form="..." id="..."/>
    <token form="..." id="..."/>
    ...
  </tokens>
</sentence>
```

where form means the surface form of a token. How do we guarantee that the XML given to berkeleyparser satisfies this form?

Currently, Jigg manages these dependencies between annotators using the concept of Requirement, which we also borrowed from Stanford CoreNLP. Each annotator has a field called requires, which specifies the type of necessary annotations that must be given before running it. In berkeleyparser it is defined as follows:

```
override def requires:Set[Requirement] =
  Set(Tokenize, Ssplit)
```

where Ssplit is an object (of Requirement type), which guarantees that sentences element (a collection of sentence elements) exists on the current annotation, while Tokenize guarantees that each sentence element has tokens element (a collection of token elements), and each token has four attributes: id, form, characterOffsetBegin, and characterOffsetEnd.

Each annotator also has requirementsSatisfied field, which declares which Requirements will be satisfied (annotated). In the above requirements,

Ssplit is given by corenlp[ssplit] while Tokenize is given by corenlp[tokenize]. In berkeleyparser, it is POS and Parse; POS guarantees that each token element has pos attribute. Before running annotation, Jigg checks whether the constructed pipeline correctly works by checking that all elements in requires for each annotator are satisfied by (included in) the requirementsSatisfied elements of the previous annotators. For example, if we run the pipeline with −annotators berkeleyparser argument, the program fails with an error message suggesting missing Requirements.

Note that currently Requirement is something just like a contract on the structure of annotated XML, and it is the author's responsibility to implement each annotator to output the correct XML structure. Currently the correspondence between each Requirement and the satisfied XML structure is managed with a documentation on the wiki of the project Github. We are seeking a more sophisticated (safe) mechanism to guarantee these correspondences in a code; one possible solution might be to define the skeletal XML structure for each Requirement, and test in each annotator whether the annotated object follows the defined structure.

4 Adding New Annotator

Here we describe how to implement a new annotator and integrate it into the Jigg pipeline. We also discuss a way to distribute a new system in Jigg.

Implementing new annotator We focus on implementation of Berkeley parser as an example to get intuition into what we should do. Annotator is the base trait[3] of all annotator classes, which defines the following basic methods:

- def annotate(annotation : Node) : Node
- def requires : Set[Requirement]
- def requirementsSatisfied : Set[Requirement]

We have already seen the roles of requires and requirementsSatisfied in Section 3.2. Note that in many cases including the Berkeley parser, annotation is performed on each *sentence* independently. For this type of annotation, we provide a useful trait SentenceAnnotator, which replaces the method to be implemented from annotate to newSentenceAnnotation, which has the same signature as annotate.[4]

---

[2]One exception in the current implementation is ssplit in corenlp, which breaks the result of tokenize (one very long tokenized sentence) into several sentences.

[3]Trait is similar to interface in Java.

[4]This trait implements annotate to traverse all sentences and replace them using newSentenceAnnotation method.

```
package jigg.pipeline
import ...

// By supporting a constructor with signature
// (String, Properties), the annotator can be
// instantiated dynamically using reflection.
class BerkeleyParserAnnotator(
  override val name: String,
  override val props: Properties) extends SentenceAnnotator {

  // Instantiate a parser by reading the gramar file.
  val parser: CoarseToFineMaxRuleParser = ...

  override def newSentenceAnnotation(sentence: Node): Node = {

    val tokens: Node = (sentence \ "tokens").head
    val tokenSeq: Seq[Node] = tokens \ "token"

    // (1) Get a list of surface forms.
    val formSeq: Seq[String] = tokenSeq.map(_ \@ "form")

    // (2) Parse the sentence by calling the API.
    val binaryTree: Tree[String] = parser.
      getBestConstrainedParse(formSeq.asJava, null, null)
    val tree =
      TreeAnnotations.unAnnotateTree(binaryTree, true)

    // (3) Convert the output tree into annotation.
    val taggedTokens = addPOSToTokens(tree, tokens)
    val parse = treeToNode(tree, tokenSeq)

    // (4) Return a new sentence node with updated
    // child elements.
    XMLUtil.addOrOverrideChild(
      sentence, Seq(newTokens, parseNode))
  }
  // Return the new tokens element on which each element has
  // pos attributes.
  def addPOSToTokens(tree: Tree[String], tokens: Node): Node
    = { ... }

  // Convert the Tree object in Berkeley parser into XML.
  def treeToNode(
    tree: Tree[String], tokenSeq: Seq[Node]): Node = { ... }

  override def requires = Set(Tokenize)
  override def requirementsSatisfied = Set(POS, Parse)
}
```

Figure 6: Core parts in BekeleyParserAnnotator.

Figure 6 shows an excerpt of essential parts in BerkeleyParserAnnotator. It creates a parser object in the constructor, and then in each newSentenceAnnotation, it first extracts a sequence of (yet annotated) tokens (1), gets a tree object from the parser (2), converts the tree into Scala XML object (3), and returns the updated sentence XML object (4). This workflow to encode to and decode from the API-specific objects is typical when implementing new annotators.

Calling with reflection The class in Figure 6 has a constructor with the signature (String, Properties), which allows us to instantiate the class dynamically using reflection. To do this, a user has to add a new property prefixed with customAnnotatorClass (the same as Stanford CoreNLP). In the case above, the property

customAnnotatorClass.berkeleyparser : jigg.pipeline.BerkeleyParser

makes it possible to load the implemented annotator with the name berkeleyparser.

Distributing new annotators An ultimate goal of Jigg is that the developers of a new tool in a pipeline distribute their system along with the wrapper (Jigg annotator) when releasing the software. If the system is JVM-based, the most stable way to integrate it is releasing the annotator (along with the software) into Maven repositories. Then, a user can build an extended Jigg by adding the dependency to it. For example, now the annotator for the MST parser is implemented, but is not included in Jigg, as it is a relatively old system. One way to extend Jigg with this tool is to prepare another project, on which its build.sbt may contain the following lines:[5]

```
libraryDependencies ++= Seq(
  "com.github.mynlp" % "jigg" % "VVV",
  "com.github.mynlp" % "jigg-mstparser" % "0.1-SNAPSHOT")
```

Jigg itself focuses more on the central NLP tools for wider users, but one can obtain the customized Jigg in this way.

Tools beyond JVM So far we have only dealt with JVM softwares such as Stanford CoreNLP, but Jigg can also wraps the softwares written in other languages such as C++ and python. In fact, many existing tools for Japanese are implemented in C or C++, and Jigg provides wrappers for those softwares. One problem of these languages is that installation is sometimes hard due to complex dependencies to other libraries. We thus put a priority on supporting the tool written in JVM languages in particular on Maven first, which can be safely incorporated in general.

5 Comparison to Stanford CoreNLP

As we have seen so far, Jigg follows the software design of Stanford CoreNLP in many respects. Finally, in this section, we highlight the important differences between two approaches.

Annotated objects Conceptually this is the most crucial difference as we mentioned in Section 1. In Stanford CoreNLP, each annotator manipulates an object called CoreMap. A clear advantage of this data structure is that one can take out a *typed* data structure, such as a well implemented Sentence or Graph object, which is easy

---

Another advantage of this trait is that annotations are automatically performed in parallel if the code is thread-safe. One can also prohibit this behavior by overriding nThreads variable by 1 in the annotator class.

[5]To call a new annotator, a user have to give a class path to the annotator with the property. Note that the mappings for the built-in annotators such as berkeleyparser are preserved in the Jigg package, so they can be used without any settings.

to use. In Jigg's XML, on the other hand, one accesses the fields through literals (e.g., $\backslash @$ $''pos''$ to get the POS attribute of a token). This may suggests Jigg needs more careful implementation for each annotator. However, we note that the problem can be alleviated by adding a simple unit test, which we argue is important as well in other platforms.

The main advantage of using Scala XML as a primary object is its flexibility for adapting to new types of annotations. It is just an XML object, so there is no restriction on the allowed structure. This is not the case in Stanford CoreNLP, where each element in CoreMap must be a proper data structure defined in the library, which means that the annotation that goes beyond the assumption of Stanford CoreNLP is difficult to support. Even if we define a new data structure in CoreMap, another problem occurs when outputting the annotation into other formats such as XML. In Stanford CoreNLP, this output component is hard-coded in the outputter class, which is difficult to extend. This is the problem that we encountered when we explored an extension to Stanford CoreNLP for Japanese processing pipeline as our initial attempt. Historically in Japanese NLP, the basic analyzing unit is called *bunsetsu*, which is a kind of chunk; a syntactic tree is often represented as a dependency tree on bunsetsu. Jigg is preferable to handle these new data structures, which go beyond the assumption on typical NLP focusing primarily on English, and we believe this flexibility make Jigg suitable for an integration framework, which has no restrictions on the applicable softwares and languages.

Output format Another small improvement is that our XML output format (Figure 3) is (we believe) more machine-friendly. For example, in Stanford CoreNLP, the parse element is just a Lisp-style tree like (S (NP (DT This)) ((VBZ is) (NP (DT a) (NN cat))) (. .)), which is parsable elements in Jigg. For some attribute names we employ different names, e.g., surface form is called form in Jigg instead of word in Stanford CoreNLP. We decide these names basically following the naming convention found in Universal Dependencies[6], which we expect becomes the standard in future NLP. Finally, now we implement each wrapper so that each id attribute is unique across the XML, which is not the case in Stanford CoreNLP. This makes search of elements more easier.

---

[6]http://universaldependencies.org/docs/

6 Conclusion

We presented Jigg, an open source framework for an easy natural language processing pipeline both for system developers and users. We hope that this platform facilitates distribution of a new high quality system on the pipeline to wider users.

Acknowledgments

This work was supported by CREST, JST.

References

David A. Ferrucci and Adam Lally. 2004. Uima: an architectural approach to unstructured information processing in the corporate research environment. *Natural Language Engineering*, 10(3-4):327–348.

Y. Kano, M. Miwa, K. B. Cohen, L. E. Hunter, S. Ananiadou, and J. Tsujii. 2011. U-compare: A modular nlp workflow construction and evaluation system. *IBM Journal of Research and Development*, 55(3):11:1–11:10, May.

Taku Kudo, Kaoru Yamamoto, and Yuji Matsumoto. 2004. Applying conditional random fields to japanese morphological analysis. In Dekang Lin and Dekai Wu, editors, *EMNLP*, pages 230–237, Barcelona, Spain, July.

Christopher Manning, Mihai Surdeanu, John Bauer, Jenny Finkel, Steven Bethard, and David McClosky. 2014. The stanford corenlp natural language processing toolkit. In *ACL: System Demonstrations*, pages 55–60, Baltimore, Maryland, June.

Ryan McDonald, Fernando Pereira, Kiril Ribarov, and Jan Hajic. 2005. Non-projective dependency parsing using spanning tree algorithms. In *HLT-EMNLP*, October.

Joakim Nivre, Johan Hall, and Jens Nilsson. 2006. Maltparser: a data-driven parser-generator for dependency parsing. In *LREC*.

Slav Petrov and Dan Klein. 2007. Improved inference for unlexicalized parsing. In *HLT-NAACL*, pages 404–411, Rochester, New York, April.

Marta Recasens, Marie-Catherine de Marneffe, and Christopher Potts. 2013. The life and death of discourse entities: Identifying singleton mentions. In *NAACL: HLT*, pages 627–633, Atlanta, Georgia, June.

Richard Socher, John Bauer, Christopher D. Manning, and Ng Andrew Y. 2013. Parsing with compositional vector grammars. In *ACL*, pages 455–465, Sofia, Bulgaria, August.

Kristina Toutanova, Dan Klein, Christopher D. Manning, and Yoram Singer. 2003. Feature-rich part-of-speech tagging with a cyclic dependency network. In *NAACL: HLT*, pages 173–180, Morristown, NJ, USA.

Sumire Uematsu, Takuya Matsuzaki, Hiroki Hanaoka, Yusuke Miyao, and Hideki Mima. 2013. Integrating multiple dependency corpora for inducing wide-coverage japanese ccg resources. In *ACL*, pages 1042–1051, Sofia, Bulgaria, August.

An Advanced Press Review System Combining Deep News Analysis and Machine Learning Algorithms

Danuta Ploch, Andreas Lommatzsch, and Florian Schultze
DAI-Labor, Technische Universität Berlin
Ernst-Reuter-Platz 7, 10587 Berlin, Germany
{danuta.ploch, andreas.lommatzsch}@dai-labor.de,
florian.schultze@campus.tu-berlin.de

Abstract

In our media-driven world the perception of companies and institutions in the media is of major importance. The creation of press reviews analyzing the media response to company-related events is a complex and time-consuming task. In this demo we present a system that combines advanced text mining and machine learning approaches in an extensible press review system. The system collects documents from heterogeneous sources and enriches the documents applying different mining, filtering, classification, and aggregation algorithms. We present a system tailored to the needs of the press department of a major German University. We explain how the different components have been trained and evaluated. The system enables us demonstrating the live analyzes of news and social media streams as well as the strengths of advanced text mining algorithms for creating a comprehensive media analysis.

1 Introduction

The analysis of news related to companies and institution is a complex task often performed by human experts. Due to the growing amount of news and articles published in social media, large collections of data must be analyzed. In order to support the efficient creation of press reviews powerful tools are needed for the automatic aggregation and deep analysis of news. This motivates us to develop an extensible framework allowing us to combine advanced machine learning algorithms for filtering, extracting, and visualizing relevant information.

1.1 The analyzed Scenario

In this work we present a system developed for the press department of the Berlin Institute of Technology (TUB). The system should be able to collect news as well as social media articles related to the TUB or to any other of the Berlin's universities. The system is subject to a collection of requirements: The system should detect duplicates or texts with minor variations. Persons and faculties mentioned in news articles are of special interest for a fine-grained analysis. The system should detect known entities and create detailed statistics. Events drive the news. The system should detect and follow news related to the Berlin's universities. Readers of news often drain in information. The system should aggregate and visualize relevant documents in a concise way by computing key figures (e.g. describing the sentiment score for news) and calculating statistics giving a quick overview on the characteristics of the news stream. The results of the news analysis should be accessible in a web application.

1.2 Challenges

The automatic creation of press reviews leads to several challenges. The system has to integrate all important sources and to filter irrelevant documents. A specific challenge is that abbreviations are often used for institutions having a long name. In our scenario the "Technische Universität Berlin" is frequently called "TUB" or "TU". The press review system must infer from the context whether an article is relevant or not. The automatic analysis and enrichment requires a variety of algorithms, including duplicates detection, identification and disambiguation of named entities, and sentiment analysis. The sentiment analysis for news articles is a hard challenge since most journalists seek to write objectively. Nevertheless, news induces emotions relevant in the automatic analysis of news documents. Since the system has

109

Proceedings of the 54th Annual Meeting of the Association for Computational Linguistics—System Demonstrations, pages 109–114,
Berlin, Germany, August 7-12, 2016. ©2016 Association for Computational Linguistics

been developed for a major German university, the language analysis focuses on German texts.

1.3 Structure of the Work

The remaining work is structured as follows. In Section 2 we explain the basics of text mining algorithms and discuss existing press review systems. The architecture and the implemented algorithms are presented in Section 3. In Section 4 the visualization of the elicited data is described in further detail. Section 5 explains the most important use cases and presents the evaluation results with respect to the functionality of the press review portal. A conclusion and an outlook to future work is given in Section 6.

2 Related Work

We review advanced text mining algorithms and existing press review systems. There are a lot of commercial press review systems such as `http://www.bluereport.net/de/`, `http://www.pressemonitor.de/` or `https://www.ausschnitt.de/`. The systems focus on printed newspapers but also provide press reviews for online published articles. Traditionally, the systems provide excerpts related to predefined search terms. In general, the companies offer a wide variety of analysis services but the applied algorithms are neither open nor explained. With the pricing models in mind a lot of work is still performed by human experts. Based on the companies' information policy and the marketing language on the websites it is unclear to what extent machine learning or text mining algorithms are used.

Several research-oriented systems complement commercial press review systems. An exemplary application for large scale news analysis is LYDIA. LYDIA focuses on named entity detection. Its key feature is answering questions such as "who is being talked about, by whom, when, and where?" (Lloyd et al., 2005). The SEMANTIC PRESS system (Picchi et al., 2008) uses an alternative approach. It presents the most discussed themes in the Italian-spoken web.

An example for German media resonance analysis is the system explained by (Scholz, 2011). It focuses on entity extraction and sentiment analysis. Similar researches were done by (Hanjalic et al., 1998) and (Zhang et al., 2009).

3 Approach

We develop an open framework enabling us integrating different information sources and machine learning algorithms. The system allows us considering news portals, search engines, RSS feeds, and messages published on TWITTER. We deploy a flexible processing pipeline enriching freshly crawled documents as well as a batch engine used for clustering and generating newsletters. Our framework is open for the integration of new sources and algorithms allowing us incrementally extending and improving our system.

3.1 System Architecture

The structure of the developed system is shown in Fig. 1. The system consists of four major building blocks. The crawler component collects potentially relevant documents and tweets. The documents are persisted in a database. The processing components enrich the crawled documents and run several different machine learning algorithms. Based on the meta-data and the computed annotations the relevance of documents is computed and near duplicates are identified. The batch processing pipeline is a second pipeline used for processing documents from the database in predefined intervals. Both processing pipelines can be easily extended. The use of a database decouples the crawling from the processing allowing an efficient and concurrent computation of annotations.

The enriched documents are presented to the user in a web application and summarized in a periodically created newsletter.

3.2 Text Mining Components

In this Section we present the algorithms implemented for the different components in detail and discuss specific adaptations.

Validation

Several crawlers collect potentially relevant documents subsequently analyzed by the validation component. The crawlers use APIs of major search engines and the TWITTER streaming API. We define for each source a component optimizing the queries in order to ensure that all relevant documents are crawled (taking into account the limits of the sources). Due to the fact that several sources only support simple term queries (instead of phrase queries), an additional filtering is required. For this purpose we manually labeled

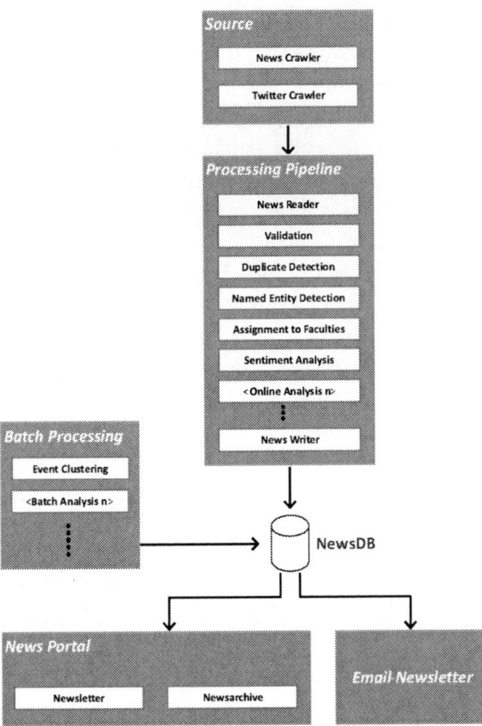

Figure 1: The figure visualizes the system architecture. Potentially relevant news documents and twitter messages collected by the *crawlers* are stored in the *news database*. The *Processing Pipeline* applies different text mining algorithms to each new document. The *Batch Processing* is executed on all documents periodically. The elicited data and documents are represented by a second application, the *News-Portal* which is built with GROOVY and GRAILS.

the documents crawled in a time frame of 2 weeks as relevant or irrelevant. Based on this dataset we trained a rule-based classifier considering phrases and context data for filtering out irrelevant documents. The filtering is especially important for handling abbreviations frequently used for referring to Berlin's universities.

Deduplication

Due to the applied architecture for collecting documents, similar documents might be crawled multiple times from different sources. Hence, we need to integrate a deduplication component identifying (near) duplicates. For ensuring an efficient processing of large text collections we implemented the *Rabin fingerprint algorithm* (Rabin and others, 1981). The algorithm randomly selects a prede-

fined number of text shingles and computes the hash codes. Duplicates are identified by counting the fraction of identical shingles in two documents. We adjust the optimal parameter settings (shingle size, number of considered shingles) on a validation dataset.

Named Entity Detection

The named entity detection component recognizes and disambiguates persons mentioned in news articles. For the recognition part it uses several components from "Stanford CoreNLP" which are explained in (Manning et al., 2014). In particular, the component applies the parser, POS-tagger, and Named Entity Recognizer (NER) to detect mentions of professors, researchers and other university-related experts mentioned in the news articles. Based on the output of the "Stanford CoreNLP" tools the module enriches each identified person with their titles and associated organization, provided the news article contains the necessary information within a window of n words. In addition, the person's name is decomposed into a given name and a surname. In order to identify person mentions unambiguously the module applies local and global disambiguation strategy. The local disambiguation resolves co-referent person mentions within one news article. It assembles a representation of each person as complete as possible. The global disambiguation performs a cross-document co-reference resolution. It considers all person attributes and words calculated from the text surrounding a person mention. Each person from a news article is compared to entries already stored in the database. In the course of similarity calculation all types of information (person attributes and bag-of-word) are weighted differently. If the similarity between a newly detected person and a person from the database exceeds a predefined threshold, the persons are merged in the database. Otherwise, a new person entry is created.

Assignment of Faculties

Usually, universities are structured in several faculties. The presence of single faculties in the media may be an important quality indicator for the universities. Our approach to assigning news articles to a faculty is person-based. Therefore, we first gather the names of all employees from the faculty websites. In this way we create a register of person names aligned with faculty affiliation.

In order to measure the media response of a specific faculty, the implemented component analyzes news articles according to mentions of persons related to the faculty. The implementation of our approach bases on an inverted index containing each document's full text. We search the documents for person names from our register. If our algorithm identifies a faculty-related person, it assigns the news article to the corresponding faculty.

Event Detection

The event detection component clusters news articles dealing with one concrete news event such as the *Queen's Lecture* or the *Long Night of the Sciences* in Berlin. Our approach uses a combination of the *Canopy* and the *k-means* algorithm for clustering which is described by (McCallum et al., 2000). In order to improve the accuracy of the clustering we enable a part-of-speech tagger. We exclude all words that do not contribute to the content like articles, conjunctions, and prepositions; we proceed with the resulting subset of the text. Since the k-means algorithm needs to be initialized with a fixed number of clusters k our component performs two stages. First, the component estimates the number of clusters by applying Canopy. We adjust Canopy's hyper-parameters on a manually annotated validation dataset. Then, the calculated canopies serve as input centroids for the second step, the k-means clustering. Finally, each cluster corresponds to a real-life event.

Sentiment Analysis

Despite of the objective nature of news articles, they are still a valuable source of sentiment information. They may express opinions of cited entities or may contain content influencing the reader's perception regarding a university. Our system incorporates two sentiment analysis components.

The first component implements a lexicon-based approach. It uses the SentiWS sentiment dictionary (Remus et al., 2010) containing positively and negatively connoted words with positive and negative scores respectively. In order to calculate the sentiment score of an entire news article it counts the values of positive and negative words occurring in the news article. The component takes into account negation by exploiting a list of inverting words. If an inverting word precedes a positive or negative connoted word, it changes its polarity.

The second approach uses machine learning techniques. We build a training dataset with about 2,400 randomly selected sentences from crawled documents. We annotate the sentences to have a positive, negative, or neutral sentiment. For the annotation we use the rules from (Clematide et al., 2012). Based on the created dataset we train a Multi-nominal Naive Bayes classifier able to classify each sentence of a news article into one of the three sentiment classes. We represent each sentence in the vector space model applying common text preprocessing steps. Beside unigrams we also include bigrams into the vectors to cover sentiment-related expressions such as "very good". The overall sentiment of a news article is computed based on all single sentence classifications. The classifier achieves promising results providing deep insights into the sentiment distribution within a news article. A more detailed explanation can be found in (Bütow et al., 2016).

4   Visualization

We implemented a web-based user interface visualizing the collected and annotated documents and tweets. The web portal provides two major views. (1) The *Newsletter* or *live* view shows the most recently collected news. (2) The *Newsarchive* view aggregates documents collected in the past and allows the creation of statistics as well as the visualization of events identified by clustering news related to one topic.

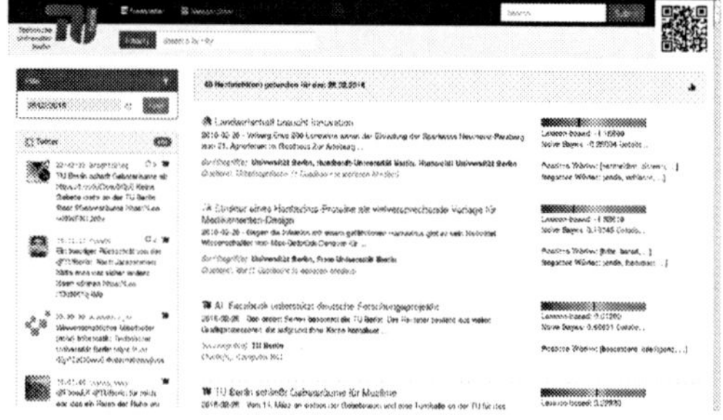

Figure 2: The Figure shows the front page of the system. It visualizes the Twitter messages on the left sidebar, the news articles in the middle and the corresponding sentiments on the right-hand side. The information for each displayed document are the title, a snippet, the date, the keywords used by the crawler and the source. A filter box is placed above the tweets allowing users filtering tweets by date and universities.

The *live* view shown in Figure 2 helps to explore the news on a daily basis. It gives users a fast overview of the most recently published news articles, shows which sources publish news related to the Berlins universities and visualizes the most important key figures. The view presents the documents as a list, each document provided with the extracted meta-data, such as the corresponding universities. If a document deals with the Berlin Institute of Technology, the faculty connected with the news item is also listed. In addition, the computed sentiment score and a short explanation for the sentiment score are displayed. A statistic showing the aggregated sentiment scores for one day for the major Berlins universities is presented in Figure 4.

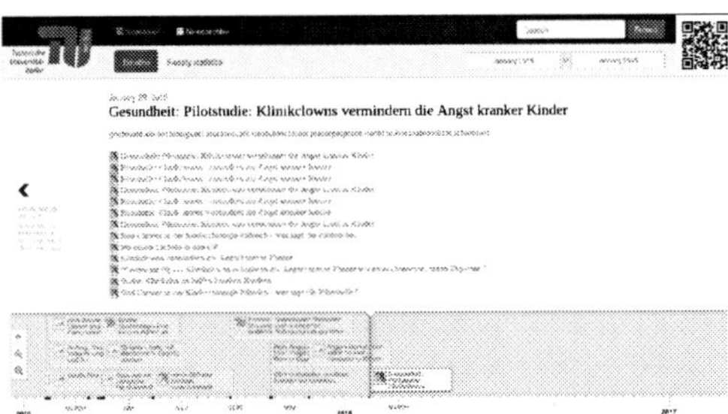

Figure 3: The Figure shows the time-line as one part of the news archive. At the bottom the timeline arranges different clusters of messages. Each cluster has an icon assigned to the related university and a title derived a document of the cluster. A selected cluster appears above the time-line with its corresponding news articles, the date and the ten most frequent terms in that cluster.

The *archive* view allows users analyzing the documents collected in the past. Users can search for documents or analyze the stream of news in detail. A powerful tool helping users to identify the most important events is the view that groups news documents by events on a timeline (Figure 3). The view lists all articles related to the selected events and shows the related institutions. The archive view also provides statistics. Figure 6 visualizes the number of documents related to the faculties of the TUB in a predefined time frame. These diagram supports a quick comparison of different faculties.

In addition to the statistics aggregating information collected over a timeframe, the systems provides views giving insights into single news articles. As discussed, we implemented a sentiment classifier working based on sentences. The senti-

ments scores computed for each sentence are visualized in Figure 5.

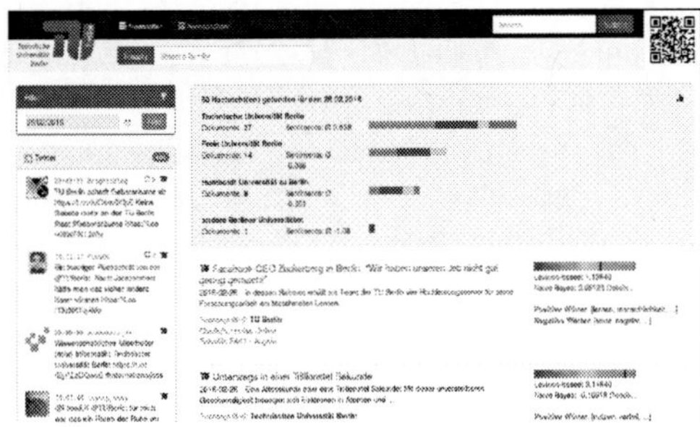

Figure 4: The Figure visualizes a diagram summarizing the results of the news aggregation and sentiment analysis for the current day. The diagram shows the distribution of the positive, negative, and neutral documents assigned to the corresponding university. In addition, the number of collected documents and the average sentiment scores are shown in this panel.

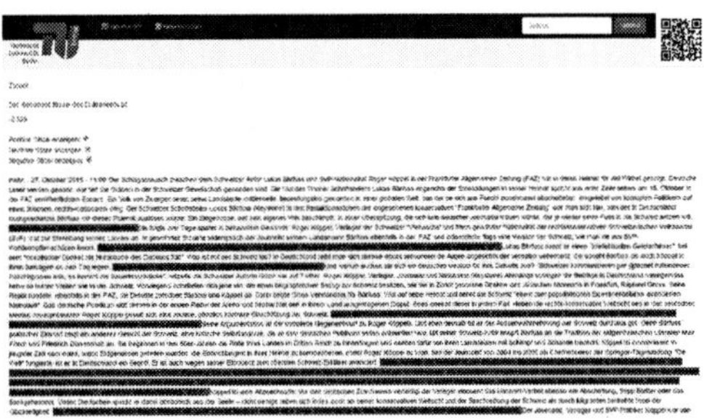

Figure 5: The Figure visualizes the sentiments computed for each sentence in a document. Sentences classified as negative are shaded in red; sentences classified as positive are shaded in green. The checkbox above the full text allows users to hide positive, negative, and neutral sentences.

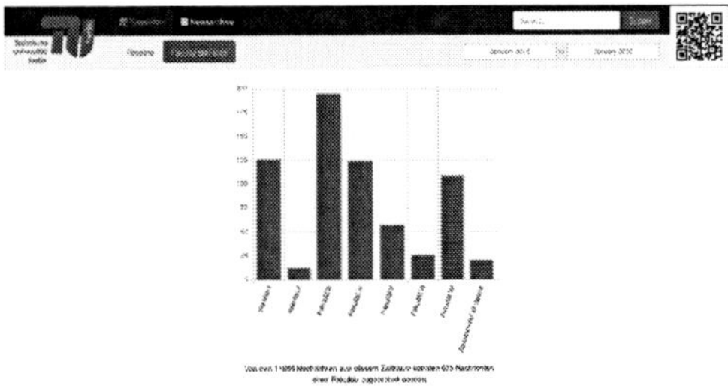

Figure 6: The Figure visualizes the number of news articles related to the "Technische Universiät Berlin" depending on the different faculties.

5 The Demonstration

The demo is accessible at `http://presse.dai-labor.de/pressreview/` with the following credentials: username `demo` and password `pressespiegel`.

The system follows the live news stream and allows users discovering the most recent news as well analyzing documents collected in the past. The web applications provides views for "regular" users but also detailed information and statistics for experts giving more fine-grained insights in the applied methods.

6 Conclusion and Future Work

We developed a powerful system that fulfills the requirements of a press review in the context of Berlin's universities. The system combines several different text mining algorithms and incorporates various visualizations helping users understanding the news and social media contributions. The system is open (upon request). It allows accessing the documents and their annotations by querying the database. The system can be extended by adding new modules to the processing pipelines. Hence, the system can be easily adapted for the specific requirements of other companies and for computing additional metrics. As future work we plan to conduct comprehensive user studies in order to optimize the algorithms to the needs of our users. We continuously work on adding blogs and RSS feeds providing information potentially relevant for our use case. We also plan an improved support for documents in other languages. Considering the identification of relevant persons, we aim to create an extended entity dataset and train a deep neural network. Furthermore, we plan the integration of additional machine learning algorithms for summarizing multiple documents related to events as well as algorithms for tracking the evolution of topics and sentiments over longer time frames.

Acknowledgments

The research leading to these results was performed in the CrowdRec project, which has received funding from the European Union Seventh Framework Programme FP7/2007-2013 under grant agreement No. 610594.

References

Florian Bütow, Florian Schultze, and Leopold Strauch. 2016. Sentiment Analysis with Machine Learning Algorithms on German News Articles. Technical report, Berlin Institute of Technology, AOT. http://www.dai-labor.de/publikationen/1052.

Simon Clematide, Stefan Gindl, Manfred Klenner, Stefanos Petrakis, Robert Remus, Josef Ruppenhofer, Ulli Waltinger, and Michael Wiegand. 2012. MLSA – A Multi-layered Reference Corpus for German Sentiment Analysis. In *Procs. of the 8th Intl. Conf. on Lang. Res. and Evaluation*, pages 3551–3556.

Alan Hanjalic, Reginald L. Lagendijk, and Jan Biemond. 1998. Semiautomatic news analysis, indexing, and classification system based on topic preselection. *Proc. SPIE*, 3656:86–97.

Levon Lloyd, Dimitrios Kechagias, and Steven Skiena. 2005. Lydia: A system for large-scale news analysis. In *String Processing and Information Retrieval*, pages 161–166. Springer.

Christopher D. Manning, Mihai Surdeanu, John Bauer, Jenny Rose Finkel, Steven Bethard, and David McClosky. 2014. The Stanford CoreNLP Natural Language Processing Toolkit. In *ACL (System Demonstrations)*, pages 55–60.

Andrew McCallum, Kamal Nigam, and Lyle H. Ungar. 2000. Efficient clustering of high-dimensional data sets with application to reference matching. In *Procs. of the 6th ACM SIGKDD Intl. Conf. on Knowledge Discovery and Data Mining*, KDD '00, pages 169–178, NY, USA. ACM.

Eugenio Picchi, S Cucurullo, E Sassolini, and Francesca Bertagna. 2008. Mining the news with semantic press. *Procs. of the 8th Intl. Conf. on Language Resources and Evaluation*, pages 141–144.

Michael O Rabin et al. 1981. *Fingerprinting by random polynomials*. Center for Research in Computing Techn., Aiken Computation Laboratory, Univ.

Robert Remus, Uwe Quasthoff, and Gerhard Heyer. 2010. SentiWS - A Publicly Available German-language Resource for Sentiment Analysis. In *Proc. of the Intl. Conf. on Language Resources and Evaluation, LREC 2010, 17-23 May 2010, Valletta, Malta*. European Language Resources Association.

Thomas Scholz. 2011. Ein Ansatz zu Opinion Mining und Themenverfolgung für eine Medienresonanzanalyse. In *Procs. of the 23rd GI-WS Grundlagen von Datenbanken*, pages 7–12. issn: 1613-0073.

Yulei Zhang, Yan Dang, Hsinchun Chen, Mark Thurmond, and Cathy Larson. 2009. Automatic online news monitoring and classification for syndromic surveillance. *Decision Support Systems*, 47(4):508–517. Smart Business Networks: Concepts and Empirical Evidence.

Personalized Exercises for Preposition Learning

John Lee, Mengqi Luo
The Halliday Centre for Intelligent Applications of Language Studies
Department of Linguistics and Translation
City University of Hong Kong
{jsylee, mengqluo}@cityu.edu.hk

Abstract

We present a computer-assisted language learning (CALL) system that generates fill-in-the-blank items for preposition usage. The system takes a set of carrier sentences as input, chooses a preposition in each sentence as the key, and then automatically generates distractors. It personalizes item selection for the user in two ways. First, it logs items to which the user previously gave incorrect answers, and offers similar items in a future session as review. Second, it progresses from easier to harder sentences, to minimize any hindrance on preposition learning that might be posed by difficult vocabulary.

1 Introduction

Many learners of English find it challenging to master the use of prepositions. Preposition usage is a frequent error category in various learner corpora (Izumi et al., 2003; Dahlmeier et al., 2013; Lee et al., 2015); indeed, entire exercise books have been devoted to training learners on preposition usage (Watcyn-Jones and Allsop, 2000; Yates, 2010). To address this area of difficulty, we present a system that automatically generates fill-in-the-blank (FIB) preposition items with multiple choices.

Also known as gap-fill or cloze items, FIB items are a common form of exercise in computer-assisted language learning (CALL) applications. Table 1 shows an example item designed for teaching English preposition usage. It contains a sentence, "The objective is to kick the ball into the opponent's goal", with the preposition "into" blanked out; this sentence serves as the *stem* (or *carrier sentence*). It is followed by four choices for the blank, one of which is the *key* (i.e., the

correct answer), and the other three are distractors. These choices enable the CALL application to provide immediate and objective feedback to the learner.

Traditional exercise books no longer meet all the needs of today's learners. The pedagogical benefits of using authentic textual material have been well documented (Larimer and Schleicher, 1999; Erbaggio et al., 2012). One recent approach turns text on web pages into slot-fill items (Meurers et al., 2010). By offering the learner the freedom to choose his or her own preferred text, this approach motivates the learner to complete the exercises.

Our system automatically constructs FIB preposition items from sentences in Wikipedia, a corpus that contains authentic language. As more users own mobile devices, mobile applications are now among the most efficient ways to provide on-demand language learning services. Although user attention on mobile devices can be brief and sporadic, each FIB item can be completed within a short time, and therefore our system offers an educational option for users to spend their idle moments. Focusing on prepositions, the system generates distractors based on error statistics compiled from learner corpora. Further, it maintains an estimate of the user's vocabulary level, and tai-

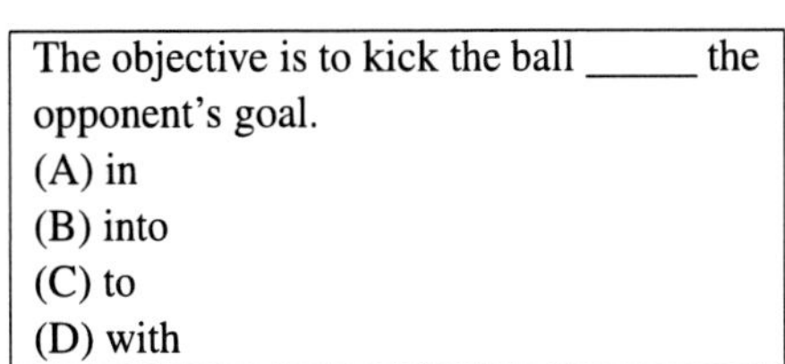

Table 1: An automatically generated fill-in-the-blank item, where "into" is the key, and the other three choices are distractors.

Proceedings of the 54th Annual Meeting of the Association for Computational Linguistics—System Demonstrations, pages 115–120,
Berlin, Germany, August 7-12, 2016. ©2016 Association for Computational Linguistics

lors item selection to address his or her areas of weakness. To the best of our knowledge, this is the first system that offers these personalization features for preposition items.

The rest of the paper is organized as follows. Section 2 reviews previous work. Section 3 outlines the algorithms for generating the fill-in-the-blank items. Section 4 gives details about the personalization features in the item selection process. Section 5 reports implementation details and evaluation results.

2   Previous work

The Internet presents the language learner with an embarassment of riches. A plethora of CALL websites—*Duolingo*, *LearnEnglish Grammar* by the British Council, or *Rosetta Stone*, to name just a few—provide a variety of speaking, listening, translation, matching and multiple choice exercises. In these exercises, the carrier sentences and other language materials are typically handcrafted. As a result, the number of items are limited, the language use can sometimes lack authenticity, and the content may not match the users' individual interests.

Promoting use of authentic material, the WERTi system provides input enhancement to web pages for the purpose of language learning (Meurers et al., 2010). It highlights grammatical constructions on which the user needs practice, and turns them into slot-fill exercises. It handles a wide range of constructions, including prepositions, determiners, gerunds, to-infinitives, wh-questions, tenses and phrasal verbs. On the one hand, the system offers much flexibility since it is up to the user to select the page. On the other, the selected text does not necessarily suit the user in terms of its language quality, level of difficulty and the desired grammatical constructions.

A number of other systems use text corpora to create grammar exercises. The KillerFiller tool in the VISL project, for example, generates slot-fill items from texts drawn from corpora (Bick, 2005). Similar to the WERTi system, an item takes the original word as its only key, and does not account for the possibility of multiple correct answers.

Other systems attempt to generate distractors for the key. Chen et al. (2006) manually designed patterns for this purpose. Smith et al. (2010) utilized a thesuarus, while Zesch and Melamud (2014) developed context-sensitive rules.

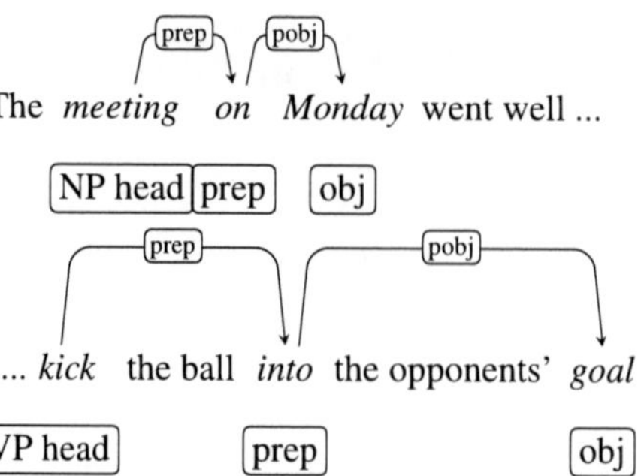

Figure 1: Parse tree for example carrier sentences. Distractors are generated on the basis of the prepositional object ("obj"), and the NP head or VP head to which the prepositional phrase is attached (Section 3). See Table 1 for the item produced from the bottom sentence.

Unlike our approach, they did not adapt to the learner's behavior. While some of these systems serve to provide draft FIB items for teachers to post-edit (Skory and Eskenazi, 2010), most remain research prototypes.

A closely related research topic for this paper is automatic correction of grammatical errors (Ng et al., 2014). While the goal of distractor generation is to identify words that yield incorrect sentences, it is not merely the inverse of the error correction task. An important element of the distractor generation task is to ensure that distractor appears plausible to the user. In contrast to the considerable effort in developing tools for detecting and correcting preposition errors (Tetreault and Chodorow, 2008; Felice and Pulman, 2009), there is only one previous study on preposition distractor generation (Lee and Seneff, 2007). Our system builds on this study by incorporating novel algorithms for distractor generation and personalization features.

3   Item creation

The system considers all English sentences in the Wikicorpus (Reese et al., 2010) that have fewer than 20 words as carrier sentence candidates. In each candidate sentence, the system scans for prepositions, and extracts two features from the linguistic context of each preposition:

- The **prepositional object**. In Figure 1, for example, the words "Monday" and "goal" are respectively the prepositional objects of the keys, "on" and "into".

Co-occurrence method
... *kicked* the chair *with* ...
... *kicked* the can *with* ...
... *with* the *goal* of ...
Learner Error method
... *kicked* it <error>*in*</error> the *goal*.
... *kick* the ball <error>*in*</error> the other team's *goal*.
Learner Revision method
... *kick* the ball *to* his own *goal*.
... *kick* the ball *into* the *goal*.
... *kick* the ball *to* the *goal*.
... *kick* it *towards* the *goal*.

Table 2: The Co-occurrence method (Section 3.1) generates "with" as the distractor for the carrier sentence in Figure 1; the Learner Error method (Section 3.2) generates "in"; the Learner Revision method (Section 3.3) generates "to".

- The head of the noun phrase or verb phrase (**NP/VP head**) to which the prepositional phrase (PP) is attached. In Figure 1, the PP "into the opponents' goal" is attached to the VP head "kick"; the PP "on Monday" is attached to the NP head "meeting".

In order to retrieve the preposition, the prepositional object, and the NP/VP head (cf. Section 3), we parsed the Wikicorpus, as well as the corpora mentioned below, with the Stanford parser (Manning et al., 2014). The system passes the two features above to the following methods to attempt to generate distractors. If more than one key is possible, it prefers the one for which all three methods can generate a distractor.

3.1 Co-occurrence method

This method requires co-occurrence statistics from a large corpus of well-formed English sentences. It selects as distractor the preposition that co-occurs most frequently with *either* the prepositional object *or* the NP/VP head, but not both. As shown in Table 2, this method generates the distractor "with" for the carrier sentence in Figure 1, since many instances of "kick ... with" and "with ... goal" are attested. The reader is referred to Lee and Seneff (2007) for details.

Our system used the English portion of Wikicorpus (Reese et al., 2010) to derive statistics for this method.

3.2 Learner error method

This method requires examples of English sentences from an error-annotated learner corpus. The corpus must indicate the preposition errors, but does not need to provide corrections for these errors. The method retrieves all sentences that have a PP with the given prepositional object and attached to the given NP/VP head, and selects the preposition that is most frequently marked as wrong.

To derive statistics for this method, our system used the NUS Corpus of Learner English (Dahlmeier et al., 2013), the EF-Cambridge Open Language Database (Geertzen et al., 2013) and a corpus of essay drafts written by Chinese learners of English (Lee et al., 2015).

3.3 Learner revision method

Finally, our system exploits the revision behavior of learners in their English writing. This method requires draft versions of the same text written by a learner. It retrieves all learner sentences in a draft that contains a PP with the given prepositional object, and attached to the given NP/VP head. It then selects as distractor the preposition that is most often edited in a later draft. As shown in Table 2, this method generates the distractor "to" for the carrier sentence in Figure 1, since it is most often edited in the given linguistic context. The reader is referred to Lee et al. (2016) for details.

To derive statistics for this method, our system also used the aforementioned corpus of essay drafts.

4 Item selection

Learners benefit most from items that are neither too easy nor too difficult. Following principles from adaptive testing (Bejar et al., 2003), the system tracks the user's performance in order to select the most suitable items. It does so by considering the vocabulary level of the carrier sentence (Section 4.1) and the user's previous mistakes (Section 4.2).

4.1 Sentence difficulty

A potential pitfall with the use of authentic sentences, such as those from Wikipedia, is that difficult vocabulary can hinder the learning of preposition usage. To minimize this barrier, the system starts with simpler carrier sentences for each new user, and then progresses to harder ones.

For simplicity, we chose to estimate the difficulty of a sentence with respect to its vocabulary.[1] Specifically, we categorized each word into one of ten levels, using graded vocabulary lists compiled by the Hong Kong Education Bureau (2012) and the Google Web Trillion Word Corpus.[2] The lists consist of about 4,000 words categorized into four sets, namely, those suitable for students in junior primary school, senior primary, junior secondary, or senior secondary. Levels 1 to 4 correspond to these four sets. If the word does not belong to these sets, it is classified at a level between 5 and 10, according to decreasing word frequency in the Google corpus. The difficulty level of a sentence is then defined as the level of its most difficult word.

For each new user, the system starts with sentences at Level 4 or lower. It keeps track of his or her performance for the last ten items. If the user gave correct answers for more than 60% of the items from the current level, the system increments the difficulty level by one. Otherwise, it decreases the difficulty level by one.

4.2 Preposition difficulty

In Figure 2, the system presents an item to the user. If the user selects a distractor rather than the key, he or she is informed by a pop-up box (Figure 3), and may then make another attempt. At this point, the user may also request to see a "similar" item to reinforce the learning of the preposition usage (Figure 4). Two items are defined as "similar" if they have the same preposition as key, and the same prepositional object and NP/VP head.

The system records all items to which the user gave incorrect answers; we will refer to this set of items as the "wrong list". When the user logs in next time, the system begins with a review session. For each item in the "wrong list", it retrieves a "similar" item from the database (Figure 4), thus facilitating the user in reviewing prepositional usage with which he had difficulty in a previous session. If the user now successfully chooses the key,

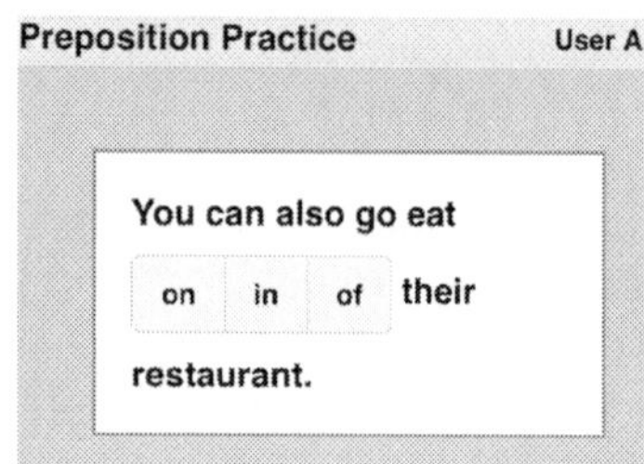

Figure 2: The system displays a carrier sentence with the key "in" and the distractors "on" and "of".

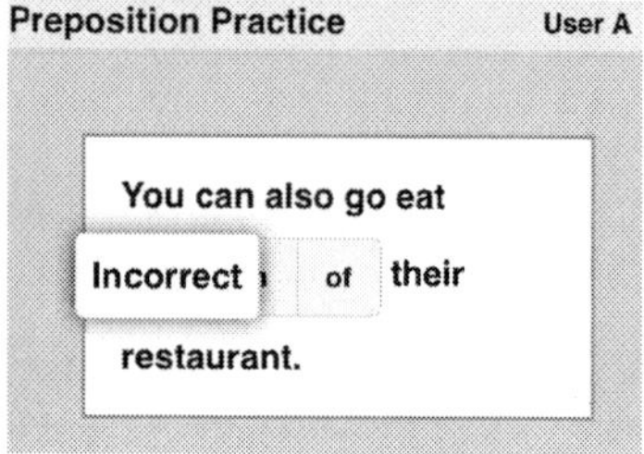

Figure 3: After the user selected the distractor "on" for the item in Figure 2, a pop-up box alerts the user.

the item is taken off the "wrong list". After the review session, the system resumes random selection of items within the estimated level of sentence difficulty, as described in the last section.

5   Implementation and evaluation

5.1   Architecture

We used the MySQL database, and JSP for the website backend. There are three main tables. The *Question* table stores all carrier sentences selected from the English portion of the Wikicorpus (Reese et al., 2010). To expedite item retrieval and identification of "similar" items, the table stores the key, prepositional object and NP/VP head of each item, as well as the difficulty level of the carrier sentence.

The *Answer* table stores the distractors for each item. Currently, the distractors do not change according to user identity, but we anticipate a future version that personalizes the distractors with respect to the user's mother tongue.

The *User* table stores the user profile. Information includes the user's personal "wrong list", his or her estimated vocabulary level, as well as login time stamps.

---

[1] The difficulty level of a sentence depends also on syntactic and semantic features. Most metrics for measuring readability, however, have focused on the document rather than the sentence level (Miltsakaki and Troutt, 2008; Pitler and Nenkova, 2008).

[2] http://norvig.com/ngrams/

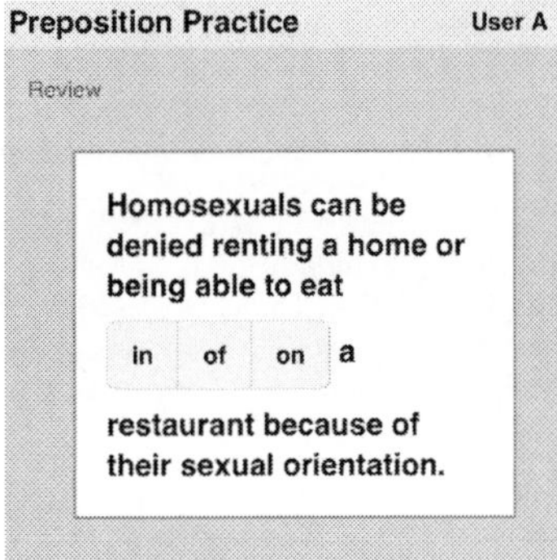

Figure 4: As review for the user, the system offers an item that is similar to the one in Figure 2, which also has "in" as the key, "eat" as the VP head and "restaurant" as the prepositional object.

5.2 Interface

For a better user experience on mobile devices, we used JQuery Mobile for interface development. At the start page, the user can register for a new account, or log in with an existing user name and password. Alternatively, the user can choose to access the system as a guest. In this case, he or she would be treated as a new user, but no user history would be recorded.

The user can attempt an arbitrary number of preposition items before logging out. Each item is presented on its own page, with the distractor and key displayed in random order (Figure 2). The user chooses the best preposition by tapping on its button. If the answer is correct, the system advances to the next item; otherwise, it informs the user via a pop-up box (Figure 3), and then flags the distractor in red. The user may try again until he or she successfully chooses the key.

5.3 Evaluation

To assess system quality, we asked two professional English teachers to annotate a set of 400 items, which included both automatically generated and human-crafted items. For each choice in an item, the teachers judged whether it is correct or incorrect. They did not know whether each choice was the key or a distractor. They may judge one, multiple, or none of the choices as correct.

A distractor is called "reliable" if it yields an incorrect sentence. As reported in Lee et al. (2016), the proportion of distractors judged reliable reached 97.4% for the Learner Revision method, 96.1% for the Co-occurrence method, and 95.6% for the Learner Error method.

For each incorrect choice, the two annotators further assessed its plausibility as a distractor from their experience in teaching English to native speakers of Chinese. They may label it as either "obviously wrong", "somewhat plausible", or "plausible". The Learner Error method produced the best distractors, with 51.2% rated "plausible", followed by the Learner Revision method (45.4%) and the Co-occurrence method (34.6%). The number of plausible distractors per item among the automatically generated items compares favourably to the human-crafted ones (Lee et al., 2016).

6 Conclusion

We have presented a CALL system that turns sentences from Wikipedia into fill-in-the-blank items for preposition usage. Using statistics from both standard and learner corpora, it generates plausible distractors to provide multiple choices.

The system tailors item selection for individual learners in two ways. First, it chooses carrier sentences that matches the learner's estimated vocabulary level. Second, to facilitate learning, it offers review sessions with items that are similar to those with which the learner previously demonstrated difficulty.

In future work, we plan to extend the system coverage beyond preposition to other common learner error types.

Acknowledgments

We thank the reviewers for their very helpful comments. This work was supported in part by an Applied Research Grant (Project no. 9667115) from City University of Hong Kong.

References

Isaac I. Bejar, René R. Lawless, Mary E. Morley, Michael E. Wagner, Randy E. Bennett, and Javier Revuelta. 2003. A Feasibility Study of On-the-Fly Item Generation in Adaptive Testing. *The Journal of Technology, Learning, and Assessment*, 2(3).

Eckhard Bick. 2005. Grammar for Fun: IT-based Grammar Learning with VISL. In P. Juel, editor, *CALL for the Nordic Languages*, pages 49–64. Copenhagen: Samfundslitteratur, Copenhagen Studies in Language.

Hong Kong Education Bureau. 2012. *Enhancing English Vocabulary Learn-*

ing and Teaching at Secondary Level. http://www.edb.gov.hk/vocab_learning_sec.

Chia-Yin Chen, Hsien-Chin Liou, and Jason S. Chang. 2006. FAST: An Automatic Generation System for Grammar Tests. In *Proc. COLING/ACL Interactive Presentation Sessions*.

Daniel Dahlmeier, Hwee Tou Ng, and Siew Mei Wu. 2013. Building a Large Annotated Corpus of Learner English: The NUS Corpus of Learner English. In *Proc. 8th Workshop on Innovative Use of NLP for Building Educational Applications*.

Pierluigi Erbaggio, Sangeetha Gopalakrishnan, Sandra Hobbs, and Haiyong Liu. 2012. Enhancing Student Engagement through Online Authentic Materials. *The International Association for Language Learning Technology Journal*, 42(2):27–51.

Rachele De Felice and Stephen Pulman. 2009. Automatic Detection of Preposition Errors in Learner Writing. *CALICO Journal*, 26(3):512–528.

Jeroen Geertzen, Theodora Alexopoulou, and Anna Korhonen. 2013. Automatic Linguistic Annotation of Large Scale L2 Databases: The EF-Cambridge Open Language Database (EFCAMDAT). In *Proc. 31st Second Language Research Forum (SLRF)*.

Emi Izumi, Kiyotaka Uchimoto, Toyomi Saiga, Thepchai Supnithi, and Hitoshi Isahara. 2003. Automatic Error Detection in the Japanese Learners' English Spoken Data. In *Proc. ACL*.

Ruth E. Larimer and Leigh Schleicher. 1999. *New Ways in Using Authentic Materials in the Classroom*. Teachers of English to Speakers of Other Languages, Inc., Alexandria, VA.

John Lee and Stephanie Seneff. 2007. Automatic Generation of Cloze Items for Prepositions. In *Proc. Interspeech*.

John Lee, Chak Yan Yeung, Amir Zeldes, Marc Reznicek, Anke Lüdeling, and Jonathan Webster. 2015. CityU Corpus of Essay Drafts of English Language Learners: a Corpus of Textual Revision in Second Language Writing. *Language Resources and Evaluation*, 49(3):659–683.

John Lee, Donald Sturgeon, and Mengqi Luo. 2016. A CALL System for Learning Preposition Usage. In *Proc. ACL*.

Christopher D. Manning, Mihai Surdeanu, John Bauer, Jenny Finkel, Steven J. Bethard, and David McClosky. 2014. The Stanford CoreNLP Natural Language Processing Toolkit. In *Proc. ACL System Demonstrations*, pages 55–60.

Detmar Meurers, Ramon Ziai, Luiz Amaral, Adriane Boyd, Aleksandar Dimitrov, Vanessa Metcalf, and Niels Ott. 2010. Enhancing Authentic Web Pages for Language Learners. In *Proc. Fifth Workshop on Innovative Use of Nlp for Building Educational Applications*.

Eleni Miltsakaki and Audrey Troutt. 2008. Real Time Web Text Classification and Analysis of Reading Difficulty. In *Proc. Third Workshop on Innovative Use of NLP for Building Educational Applications*.

Hwee Tou Ng, Siew Mei Wu, Ted Briscoe, Christian Hadiwinoto, Raymond Hendy Susanto, and Christopher Bryant. 2014. The CoNLL-2014 Shared Task on Grammatical Error Correction. In *Proc. 8th Conference on Computational Natural Language Learning: Shared Task*, pages 1–14.

Emily Pitler and Ani Nenkova. 2008. Revisiting Readability: a Unified Framework for Predicting Text Quality. In *Proc. EMNLP*.

Samuel Reese, Gemma Boleda, Montse Cuadros, Lluís Padró, and German Rigau. 2010. Wikicorpus: A Word-Sense Disambiguated Multilingual Wikipedia Corpus. In *Proc. LREC*.

Adam Skory and Maxine Eskenazi. 2010. Predicting Cloze Task Quality for Vocabulary Training. In *Proc. NAACL HLT 2010 Fifth Workshop on Innovative Use of NLP for Building Educational Applications*.

Simon Smith, P. V. S. Avinesh, and Adam Kilgarriff. 2010. Gap-fill Tests for Language Learners: Corpus-Driven Item Generation. In *Proc. 8th International Conference on Natural Language Processing (ICON)*.

Joel Tetreault and Martin Chodorow. 2008. The Ups and Downs of Preposition Error Detection in ESL Writing. In *Proc. COLING*.

Peter Watcyn-Jones and Jake Allsop. 2000. *Test Your Prepositions*. Penguin Books Ltd.

Jean Yates. 2010. *The Ins and Outs of Prepositions*. Hauppauge, New York : Barron's.

Torsten Zesch and Oren Melamud. 2014. Automatic Generation of Challenging Distractors Using Context-Sensitive Inference Rules. In *Proc. Workshop on Innovative Use of NLP for Building Educational Applications (BEA)*.

My Science Tutor: Learning Science with a Conversational Virtual Tutor

Sameer Pradhan   Ron Cole   Wayne Ward

Boulder Learning, Inc.

Boulder, CO

{pradhan,rcole,wward}@boulderlearning.com

Abstract

This paper presents a conversational, multimedia, virtual science tutor for elementary school students. It is built using state of the art speech recognition and spoken language understanding technology. This virtual science tutor is unique in that it elicits self-explanations from students for various science phenomena by engaging them in spoken dialogs and guided by illustrations, animations and interactive simulations. There is a lot of evidence that self-explanation works well as a tutorial paradigm, Summative evaluations indicate that students are highly engaged in the tutoring sessions, and achieve learning outcomes equivalent to expert human tutors. Tutorials are developed through a process of recording and annotating data from sessions with students, and then updating tutor models. It enthusiastically supported by students and teachers. Teachers report that it is feasible to integrate into their curriculum.

1   Introduction

According to the 2009 National Assessment of Educational Progress (NAEP, 2009), only 34 percent of fourth-graders, 30 percent of eighth-graders, and 21 percent of twelfth-graders tested as proficient in science. Thus, over two thirds of U.S. students are not proficient in science. The vast majority of these students are in low-performing schools that include a high percentage of disadvantaged students from families with low socioeconomic status, which often include English learners with low English language proficiency. Analysis of the NAEP scores in reading, math and science over the past twenty years indicate that this situation is getting worse. For example, the gap between English learners and English-only students, which is over one standard deviation lower for English learners, has increased rather than decreased over the past 20 years. Moreover, science instruction is often underemphasized in U.S. schools, with reading and math being stressed.

The Program for International Student Assessment (PISA), coordinated by the Organization for Economic Cooperation and Development (OECD), is administered every three years in 65 countries across the world. According to their findings in 2012, the U.S. average science score was not measurably different from the OECD average.

Our approach to address this problem is a conversational multimedia virtual tutor for elementary school science. The operating principles for the tutor are grounded on research from education and cognitive science where it has been shown that eliciting self-explanations plays an important role (Chi et al., 1989; Chi et al., 1994; Chi et al., 2001; Hausmann and VanLehn, 2007a; Hausmann and VanLehn, 2007b). Speech, language and character animation technologies play a central role because the focus of the system is on engagement and spoken explanations by students during spoken dialogs with the virtual tutor. Summative evaluations indicate that students are highly engaged in the tutoring sessions, and achieve learning outcomes equivalent to expert human tutors (Ward et al., 2011; Ward et al., 2013). Surveys of participating teachers indicate that it is feasible to incorporate the intervention into their curriculum. Also, importantly, most student surveys indicate enthusiastic support for the system.

Tutorials are developed through an iterative process of recording, annotating and analyzing logs from sessions with students, and then updating tutor models. This approach has been used to de-

Proceedings of the 54th Annual Meeting of the Association for Computational Linguistics—System Demonstrations, pages 121–126,
Berlin, Germany, August 7-12, 2016. ©2016 Association for Computational Linguistics

velop over 100 tutorial dialog sessions, of about 15 minutes each, in 8 areas of elementary school science.

My Science Tutor (MyST) provides a supplement to normal classroom science instruction that immerses students in a multimedia environment with a virtual science tutor that models an engaging and effective human tutor. The focus of the program is to improve each student's engagement, motivation and learning by helping them learn to visualize, reason about and explain science during conversations with the virtual tutor. The learning principles embedded in MyST are consistent with conclusions and recommendations of the National Research Council Report, "Taking Science to School: Learning and Teaching Science in Grades K-8" (NRC, 2007), which emphasizes the critical importance of scientific discourse in K-12 science education. The report identifies the following crucial principles of scientific proficiency:

Students who are proficient in science:

1. *Know, use, and interpret* scientific explanations of the natural world;

2. *Generate and evaluate* scientific evidence and explanations;

3. *Understand* the nature and development of scientific knowledge; and

4. *Participate productively* in scientific practices and discourse.

The report also emphasizes that scientific inquiry and discourse is a learned skill, so students need to be involved in activities in which they learn appropriate norms and language for productive participation in scientific discourse and argumentation.

2 The MyST Application

MyST provides students with the scaffolding, modeling and practice they need to learn to reason and talk about science. Students learn science through natural spoken dialogs with the virtual tutor Marni, a 3-D computer character. Marni asks students open-ended questions related to illustrations, silent animations or interactive simulations displayed on the computer screen.

Figure 1 shows the student's screen with Marni asking questions about media displayed in a tutorial. The student's computer shows a full screen window that contains Marni, a display area for presenting media and a display button that indicates the listening status of the system. Marni produces accurate visual speech, with head and face movements that are synchronized with her speech. The media facilitate dialogs with Marni by helping students visualize the science they are discussing. The primary focus of dialogs is to elicit explanations from students. MyST compares the student's spoken explanations to reference explanations for the lesson by matching the extracted *semantic roles* using the Phoenix parser (Ward, 1991), then presents follow-on questions and media, to help the student construct a correct explanation of the phenomena being studied. The virtual tutor Marni, who speaks with a recorded human voice, is designed to model an effective human tutor that the student can relate to and work with to learn science. MyST provides a non-threatening and supportive environment for students to express their ideas. The dialogs scaffold learning by providing students with support when needed until they can apply new skills and knowledge independently.

MyST is intended to be used as an intervention for struggling students, with intended users being K-12 science students. While it should prove a benefit to all students, struggling students should benefit most. Depending on the recording conditions and ambient noise, as well as the characteristics of the student and session, the recognition word error rate ranges from low 20s to mid-40s. MyST will contain tutorials for 3 topics per grade, with content aligned with NGSS. For each topic, students engage in an average of 10 spoken dialog sessions with the tutor, lasting approximately 20 minutes each. oThe MyST tutorial sessions are in addition to the normal classroom instruction for the module. Tutoring sessions can be assigned as homework or during regular school hours, at the teacher's discretion. In the initial studies, tutoring was always done during regular school hours. Teachers specify the space in the school to be used, generally any relatively quiet room. Students are sent to use the system a few at a time, depending on how many computers are available (5 computers per classroom were used in the efficacy study). All students are given a demo at the beginning of the school year and given a chance to ask questions. Teachers schedule time for students, but students log on and use the system without supervi-

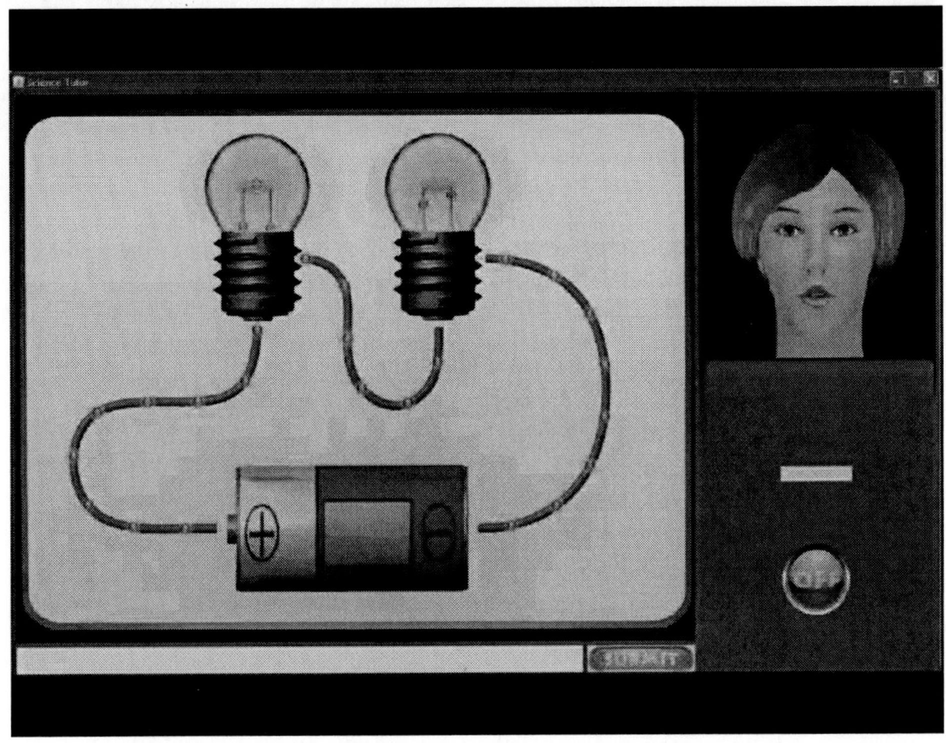

Figure 1: A snapshot of the screen as seen by a student.

sion, so it has minimal impact on teacher time or other human resources. In studies thus far, surveys report that teachers did not have problems using the system and it did not interfere with their other activities.

The application will eventually be deployed using a Software as a Service (SaaS) model. It will run on a server and students will access it through their browser. If internet service is not available or reliable, it can be run stand-alone and the data uploaded when service is available. Both content and user populations will evolve and system models need to incorporate dynamic adaptation in an efficient way. Data from all user sessions is logged in a database and is available for continuous evaluation and re-training of system models. The system is designed to work well even if it doesn't understand the user, but becomes more engaging and efficient as it understands the user better. As training data grows model parameters become more accurate and more explicit models are trained, such as acoustic models for ELL students. Unsupervised training is combined with active learning to op-

timize use of the data for tuning system models. Teachers in the initial studies did not feel that they would have a problem implementing the system.

3 Theoretical Framework

The theory of change, and theoretical and empirical support Science curricula are structured with new concepts building on those already encountered. Struggling students fall further and further behind if they don't understand the content of each topic. Research has demonstrated that human tutors are effective (Bloom, 1984; Madden and Slavin, 1989), media presentations are effective (Mayer, 2001) and QtA dialog strategies are effective (Murphy and Edwards, 2005). A system that emulates a human tutor using media presentations to focus a student's attention and conducting a QtA-style dialog with the student should also be effective. This additional time spent thinking and talking about the science concepts covered in class will enable students who would have fallen behind to understand the content of the current investigation so they will be prepared to participate in and understand subsequent topics. Student learning will increase because they are excited about and engaged by interesting and informative presentations that help them visualize and understand the science and because they will learn to engage in conversations in which they construct, reflect on and revise mental models and explanations about the science they are seeing and trying to explain. MyST dialogs are designed to provide students with understandable multimedia scenarios, explanations and challenges and a supportive social context for communication and learning. Science is introduced through scenarios that students can relate to and make sense of, and provide a context for introducing and using science vocabulary and making connections between vocabulary, objects, concepts and their prior knowledge. Multimedia learning tools show and explain science, and then enable students to revisit the media and explain the science in their own words.

Research has demonstrated that having students produce explanations improves learning (Chi et al., 1989; Chi et al., 2001; King, 1994; King et al., 1988; Palincsar and Brown, 1984). In a series of studies, Chi et al. (1989; 2001) found that having college students generate self-explanations of their understanding of physics problems improved learning. Self-explanation also improved learning about the circulatory system by eighth grade students in a controlled experiment (Chi et al., 1994). Hausmann and Van Lehn (2007a; 2007b) note that: "self-explaining has consistently been shown to be effective in producing robust learning gains in the laboratory and in the classroom." Experiments by Hausmann and Van Lehn (Hausmann and VanLehn, 2007a) indicate that it is the process of actively producing explanations, rather than the accuracy of the explanations, that makes the biggest contribution to learning.

4   Semantic Underpinnings

The patterns used in MyST to extract frames from student responses are trained from annotated data. The specification of tutorial semantics begins with creating a narrative. A tutorial narrative is a set of natural language statements that express the concepts to be discussed in as simple a form as possible. These do not represent the questions that the system asks, but are the set of points that the student should express.

The narrative represents what an ideal explanation from a student would look like. The narrative statements are manually annotated to reflect the desired semantic parses. These parsed statements define the domain of the tutorial. The initial grammar patterns are extracted from the narratives and have all of the roles and entities that will be discussed, but only a few (or one) ways of expressing them. As the system is used, the grammar is expanded to cover the various ways students articulate their understandings of the science concepts. This is done by annotating recordings of student responses generated in real use. So the life cycle of the natural language processing model for a module is:

1. Create and annotate a narrative to define the domain of the tutorial
2. Field the system to collect data from real users
3. Sample incoming data and annotate
4. Evaluate current model and re-train
5. Repeat step 3-4 as long as the module is used

As the system is used, it logs all transactions and records student speech. When tutorials are deployed for live use, incoming data are processed automatically to assess system confidence in the interpretation of student responses. High-confidence items are added to the training database, and low confidence sessions are selected for transcription and annotation. The system also provides a text input mode that students can use to interact with the Avatar. Once annotated, the data are added to the training set and system models (acoustic models, language models and extraction patterns) are retrained. Periodically, data are sampled for test sets and a learning curve is plotted for each module. All elements of this process are automatic except for transcription and annotation.

The semantics of each domain are constrained, but student responses can vary greatly in the ways they choose to express concepts and terms. It takes time, effort and data to get good coverage of student responses. Semantic annotation for the system consists of annotating:

Entities—*The basic concepts talked about in the session and the phrases that would be considered synonyms.* Electricity could be expressed as electricity, energy, power, current or electrical energy. Coverage of term synonyms from annotated data is generally achieved fairly quickly. **Roles**— *How the entities in an event or concept are related* *to each other.* The larger problem is to attain coverage of the patterns discriminating between possible role assignments. Not only is there more disfluency and variability here, annotating them is a more difficult task for someone not trained to do it. Currently, it takes about one hour for a highly-trained annotator to mark up the data collected in a single 20-minute tutorial session.

5   Extrinsic Evaluation

An assessment was conducted in schools to compare learning gains from human tutoring and MyST tutoring to business-as-usual classrooms. Learning gain was measured using standardized assessments given to students in each condition before and after each science module. Both tutoring conditions had significantly higher learning gains than the control group. While the effect size for human tutors vs. control (d=0.68) was larger than for MyST vs. control (d=0.53), statistical tests supported the hypothesis of no significant difference between the two.

A simple two-group comparison using a Repeated Measures ANOVA shows a statistically significant effect at F=46.4, df 1,759, p <.0001 favoring the treatment group. The interaction between group and module was also significant at F=9.5, p < .001. We also used an Analysis of Covariance (ANCOVA) to compare post-test scores. This procedure adjusts for pre-test differences while comparing the post-test average scores. The two-group comparison was significant at F=7.4, df 1,768, p=.018. We also saw a significant interaction between treatment group and module with F=12.4, df 3,768. Testing the main effects with a hierarchical mixed model with students nested within classrooms we found a significant effect for the treatment group at F=6.2, df 1,217,662, p=0.013. No significant interaction effect was found for module by group.

A written survey was given to the students who participated in the gas. Measures were taken to avoid bias wherein students give overly positive answers to questionnaires. The survey included questions that asked for ratings of student experience and impressions of the program and its usability. Across schools, 47% of students said they would like to talk with Marni after every science investigation, 62% said they enjoyed working with Marni "a lot," and 53% selected "I am more excited about science" after using the program. Only 4% felt that the tutoring did not help. Teachers were asked for anonymous feedback to help assess the feasibility of an intervention using the system and their perceptions of the impact of the system. A teacher survey was given to all participating teachers directly after their students completed tutoring. The survey asked teachers about the perceived impact of using Marni for student learning and engagement, impacts on instruction and scheduling, willingness to potentially adopt Marni as part of classroom instruction, and overall favorability toward participating in the research project. Teachers answered items related to potential barriers in implementing new technology in the classroom. 100% of responding teachers said that they felt it had a positive impact on their students, they would be interested in the program if it were available and they would recommend it to other teachers. 93% said that they would like to participate in the project again. 74% indicated that they would like to have all of their students use the system (not just struggling students). Following these studies, Boulder Learning combined the best elements of the initial systems into the current MyST system, and with continued funding from IES (Cognition and Student Learning Goal 3), is conducting an efficacy study. We are currently in the 3rd year of a 4 year study. While data collection will continue for another year, preliminary results support the learning gain performance from the initial studies.

6   MyST Conversations Corpus of Student Speech (MCCSC)

We are making a cleaned up version of the corpus available to the research community[1] for free and for commercial use at a pre-determined cost. The first release of the corpus v0.1.0 comprises 298 hours of speech out of which 198 hours are manually transcribed. This covers roughly 1.4 million words of text. We are in the process of cleaning up about the same amount of collected data for future distribution.

7   Future Work

In the near future we plan to evaluate applying a statistical labeler trained on existing corpora to the task of Role assignment. This approach should provide increased robustness to novel input and substantially reduce the human annotation effort required to attain a given level of coverage. The

---

[1]`http://corpora.boulderlearning.com/myst`

Proposition Bank (PropBank) provides a corpus of sentences annotated with domain-independent semantic roles (Palmer et al., 2005). PropBank has been widely used for the development of machine learning based Semantic Role Labeling (SRL) systems. Pradhan et al. (2005) used a rich set of syntactic and semantic features to obtain a performance with F-score in the low-80s. It has been an integral component of most question answering systems for the past decade. Since its first application to the newswire text, PropBank has been extended to cover many more predicates and diverse genres in the DARPA OntoNotes project (Weischedel et al., 2011; Pradhan et al., 2013) and the DARPA BOLT program. We plan to map Prop-Bank SRL output onto MyST frames. Domain specific entity patterns will still need to be applied to produce the canonical extracted form, but that is a much simpler task than role assignment and one more suited to non-linguists.

References

B. Bloom. 1984. The 2 sigma problem: The search for methods of group instruction as effective as one-to-one tutoring. *Educational Researcher*, 13(6):4–16.

M. Chi, M. Bassok, M. Lewis, P. Reimann, R. Glaser, and Alexander. 1989. Self-explanations: How students study and use examples in learning to solve problems. *Cognitive Science*, 13(2).

M. Chi, N. De Leeuw, M. Chiu, and C. LaVancher. 1994. Eliciting self-explanations improves understanding. *Cognitive Science*, 18(3):439–477.

M. T. H. Chi, S. A. Siler, H. Jeong, T. Yamauchi, and R. G. Hausmann. 2001. Learning from human tutoring. *Cognitive Science*, 25(4):471–533.

R. G. M. Hausmann and K. VanLehn. 2007a. Explaining self-explaining: A contrast between content and generation. *Artificial Intelligence in Education*, pages 417–424.

R. G. M. Hausmann and K. VanLehn. 2007b. Self-explaining in the classroom: Learning curve evidence. In *29th Annual Conference of the Cognitive Science Society*, Mahwah, NJ.

A. King, A. Staffieri, and A. Adelgais. 1988. Mutual peer tutoring: Effects of structuring tutorial interaction to scaffold peer learning. *Journal of Educational Psychology*, 90(1):134–152.

A. King. 1994. Guiding knowledge construction in the classroom: Effects of teaching children how to question and how to explain. *American Educational Research Journal*, 31(2).

N. A. Madden and R. E. Slavin. 1989. Effective programs for students at risk. In R. E. Slavin, N. L. Karweit, and N. A. Madden, editors, *Effective pull-out programs for students at risk*. Allyn and Bacon.

R. Mayer. 2001. *Multimedia Learning*. Cambridge University Press., Cambridge, U.K.

P. K. Murphy and M. N.b Edwards. 2005. What the studies tell us: A meta-analysis of discussion approaches. In *American Educational Research Association*, Montreal, Canada.

National Research Council. NRC. 2007. Taking science to school: Learning and teaching science in grades k-8. In R. A. Duschl, H. A. Schweingruber, and A. W. Shouse, editors, *Committee on Science Learning Kindergarten through Eighth Grade. Washington D.C.* The National Academies Press.

A. Palincsar and A. Brown. 1984. Reciprocal teaching of comprehension-fostering and comprehension-monitoring activities. *Cognition and Instruction*, 1(2).

Martha Palmer, Daniel Gildea, and Paul Kingsbury. 2005. The Proposition Bank: An annotated corpus of semantic roles. *Computational Linguistics*, 31(1):71–106.

Sameer Pradhan, Kadri Hacioglu, Valerie Krugler, Wayne Ward, James Martin, and Dan Jurafsky. 2005. Support vector learning for semantic argument classification. *Machine Learning*, 60(1):11–39.

Sameer Pradhan, Alessandro Moschitti, Nianwen Xue, Hwee Tou Ng, Anders Björkelund, Olga Uryupina, Yuchen Zhang, and Zhi Zhong. 2013. Towards robust linguistic analysis using OntoNotes. In *Proceedings of the Seventeenth Conference on Computational Natural Language Learning*, pages 143–152, Sofia, Bulgaria, August.

W. Ward, R. Cole, D. Bolanos, C. Buchenroth-Martin, E. Svirsky, S. V. Vuuren, and L. Becker. 2011. My science tutor: A conversational multimedia virtual tutor for elementary school science. *ACM Trans. Speech Lang. Process.*, 7(4).

Wayne Ward, Ron Cole, Daniel Bolanos, C. Buchenroth-Martin, E. Svirsky, and Tim Weston. 2013. My science tutor: A conversational multimedia virtual tutor. *Journal of Educational Psychology*, 105(4):1115–1125.

W Ward. 1991. Understanding spontaneous speech: the phoenix system. In *Acoustics, Speech, and Signal Processing, 1991. ICASSP-91., 1991 International Conference on*, pages 365–367 vol.1, April.

Ralph Weischedel, Eduard Hovy, Mitchell Marcus, Martha Palmer, Robert Belvin, Sameer Pradhan, Lance Ramshaw, and Nianwen Xue. 2011. OntoNotes: A large training corpus for enhanced processing. In Joseph Olive, Caitlin Christianson, and John McCary, editors, *Handbook of Natural Language Processing and Machine Translation: DARPA Global Autonomous Language Exploitation*. Springer.

`pigeo`: A Python Geotagging Tool

Afshin Rahimi, Trevor Cohn, and **Timothy Baldwin**
Department of Computing and Information Systems
The University of Melbourne
arahimi@student.unimelb.edu.au
{t.cohn, tbaldwin}@unimelb.edu.au

Abstract

We present `pigeo`, a Python geolocation prediction tool that predicts a location for a given text input or Twitter user. We discuss the design, implementation and application of `pigeo`, and empirically evaluate it. `pigeo` is able to geolocate informal text and is a very useful tool for users who require a free and easy-to-use, yet accurate geolocation service based on pre-trained models. Additionally, users can train their own models easily using `pigeo`'s API.

1 Introduction

Geolocation is the task of identifying a location for a user or document, and has applications in local search, recommender systems (Ho et al., 2012), targeted advertising (Lim and Datta, 2013), health monitoring (Paul et al., 2015), rapid disaster response (Ashktorab et al., 2014), and research with a regional restriction (Gutierrez et al., 2015), noting the potential privacy concerns associated with any such application (De Cristofaro et al., 2012). While primary service providers such as Twitter and Google are able to use metadata such as IP addresses, WiFi traces and direct access to a GPS signal to geolocate their users, this data is generally not available to third parties. This paper introduces a resource that can be used to geolocate users given textual messages generated by them, and the interactions between users encoded in those messages, focused particularly at Twitter data.

Both language use and social ties are geographically biased, and thus can be used to recover the location of a user or a document. Previous research has shown that the geographical bias in language use can be used in supervised text-based geolocation models, to learn associations between textual features and different regions based on large-scale collections of geotagged documents/tweets (Wing and Baldridge, 2011; Han et al., 2012; Maier and Gómez-Rodrıguez, 2014). Given an unseen piece of text or the text content of a user's timeline, the trained classifier can predict the most likely location(s) associated with the input.

Although social media services such as Twitter remove the geographical barrier for users to communicate, the majority of user interactions are still local (Backstrom et al., 2010). This geographical bias can be utilised to geolocate a user by analysing their social interactions. Based on the assumption that social interactions are more likely to be local, a user should be geographically close to their connections. The simplest approach to geolocation is to use the median location of a user's friends. Recent studies have shown that using both network and text information can improve the coverage and keep the predictions accurate simultaneously (Rahimi et al., 2015b).

Despite the widespread use of geolocation, most services are proprietary, overly-simplistic, or complicated to use. Supervised classification models often require huge amounts of geotagged data and large amounts of computing power to be trained. The performance is also heavily dependent on hyperparameter tuning, making the training procedure more challenging for end-users.

In this paper we introduce `pigeo`, a Python geolocation tool that has the following characteristics: (1) it comes with a pre-trained text-based model; (2) it is easy to use; (3) it has been tuned, benchmarked and proven to be accurate; (4) it supports both informal and formal text input; (5) it directly supports Twitter user geolocation; and (6) it has an easy-to-use RESTful API. `pigeo` is available at http://github.com/afshinrahimi/pigeo.

Proceedings of the 54th Annual Meeting of the Association for Computational Linguistics—System Demonstrations, pages 127–132,
Berlin, Germany, August 7-12, 2016. ©2016 Association for Computational Linguistics

2 Background and Related Work

Prior work on geolocation falls broadly into two main categories: text-based and network-based methods. Both approaches use geotagged samples, and predict the location of an unseen document or user based on the trained model. Those approaches usually use GPS tags or user profile location fields as the ground truth both for training and evaluating the model. Geographical bias in language use is most evident for countries with different languages (e.g. Germany versus China), but also exists for countries which share the same languages (e.g. in the spelling of *centre* vs. *center* in British vs. American English). The linguistic geographical bias is not limited to these obvious cases, however, and includes the use of toponyms, names of people, sport teams, and dialectal terms. These differences in use of language can be captured in text-based geolocation models. Previous work have used topic models (Eisenstein et al., 2010) and supervised flat (Wing and Baldridge, 2011; Han et al., 2012; Han et al., 2013; Han et al., 2014; Rahimi et al., 2015b) and hierarchical (Wing and Baldridge, 2014) classification models. The main idea is to learn the geographical distribution of a given word across different locations from training data, and use it to predict a location for a new user.

Social ties have also been used for social media user geolocation. Backstrom et al. (2010) showed that Facebook users tend to interact more with nearby people ("location homophily"), and used this property to geolocate users based on the location of their friends, hence popularising network-based geolocation approaches. A graph is usually built based on Facebook friendship (Backstrom et al., 2010), Twitter follows (Rout et al., 2013), Twitter reciprocal @-mentions (Jurgens, 2013), or Twitter @-mentions (Rahimi et al., 2015b). The problem can also be formulated as classification (Rout et al., 2013) or regression over real-valued coordinates (Jurgens, 2013; Rahimi et al., 2015b). In classification models, the location label set can be pre-existing regional boundaries (e.g. countries or cities) or automatically generated through discretisation (e.g. a k-d tree). The label distribution of friends is then averaged and used as the location of a given user. In a regression model, the median coordinates of the friends of a user are often used for prediction.

Network-based models are generally more ac-curate than text-based models but can't geolocate users who don't interact with training users, which is the case for more than 30% of users in the case of reciprocal Twitter @-mentions (Jurgens et al., 2015). Relaxing the requirement on reciprocity increases the coverage of users, at the expense of lower accuracy (Rahimi et al., 2015a).

There are several other geolocation services and libraries which focus on Twitter, including `pigeoTextGrounder` (Wing and Baldridge, 2014) with a focus on targeted advertising, `pigeoCarmen` (Dredze et al., 2013) with a focus on help monitoring, `pigeoMapAffil` (Torvik, 2015) for affiliation mapping, and `pigeoTweedr` (Ashktorab et al., 2014) for rapid disaster response. Many companies have their own proprietary geolocation service, which are either not available for public use or not open source. In `pigeo`, we provide trained a text-based classification model and network-based regression model for geolocation prediction, which has been benchmarked against standard datasets.

3 Methodology

`pigeo` uses two pre-trained models for geolocation: (1) `LR-WORLD` and (2) `LP-WORLD`. Both are trained on TWITTER-WORLD-EX, an extended version of the TWITTER-WORLD dataset (Han et al., 2012).

3.1 Data

We use TWITTER-WORLD-EX to train both the text-based classification and the network-based regression model. TWITTER-WORLD-EX is a Twitter dataset with global coverage (Han et al., 2012), comprising 1.3M geotagged users (188M tweets), of which 10K are held out for each of development and testing. The dataset contains predominantly English text, but also includes a rich variety of other languages. In TWITTER-WORLD, the location representation was cities, based on GEONAMES. For our purposes, we modify this to 930 clusters based on a k-d tree, to derive a smaller number of classes and remove class imbalance. Given that the dataset is about 5 years old, we expect the off-the-shelf performance to be degraded on newer tweets (Dredze et al., 2016), particularly in the case of the network-based model (Jurgens et al., 2015).

`LR-WORLD` is a text-based classification model trained over TWITTER-WORLD-EX. The training users of TWITTER-WORLD-EX are clustered into 930 regions with roughly the same number of users per region (about 2400), using a k-d tree. This results in many small regions/clusters in highly populated areas such as NYC, and a few large regions in sparsely-populated areas or areas with few Twitter users, such as the Sahara desert and China. The region IDs are then used as labels for all the users in that region. We use a bag-of-unigrams model of text with binary term frequency, inverse document frequency and l_2 normalisation of samples to create user vectors. Log loss is used with ElasticNet regularisation (90% l_1) as the cost function to train the model using stochastic gradient descent. Given an unseen text sample, one can vectorise the sample and use the classifier to predict a region/label or a probability distribution over regions. The predicted label(s) can be mapped to coordinates or locations.

The `LP-WORLD` model is a network-based regression model, also trained on TWITTER-WORLD-EX. An @-mention network is built over the dataset, and the real-valued coordinates of the training users are iteratively propagated to all the mentioned users. The location of each user is set to the weighted median latitude and weighted median longitude of all its connections. The edge weights are initially binary but are then normalised by dividing them by the product of the degree of the two corresponding nodes. The algorithm converges after 5 iterations. The predicted coordinates for all users are stored in a gzipped Python pickled dictionary for later use by `pigeo`. The Twitter user names are hashed by the MD5 algorithm for privacy reasons. The collision probability for MD5 hashing is very low and we didn't experience any collisions for our 7M nodes. Given an unseen Twitter user, the timeline of the user is downloaded and the @-mentions are extracted. The hashed content of each @-mention is looked up in the saved user-coordinate mapping to see if any predictions are available. The median latitude and longitude of geolocated @-mention connections are then predicted as the Twitter user location.

Although we experiment with the `LP-WORLD` model in this paper, we are unable to distribute it, due to Twitter's terms of service. It is possible, however, for a user to use `pigeo` to train their own network model by providing data in the format described in Section 4.

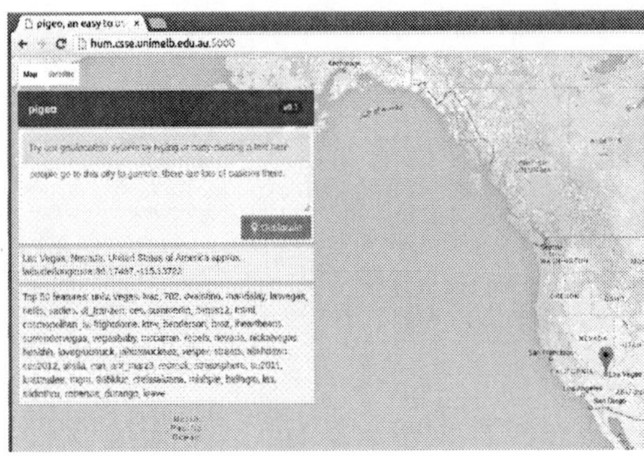

Figure 1: `pigeo`'s web interface. Given a piece of text or a single Twitter user, it geolocates it and returns the description and coordinates of the predicted location and its most important textual features in the model.

4 System Architecture

The main feature of `pigeo` is the ability to use the trained text-based classification network-based regression models that are distributed with the library, for geolocation of both text documents and Twitter users. Additionally, however, the library supports the training and storage of new text-based classification models. The `pigeo` tool is written in Python 2.7 and consists of: (1) the main `pigeo.py` script; (2) `params.py`, which stores the global parameters; (3) `twitterapi.py`, which uses `pigeo` to connect to Twitter; and (4) an `index.html` file, which is used by the web service. The tool returns a JSON string with fields such as `latitude`, `longitude`, `city` and `label_distribution`. `pigeo.py` packages all the main functions that are required by `pigeo`. It can be used in 3 modes: (1) Shell mode; (2) Web mode; and (3) Library mode.

Shell mode: Shell mode is activated as follows:

```
> python pigeo.py --mode shell
```
It takes an input text, geolocates it, and returns the result in JSON format. Shell mode uses the trained `LR-WORLD` model stored in `./models/world` and is best suited for testing `pigeo`.

Web mode: Web mode is activated by running:

```
> python pigeo.py --mode web
```
`pigeo` uses Flask, a lightweight Python web framework, to provide web access to end-users. The default host and port are 127.0.0.1 and 5000, respectively, which can be modified using the `--host` and `--port` options on the

```
import pigeo

# load the world model (default)
pigeo.load_model()

# geolocate a sentence
pigeo.geo("gamble casino city")

# geolocate a Twitter user
pigeo.geo('@POTUS')

# geolocate a list of texts
pigeo.geo(['city centre', 'city center'])
```

Figure 2: An illustration of Library mode

```
import pigeo

# train a model and save it in 'example'
pigeo.train_model(['text1', 'text2'],
[(lat1, lon1), (lat2, lon2)],
num_classes=2, model_dir='example')

# load and use the new model
pigeo.load_model(model_dir='example')
```

Figure 3: An illustration of training a model

```
import pigeo

# load lpworld
pigeo.load_lpworld()

# geolocate a Twitter user
pigeo.geo_lp('@potus')
```

Figure 4: An illustration of Twitter user geolocation using the network model

command line. When the service is running, the user can use the web service by opening `http://127.0.0.1:5000` via a web browser on their local machine shown, as illustrated in Figure 1. Alternatively, the users are able to use the `curl` command to geolocate a text or a Twitter user:

```
> curl 127.0.0.1:5000/geo?text='beach'
```

Library mode: `pigeo` can also be used as a library. This is the suggested way of using it if many documents are needed to be geolocated, because the batch functionality is only available in this mode. Note that running the `pigeo.geo` function in a loop is not as efficient as running it with a list argument (in **Batch mode**). The code snippet in Figure 2 shows how `pigeo` can be used in Library mode.

Twitter user geolocation: `pigeo` takes the user name of a Twitter user, crawls their timeline, and geolocates them on the basis of that data. This can be done in any of Shell, Web or Library modes, but requires an internet connection and valid Twitter authentication information (Twitter keys, tokens and secrets) which should be set in `twitterapi.py`.

Training a new model: Training a new model is possible in Library mode, using scikit-learn (Pedregosa et al., 2011) both for feature extraction and training the model. The training data consists of a list of text samples and a list of corresponding coordinates as a (latitude, longitude) tuple. Given the number of desired classes, `pigeo` discretises the training points and assigns a class to each training sample. The bag-of-unigram features are extracted using `TfidfVectorizer` and the model is

trained by `SGDClassifier` with log loss and ElasticNet regularisation. The end-user can manually tune the regularisation parameters using a held-out development set. The procedure for training is illustrated in Figure 3.

Network-based model: geolocation with the network-based model can be done similarly to LR-WORLD, but since the data is not recent, the results might not be as accurate as reported in Section 5. Given a Twitter user, the timeline is downloaded and the @-mentions are matched with the hashed user account names. The median location of the matched users is returned as the prediction. The procedure is illustrated in Figure 4.

4.1 Trained models

The trained LR-WORLD model distributed with `pigeo`, and we additionally document the LP-WORLD, in terms of the files, formats and characteristics of the model.

LR-WORLD contains 4 gzipped pickle files:

- `clf.pkl.gz` is a scikit-learn `SGDClassifier` instance trained on TWITTER-WORLD-EX, whose projection matrix is converted to a Scipy sparse matrix for scalability.

- `vectorizer.pkl.gz` is a scikit-learn `TfidfVectorizer` instance fitted to TWITTER-WORLD-EX which, given a text, extracts the bag-of-unigram features with binary term frequency, inverse document frequency and l_2 normalisation of samples. Terms which occur in less than 10 documents are excluded.

- `coordinate_address.pkl.gz` is a dictionary that, given a (latitude, longitude) coordinate tuple, returns an address. It only covers the coordinates of the `LR-WORLD` classes and is based on geopy's OpenStreetMap API.

- `label_coordinate.pkl.gz` is a dictionary containing the classes/regions of the `LR-WORLD` model and their corresponding latitude/longitude tuple, which is the median of all the training points in that class.

LP-WORLD is made up of a single gzipped pickle file `userhash_coordinate.pkl.gz`, which is a dictionary of users mapped to predicted locations using label propagation over real-valued coordinates of TWITTER-WORLD-EX dataset. As we are unable to distribute this model, the user needs to provide it themselves.

5 Evaluation

We evaluate the performance of `LR-WORLD` and `LP-WORLD` model based on 3 evaluation measures used in previous research (Cheng et al., 2010; Eisenstein et al., 2010): the mean error (Mean), median error (Median), and the accuracy of geolocation within 161km of the actual location (Acc@161).

Note that lower values are better for Mean and Median, and higher values are better for Acc@161. The performance for the `LR-WORLD` and `LP-WORLD` models is shown in Table 1. Because there are no published results over TWITTER-WORLD-EX, we compared the performance of the models with previous work based on TWITTER-US (Wing and Baldridge, 2011).

6 Conclusion

We introduced `pigeo`, an easy-to-use, accurate Python geolocation tool which is able to geolocate both text and Twitter users based on two trained geolocation models: `LR-WORLD` and `LP-WORLD`. We described the implementation details of `pigeo`, and evaluated it on a standard Twitter geolocation dataset. It is our hope that

	Acc@161	Mean	Median
TWITTER-WORLD-EX dataset			
LR-WORLD	0.62	818	31
LP-WORLD	0.67	829	4
TWITTER-US dataset			
LR-NA	0.51	636	148
LP-NA	0.50	610	144
Wing and Baldridge (2014)	0.49	703	170

Table 1: The performance of the `LR-WORLD` text-based classification model and the `LP-WORLD` network-based regression model over the test set of TWITTER-WORLD-EX. The model performance over TWITTER-US is compared to previous work.

`pigeo` will provides researchers with an accurate off-the-shelf baseline geolocation model for applications which require geolocation.

References

Zahra Ashktorab, Christopher Brown, Manojit Nandi, and Aron Culotta. 2014. Tweedr: Mining Twitter to inform disaster response. In *Proceedings of The 11th International Conference on Information Systems for Crisis Response and Management (ISCRAM 2014)*, pages 354–358, University Park, USA.

Lars Backstrom, Eric Sun, and Cameron Marlow. 2010. Find me if you can: improving geographical prediction with social and spatial proximity. In *Proceedings of the 19th International Conference on World Wide Web (WWW 2010)*, pages 61–70, Raleigh, USA.

Zhiyuan Cheng, James Caverlee, and Kyumin Lee. 2010. You are where you tweet: a content-based approach to geo-locating Twitter users. In *Proceedings of the 19th ACM International Conference Information and Knowledge Management (CIKM 2010)*, pages 759–768, Toronto, Canada.

Emiliano De Cristofaro, Claudio Soriente, Gene Tsudik, and Albert Williams. 2012. Hummingbird: Privacy at the time of Twitter. In *Proceedings of the 2012 IEEE Symposium on Security and Privacy (SP)*, pages 285–299, San Francisco, USA.

Mark Dredze, Michael J Paul, Shane Bergsma, and Hieu Tran. 2013. Carmen: A twitter geolocation system with applications to public health. In *Proceedings of the AAAI 2013 Workshop on Expanding the Boundaries of Health Informatics Using AI (HIAI)*, pages 20–24, Bellevue, USA.

Mark Dredze, Miles Osborne, and Prabhanjan Kambadur. 2016. Geolocation for Twitter: Timing matters. In *Proceedings of the North American Chapter of the Association for Computational Linguistics (NAACL 2016)*, San Diego, USA.

Jacob Eisenstein, Brendan O'Connor, Noah A Smith, and Eric P Xing. 2010. A latent variable model for geographic lexical variation. In *Proceedings of the 2010 Conference on Empirical Methods in Natural Language Processing (EMNLP 2010)*, pages 1277–1287, Boston, USA.

Carlos Gutierrez, Paulo Figueiras, Pedro Oliveira, Ruben Costa, and Ricardo Jardim-Goncalves. 2015. Twitter mining for traffic events detection. In *Science and Information Conference (SAI), 2015*, pages 371–378.

Bo Han, Paul Cook, and Timothy Baldwin. 2012. Geolocation prediction in social media data by finding location indicative words. In *Proceedings of the 24th International Conference on Computational Linguistics (COLING 2012)*, pages 1045–1062, Mumbai, India.

Bo Han, Paul Cook, and Timothy Baldwin. 2013. A stacking-based approach to Twitter user geolocation prediction. In *Proceedings of the 51st Annual Meeting of the Association for Computational Linguistics (ACL 2013): System Demonstrations*, pages 7–12, Sofia, Bulgaria.

Bo Han, Paul Cook, and Timothy Baldwin. 2014. Text-based Twitter user geolocation prediction. *Journal of Artificial Intelligence Research*, 49:451–500.

Shen-Shyang Ho, Mike Lieberman, Pu Wang, and Hanan Samet. 2012. Mining future spatiotemporal events and their sentiment from online news articles for location-aware recommendation system. In *Proceedings of the First ACM SIGSPATIAL International Workshop on Mobile Geographic Information Systems*, pages 25–32, Redondo Beach, USA.

David Jurgens, Tyler Finethy, James McCorriston, Yi Tian Xu, and Derek Ruths. 2015. Geolocation prediction in twitter using social networks: A critical analysis and review of current practice. In *Proceedings of the 9th International Conference on Weblogs and Social Media (ICWSM 2015)*, pages 188–197, Oxford, UK.

David Jurgens. 2013. That's what friends are for: Inferring location in online social media platforms based on social relationships. In *Proceedings of the 7th International Conference on Weblogs and Social Media (ICWSM 2013)*, pages 273–282, Boston, USA.

Kwan Hui Lim and Amitava Datta. 2013. A topological approach for detecting twitter communities with common interests. In *Ubiquitous Social Media Analysis*, pages 23–43. Springer.

Wolfgang Maier and Carlos Gómez-Rodrıguez. 2014. Language variety identification in Spanish tweets. In *Proceedings of the EMNLP2014 Workshop on Language Technology for Closely Related Languages and Language Variants*, pages 25–35, Doha, Qatar.

Michael J Paul, Mark Dredze, David A Broniatowski, and Nicholas Generous. 2015. Worldwide influenza surveillance through twitter. In *AAAI Workshop on the World Wide Web and Public Health Intelligence*, Austin, USA.

Fabian Pedregosa, Gaël Varoquaux, Alexandre Gramfort, Vincent Michel, Bertrand Thirion, Olivier Grisel, Mathieu Blondel, Peter Prettenhofer, Ron Weiss, Vincent Dubourg, et al. 2011. Scikit-learn: Machine learning in Python. *The Journal of Machine Learning Research*, 12:2825–2830.

Afshin Rahimi, Trevor Cohn, and Timothy Baldwin. 2015a. Twitter user geolocation using a unified text and network prediction model. In *Proceedings of the 53rd Annual Meeting of the Association for Computational Linguistics — 7th International Joint Conference on Natural Language Processing (ACL-IJCNLP 2015)*, pages 630–636, Beijing, China.

Afshin Rahimi, Duy Vu, Trevor Cohn, and Timothy Baldwin. 2015b. Exploiting text and network context for geolocation of social media users. In *Proceedings of the 2015 Conference of the North American Chapter of the Association for Computational Linguistics — Human Language Technologies (NAACL HLT 2015)*, pages 1362–1367, Denver, USA.

Dominic Rout, Kalina Bontcheva, Daniel Preoţiuc-Pietro, and Trevor Cohn. 2013. Where's @wally?: A classification approach to geolocating users based on their social ties. In *Proceedings of the 24th ACM Conference on Hypertext and Social Media (Hypertext 2013)*, pages 11–20, Paris, France.

Vetle I Torvik. 2015. Mapaffil: A bibliographic tool for mapping author affiliation strings to cities and their geocodes worldwide. *D-Lib Magazine*, 21(11):9.

Benjamin P Wing and Jason Baldridge. 2011. Simple supervised document geolocation with geodesic grids. In *Proceedings of the 49th Annual Meeting of the Association for Computational Linguistics: Human Language Technologies-Volume 1 (ACL-HLT 2011)*, pages 955–964, Portland, USA.

Benjamin P Wing and Jason Baldridge. 2014. Hierarchical discriminative classification for text-based geolocation. In *Proceedings of the 2014 Conference on Empirical Methods in Natural Language Processing (EMNLP 2014)*, pages 336–348, Doha, Qatar.

Creating Interactive Macaronic Interfaces for Language Learning

Adithya Renduchintala and **Rebecca Knowles** and **Philipp Koehn** and **Jason Eisner**
Department of Computer Science
Johns Hopkins University
{adi.r,rknowles,phi,eisner}@jhu.edu

Abstract

We present a prototype of a novel technology for second language instruction. Our learn-by-reading approach lets a human learner acquire new words and constructions by encountering them in context. To facilitate reading comprehension, our technology presents mixed native language (L1) and second language (L2) sentences to a learner and allows them to interact with the sentences to make the sentences easier (more L1-like) or harder (more L2-like) to read. Eventually, our system should continuously track a learner's knowledge and learning style by modeling their interactions, including performance on a pop quiz feature. This will allow our system to generate personalized mixed-language texts for learners.

1 Introduction

Growing interest in self-directed language learning methods like Duolingo (von Ahn, 2013), along with recent advances in machine translation and the widespread ease of access to a variety of texts in a large number of languages, has given rise to a number of web-based tools related to language learning (ranging from dictionary apps to more interactive tools like Alpheios (Nelson, 2007) or Lingua.ly (2013)). Most of these either focus on vocabulary learning or require hand-curated lesson plans. We present a prototype of a system for learning to read in a foreign language, which presents learners with text consisting of a mix of their native language (L1) and the language they are interested in learning (L2). We refer to sentences containing a mix of L1 and L2 text as **macaronic**[1] sentences. Along the continuum from fully L1 to fully L2 text are sentences with any combination of L1 and L2 vocabulary, syntax, and (potentially) morphology.

Proponents of language acquisition through extensive reading, such as Krashen (1989), argue that much of language acquisition takes place through incidental learning—when a learner is exposed to novel vocabulary or structures and must find a way to understand them in order to comprehend the text. The trouble is that learning by reading already requires considerable L2 fluency. To bootstrap, we propose making L2 sentences more accessible to early learners by shifting these sentences along the macaronic spectrum towards L1, stopping at the "zone of proximal development" (Vygotskiĭ, 2012) where the learner is able to comprehend the text but only by stretching their L2 capacity. We aim in the future to customize macaronic sentences to each individual learner.

A reasonable concern is whether exposure to macaronic language might actually harm acquisition of correct L2 (even though our interface uses color and font to mark the L1 "intrusions" into the L2 sentence). As some reassurance, our approach is analogous to the well-established paradigm of inventive spelling (or "invented spelling"),[2] in which early writers are encouraged to write in their native language without concern for correct spelling, in part so they can more fully and happily engage with the writing challenge of composing longer and more authentic texts (Clarke, 1988). We also observe that simultaneous dual language acquisition—from multilingual and code-switched language—is common for young children in many countries, who employ code-switching in a socially appropriate way and as "a resource . . . to fill gaps in their developing

---

[1]The term "macaronic" traditionally refers to a mashup of languages, often intended to be humorous. We use this term, rather than "code-switching," since code-switching requires the speaker/writer to be fluent in both languages. Code-switching is governed by syntactic and pragmatic considerations, rather than by pedagogical or humorous ones.

[2]Spelling, like L2, is a type of linguistic knowledge that is acquired after L1 fluency and largely through incidental learning (Krashen, 1993).

Proceedings of the 54th Annual Meeting of the Association for Computational Linguistics—System Demonstrations, pages 133–138,
Berlin, Germany, August 7-12, 2016. ©2016 Association for Computational Linguistics

languages" (Genesee, 2009). Still, it remains an open question whether older students can successfully unlearn initial habits and move toward an increasingly complete and correct L2 model.

We envision our technology being used *alongside* traditional classroom L2 instruction—the same instructional mix that leads parents to accept inventive spelling (Gentry, 2000). Traditional grammar-based instruction and assessment, which use "toy" sentences in pure L2, should provide further scaffolding for our users to acquire language by reading more advanced (but macaronic) text.

We provide details of the current user interface and discuss how content for our system can be automatically generated using existing statistical machine translation (SMT) methods, enabling learners or teachers to choose their own texts to read. Our prototype is currently running on `http://www.clsp.jhu.edu:3030/` with sample content. Our interface lets the user navigate through the spectrum from L2 to L1, going beyond the single-word or single-phrase translations offered by other online tools such as Swych (2015), or dictionary-like browser plugins.

Finally, we discuss plans to extend this prototype and to integrate it with a continuously adapting user model. To this end, our companion paper (Renduchintala et al., 2016) develops an initial model of macaronic sentence comprehension by novice L2 learners, using data collected from human subjects via Amazon's Mechanical Turk service. In another paper (Knowles et al., 2016), we carry out a controlled study of comprehension of individual L2 words in isolation and in L1 context.

2 Macaronic Interface

For the purposes of this demo we assume a native English speaker (L1=English) who is learning German (L2=German). However, our existing interface can accommodate any pair of languages whose writing systems share directionality.[3] The primary goal of the interface is to empower a learner to translate and reorder parts of a confusing foreign language sentence. These translations and reorderings serve to make the German sentence more English-like. The interface also permits reverse transformations, letting the curious learner "peek ahead" at how specific English words and constructions would surface in German.

---

[3]We also assume that the text is segmented into words.

Der Preis ist nach Georg Büchner benannt .

(a) Initial sentence state.

Der Preis ist nach Georg Büchner benannt .

(b) Mouse hovered under `Preis`.

Der *prize* ist nach Georg Büchner benannt .

(c) `Preis` translated to `prize`.

Der *prize* ist nach Georg Büchner benannt .

(d) Mouse hovered above `prize`. Clicking above will revert the sentence back to the initial state 1a.

Der *prize* ist nach Georg Büchner *named* .

(e) Sentence with 2 different words translated into English

Figure 1: Actions that translate words.

Using these fundamental interactions as building blocks, we create an interactive framework for a language learner to explore this continuum of "English-like" to "foreign-like" sentences. By repeated interaction with new content and exposure to recurring vocabulary items and linguistic patterns, we believe a learner can pick up vocabulary and other linguistic rules of the foreign language.

2.1 Translation

The basic interface idea is that a line of macaronic text is equipped with hidden interlinear annotations. Notionally, English translations lurk below the macaronic text, and German ones above.

The *Translation* interaction allows the learner to change the text in the macaronic sentence from one language to another. Consider a macaronic sentence that is completely in the foreign state (i.e.,, entirely in German), as shown in Fig. 1a. Hovering on or under a German word shows a *preview* of a translation (Fig. 1b). Clicking on the preview will cause the translation to "rise up" and replace the German word (Fig. 1c).

To translate in the reverse direction, the user can hover and click above an English word (Fig. 1d).

Since the same mechanism applies to all the words in the sentence, a learner can manipulate translations for each word independently. For example, Fig. 1e shows two words in English.

The version of our prototype displayed in Figure 1 blurs the preview tokens when a learner is hovering above or below a word. This blurred preview acts as a visual indication of a potential change to the sentence state (if clicked) but it also

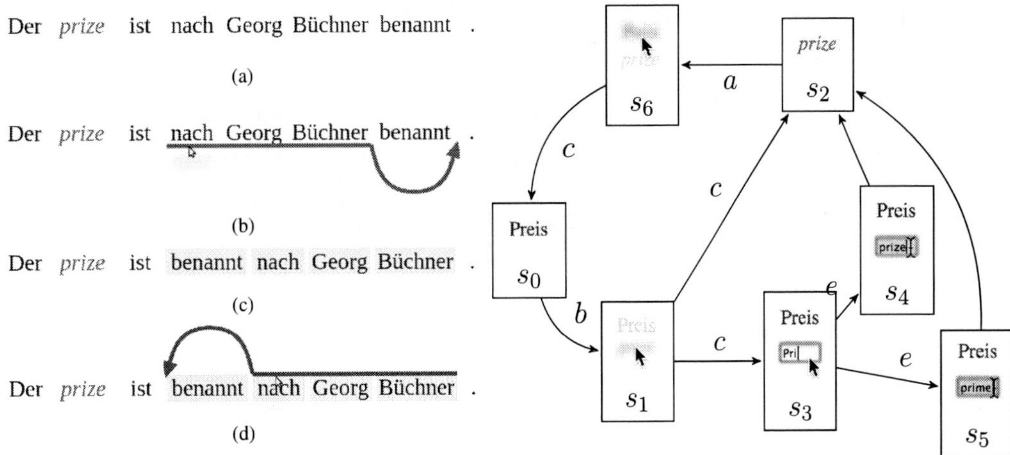

Figure 2: Actions that reorder phrases.

Figure 3: State diagram of learner interaction (edges) and system's response(vertices). Edges can be traversed by clicking (c), hovering above (a), hovering below (b) or the enter (e) key. Unmarked edges indicate an automatic transition.

gives the learner a chance to think about what the translation might be, based on visual clues such as length and shape of the blurred text.

2.2 Reordering

When the learner hovers slightly *below* the words nach Georg Büchner a *Reordering* arrow is displayed (as shown in Figure 2). The arrow is an indicator of reordering. In this example, the German past participle benannt appears at the end of the sentence (the conjugated form of the verb is ist benannt, or is named); this is the grammatically correct location for the participle in German, while the English form should appear earlier in the equivalent English sentence.

Similar to the translation actions, reordering actions also have a directional attribute. Figure 2b shows a German-to-English direction arrow. When the learner clicks the arrow, the interface rearranges all the words involved in the reordering. The new word positions are shown in 2c. Once again, the user can undo: hovering just *above* nach Georg Büchner now shows a gray arrow, which if clicked returns the phrase to its German word order (shown in 2d).

German phrases that are not in original German order are highlighted as a warning (Figure 2c).

2.3 "Pop Quiz" Feature

So far, we have described the system's standard responses to a learner's actions. We now add occasional "pop quizzes." When a learner hovers below a German word (s_0 in Figure 3) and clicks the blurry English text, the system can either reveal the translation of the German word (state s_2) as described in section 2.1 or quiz the learner (state s_3). We implement the quiz by presenting a text input box to the learner: here the learner is expected to type what they believe the German word means. Once a guess is typed, the system indicates if the guess is correct (s_4) or incorrect(s_5) by flashing green or red highlights in the text box. The box then disappears (after 700ms) and the system automatically proceeds to the reveal state s_2. As this imposes a high cognitive load and increases the interaction complexity (typing vs. clicking), we intend to use the pop quiz infrequently.

The pop quiz serves two vital functions. First, it further incentivizes the user to retain learned vocabulary. Second, it allows the system to update its model of the user's current L2 lexicon, macaronic comprehension, and learning style; this is work in progress (see section 4.2).

2.4 Interaction Consistency

Again, we regard the macaronic sentence as a kind of interlinear text, written between two mostly invisible sentences: German above and English below. In general, hovering above the macaronic sentence will reveal German words or word orders, which fall down into the macaronic sentence upon clicking. Hovering below will reveal English translations, which rise up upon clicking.

The words in the macaronic sentence are colored according to their language. We want the user to become accustomed to reading German, so the German words are in plain black text by de-

Action	Direction	Trigger	Preview	Preview Color	Confirm	Result
Translation	E-to-G	Hover above English	Blurry German translation above	Gray Blur	Click on Blurry Text	translation replaces English word(s)
	G-to-E	Hover under German token	Blurry English translation below	Blue Blur	Click on Blurry Text	translation replaces German word(s)
Reordering	E-to-G	Hover above token	Arrow above reordering tokens	Gray Arrow	Click on Arrow	tokens reorder
	G-to-E	Hover under token	Arrow below reordering tokens	Blue Arrow	Click on Arrow	tokens reorder

Table 1: Summary of learner triggered interactions in the Macaronic Interface.

fault, while the English words use a marked color and font (italic blue). Reordering arrows also follow the same color scheme: arrows that will make the macaronic sentence more "German-like" are gray, while arrows that make the sentence more "English-like" are blue. The summary of interactions is shown in Table 1.

3 Constructing Macaronic Translations

In this section, we describe the details of the underlying data structures needed to allow all the interactions mentioned in the previous section. A key requirement in the design of the data structure was to support orthogonal actions in each sentence. Making all translation and reordering actions independent of one another creates a large space of macaronic states for a learner to explore.

At present, the input to our macaronic interface is bitext with word-to-word alignments provided by a phrase-based SMT system (or, if desired, by hand). We employ Moses (Koehn et al., 2007) to translate German sentences and generate phrase alignments. News articles written in simple German from `nachrichtenleicht.de` (Deutschlandfunk, 2016) were translated after training the SMT system on the WMT15 German-English corpus (Bojar et al., 2015).

We convert the word alignments into "minimal alignments" that are either one-to-one, one-to-many or many-to-one.[4] This step ensures consistent reversibility of actions and prevents large phrases from being translated with a single click.[5] The resulting bipartite graph can be regarded as

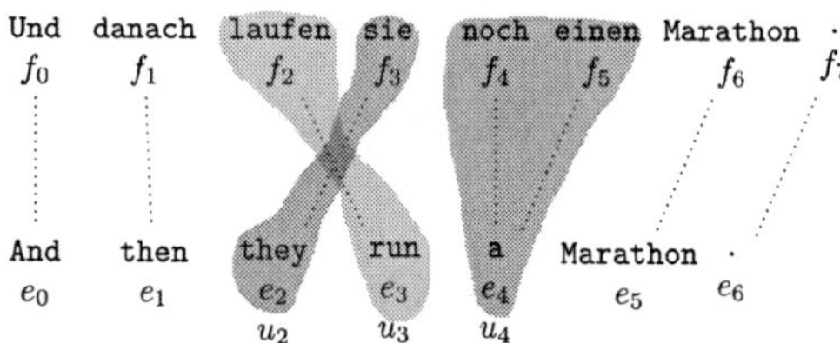

Figure 4: The dotted lines show word-to-word alignments between the German sentence $f_0, f_1, \ldots, f_7$ and its English translation $e_0, e_1, \ldots, e_6$. The figure highlights 3 of the 7 units: u_2, u_3, u_4.

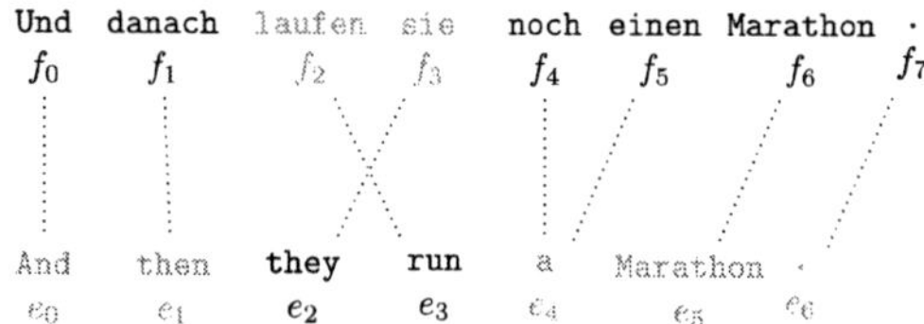

Figure 5: A possible state of the sentence, which renders a subset of the tokens (shown in black). The rendering order (section 3.2) is not shown but is also part of the state. The string displayed in this case is "Und danach *they run* noch einen Marathon." (assuming no reordering).

a collection of connected components, or *units* (Fig. 4).[6]

3.1 Translation Mechanism

In a given state of the macaronic sentence, each unit is displayed in either English or German. A translation action toggles the display language of the unit, leaving it in place. For example, in Figure 5, where the macaronic sentence is currently displaying $f_4 f_5$ = noch einen, a translation action will replace this with e_4 = a.

3.2 Reordering Mechanism

A reordering action changes the unit order of the current macaronic sentence. The out-

---

[4]For each many-to-many alignment returned by the SMT system, we remove alignment edges (lowest probability first) until the alignment is no longer many-to-many. Then we greedily add edges from unaligned tokens (highest probability first), subject to not creating many-to-many alignments and subject to minimizing the number of crossing edges, until all tokens are aligned.

[5]Preliminary experiments showed that allowing large phrases to translate with one click resulted in abrupt jumps in the visualization, which users found hard to follow.

[6]In the sections below, we gloss over cases where a unit is discontiguous (in one language). Such units are handled specially (we omit details for reasons of space). If a unit would fall outside the bounds of what our special handling can handle, we fuse it with another unit.

put string "Und danach `they run` noch
`einen Marathon.`" is obtained from Figure
5 only if unit u_2 (as labeled in Figure 4) is rendered (in its current language) to the left of unit
u_3, which we write as $u_2 < u_3$. In this case, it is
possible for the user to change the order of these
units, because $u_3 < u_2$ in German. Table 2 shows
the 8 possible combinations of ordering and translation choices for this pair of units.

String Rendered	Unit Ordering
`...they run...`	
`...they laufen...`	$\{u_2\} < \{u_3\}$
`...sie run...`	
`...sie laufen...`	
`...run they...`	
`...run sie...`	$\{u_2\} > \{u_3\}$
`...laufen they...`	
`...laufen sie...`	

Table 2: Generating reordered strings using units.

The space of possible orderings for a sentence
pair is defined by a bracketing ITG tree (Wu,
1997), which transforms the German ordering of
the units into the English ordering by a collection of nested binary swaps of subsequences.[7] The
ordering state of the macaronic sentence is given
by the subset of these swaps that have been performed. A reordering action toggles one of the
swaps in this collection.

Since we have a parser for German (Rafferty
and Manning, 2008), we take care to select an
ITG tree that is "compatible" with the German
sentence's dependency structure, in the following
sense: if the ITG tree combines two spans A and
B, then there are not dependencies from words in
A to words in B *and* vice-versa.

4 Discussion and Future Work

4.1 Machine Translation Challenges

When the English version of the sentence is produced by an MT system, it may suffer from MT
errors and/or poor alignments.

Even with correct MT, a given syntactic construction may be handled inconsistently on different occasions, depending on the particular words
involved (as these affect what phrasal alignment
is found and how we convert it to a minimal alignment). Syntax-based MT could be used to design a
more consistent interface that is also more closely
tied to classroom L2 lessons.

Cross-linguistic divergences in the expression
of information (Dorr, 1994) could be confusing.
For example, when moving through macaronic
space from `Kaffee gefällt Menschen`
(coffee pleases humans) to its translation *humans
like coffee*, it may not be clear to the
learner that the reordering is triggered by the
fact that `like` is not a literal translation of
`gefällt`. One way to improve this might be to
have the system pass smoothly through a range
of intermediate translations from word-by-word
glosses to idiomatic phrasal translations, rather
than always directly translating idioms. We might
also see benefit in guiding our gradual translations
with cognates (for example, rather than translate
directly from the German `Möhre` to the English
`carrot`, we might offer the cognate `Karotte`
as an intermediate step).

We also plan to transition through words
that are macaronic at the sub-word level. For
example, hovering over the unfamiliar German word `gesprochen` might decompose it
into `ge-sprochen`; then clicking on one of
those morphemes might yield `ge-`*talk* or
`sprech-`*ed* before reaching *talked*. This
could guide learners towards an understanding of
German tense marking and stem changes.

4.2 User Adaptation and Evaluation

We would prefer to show the learner a macaronic
sentence that provides just enough clues for the
learner to be able to comprehend it, while still
pushing them to figure out new vocabulary or new
structures. Thus, we plan to situate this interface
in a framework that continuously adapts as the
user progresses. As the user learns new vocabulary, the system will automatically present them
with more challenging sentences (containing less
L1). In (Renduchintala et al., 2016) we show that
we can predict a novice learner's guesses of L2
word meanings in macaronic sentences using a
few simple features. We will subsequently track
the user's learning by observing their mouse actions and "pop quiz" responses (section 2).

While we have had users interact with our system in order to collect data about novice learners' guesses, we are working toward an evaluation
where our system is used to supplement classroom
instruction for real foreign-language students.

---

[7]Occasionally no such ITG tree exists, in which case we
fuse units as needed until one does.

5   Conclusion

In this work we present a prototype of an interactive interface for learning to read in a foreign language. We expose the learner to L2 vocabulary and constructions in contexts that are comprehensible because they have been *partially* translated into the learner's native language, using statistical MT. Using MT affords flexibility: learners or instructors can choose which texts to read, and learners or the system can control which parts of a sentence are translated.

We are working towards integrating models of learner understanding (Renduchintala et al., 2016; Knowles et al., 2016) to produce personalized macaronic texts that give each learner just the right amount of challenge and support. In the long term, we would like to extend the approach to allow users also to *produce* macaronic language, drawing on techniques from grammatical error correction or computer-aided translation to help them gradually remove L1 features from their writing (or speech) and make it more L2-like.

Acknowledgments

This material is based upon work supported by a seed grant from the Science of Learning Institute at Johns Hopkins University, and also by a National Science Foundation Graduate Research Fellowship (Grant No. DGE-1232825) to the second author. We would like to thank Chadia Abras for useful discussions.

Supplemental Material

- A video demonstration can be found here: `https://youtu.be/d5lxyeHIDWI`
- A live sample version is here: `http://www.clsp.jhu.edu:3030/signin`

References

Ondřej Bojar, Rajen Chatterjee, Christian Federmann, Barry Haddow, Matthias Huck, Chris Hokamp, Philipp Koehn, Varvara Logacheva, Christof Monz, Matteo Negri, Matt Post, Carolina Scarton, Lucia Specia, and Marco Turchi. 2015. Findings of the 2015 Workshop on Statistical Machine Translation. In *Proceedings of the Tenth Workshop on Statistical Machine Translation*, pages 1–46.

Linda K. Clarke. 1988. Invented versus traditional spelling in first graders' writings: Effects on learning to spell and read. *Research in the Teaching of English*, pages 281–309, October.

Deutschlandfunk. 2016. nachrichtenleicht. `http://www.nachrichtenleicht.de/`. Accessed: 2015-09-30.

Bonnie J. Dorr. 1994. Machine translation divergences: A formal description and proposed solution. *Computational Linguistics*, 20(4):597–633, December.

Fred H. Genesee. 2009. Early childhood bilingualism: Perils and possibilities. *Journal of Applied Research on Learning*, 2(Article 2):1–21, April.

J. Richard Gentry. 2000. A retrospective on invented spelling and a look forward. *The Reading Teacher*, 54(3):318–332, November.

Rebecca Knowles, Adithya Renduchintala, Philipp Koehn, and Jason Eisner. 2016. Analyzing learner understanding of novel L2 vocabulary. To appear.

Philipp Koehn, Hieu Hoang, Alexandra Birch, Chris Callison-Burch, Marcello Federico, Nicola Bertoldi, Brooke Cowan, Wade Shen, Christine Moran, Richard Zens, et al. 2007. Moses: Open source toolkit for statistical machine translation. In *Proceedings of ACL: Interactive Poster and Demonstration Sessions*, pages 177–180.

Stephen Krashen. 1989. We acquire vocabulary and spelling by reading: Additional evidence for the input hypothesis. *The Modern Language Journal*, 73(4):440–464.

S. Krashen. 1993. How well do people spell? *Reading Improvement*, 30(1).

Lingua.ly. 2013. Lingua.ly. `https://lingua.ly/`. Accessed: 2016-04-04.

Mark Nelson. 2007. The Alpheios project. `http://alpheios.net/`. Accessed: 2016-04-05.

Anna N Rafferty and Christopher D Manning. 2008. Parsing three German treebanks: Lexicalized and unlexicalized baselines. In *Proceedings of the Workshop on Parsing German*, pages 40–46. Association for Computational Linguistics.

Adithya Renduchintala, Rebecca Knowles, Philipp Koehn, and Jason Eisner. 2016. User modeling in language learning with macaronic texts. In *Proceedings of ACL*.

Swych. 2015. Swych. `http://swych.it/`. Accessed: 2016-04-05.

Luis von Ahn. 2013. Duolingo: Learn a language for free while helping to translate the web. In *Proceedings of the 2013 International Conference on Intelligent User Interfaces*, pages 1–2.

Lev Vygotskiĭ. 2012. *Thought and Language (Revised and Expanded Edition)*. MIT press.

Dekai Wu. 1997. Stochastic inversion transduction grammars and bilingual parsing of parallel corpora. *Computational Linguistics*, 23(3):377–404.

Roleo: visualising thematic fit spaces on the web

Asad Sayeed and **Xudong Hong** and **Vera Demberg**
Cluster of Excellence "Multimodal Computing and Interaction"
Saarland University
66123 Saarbrücken, Germany
`{asayeed,xhong,vera}@coli.uni-saarland.de`

Abstract

In this paper, we present Roleo, a web tool for visualizing the vector spaces generated by the evaluation of distributional memory (DM) models over thematic fit judgements. A thematic fit judgement is a rating of the selectional preference of a verb for an argument that fills a given thematic role. The DM approach to thematic fit judgements involves the construction of a sub-space in which a prototypical role-filler can be built for comparison to the noun being judged. We describe a publicly-accessible web tool that allows for querying and exploring these spaces as well as a technique for visualizing thematic fit sub-spaces efficiently for web use.

1 Introduction

We developed Roleo as a web platform in order to visualize and explore the vector spaces generated by the process of thematic fit evaluation in distributional models. We define thematic fit to be a measure of the extent to which the selectional preference of a verb given a thematic role is fulfilled by a particular noun. For example, we expect "knife" to strongly fit the instrument role of "cut", but "sword" much less so, and "hammer" hardly at all. Modeling thematic fit has applications in areas like cognitive modeling and incremental parsing. Various efforts have produced human judgements of thematic fit for different combinations of verbs, roles, and nouns (Padó, 2007; Greenberg et al., 2015), and there have been a number of recent efforts to build models that correlate closely with those judgement datasets.

The most successful of these have been the Distributional Memory (DM) models (Baroni and Lenci, 2010), which are unsupervised models that produce sparse, very high-dimensional vector spaces. Recently, word embedding models with smaller numbers of dimensions have been tested, although they have yet to reach the degree of correlation with human judgements that DM models have (Baroni et al., 2014). Nevertheless, in both cases, some notion of geometric distance or similarity is used to substitute for the concept of fit.

If a geometric measure is used as the operational conceptualization of thematic fit, then we should be able to subjectively assess the quality of the space through visualization in order to gain a grasp, for example, of how easily the space is partitionable or clusterable. This capability is useful in the iterative engineering of features or for assessing the quality of training data.

A number of existing packages across many different development environments support low-dimensional projection and visualization of high-dimensional vector spaces. There are also a small number of web sites that allow word embeddings to be visualized in a low-dimensional space (Faruqui and Dyer, 2014). However, the best-performing work in vector-space thematic fit evaluation projects sub-spaces from a full tensor space given a verb and a role. Roleo is designed to query and visualize these sub-spaces in a manner that reflects the evaluation process.

Roleo is live and available for use at `http://roleo.coli.uni-saarland.de/` with two example models and an efficient visualization technique. We have furthermore made the code for it open source and available at `https://github.com/tony-hong/roleo`.

1.1 Design goals

Our goals for the Roleo software are to:

- Provide a web-based platform for the exploration of thematic fit sub-spaces based on dif-

Proceedings of the 54th Annual Meeting of the Association for Computational Linguistics—System Demonstrations, pages 139–144,
Berlin, Germany, August 7-12, 2016. ©2016 Association for Computational Linguistics

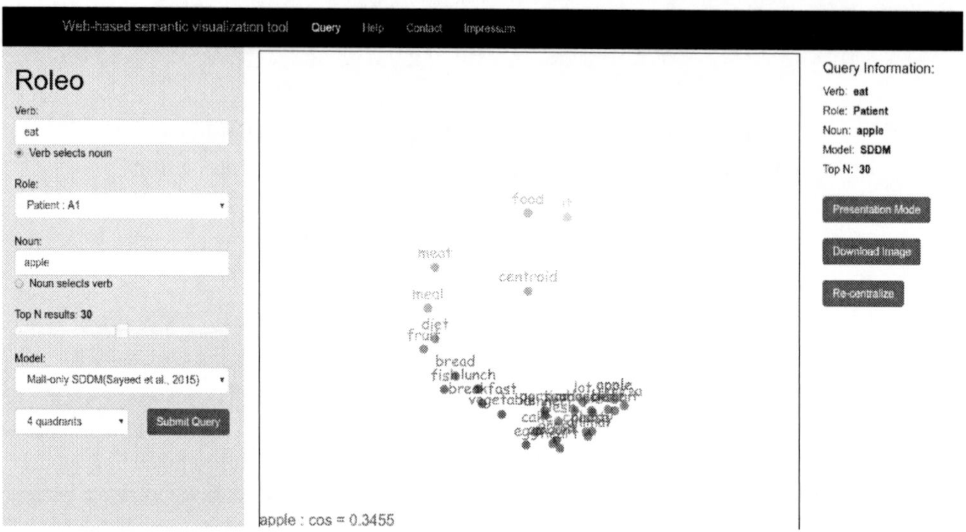

Figure 1: Initial screen on loading Roleo in a browser.

ferent vector-space modeling techniques. We begin with DM models.

- Make this type of semantic modeling accessible to other researchers via the web. This means that the interface must be reasonably user-friendly and allow visitors to test simple queries without knowing how to set all possible parameters.
- Facilitate presentations and demonstrations about thematic fit evaluation.
- Serve queries reasonably quickly, ideally at "web speed", so that it is reasonable to "play around" with the models. This puts a constraint on the kinds of projections and dimensionality reduction we can use.

2 Vector-space thematic fit modeling

2.1 Distributional Memory

The currently best-performing models on the thematic fit task, in terms of correlation with human judgements, are the Distributional Memory (DM) models, based on a technique first proposed by Baroni and Lenci (2010). A DM model is an order-3 tensor with two axes that represent words in the model's vocabulary and one axis that represents links between the words, so that the cell of the tensor is a positive real value for the occurrence of a triple <word0,link,word1>. That occurrence is an adjusted count of frequency such as Local Mutual Information (LMI). The link between the words is a connection acquired from processing a corpus,

such as with a dependency parser.

This structure was extensively tested by Baroni and Lenci on a number of semantic tasks, including on thematic fit modeling. Their procedure for thematic fit modeling was the following: given a verb v and a role r, they look up all the nouns n such that each $< v, r, n >$ LMI is within the highest 20 for v and r. Then for each n, they get a word vector w_n from the model by looking up all the word0 and link contexts that n appeared in as word1; the vector is assembled from the LMI values in those cells of the tensor. Given a candidate noun m against which to evaluate the fit with v and r, a w_m vector is similarly found. All the <word0,link> contexts are the dimensions of a subspace of the space represented by the DM tensor as a whole; they can number potentially in the millions. All the w_n vectors are summed to form a centroid that represents a "prototype" noun for that verb and role. The thematic fit of m is evaluated via the cosine similarity of w_m and the centroid.

2.2 Provided models

In our demonstration version of Roleo, we provide two models, the TypeDM model from Baroni and Lenci and the "Malt-only SDDM" model from Sayeed et al. (2015). TypeDM is trained on multiple corpora (BNC, ukWaC, and Wikipedia) that have been downloaded and parsed by Malt-Parser. The links between words that are used to form TypeDM's link axis are derived from short

MaltParser dependency paths via a partly hand-crafted rule set. As TypeDM's links are derived from a syntactic parser, we must simulate semantic roles by interpreting these links. Roleo allows for the query of agent roles (via subject links), patient roles (via object links), instrument roles (via the preposition "with"), and location roles (via the prepositions "in", "at", and "on").

Malt-only SDDM (just SDDM from now on) is derived from a set of corpora similar to that of TypeDM: BNC and ukWaC. The main difference between TypeDM and SDDM are the link types, which in SDDM are PropBank roles, derived from applying the SENNA semantic role labeller to the corpora. The links are therefore the PropBank roles that connect verbs to nouns. SENNA (Collobert and Weston, 2007), however, labels entire noun chunks with roles, often including adjectives and whole relative clauses. Sayeed et al. experiment with a number of algorithms for extracting the noun head or bare noun phrase; the best performing SENNA-based technique is to use the MaltParser dependencies produced by Baroni and Lenci, but simply as a guide for head-identification. Sayeed et al. show that PropBank-based roles and TypeDM roles help cover different aspects of the thematic fit problem.

This process can be trivially reversed to represent the plausible verbs given a noun-role combination and to produce a visualization thereof. We provide this functionality inside Roleo, although it has never so far been evaluated on any task.

3 Efficient projection

One of our design goals was to build a query tool that delivered results in times reasonable for the web with limited resources, i.e., a single-PC web server with a modern CPU. Because we are visualizing thematic fit sub-spaces constructed around a centroid, we also looked for a projection that puts the centroid at the center of the display consisting of the prototype nouns that were used to construct that centroid. We experimented with principal component analysis (PCA) and t-SNE (Van der Maaten and Hinton, 2008) and found that at DM-scale dimensionality, these took too long and were too computationally intensive to resolve a query in web-appropriate time.

For this reason, we came up with a two-dimensional projection specialized to our problem: Fraction-Cosine Vector Mapping (FCVM).

This projection is easy to calculate directly from the support s_w of each word vector w in the DM model (LMI) given the role and the verb, the support of the centroid s_c (which is just the sum of the supports of all the vectors in the top n words for that verb-role combination), and the cosine c_w of the angle between the centroid and the vector.

Let V be the set of n highest supported word vectors for the given verb-role combination. Then for each vector, we can calculate its x and y coordinates in FCVM with the following procedure. The x coordinate for a projected word vector w is the sum of proportions of contributions to s_c of all words w' with a support $s_{w'} > s_w$, meaning that the more LMI-associated w is with the verb-role combination, the closer it is to the centroid along the x-axis. That is,

$$x_w = \sum_{w' \in V} \frac{s_{w'}}{s_c} \qquad (1)$$

The y_w-coordinate is simply $1 - c_w$. This means that x_w and y_w are both in the interval $[0, 1]$ and sit in the upper right quadrant of the Cartesian plane, with the origin (corner) as the centroid. We convert these to polar coordinates (r_w, θ_w) and then optionally apply an adjustment to spread the points out. This adjustment is to multiply θ_w by a multiple of 4, sweeping them across Cartesian quadrants, in order to bring the centroid closer to a circular cloud of points representing word vectors. The factors in Roleo are 1, 4, and 32, with 4 as the default. The higher the factor, the more circular the cloud. We finally convert the polar coordinates back to rectangular. We also include an option to display the polar coordinates by directly interpreting them as rectangular coordinates. The points are also given a colour that is dependent on their θ after the multiplication factor is applied.

4 System implementation

Roleo was developed in Python using the Django web development package. The DMs are implemented as Pandas dataframes stored in indexed HDF5 tables for efficient lookup. Vector algebra is implemented in NumPy. The two-dimensional coordinates for the points that appear in the visualization are calculated server-side, currently implemented on our own host, which is a single recent PC. The image is drawn client-side and requires a recent browser (we test with Firefox and Chrome).

Queries to Roleo take 2-10 seconds, depending

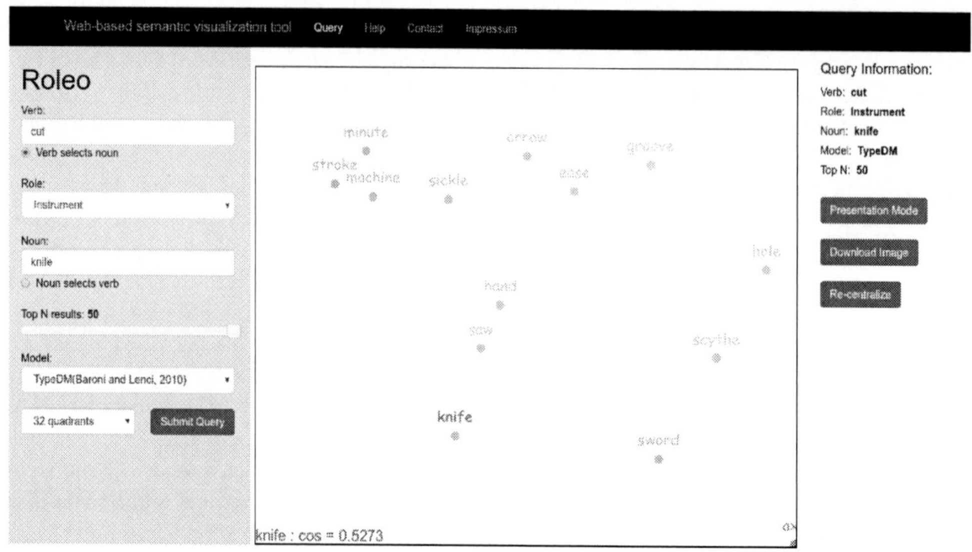

Figure 2: Zoomed-in query result for knife as instrument of cut under TypeDM with a 32-quadrant sweep and a space constructed from 50 prototype noun vectors.

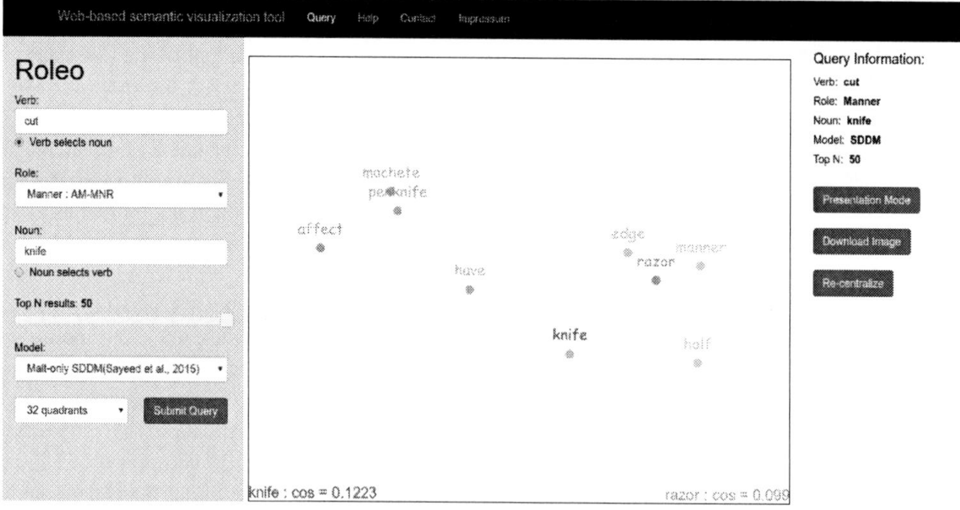

Figure 3: Zoomed-in query result for knife as ARGM-MNR of cut under SDDM with a 32-quadrant sweep and a space constructed from 50 prototype noun vectors. A touch gesture has highlighted the "razor" vector and put its cosine score on the bottom right corner.

on the number of vectors chosen by the user to form the centroid, within a tolerable range for a specialized web application.

4.1 Using Roleo

Roleo's initial screen on loading it for the first time in a browser is in figure 1. The screen is already populated with a query: how well "apple" fits as the patient of "eat"under SDDM, using 30 prototype nouns to calculate the centroid and populate the space. The 4-quadrant sweep is used to draw the canvas. Roleo is intended for use on a desktop PC or laptop or on a tablet.

Left pane Roleo's main options are shown on the left pane of the web page. There, the user can set the parameters and start the query. Fields are

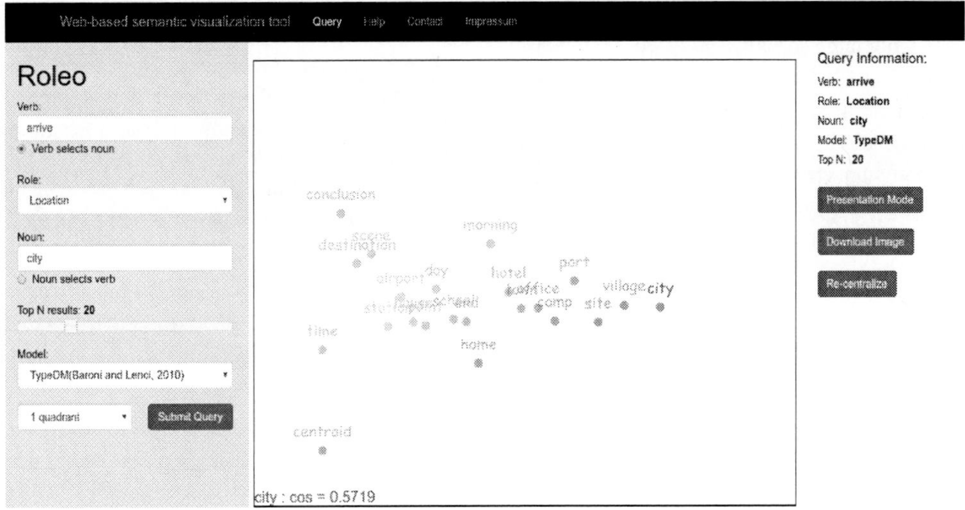

Figure 4: Query result (without zooming) for "city" as location of "arrive" under TypeDM with a 1-quadrant sweep and a space constructed from 20 prototype noun vectors.

available to enter a noun, a verb, and a role. The roles available are dependent on the model chosen. A slider allows the choice of between 10 and 50 top prototype vectors in increments of 10, and the choice of quadrant sweep size is available, including a "4-span by cosine" option, which is the direct interpretation of the polar coordinates.

The radio buttons "Verb selects noun" and "Noun selects verb" allows the user to set the direction in which the thematic fit query is executed. "Verb selects noun" is the default algorithm that chooses prototype nouns based on a verb-role combination. "Noun selects verb" allows the user to explore the choice of verbs based on a noun-role combination.

Main canvas   The central pane of the Roleo page is the canvas on which the vectors are visualized. This pane can be scrolled and zoomed via mouse or touch gestures, depending on the user's browser, operating system, and hardware. The vectors are shown as small labeled circles on the canvas, with the gray dot as the centroid, usually located in the center for the 4- and 32-quadrant sweep displays. The queried vector is highlighted in red; the labels for the other vectors appear when the canvas decides there is space for them or when they are moused over. The bottom left corner contains the cosine similarity score (with the centroid) for the queried vector, and the bottom right corner displays the cosine similarity of a moused-over or

touched vector.

Right pane   Roleo's right pane contains the details of the query currently represented on the canvas, in case the user needs a reminder of the previous field contents as they change the fields to explore the space. In addition, it contains a button to shift Roleo into a full-screen presentation mode, a button to download the depicted space as an image file, and a button ("Re-centralize") to return the current query to its default view and cancel the effect of scrolling or zooming.

4.2   Example lookups

Figures 2 and 3 contain queries about "cut" and "knife" for TypeDM and SDDM respectively. For TypeDM, we chose the instrument role; for SDDM, we chose manner (PropBank "ARGM-MNR"). With TypeDM, we see items that are knife-like. Most of what appears there that is *not* knife-like can be used with the preposition "with", as we have defined the instrument role for querying TypeDM (section 2.2). Other parts of the space not depicted here contain less knife-like items, such as a region where "chainsaw", "clipper", "mower", and "grinder" are close to one another.

For SDDM, we also see knife-like instruments, but we see "half" and "manner", as in "cut in half" and "cut in a manner", also a result of PropBank. There is also probable noise in both cases (e.g.

"have", "hole"), as these spaces are ultimately derived from large corpora.

Figure 4 is a 1-quadrant, 20-prototype view of the "arrive"-location combination given a queried noun of "city" under TypeDM. This is therefore a rectangular view. Given the FCVM projection, "city" is in the middle of the group along the y-axis, meaning that it is the middle of the group for cosines. However, it is far along the x-axis, meaning that it had comparatively low LMI score with respect to "arrive" and the location role.

5 Demonstration

The centrepiece of our demonstration at the conference is a laptop or other computer display that allows conference visitors to interact with Roleo, as we explain its capabilities and advantages and explore different vector spaces with the help of an associated poster.

6 Future work

Roleo is under active development, and we intend to include significant additional features. Among these:

Adding models We plan to add more models, including newer, dense word-embedding spaces for comparison, in order to help us diagnose why these spaces seem to perform less well than DMs on the thematic fit task (Baroni et al., 2014).

More visualizations FCVM provides a way to project high-dimensional vector spaces down to two dimensions in a reasonable time for web use on a single thread on a single server. It principally represents the location of a vector with respect to the centroid, which is ideal for thematic fit modeling, and it leads to a tendency for vectors related via the verb to be close to one another. However, it loses a direct geometric or probabilistic interpretation of the proximity of vectors. Therefore, we are investigating the possibility of adapting FCVM and more processor-intensive procedures like t-SNE and PCA to one another. Currently, we are testing a lightweight SVD-based visualization algorithm that still centers points around the centroid; although it is more computationally intensive than FCVM, our preliminary observations are that it produces more well-defined clusters in acceptable time.

References

Marco Baroni, Georgiana Dinu, and Germán Kruszewski. 2014. Don't count, predict! a systematic comparison of context-counting vs. context-predicting semantic vectors. In *Proceedings of the 52nd Annual Meeting of the Association for Computational Linguistics*. volume 1, pages 238–247.

Marco Baroni and Alessandro Lenci. 2010. Distributional memory: A general framework for corpus-based semantics. *Computational Linguistics* 36(4):673–721.

Ronan Collobert and Jason Weston. 2007. Fast semantic extraction using a novel neural network architecture. In *Proceedings of the 45th Annual Meeting of the Association of Computational Linguistics*. Association for Computational Linguistics, Prague, Czech Republic, pages 560–567.

Manaal Faruqui and Chris Dyer. 2014. Community evaluation and exchange of word vectors at wordvectors.org. In *Proceedings of the 52nd Annual Meeting of the Association for Computational Linguistics: System Demonstrations*. Association for Computational Linguistics, Baltimore, USA.

Clayton Greenberg, Vera Demberg, and Asad Sayeed. 2015. Verb polysemy and frequency effects in thematic fit modeling. In *Proceedings of the 6th Workshop on Cognitive Modeling and Computational Linguistics*. Association for Computational Linguistics, Denver, Colorado, pages 48–57.

Ulrike Padó. 2007. *The integration of syntax and semantic plausibility in a wide-coverage model of human sentence processing*. Ph.D. thesis, Saarland University.

Asad Sayeed, Vera Demberg, and Pavel Shkadzko. 2015. An exploration of semantic features in an unsupervised thematic fit evaluation framework. In *IJCoL vol. 1, n. 1 december 2015: Emerging Topics at the First Italian Conference on Computational Linguistics*. Accademia University Press, pages 25–40.

Laurens Van der Maaten and Geoffrey Hinton. 2008. Visualizing data using t-sne. *Journal of Machine Learning Research* 9(2579-2605):85.

MediaGist: A cross-lingual analyser of aggregated news and commentaries

Josef Steinberger
University of West Bohemia
Faculty of Applied Sciences
Department of Computer Science and Engineering, NTIS Center
Univerzitni 8, 30614 Pilsen, Czech Republic
`jstein@kiv.zcu.cz`

Abstract

We introduce MediaGist, an online system for crosslingual analysis of aggregated news and commentaries based on summarization and sentiment analysis technologies. It is designed to assist journalists to detect and explore news topics, which are controversially reported or discussed in different countries. News articles from current week are clustered separately in currently 5 languages and the clusters are then linked across languages. Sentiment analysis provides a basis to compute controversy scores and summaries help to explore the differences. Recognized entities play an important role in most of the system's modules and provide another way to explore the data. We demonstrate the capabilities of MediaGist by listing highlights from the last week and present a rough evaluation of the system.

1 Introduction

News portals publish thousands of articles every day in various languages. Making sense out of such data without automated tools is impossible.

There are many news aggregators/analysers and each of them has its strengths. Google News aggregates headlines and displays the stories according to each reader's interests. IBM Watson News Explorer gives a more analytical way to read news through linked data visualizations. Europe Media Monitor (EMM) produces a summary of news stories clustered near realtime in various languages and compares how the same events have been reported in the media written in different languages.

However, there is another source of information at the news sites – commentaries – which contain very valuable public opinion about the news top-ics and has not been explored enough yet. Including commentaries opens many new use cases for journalists, agencies, which study public opinion, and partially also for readers. Controversial topics, such as the refugee crisis in Europe, or the Volkswagen's emission scandal, and their perception in different countries might be itself a source for reporting. Focusing on such topics should bring more traffic and rich discussions to the news portals. International agencies or political institutions will find useful the comparisons when studying particular public opinions. Crosslingually-organized news and commentaries will be useful for readers living in a multicultural environment, as they can quickly find and understand different views on the controversial topics.

MediaGist[1] builds on the ideas of news aggregators, but adds the comments' dimension. It continuously gathers metadata about news articles and their commentaries, currently in 5 languages. Articles from current week are clustered monolingually several times a day. It extracts entities, labels news and commentaries with sentiment scores and generates summaries on both sides. It also links the clusters across languages, similarly to EMM. Having aggregated news on one side and commentaries on the other side, it compares the information by sentiment analysis and summarization. A different sentiment of news and commentaries indicate a controversial topic and summaries help to identify the difference qualitatively. The crosslingual links allow to discover and explore topics, which are controversially reported or discussed in different countries.

The next section (2) relates MediaGist to the current news aggregation or analytics solutions. Section 3 describes MediGist from inside. The

---

[1]MediaGist is running at: `http://mediagist.eu`. A screencast video can be found at: `https://www.youtube.com/watch?v=ONtKw_16_X4`.

Proceedings of the 54th Annual Meeting of the Association for Computational Linguistics—System Demonstrations, pages 145–150,
Berlin, Germany, August 7-12, 2016. ©2016 Association for Computational Linguistics

overall architecture is followed by a description of the NLP pipeline. Section 4 gives an overview of the system's functionality and shows highlights from the last week, followed by a rough evaluation of the system, conclusions and future plans.

2   Related sites

Google News[2] is an automatic service that aggregates headlines from more than 50K news sources worldwide, groups similar stories together, and displays them according to each reader's interests. The content is selected and ranked using many factors, e.g. coverage, freshness, location, relevance and diversity of the story. There are more than 70 regional editions in many different languages.

IBM Watson News Explorer[3] gives a more analytical way to read news. It gathers 250k articles a day from 70k sources and converts the unstructured text into entities and concepts, and connects the dots through linked data visualizations.

EMM NewsBrief[4] is a summary of news stories (news clusters) from around the world, automatically classified according to thousands of criteria. It is updated every 10 minutes, and over 100k articles in 50+ languages run through it a day. It automatically detects the stories that are the most reported in each language at the moment. The Alert system presents the stories in many different classifications (Atkinson and van der Goot, 2009).

The second EMM's technology, NewsExplorer[5], allows to see the major news stories in various languages for any specific day and to compare how the same events have been reported in different languages (Steinberger et al., 2009). It shows the most mentioned names and other automatically derived information, eg. variant name spellings or a list of related entities (Pouliquen and Steinberger, 2009).

To summarize, the current systems gather masses of news articles and cluster them into stories. Some systems do it in many languages, and few link the stories across languages. Analytical solutions add information extraction (locations, entities, relations or categories). However, they do not integrate commentaries, which complement well the stories with public opinion. MediaGist adds the commentaries and uses them for various monolingual or crosslingual comparisons resulting in discovering and exploring controversies in the whole data.

3   System overview

MediaGist processing starts with a crawler (see figure 1). It gathers articles and their comments from predefined news sites[6]. It creates an RSS file for each article, which goes down the NLP pipeline. The pipeline first recognizes entities, in both the article and its comments, and assigns a crosslingual id to each mention. The next step is performed by the sentiment analyser, which assigns to each article and comment a tonality score[7]. The coreference resolver then enriches the list of entity mentions by name part references and definite descriptions. Each entity mention is then assigned a sentiment score and article comments are summarized[8]. These fully annotated article RSS files enter the clustering phase. Every four hours, for each language, the clusterer takes the articles published during the current week and creates monolingual clusters. Since this step, RSS files contain information about all articles in the cluster. The crosslingual linker then adds to each cluster links to the most similar cluster in other languages. The last step is creating a summary of clustered articles and a summary of cluster's comments (already summarized per article before). The RSS now contains all information needed by the presentation layer, the MediaGist website.

3.1   NER and coreference

The named entity recognizer is based on JRC-Names[9], which is a highly multilingual named entity resource for person and organisation names (Steinberger et al., 2011c). It consists of large lists of names and their many spelling variants (up to hundreds for a single person), including across scripts (Steinberger and Pouliquen, 2009).

Because the resource does not contain many morphological variants for Czech, it was extended

---

[2]https://news.google.com/

[3]http://news-explorer.mybluemix.net/

[4]EMM (Europe Media Monitor) is developed at Joint Research Centre, European Commission: http://emm.newsbrief.eu

[5]http://emm.newsexplorer.eu

[6]Currently, it gathers data from 7 sources in 5 languages: English (theguardian.com), Czech (idnes.cz, ihned.cz, novinky.cz), Italian (corriere.it), French (lemonde.fr) and German (spiegel.de).

[7]We call a document-level sentiment 'tonality'.

[8]There can be even thousands of comments attached to a single article. This summarization step largely reduces the size of the data sent further down the pipeline.

[9]https://ec.europa.eu/jrc/en/language-technologies/jrc-names

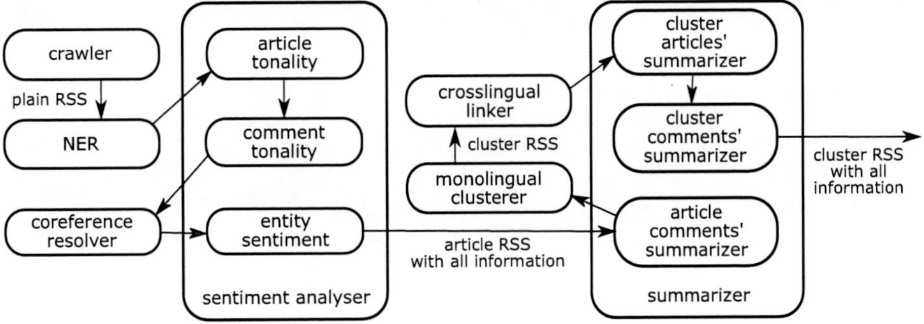

Figure 1: The architecture of MediaGist.

by an in-house rule-based morphological analyser.

Coreference resolution was inspired by (Steinberger et al., 2011a). In the cases of titles, it uses a list of person-title associations semi-automatically compiled over the past few years (Pouliquen and Steinberger, 2009).

3.2 Sentiment analysis

The sentiment analyser is used for 2 purposes. Assigning first a document-level tonality score $\langle -100; +100 \rangle$ to each article and comment, and second, a sentiment score $\langle -100; +100 \rangle$ to each entity mention. It uses highly multilingual and comparable sentiment dictionaries having similar sizes and based on a common specification, created by triangulation from English and Spanish (Steinberger et al., 2012). In the case of the tonality score, it counts subjective terms in an article, resp. a comment, and in the case of the entity score, it counts terms around entity mentions. It includes rules for using negation, intensifiers and diminishers (Steinberger et al., 2011b). Although machine learning approaches would produce better sentiment predictions, they require training data per language, and ideally per industry as well. And such data are currently expensive to create. With the rule-based approach, the system can easily process multiple languages.

3.3 Clustering and crosslingual linking

The monolingual clustering algorithm is based on agglomerative hierarchical clustering with the group average strategy (Hastie et al., 2009). The articles are represented by log-likelihood vectors of its terms and the similarity function is Cosine.

Crosslingual linking uses two kinds of features: entities and descriptors from EuroVoc[10]. EuroVoc

is a multilingual, multidisciplinary thesaurus covering the activities of the EU, the European Parliament in particular. It contains terms organized in a hierarchy in 23 EU languages. Using Eurovoc features ensures that the linked clusters share the same topic. If at the same time the clusters share the same entities[11], it is very likely that the clusters are about the same story. A similar approach as in (Steinberger, 2013).

3.4 Summarization

The summarizer is used for three steps of the pipeline. First, it summarizes article comments, then articles in the cluster and finally comments of the cluster. We use an extractive approach based on latent semantic analysis, which uses both lexical and entity features (Kabadjov et al., 2013). This approach performed well in the Multiling evaluation campaigns[12].

4 Functionality

The systems has two main views to explore the media data: cluster view and entity view. We can select a language, a period (=week) and sort the data by different criteria[13]. Each view contains highlights of the selected period in the left panel.

4.1 The cluster view

It displays title and description, taken from the central article of the cluster (see figure 2). The left part shows information about articles and the right part about commentaries. On both sides, it displays generated summaries and aggregated tonal-

---

[10]http://eurovoc.europa.eu

[11]The entity ids are unified across languages.

[12]There were already 3 editions of MultiLing's multilingual multi-document summarization shared task: 2011 (Giannakopoulos et al., 2011), 2013, and 2015 (Giannakopoulos et al., 2015).

[13]The system currently holds data from the last 24 weeks.

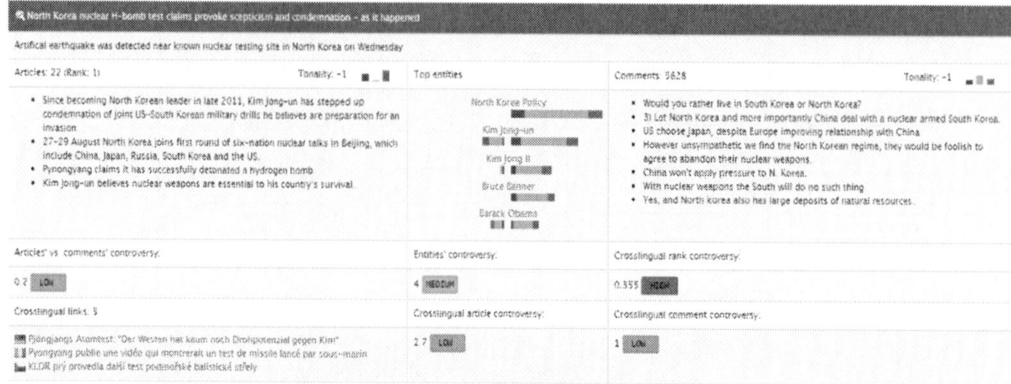

Figure 2: The top English cluster from the first week of 2016 (Jan 4th-10th). The screenshot does not include the page header, the left bar with highlights and the footer. More at http://mediagist.eu

ity figures. The central part shows entities and their sentiment in articles and comments.[14] At the bottom, you can see links to the related clusters in other languages.

MediaGist computes several controversy scores for each cluster. *Articles' vs. comments' controversy* compares tonality of articles and comments. The value correspond to the standard deviation of the two values. *Entities' controversy* compares sentiment of entity mentions in articles and comments. The value is a macro-average of standard deviations of each entity sentiment. *Crosslingual rank controversy* compares ranks of the cluster in different languages. Clusters are ranked for each language based on the number of articles. The value is a standard deviation of logarithms of the ranks. Logarithms give larger weights to the top ranks. This controversy is large if the topic is ranked at the top for some languages based on the coverage, while in other languages it is mentioned only marginally. Large *Crosslingual article controversy* indicates a large difference in articles' tonality among languages. The value is a standard deviation of average article tonalities across languages. This score says whether the topic is reported with the same tonality in different languages or not. And finally, a large *Crosslingual comment controversy* indicates topics which are discussed with different tonality across languages. The score compares average comment tonalities across languages by the standard deviation.

4.2 The entity view

The entity view displays variants of the entity found in the data (e.g. for David Bowie in week Jan 11-17, 2016: Bowie (3816 mentions), David Bowie (914), David (74), singer (60), star (46), musician (33), popstar (5), etc.). It shows the aggregated entity sentiment in articles and comments, which is compared by *Articles' vs. comments' controversy*. The sentiment is summarized by the most frequent subjective terms on both sides. Because we have also the entities linked across languages, we can compute their crosslingual controversy in articles and in comments. We can then easily find, which entities are reported or discussed with different sentiment across languages. As an example, Volkswagen is discussed negatively in Czech but positively in German (when all periods are selected).

4.3 Highlights from the last week

The most international topic during week (Mar 21-27, 2016) was *Fayal Cheffou charged over core role in Brussels bomb attacks* – covered well in all 5 languages. The English summary:

At least 31 dead and more than 200 injured in bombings claimed by Islamic State. The attackers Brothers Khalid and Ibrahim el-Bakraoui have been identified as suicide bombers at the metro station and airport respectively. Before the Brussels attacks, Belgian prosecutors said DNA evidence had identified Moroccan-born Laachraoui as an accomplice of Paris attacker Salah Abdeslam. He was one of several men detained in police raids on Thursday. "What we feared has happened," said the Belgian prime minister, Charles Michel, at a press conference.

The following story was controversial in coverage: *Ukrainian pilot given 22-year jail sentence by Russian court* – one of the top clus-

---

[14]Tonality/sentiment range is: $\langle -100; +100 \rangle$, green column = positive, orange = neutral, red = negative.

ters in Czech but only few articles in English and French. The same topic was seen as controversially reported as well – the tonality of Czech articles was much more negative than English and French ones. A controversially discussed topic: *Sanders: 'We have a path towards victory' after win Washington caucuses* – while positive in English, negative in Czech. Reasons of the controversy can be found in the summaries.

Controversial entity in articles: *Donald Trump* – negative in English, close to neutral in Italian and French and positive in German and Czech. Difference between sentiment in articles and comments: *John Key* – positive in articles but negative in comments (English). Controversial entity in comments: *George W. Bush* – while the sentiment is balanced in English, it is negative in Czech and positive in German. The most frequent sentiment terms indicate the reasons: English: *good, helped, better, evil, violence*; German: *liebesmüh* (love effort), *deutlich besser* (clearly better), Czech: *zločiny* (crimes), *odsuzovat* (accusing), *špatný* (bad).

5 Evaluation

We present a rough evaluation of the key modules of the system. We discus results of NER, coreference, sentiment analysis and summarization obtained in the previous research. In the case of clustering, crosslingual linking and controversy predictions we validated the system output to get the first insight of their accuracy.

5.1 NER and coreference

The precision of the applied NER and coreference was measured in Steinberger et al. (2011a). From the current MediaGist's languages, person recognition performs best for French (98.4%) and worst for Italian (92.1%). The coreference module resolves name parts at precision of 98% and person title references at 70%. As the title references have not been continuously updated yet, several wrong references are caused by the missing temporal dimension.

5.2 Sentiment analysis

The accuracy of the sentiment analyser in all MediaGist's languages was measured in Steinberger et al. (2011b). For news sentences and entity targets, we got the best accuracy for English (74%) and the worst for Italian (66%). However, in the case of aggregating the polarities per entity and considering only entities with a larger difference between positive and negative mentions (extremely polar entities), 78% of entity classifications across all languages were correct.

5.3 Summarization

The LSA-based summarizer was evaluated during the last edition of the Multiling's multi-document summarization shared task (Giannakopoulos et al., 2015) as the top performing system overall (it received the lowest sum of ranks over all 10 languages). From the MediaGist's languages, it performed best in Czech, English and French. German and Italian was not included.

5.4 Clustering and crosslingual linking

In the case of clustering and crosslingual linking, we asked two annotators to validate the output of the system. The annotators were not fluent speakers in all 5 languages, but they had enough knowledge to judge the task. We selected the top 5 English clusters from the first 4 full weeks of 2016. The clusters were ranked based on the number of crosslingual links. The task of the clustering validation was to check whether the components of the cluster are relevant to the cluster's topic identified by the title of its central article. In the case of the crosslingual linking, the task was to check the similarity of the linked clusters based on their article titles. Clustering validation was found not to be that subjective, the inter-annotator kappa was .89. The validation of crosslingual links was more difficult, the annotators did not always agree (kappa was .63), mainly because of a different view on the right granularity of the topic (e.g. the clusters were both discussing the regugee crisis, but in one language it was about closing the borders and in the other about a disorder in Germany). From the total of 235 cluster components, 96% were judged as correct and from the 59 crosslingual links, 76% were pointing to the right cluster of the other language.

5.5 Controversy scores

We selected the most interesting controversy score, crosslingual comment controversy, to be judged by two annotators. For each crosslingual link evaluated in 5.4, we took the corresponding comment summaries (each in a different language) and showed them to an annotator. Her task was to assess whether the view of the topic/entities is different (controversial) in the two languages or not. The task definition was rather shallow, but still there was a fair agreement (kappa was .48). We then produced a gold controversy scores: for instance if we had a topic linked across 5 languages, there were 10 combinations judged twice. The Boolean judgements were aggregated and normalized, resulting in a score between 0 and 1. These golden scores were then compared against the system's crosslingual comment controversy scores by Pearson correlation: .51. Although the correlation is not perfect, the measure can already be useful to indicate controversy.

6 Conclusion

MediaGist uses language technology to detect controversy in world news. Sentiment analysis helps to identify controversial topics and entities across languages, and via summarization it is possible to explore them in detail. The controversy scores are much dependent on the quality of sentiment analysis. Improving the sentiment module will directly lead to better predictions. Future plans include increasing the data volume on on both vertical (sources) and horizontal (historical data) axes. This will allow to study the evolution of a news thread or of a person name. The system currently consumes raw commentaries. Representing a precise opinion of real Internet users will require to fight trolls and filter the conversations (Mihaylov et al., 2015).

Acknowledgments

This work was supported by project MediaGist, EUs FP7 People Programme (Marie Curie Actions), no. 630786. MediaGist.

References

M. Atkinson and E. van der Goot. 2009. Near real time information mining in multilingual news. In *Proceedings of the 18th International World Wide Web Conference (WWW 2009)*, pages 1153–1154, Madrid, Spain.

G. Giannakopoulos, M. El-Haj, B. Favre, M. Litvak, J. Steinberger, and V. Varma. 2011. TAC2011 MultiLing Pilot Overview. In *TAC 2011 Workshop*.

G. Giannakopoulos, J. Kubina, J. Conroy, J. Steinberger, B. Favre, M. Kabadjov, U. Kruschwitz, and M. Poesio. 2015. Multiling 2015: Multilingual summarization of single and multi-documents, online fora, and call-center conversations. In *Proceedings of the 16th Annual Meeting of the Special Interest Group on Discourse and Dialogue*, pages 270–274. ACL.

T. Hastie, R. Tibshirani, and J. Friedman. 2009. *The Elements of Statistical Learning*. Springer-Verlag.

M. Kabadjov, J. Steinberger, and R. Steinberger. 2013. Multilingual statistical news summarization. In *Multilingual Information Extraction and Summarization*, volume 2013 of *Theory and Applications of Natural Language Processing*, pages 229–252. Springer.

T. Mihaylov, G. Georgiev, and P. Nakov. 2015. Finding opinion manipulation trolls in news community forums. In *Proceedings of the 19th CoNLL*, pages 310–314. ACL.

B. Pouliquen and R. Steinberger. 2009. Automatic construction of multilingual name dictionaries. In *Learning Machine Translation*. MIT Press.

R. Steinberger and B. Pouliquen. 2009. Crosslingual named entity recognition. In *Named Entities - Recognition, Classification and Use*, volume 19 of *Benjamins Current Topics*, pages 137–164. John Benjamins Publishing Company.

R. Steinberger, B. Pouliquen, and C. Ignat. 2009. Using language-independent rules to achieve high multilinguality in text mining. In *Mining Massive Data Sets for Security*. IOS-Press, Amsterdam, Holland.

J. Steinberger, J. Belyaeva, J. Crawley, L. Della-Rocca, M. Ebrahim, M. Ehrmann, M. Kabadjov, R. Steinberger, and E. Van der Goot. 2011a. Highly multilingual coreference resolution exploiting a mature entity repository. In *Proceedings of the 8th RANLP Conference*, pages 254–260. Incoma Ltd.

J. Steinberger, P. Lenkova, M. Kabadjov, R. Steinberger, and E. van der Goot. 2011b. Multilingual entity-centered sentiment analysis evaluated by parallel corpora. In *Proceedings of the 8th RANLP Conference*, pages 770–775.

R. Steinberger, B. Pouliquen, M. Kabadjov, J. Belyaeva, and E. van der Goot. 2011c. Jrcnames: A freely available, highly multilingual named entity resource. In *Proceedings of the International RANLP Conference*. Incoma Ltd.

J. Steinberger, M. Ebrahim, M. Ehrmann, A. Hurriyetoglu, M. Kabadjov, P. Lenkova, R. Steinberger, H. Tanev, S. Vzquez, and V. Zavarella. 2012. Creating sentiment dictionaries via triangulation. *Decision Support Systems*, 53(4):689 – 694.

R. Steinberger. 2013. Multilingual and cross-lingual news analysis in the europe media monitor (emm). In *Multidisciplinary Information Retrieval*, volume 8201 of *LNCS*, pages 1–4. Springer.

GoWvis: a web application for Graph-of-Words-based text visualization and summarization

Antoine J.-P. Tixier, Konstantinos Skianis, and Michalis Vazirgiannis
Computer Science Laboratory
École Polytechnique, France

Abstract

We introduce `GoWvis`[1], an interactive web application that represents any piece of text inputted by the user as a graph-of-words and leverages graph degeneracy and community detection to generate an extractive summary (keyphrases and sentences) of the inputted text in an unsupervised fashion. The entire analysis can be fully customized via the tuning of many text preprocessing, graph building, and graph mining parameters. Our system is thus well suited to educational purposes, exploration and early research experiments. The new summarization strategy we propose also shows promise.

1 Introduction

The term independence assumption made by the traditional Bag-of-Words (BoW) representation of text comes with many limitations. One approach that challenges this assumption is the Graph-of-Words model (GoW). As shown in Figure 1, it represents a textual document as a graph whose vertices are unique terms in the document and whose edges capture term co-occurrence within a window of predetermined, fixed size, that is slided over the entire document from start to finish.

This approach is statistical, as terms are linked based on local context of co-occurrence only, regardless of any semantic or syntactic information (Distributional Hypothesis). Unlike BoW, GoW encodes term dependency and term order (via directed edges). The strength of the dependence between two words can also be captured by assigning a weight to the edge that links them. While other definitions can be used, we consider here edge

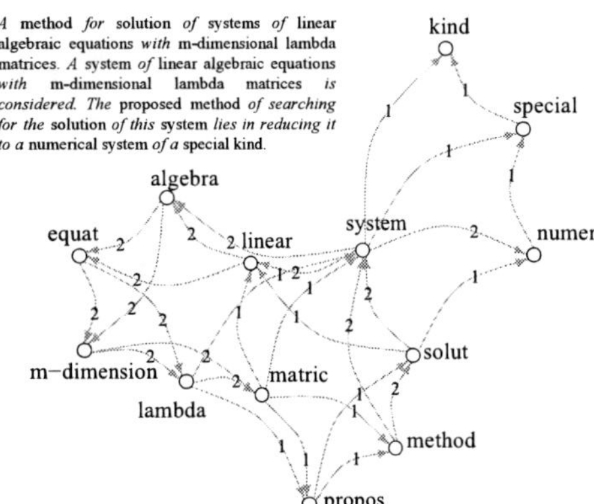

Figure 1: Graph-of-Words representation with POS-based screening, and directed, weighted edges. Non-(nouns and adjectives) in *italic*.

weights to be integers matching co-occurrence counts.

GoW can be tracked back to the works of (Mihalcea and Tarau, 2004) and (Erkan and Radev, 2004) who applied it to the tasks of unsupervised keyword extraction and extractive single document summarization. Notably, the former effort ranked nodes based on a modified version of the PageRank algorithm.

Recently, (Rousseau and Vazirgiannis, 2015) showed that degeneracy-based approaches (i.e., extracting dense, cohesive subgraphs) could outperform PageRank for unsupervised keyword extraction. We will show in subsection 3.4 how combining this strategy with graph clustering may improve summarization performance for multitopic documents. Other NLP tasks on which GoW-based approaches have reached new state-of-the-art include ad-hoc information retrieval (Rousseau and Vazirgiannis, 2013) and document classification (Rousseau et al., 2015; Malliaros and Skianis, 2015). The high success, promising potential and visual nature of the GoW representation was the impetus for the development of `GoWvis`.

---

[1] https://safetyapp.shinyapps.io/GoWvis/

Proceedings of the 54th Annual Meeting of the Association for Computational Linguistics—System Demonstrations, pages 151–156,
Berlin, Germany, August 7-12, 2016. ©2016 Association for Computational Linguistics

The remainder of this paper is organized as follows: Section 2 provides some background on graph degeneracy and community detection, Section 3 presents our system, and finally, Section 4 concludes and discusses future work.

2 Graph mining

2.1 Graph degeneracy

k-core. A core of order k (or k-core) of a graph G is a maximal connected subgraph of G in which every vertex v has at least degree k (Seidman, 1983). It is a relaxation of a clique: a k-core with $k + 1$ members is a subgraph where every two nodes are adjacent, that is, a clique (Luce and Perry, 1949). In the classical unweighted case, edge weights are not taken into account and thus the degree of a node v is simply equal to the number of its neighbors. In the weighted (or generalized) case, the degree of a vertex v is the sum of the weights of its incident edges.

k-core decomposition. The k-core decomposition of a graph G is the list of all its cores from 0 (G itself) to k_{max} (its main core). It forms a hierarchy of subgraphs that are recursively included in one another and whose cohesiveness and size respectively increases and decreases with k (Seidman, 1983). A linear (resp. linearithmic) time algorithm for k-core decomposition can be found in (Batagelj and Zaveršnik, 2002) for the unweighted (resp. weighted) case. Both algorithms implement a pruning process that removes the lowest degree node at each step.

The **core number** of a node is the highest order of a core that contains this node. Nodes with high core numbers have the desirable property of not only being central (like nodes with high degree centrality) but also part of cohesive subgraphs with other central nodes (i.e., the other members of the upper cores). For this reason, they make, among other things, influential spreaders (Kitsak et al., 2010) and good keywords (Rousseau and Vazirgiannis, 2015).

The main core of a graph yields a fast (but rough) approximation of its densest subgraph. Indeed, it may contain in some cases a very large portion of the nodes of the graph. As (Seidman, 1983) puts it, k-cores should be regarded as *seedbeds* within which it is possible to find more cohesive subgraphs.

k-truss. A triangle-based extension of k-core that yields densest subgraphs is k-truss (Cohen, 2008). More precisely, the k-truss of a graph G is the largest subgraph of G in which every edge belongs to at least $k - 2$ cycle subgraphs of length 3 (i.e., triangles). Put differently, every edge in the k-truss joins two vertices that have at least $k - 2$ common neighbors.

k-truss decomposition. The k-truss decomposition of a graph G is the set of all its k-trusses from $k - 2$ to k_{max}. The k-trusses correspond to densely connected *subsets* of the k-cores that can be viewed as their essential parts (Malliaros et al., 2016). The maximal k-truss thus yields a smaller and denser subgraph of G that better approximates its densest subgraph. Nevertheless, the finer resolution of the k-truss decomposition comes at the cost of a greater complexity, polynomial in the number of edges (Wang and Cheng, 2012).

By analogy with k-core, the **truss number** of an *edge* is the highest order of a truss the edge belongs to. By extension, we define the truss number of a *node* as the maximum truss number of its incident edges, like in (Malliaros et al., 2016).

We wrote our own implementation of weighted k-core in R (R Core Team, 2015). For unweighted k-core, we used the `igraph` package (Csardi and Nepusz, 2006), and for k-truss, the C++ implementation offered by (Wang and Cheng, 2012).

2.2 Community detection

While the k-core and k-truss decomposition algorithms converge towards the *unique* most cohesive subgraph of a graph, the task of community detection consists in clustering a graph into *multiple* groups within which connections are dense and between which they are sparse (Fortunato, 2010).

Many community detection algorithms have been proposed, of which some of the most popular are listed below. The fundamental *Modularity* function used by the first three algorithms measures the strength of the partition of a graph by comparing the number of within-group edges to the expected such number in a null model (Newman and Girvan, 2004).

The *fast greedy* algorithm (Clauset et al., 2004) merges at each step the pair of nodes that yields the largest gain in modularity until a single community remains. The best partition is the one associated with the greatest modularity value.

The *multi-level* (or *Louvain*) algorithm (Blondel et al., 2008) first aggregates each node with one of its neighbors such that the gain in modularity is maximized. Then, the groupings obtained at the first step are turned into nodes, yielding a new graph. This two-step process iterates until a peak in modularity is attained and no more change occurs.

The *walktrap* algorithm (Pons and Latapy, 2005) uses agglomerative hierarchical clustering with a random walk-based distance between vertices to obtain a set of subdivisions of the graph. The optimal clustering is given by the level of the hierarchy that maximizes modularity.

Finally, the *infomap* algorithm (Rosvall and Bergstrom, 2008) optimizes the map equation to find an optimal compression of a description of information flow in the graph. Unlike other aforementioned algorithms, *infomap* works for directed networks.

We used the R wrappers of the `igraph` C implementations of the algorithms presented above. Note that all `igraph` implementations can (optionally) take edge weights into account. Unless mentioned, all other parameters remained at their default values.

3 GoWvis

Our system was developed in R Shiny (Chang et al., 2015), and can be broken down into the four modules shown in Figure 2. The steps are sequential except the last two which are performed in parallel. In what follows, we present the tuning parameters involved at each step and discuss their individual impact (all other parameters being held constant).

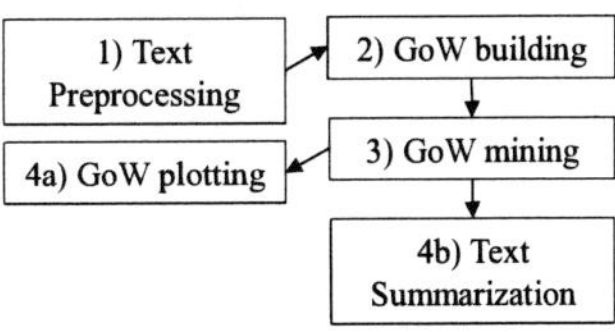

Figure 2: System architecture

3.1 Text preprocessing

The first module cleans the inputted text by (1) removing special characters, punctuation marks except the ones indicative of sentence boundary (used by the second module, see subsection 3.2) and intra-word dashes, (2) removing numbers except dates (like "2016"), and (3) tokenizing. In addition to R built-in functions, the `stringr` package (Wickham, 2015) is used here. Also, text is

split into sentences using the implementation of the Apache OpenNLP Maxent sentence detector offered by the `openNLP` R package (Hornik, 2015). The list of sentences is eventually passed to the fourth module (see subsection 3.4). Additionally, the user is provided with the following tuning parameters:

Keep only nouns and adjectives? Boolean, defaults to TRUE. Uses `openNLP`'s implementation of the Apache OpenNLP Maxent POS tagger to perform part-of-speech (POS) tagging. Then, following (Mihalcea and Tarau, 2004), only nouns and adjectives are kept.

Stopwords removal. Boolean, defaults to TRUE. Only actionable if no POS-based screening is performed. Removes common English stopwords[2] from the SMART information retrieval system.

Stemming. Boolean, defaults to TRUE. Retains only the stem of each term by implementing Porter's stemmer with the R `SnowballC` package (Bouchet-Valat, 2014). For instance, when stemming is performed, *win* and *winning* are both collapsed to *win*. Stemming thus tends to yield smaller and denser graphs.

The unique words that passed the aforelisted preprocessing steps are then used as the nodes of the graph-of-words.

3.2 Graph-of-Words building

The graph-of-words is constructed by adding edges between the n nodes previously obtained. Complexity is $O(nW)$ where W is window size. The module offers the following tuning parameters:

Window size. Integer between 2 and 12, defaults to 3. Specifies the size of the window slided over the document. Values around 3 and 4 have been reported to work well (Mihalcea and Tarau, 2004; Malliaros and Skianis, 2015). Note that the larger the window, the denser the graph, since more edges are created while the number of nodes remains constant.

Build on processed text? Boolean, defaults to TRUE. Whether the window should be slided over the (1) processed or the (2) unprocessed text. May yield very different results, depending on the preprocessing steps that have been applied. Indeed,

---

[2]`http://jmlr.org/papers/volume5/`
`lewis04a/all-smart-stop-list/english.`
`stop`

two words that are initially very distant in the original, *unprocessed* text and whose co-occurence would therefore not be captured may end up close to each other in the *processed* text if many words between them (e.g., stopwords) were removed as a result of preprocessing. Consequently, building the graph from the processed text tends to link more distant words and produce denser graphs than when using the unprocessed text.

Overspan sentences? Boolean, defaults to TRUE. If FALSE, an edge between two co-occurring words is only created (or if the edge already exists, its weight is only incremented) if the two words belong to the same sentence. The punctuation marks ".", ";", "!", "?", and "..." are used here as sentence boundaries.

Color. List, defaults to `heat`. A set of five built-in R palettes to color the nodes of the graph, including the color-blind-friendly `gray.colors`. Node colors match their core (or truss) number (also indicated in a legend) and go darker as k increases.

3.3 Graph-of-Words mining

This module analyzes the graph-of-words returned at the previous step using graph degeneracy and community detection. The user can tweak the following parameters to customize the analysis:

Degeneracy. List, defaults to "weighted k-core". Choice of the graph decomposition method, among "k-core", "weighted k-core", and "k-truss". If "weighted k-core" is selected, the edge weights appear as edge labels in the plot.

Directed? Boolean, defaults to TRUE. Whether edge direction should be taken into account in computing node degree. Only actionable if a degree-based degeneracy algorithm has been selected (i.e., any but "k-truss"). When TRUE, edges in the plot feature arrows indicating their direction.

Mode. List, defaults to "all". Which of the incident edges of a node should be taken into account in computing its degree, between "all" (all edges), "in" (incoming edges only), or "out" (outgoing edges only). Only actionable if edge direction is taken into account, and only impacts the output of the k-core algorithms. Note that the default value "all" gives the same results as when edge direction is ignored, but generates a plot with arrow edges.

Community detection? List, defaults to "none".

Choice of the graph clustering algorithm, among "fast greedy", "louvain", "walktrap", "infomap", and "none". If not "none", each main community (see *size threshold* parameter below) is separately degenerated. If "walktrap", the user can select the length of the random walks between 2 and 8 (defaults to 4). If "infomap", the user can specify whether edge direction should be taken into account. Clustering increases coverage for multitopic documents.

Weighted? Boolean, defaults to FALSE. Whether edge weights should be used by the community detection algorithm. Only actionable if the community detection parameter is not "none". If TRUE, the edge weights appear as edge labels in the plot.

Size threshold. Numeric (from 0.4 to 1.0, by 0.1), defaults to 0.8. Only actionable if the community detection parameter is not "none". Percentile size threshold used to determine which communities should be considered to be *main* ones. For instance, the default value of 0.8 retains as main communities the ones whose sizes (i.e., number of nodes) exceed that of 80% of all detected communities. As will be further illustrated in subsection 3.4, this parameter enables the user to chose whether the summary should cover only the *major* or also the *subtle* topics of the document. Nonetheless, diminishing *size threshold* increases the risk of including irrelevant (or noise) topics in the summary.

3.4 Text summarization

The fourth module uses the results from the previous step (graph mining) to (1) extract keyphrases from and (2) select a subset of the original sentences in the document inputted by the user in an unsupervised manner. It is performed in parallel with the graph plotting module (see subsection 3.5).

1. Keyphrase extraction. The terms whose core (or truss) number is exactly equal to $k_{max} - p$ are used as seeds from which keyphrases (n-grams) are reconstructed. p is an integer parameter between 0 and 10 that lets the user navigate the core (or truss) hierarchy up and down. If $p = 0$ (the default), the main core is used. Whenever $k_{max} \leq p$, the user is informed that their selection is empty. In practice, one would want to retain all the words whose core (or truss) number is at least equal to $k_{max} - p$, that is, the members of the $(k_{max} - p)$-core (or truss), and this is indeed what we do for sentence selection (see "Sentence selection" paragraph below). Here though, we only use a single slice of the hierarchy (called a *shell*) to make it clear for the user how the process of keyword extraction and keyphrase reconstruction works.

Reconciliation is then performed by pasting together the seeds that are found adjacent in the original, unprocessed text. For example, if "algebra" and "linear" both belong to the selected shell and "linear algebra" is present in the text, the two seeds are collapsed and added to the set of candidate keyphrases. Duplicates and keyphrases included in higher order keyphrases are then discarded.

When community detection is used, as already explained, each main community is separately degenerated. The entire process of keyterm extraction and keyphrase reconstruction is then run for each main community, ensuring that keyphrases cover the main topics in the document.

Example. We created a two-topic 925-word document[3] by drawing and intertwining an equal number of sentences from two Wikipedia articles, one about the website *Stack Overflow* (SO) and one about *pizza*. With all default parameters, the keyphrases extracted are all about SO: *stack overflow, user, answer question...* However, still with all default parameters, by simply enabling community detection (e.g., with "fast greedy"), the two topics are detected (*answer question, pizza margherita, queen margherita*).

Related work. Similarly, (Bougouin et al., 2013) have used clustering and graph mining for keyphrase extraction, but the other way around. They first group candidate keyphrases into topics via hierarchical clustering (with a word overlap distance), and then apply PageRank on a complete graph with topic nodes and edge weights based on keyphrase offset positions. Closer to our approach is that of (Grineva et al., 2009). Like us, they also observe that terms tend to cluster based on topic and that the largest communities correspond to the main themes in the document. However, they use a complete graph where edges are weighted based on Wikipedia-based semantic relatedness. Additionally, they select *all* the terms in the top-ranked communities whereas we extract only a highly cohesive subgraph from each main group.

---

[3]https://github.com/Tixierae/examples/blob/master/sopz.txt

2. Sentence selection. Unlike for keyphrase extraction, the entire $k_{max} - p$ core (or truss) is used here as seedbed. Representative members are drawn from the list of sentences extracted from the original document (in subsection 3.1) following a three-step process: (1) sentences that do not contain any term belonging to the selected core (or truss) are pruned out, (2) the remaining sentences are ranked in decreasing order according to how many *different* central terms they feature, and finally, (3) sentences are selected one at a time from the top until a certain *summary length* has been reached. If two or more sentences have the same rank, the longest and least redundant is selected, where length is the number of words in the sentence and redundancy is computed in terms of word overlap with the current summary (stemming and stopword removal are performed based on user selection). The *summary length* tuning parameter is a decimal number (between 0.01 and 0.51, by 0.05, defaults to 0.01) indicating the percentage of total candidate sentences (from step 2 above) to include in the summary. Again, if community detection is performed, the process is run separately for each community, enabling coverage of the main topics in the document. In the previous example, using community detection generates a 11:1 compression ratio summary covering both themes (not shown here due to space limitations).

3.5 Graph plotting

Done in parallel with text summarization. Plots an interactive, dynamic browser-based representation of the graph-of-words using `igraph` and the `visNetwork` R package (Almende B.V. and Thieurmel, 2016).

4 Conclusion and next steps

We have presented `GoWvis`, a freely accessible web application providing an engaging illustration of the GoW concept and how it can be applied to unsupervised extractive single document summarization. Through trial and error, users can navigate the parameter space and develop an intuition as for which parameter values may be optimal for a given task and the particular type of text at hand. Future work should add support for directed degeneracy algorithms (Giatsidis et al., 2011). While showing promise, our summarization approach needs refinement and formal experiments to quantify how it compares to the state-of-the-art. When $p > 0$, taking into account the core (or truss) numbers of terms could yield better sentence ranking.

References

Almende B.V. and Benoit Thieurmel, 2016. *visNetwork: Network Visualization using 'vis.js' Library*. R package version 0.2.1.

Vladimir Batagelj and Matjaž Zaveršnik. 2002. Generalized cores. *arXiv preprint cs/0202039*.

Vincent D Blondel, Jean-Loup Guillaume, Renaud Lambiotte, and Etienne Lefebvre. 2008. Fast unfolding of communities in large networks. *Journal of statistical mechanics: theory and experiment*, 2008(10):P10008.

Milan Bouchet-Valat, 2014. *SnowballC: Snowball stemmers based on the C libstemmer UTF-8 library*. R package version 0.5.1.

Adrien Bougouin, Florian Boudin, and Béatrice Daille. 2013. Topicrank: Graph-based topic ranking for keyphrase extraction. In *International Joint Conference on Natural Language Processing (IJCNLP)*, pages 543–551.

Winston Chang, Joe Cheng, JJ Allaire, Yihui Xie, and Jonathan McPherson, 2015. *shiny: Web Application Framework for R*. R package version 0.12.2.

Aaron Clauset, Mark EJ Newman, and Cristopher Moore. 2004. Finding community structure in very large networks. *Physical review E*, 70(6):066111.

Jonathan Cohen. 2008. Trusses: Cohesive subgraphs for social network analysis. *National Security Agency Technical Report*, page 16.

Gabor Csardi and Tamas Nepusz. 2006. The igraph software package for complex network research. *InterJournal*, Complex Systems:1695.

Günes Erkan and Dragomir R Radev. 2004. Lexrank: Graph-based lexical centrality as salience in text summarization. *Journal of Artificial Intelligence Research*, pages 457–479.

Santo Fortunato. 2010. Community detection in graphs. *Physics reports*, 486(3):75–174.

Christos Giatsidis, Dimitrios M Thilikos, and Michalis Vazirgiannis. 2011. D-cores: Measuring collaboration of directed graphs based on degeneracy. In *Data Mining (ICDM), 2011 IEEE 11th International Conference on*, pages 201–210. IEEE.

Maria Grineva, Maxim Grinev, and Dmitry Lizorkin. 2009. Extracting key terms from noisy and multitheme documents. In *Proceedings of the 18th international conference on World wide web*, pages 661–670. ACM.

Kurt Hornik, 2015. *openNLP: Apache OpenNLP Tools Interface*. R package version 0.2-5.

Maksim Kitsak, Lazaros K Gallos, Shlomo Havlin, Fredrik Liljeros, Lev Muchnik, H Eugene Stanley, and Hernán A Makse. 2010. Identification of influential spreaders in complex networks. *Nature physics*, 6(11):888–893.

R Duncan Luce and Albert D Perry. 1949. A method of matrix analysis of group structure. *Psychometrika*, 14(2):95–116.

Fragkiskos D Malliaros and Konstantinos Skianis. 2015. Graph-based term weighting for text categorization. In *Proceedings of the 2015 IEEE/ACM International Conference on Advances in Social Networks Analysis and Mining 2015*, pages 1473–1479. ACM.

Fragkiskos D Malliaros, Maria-Evgenia G Rossi, and Michalis Vazirgiannis. 2016. Locating influential nodes in complex networks. *Scientific reports*, 6:19307.

Rada Mihalcea and Paul Tarau. 2004. Textrank: Bringing order into texts. Association for Computational Linguistics.

Mark EJ Newman and Michelle Girvan. 2004. Finding and evaluating community structure in networks. *Physical review E*, 69(2):026113.

Pascal Pons and Matthieu Latapy. 2005. Computing communities in large networks using random walks. In *Computer and Information Sciences-ISCIS 2005*, pages 284–293. Springer.

R Core Team, 2015. *R: A Language and Environment for Statistical Computing*. R Foundation for Statistical Computing, Vienna, Austria.

Martin Rosvall and Carl T Bergstrom. 2008. Maps of random walks on complex networks reveal community structure. *Proceedings of the National Academy of Sciences*, 105(4):1118–1123.

François Rousseau and Michalis Vazirgiannis. 2013. Graph-of-word and tw-idf: new approach to ad hoc ir. In *Proceedings of the 22nd ACM international conference on Conference on information & knowledge management*, pages 59–68. ACM.

François Rousseau and Michalis Vazirgiannis. 2015. Main core retention on graph-of-words for single-document keyword extraction. In *Advances in Information Retrieval*, pages 382–393. Springer.

François Rousseau, Emmanouil Kiagias, and Michalis Vazirgiannis. 2015. Text categorization as a graph classification problem. In *ACL*, volume 15, page 107.

Stephen B Seidman. 1983. Network structure and minimum degree. *Social networks*, 5(3):269–287.

Jia Wang and James Cheng. 2012. Truss decomposition in massive networks. *Proceedings of the VLDB Endowment*, 5(9):812–823.

Hadley Wickham, 2015. *stringr: Simple, Consistent Wrappers for Common String Operations*. R package version 1.0.0.

LiMoSINe pipeline: Multilingual UIMA-based NLP platform

Olga Uryupina[1], Barbara Plank[2], Gianni Barlacchi[1,3],
Francisco Valverde Albacete[4], Manos Tsagkias[5], Antonio Uva[1], and Alessandro Moschitti[6,1]

[1]Department of Information Engineering and Computer Science, University of Trento, Italy
[2]University of Groningen, The Netherlands
[3]SKIL - Telecom Italia, Trento, Italy
[4]Dept. Teoria de Señal y Comunicaciones, Universidad Carlos III de Madrid, Spain
[5]904Labs, Amsterdam, The Netherlands
[6]Qatar Computing Research Institute

`uryupina@gmail.com, b.plank@rug.nl, gianni.barlacchi@unitn.it,`
`fva@tsc.uc3m.es, manos@904labs.com,`
`antonio.uva@unitn.it, amoschitti@gmail.com`

Abstract

We present a robust and efficient parallelizable multilingual UIMA-based platform for automatically annotating textual inputs with different layers of linguistic description, ranging from surface level phenomena all the way down to deep discourse-level information. In particular, given an input text, the pipeline extracts: sentences and tokens; entity mentions; syntactic information; opinionated expressions; relations between entity mentions; co-reference chains and wikified entities. The system is available in two versions: a standalone distribution enables design and optimization of user-specific sub-modules, whereas a server-client distribution allows for straightforward high-performance NLP processing, reducing the engineering cost for higher-level tasks.

1 Introduction

With the growing amount of textual information available on an everyday basis, Natural Language Processing gets more and more large-scale. Moreover, a lot of effort has been invested in the recent years into the development of multi- and cross-lingual resources. To efficiently use large amounts of data for high-level tasks, e.g., for Information Extraction, we need robust parallelizable multilingual preprocessing pipelines to automatically annotate textual inputs with a variety of linguistic structures. To address the issue, we present the LiMoSINe Pipeline—a platform developed by the FP7 EU project LiMoSINE: Linguistically Motivated Semantic aggregation engiNes.

Several platforms and toolkits for NLP preprocessing have been made available to the research community in the past decades. The most commonly used ones are OpenNLP[1], FreeLing (Padró and Stanilovsky, 2012) and GATE (Cunningham et al., 2011). In addition, many research groups publicly release their pre-

---

[1] `http://opennlp.apache.org`

processing modules. These approaches, however, pose several problems:

- most of these tools require a considerable effort for installation, configuration and getting familiar with the software,
- parallelization might be an issue,
- for languages other than English, many modules are missing, while the existing ones often have only a moderate performance level.

In the LiMoSINe project, we focus on high-performance NLP processing for four European languages: English, Italian, Spanish and Dutch. We combine state-of-the-art solutions with specifically designed in-house modules to ensure reliable performance. Using the UIMA framework, we opt for a fully parallelizable approach, making it feasible to process large amounts of data. Finally, we release the system in two versions: a client application connects to the pipeline installed on the LiMoSINe server to provide the users with all the annotation they require. This does not require any advanced installation or configuration of the software, thus reducing the engineering cost for the potential stake holders. A local installation of the pipeline, on the contrary, requires some effort to get familiar with the system, but it also gives users a possibility to integrate their own modules, thus allowing for a greater flexibility. The pipeline is available at `http://ikernels-portal.disi.unitn.it/projects/limosine/`.

2 LiMoSINe pipeline: overall structure

Our platform supports various levels of linguistic description, representing a document from different angles. It should therefore combine outputs of numerous linguistic preprocessors to provide a uniform and deep representation of a document's semantics. The overall structure of our pipeline is shown on Figure 1. This complex structure raises an issue of the compatibility between preprocessors: with many NLP modules around—publicly available, implemented by the LiMoSINe partners or designed by potential stakeholders—it becomes virtually impossible to ensure that

Proceedings of the 54th Annual Meeting of the Association for Computational Linguistics—System Demonstrations, pages 157–162,
Berlin, Germany, August 7-12, 2016. ©2016 Association for Computational Linguistics

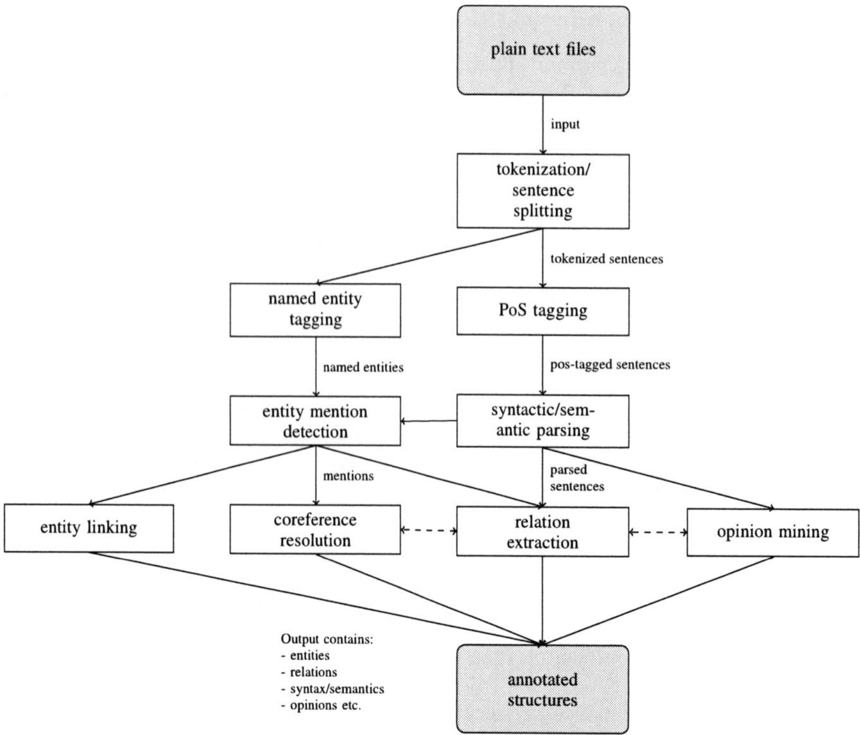

Figure 1: LiMoSINe pipeline architecture

any two modules have the same input/output format and thus can be run as a pipeline.

We have focused on creating a platform that allows for straightforward incorporation of various tools, coordinating their inputs and outputs in a uniform way. Our LiMoSINe Pipeline is based on Apache UIMA—a framework for Unstructured Information Management.[2] UIMA has been successfully used for a number of NLP projects, e.g., for the IBM Watson system (Ferrucci et al., 2010).

One of the main features of UIMA is its modularity: the individual annotators only incrementally update the document representation ("CAS"), but do not interact with each other. This allows for a straightforward deployment of new components: to add a new module to a UIMA system, one only has to create a wrapper converting its input and output objects into CAS structures. Moreover, UIMA allows for full parallelization of the processing flow, which is especially crucial when we aim at annotating large amounts of data.

UIMA-based systems can be deployed both locally or remotely. To run a UIMA application on a local machine, the user should follow the instructions on the UIMA web site to download and install UIMA. The

LiMoSINe Pipeline should then be downloaded and run. While this requires some engineering effort, such an approach would allow the user to implement and integrate their own modules into the existing pipeline, as well as to re-optimize (e.g., retraining a parser to cover a specific domain).

A client-server version of the pipeline has been installed on the LiMoSINe server. The client application can be downloaded from the pipeline website. The users do not need to install any UIMA-related software to use this service. While this approach does not provide the flexibility of a local installation, it allows the users to obtain state-of-the-art NLP annotations for their textual inputs at no engineering cost at all. This might provide a valuable support for projects focusing on higher-level tasks, for example, on Question Answering, especially for languages other than English, considerably reducing the effort required for implementing and integrating all the preprocessing components needed.

3 Integrated modules

The LiMoSINe project has focused on four European languages: English, Italian, Spanish and Dutch. For all these languages, we have created a platform that provides robust parallelizable NLP processing up to the

---

[2]http://uima.apache.org/

syntactic parsing level. This already allows to create complex structural representations of sentences, to be used for higher-level tasks, such as Opinion Mining or Question Answering (cf. Section 4 below). In addition, where possible, we have integrated deeper semantic and discourse-level processing, such as relation extraction, coreference, opinion mining and entity linking. Table 1 provides an overview of all the currently supported modules.

The feasibility of our approach depends crucially on the performance of linguistic processors for a specific language and on the availability of the manually annotated data. Despite a growing interest in the multilingual processing in the NLP community, for a number of tasks no robust processors are available for languages other than English and for some others even a generic model cannot be retrained due to the lack of data. While we tried to rely as much as possible on the state-of-the-art technology, we had to implement or re-optimize a number of preprocessors.

3.1 English

Stanford tools. To provide basic preprocessing, required by our high-level components, we created UIMA wrappers for several Stanford NLP tools (Manning et al., 2014): the tokenizer, the parser and the named entity analyzer.

Entity Mention Detector. Both coreference resolver and relation extractor require information on *mentions*—textual units that correspond to real-world objects. Even though some studies focus on specific subtypes of mentions (for example, on pronominal coreference or on relations between named entities), we believe that a reliable pipeline should provide information on all the possible mentions.

An entity mention detector (EMD), covering a wide variety of mentions, has been developed at the University of Trento as a part of BART (see below). A more recent version has been proposed for the CoNLL-2011/2012 Shared Tasks (Uryupina et al., 2011; Uryupina et al., 2012). It is a rule-based system that combines the outputs of a parser and an NE-tagger to extract mention boundaries (both full and minimal nominal spans) and assign mention types (name, nominal or pronoun) and semantic classes (inferred from WordNet for common nouns, from NER labels for proper nouns). We are currently planning to integrate learning-based EMD (Uryupina and Moschitti, 2013) to cover additional languages, in particular, Arabic.

Opinion Mining. The opinion expression annotator is a system developed at the University of Trento by Johansson and Moschitti (2011). It extracts fine-grained opinion expressions together with their polarity. To extract opinion expressions, it uses a standard sequence labeler for subjective expression markup similar to the approach by (Breck et al., 2007). The system has been developed on the MPQA corpus that contains news articles. It internally uses the syntactic/semantic LTH dependency parser of (Johansson and Nugues, 2008). The opinion mining tool thus requires CoNLL-2008-formatted data as input, as output by the parser, and as such needs pre-tokenized and tagged input.

Relation Extraction. The relation extractor (RE) is a tree-kernel based system developed at the University of Trento (Moschitti, 2006; Plank and Moschitti, 2013). Tree kernel-based methods have been shown to outperform feature-based RE approach (Nguyen et al., 2015). The system takes as input the entity mentions detected by the EMD module (which provides information on the entity types, i.e. PERSON, LOCATION, ORGANIZATION or ENTITY).

The first version of the relation extractor was trained on the ACE 2004 data. It provides the following binary relations as output: Physical, Personal/Social, Employment/Membership, PER/ORG Affiliation and GPE Affiliation.

An extended version of the Relation Extractor includes an additional model trained on the CoNLL 2004 data (Roth and Yih, 2004) following the setup of Giuliano et al. (2007). The model uses a composite kernel consisting of a constituency-based path-enclosed tree kernel and a linear feature vector encoding local and global contexts (Giuliano et al., 2007). The CoNLL 2004 model contains the following relations: LiveIn, LocatedIn, WorkFor, OrgBasedIn, Kill.

Both models exhibit state-of-the art performance. For the ACE 2004 data, experiments are reported in (Plank and Moschitti, 2013). For the CoNLL 2004 data, our model achieves results comparable to or advancing the state-of-the-art (Giuliano et al., 2007; Ghosh and Muresan, 2012).

Coreference Resolution. Our coreference resolution Analysis Engine is a wrapper around BART—a toolkit for Coreference Resolution developed at the University of Trento (Versley et al., 2008; Uryupina et al., 2012). It is a modular anaphora resolution system that supports state-of-the-art statistical approaches to the task and enables efficient feature engineering. BART implements several models of anaphora resolution (mention-pair and entity-mention; best-first vs. ranking), has interfaces to different machine learners (MaxEnt, SVM, decision trees) and provides a large set of linguistically motivated features, along with the possibility to design new ones.

Entity Linking. The Entity Linking Analysis Engine ("Semanticizer") makes use of the Entity Linking Web Service developed by the University of Amsterdam

Annotator	English	Italian	Spanish	Dutch
tokenizer	Stanford	TextPro	IXA	xTas/Frog
POS-tagger	Stanford	TextPro	IXA	xTas/Frog
NER	Stanford	TextPro	IXA	xTas/Frog
Parsing	Stanford, LTH	FBK-Berkeley	IXA	xTas/Alpino
Entity Mention Detection	BART	BART-Ita	-	-
Opinion Mining	Johansson&Moschitti (2001)	-	-	-
Relation Extraction	RE-UNITN	RE-UNITN unlex	-	-
Coreference	BART	Bart-Ita	-	-
Entity Linking	Semanticizer	Semanticizer	Semanticizer	Semanticizer

Table 1: Supported modules for different languages

(Meij et al., 2012). The web service supports automatic linking of an input text to Wikipedia articles: the output of the web service API is a list of IDs of recognized articles, together with confidence scores as well as the part of the input text that was matched. This entity linking module can be considered as cross-lingual and cross-document co-reference resolution, since entity mentions in documents in different languages are disambiguated and linked to Wikipedia articles. Each annotation unit corresponds to a span in the document and is labeled with two attributes: the corresponding Wikipedia ID and the system's confidence.

3.2 Italian

For Italian, we have been able to integrate language-specific processors for tokenization, sentence splitting, named entity recognition, parsing, mention detection and coreference. For relation extraction, we have followed a domain adaptation approach, transferring an unlexicalized model learned on the English data. A detailed description of our annotators for Italian is provided below.

TextPro wrapper. To provide basic levels of linguistic processing, we rely on TextPro—a suite of Natural Language Processing tools for analysis of Italian (and English) texts (Pianta et al., 2008). The suite has been designed to integrate various NLP components developed by researchers at Fondazione Bruno Kessler (FBK). The TextPro suite has shown exceptional performance for several NLP tasks at multiple EvalIta competitions. Moreover, the toolkit is being constantly updated and developed further by FBK. We can therefore be sure that TextPro provides state-of-the-art processing for Italian.

TextPro combines rule-based and statistical methods. It also allows for a straightforward integration of task-specific user-defined pre- and post-processing techniques. For example, one can customize TextPro to provide better segmentation for web data.

TextPro is not a part of the LiMoSINe pipeline, it can be obtained from FBK and installed on any platform in a straightforward way. No TextPro installation is needed for the client version of the semantic model.

Parsing. A model has been trained for Italian on the Torino Treebank data[3] using the Berkeley parser by the Fondazione Bruno Kessler. The treebank being relatively small, a better performance can be achieved by enforcing TextPro part-of-speech tags when training and running the parser. Both the Torino Treebank itself and the parsing model use specific tagsets that do not correspond to the Penn TreeBank tags of the English parser. To facilitate cross-lingual processing and enable unlexicalized cross-lingual modeling for deep semantic tasks, we have mapped these tagsets to each other.

Entity Mention Detection. We have adjusted our Entity Mention Detection analysis engine to cover the Italian data. Similarly to the English module, we use BART to heuristically extract mention boundaries from parse trees. However, due to the specifics of the Torino Treebank annotation guidelines, we had to change the extraction rules substantially.

Relation Extraction. Since no relation extraction datasets are available for Italian, we have opted for a domain adaptation solution, learning an unlexicalized model on the English RE data. This model aims at capturing structural patterns characteristic for specific relations through tree kernel-based SVMs. This solution requires some experiments on making English and Italian parse trees more uniform, for example, on translating the tagsets. We extract tree-based patterns for CoNLL-2004 relations (see above) from the unlexicalized variant of the English corpus and then run it on modified Italian parse trees. Clearly, this model cannot provide robust and accurate annotation. It can, however, be used as a benchmark for supervised RE in Italian. To improve the model's precision, we have restricted its coverage to named entities in contrast to all the nominal mentions used by the English RE models.

Coreference Resolution. A coreference model for BART has been trained on the Italian portion of the SemEval-2010 Task 1 dataset (Uryupina and Moschitti, 2014). Apart from retraining the model, we have incorporated some language-specific features to account,

---

[3]http://www.di.unito.it/~tutreeb/

for example, for abbreviation and aliasing patterns in Italian. The Italian version of BART, therefore, is a high-performance language-specific system. It has shown reliable performance at the recent shared tasks for Italian, in particular, at the SemEval-2010 Task 1 (Broscheit et al., 2010) and at the EvalIta 2009 (Biggio et al., 2009).

Both our English and Italian coreference modules are based on BART. Their configurations (parameter settings and features) have been optimized separately to enhance the performance level on a specific language. Since BART is a highly modular toolkit itself and its language-specific functionality can be controlled via a *Language Plugin*, no extra BART installation is required to run the Italian coreference resolver.

3.3 Spanish

We have tested two publicly available toolkits supporting language processing in Spanish: OpenNLP and IXA (Agerri et al., 2014). The latter has shown a better performance level and has therefore been integrated for the final release of the LiMoSINe pipeline.

For tokenization, we rely on the `ixa-pipe-tok` library (version 1.5.0) from the IXA pipes project. Since it uses FSA technology for the tokenization and a rule-based segmenter, it is fast (tokenizing around 250K words/s) and expected to be valid accross several dialects of Spanish (Agerri et al., 2014).

The POS tags are assigned by using the IXA model for Maximum Entropy POS tagging, and reported to provide 98.88% accuracy (Agerri et al., 2014). Lemmatization uses the morfologik-stemming toolkit, based on FSA for a lower memory footprint (up to 10% the size of a full-fledged dictionary).

Named entities (PERSON, LOCATION, ORGANIZATION and MISC) are annotated using the Maximum Entropy model of IXA trained on the CONLL 2002 dataset and tags.

Finally, the IXA pipeline provides a module for constituency parsing trained on the (Iberian) Spanish section of the AnCora corpus.

3.4 Dutch

For Dutch, we have been able to integrate language-specific processors for tokenization, sentence splitting, lemmatization, named entity recognition, dependency tree, and part-of-speech tagging.

To provide basic levels of linguistic processing, we rely on xTas—a text analysis suite for English and Dutch (de Rooij et al., 2012). The suite has been designed to integrate various NLP components developed by researchers at University of Amsterdam and is extendable to work with components from other parties. xTas is designed to leverage distributed environments for speeding up computationally demanding NLP tasks

and is available as a REST web service. xTas and instructions on how to install it and set it up can be found at `http://xtas.net`.

Most of the Dutch processors at xTas come from Frog, a third-party module. Frog, formerly known as Tadpole, is an integration of memory-based NLP modules developed for Dutch (van den Bosch et al., 2007). All NLP modules are based on Timbl, the Tilburg memory-based learning software package. Most modules were created in the 1990s at the ILK Research Group (Tilburg University, the Netherlands) and the CLiPS Research Centre (University of Antwerp, Belgium). Over the years they have been integrated into a single text processing tool. More recently, a dependency parser, a base phrase chunker, and a named-entity recognizer module were added.

For dependency parsing, xTas uses Alpino, a third-party module.[4] Annotation typically starts with parsing a sentence with the Alpino parser, a wide coverage parser of Dutch text. The number of parses that is generated is reduced through interactive lexical analysis and constituent marking. The selection of the best parse is done efficiently with the parse selection tool.

4 Conclusion and Future/Ongoing work

In this paper, we have presented the LiMoSINe pipeline—a platform supporting state-of-the-art NLP technology for English, Italian, Spanish and Dutch. Based on UIMA, it allows for efficient parallel processing of large volumes of text. The pipeline is distributed in two versions: the client application is oriented to potential users that need high-performance standard tools at a zero engineering cost. The local version, on the contrary, requires some installation and configuration effort, but in return it offers a great flexibility in implementing and integrating user-specific modules.

Since the beginning of the LiMoSINe project, the platform has been used for providing robust preprocessing for a variety of high-level tasks. Thus, we have recently shown how structural representations, extracted with our pipeline, improve multilingual opinion mining on YouTube (Severyn et al., 2015) or crossword puzzle resolution (Barlacchi et al., 2014).

The pipeline has been adopted by other parties, most importantly by the joint QCRI and MIT project IYAS (Interactive sYstem for Answer Selection). IYAS focuses on Question Answering, showing that representations, based on linguistic preprocessing, significantly outperform more shallow methods (Tymoshenko and Moschitti, 2015; Tymoshenko et al., 2014).

As part of the LiMoSINe project, we have created the LiMoSINe Common Corpus: a large collection of documents downloaded from different web resources

---

[4] `http://www.let.rug.nl/vannoord/alp/Alpino/`

in any of the four addressed languages. These data were annotated automatically. We illustrate the processing capabilities of our pipeline on the Spanish part of the corpus (EsLCC). To this end, we developed a UIMA Collection Processing Engine (CPE). Once the EsLCC was downloaded it was first tidied up with Apache Tika. The pipeline was then applied to clean text. It was capable of processing the approximately 103K EsLCC documents in a little bit more than 24 hours on an Ubuntu 14.04 with 16GB of RAM, on an Intel $i7$@3.50GHz $\times$ 8 core box.

Currently, the QCRI team is working on extending the pipeline, integrating various preprocessing modules for Arabic.

5 Acknowledgements

This work has been supported by the EU Projects FP7 LiMoSINe and H2020 5G-CogNet.

References

R. Agerri, J. Bermudez, and G. Rigau. 2014. IXA pipeline: Efficient and ready to use multilingual NLP tools. In *LREC*.

G. Barlacchi, M. Nicosia, and A. Moschitti. 2014. Learning to rank answer candidates for automatic resolution of crossword puzzles. In *CoNLL-2014*.

S. M. Bernaola Biggio, C. Giuliano, M. Poesio, Y. Versley, O. Uryupina, and R. Zanoli. 2009. Local entity detection and recognition task. In *EvalIta-2009*.

E. Breck, Y. Choi, and C. Cardie. 2007. Identifying expressions of opinion in context. In *IJCAI*.

S. Broscheit, M. Poesio, S.P. Ponzetto, K.J. Rodriguez, L. Romano, O. Uryupina, and Y. Versley. 2010. BART: A multilingual anaphora resolution system. In *SemEval*.

H. Cunningham, D. Maynard, K. Bontcheva, V. Tablan, N. Aswani, I. Roberts, G. Gorrell, A. Funk, A. Roberts, D. Damljanovic, T. Heitz, M.A. Greenwood, H. Saggion, J. Petrak, Y. Li, and W. Peters. 2011. *Text Processing with GATE (Version 6)*.

O. de Rooij, J. van Gorp, and Maarten de Rijke. 2012. xtas: Text analysis in a timely manner. In *DIR 2012: 12th Dutch-Belgian Information Retrieval Workshop*.

D.A. Ferrucci, E.W. Brown, J. Chu-Carroll, J. Fan, D. Gondek, A. Kalyanpur, A. Lally, J.W. Murdock, E. Nyberg, J.M. Prager, N. Schlaefer, and Ch.A. Welty. 2010. Building Watson: An overview of the DeepQA project. *AI Magazine*, pages 59–79.

D. Ghosh and S. Muresan. 2012. Relation classification using entity sequence kernels. In *COLING 2012*, pages 391–400.

C. Giuliano, A. Lavelli, and L. Romano. 2007. Relation extraction and the influence of automatic named-entity recognition. *ACM Trans. Speech Lang. Process.*, 5(1).

R. Johansson and A. Moschitti. 2011. Extracting opinion expressions and their polarities – exploration of pipelines and joint models. In *ACL*.

R. Johansson and P. Nugues. 2008. Dependency-based semantic role labeling of PropBank. In *EMNLP*.

C.D. Manning, M. Surdeanu, J. Bauer, J. Finkel, S.J. Bethard, and D. McClosky. 2014. The Stanford CoreNLP natural language processing toolkit. In *ACL System Demonstrations*.

E. Meij, W. Weerkamp, and M. de Rijke. 2012. Adding semantics to microblog posts. In *WSDM*.

A. Moschitti. 2006. Efficient convolution kernels for dependency and constituent syntactic trees. *Machine Learning: ECML 2006*.

T.H. Nguyen, B. Plank, and R. Grishman. 2015. Semantic representations for domain adaptation: A case study on the tree kernel-based method for relation extraction. In *ACL*.

L. Padró and E. Stanilovsky. 2012. Freeling 3.0: Towards wider multilinguality. In *LREC*, Istanbul, Turkey, May. ELRA.

E. Pianta, Ch. Girardi, and R. Zanoli. 2008. The TextPro tool suite. In *LREC*.

B. Plank and A. Moschitti. 2013. Embedding semantic similarity in tree kernels for domain adaptation of relation extraction. In *ACL*.

D. Roth and W. Yih. 2004. A linear programming formulation for global inference in natural language tasks. In *CoNLL*.

Aliaksei Severyn, Alessandro Moschitti, Olga Uryupina, and Barbara Plank. 2015. Multilingual opinion mining on YouTube. *Information Processing and Management*.

K. Tymoshenko and A. Moschitti. 2015. Assessing the impact of syntactic and semantic structures for answer passages reranking. In *ACM CIKM*.

K. Tymoshenko, A. Moschitti, and A. Severyn. 2014. Encoding semantic resources in syntactic structures for passage reranking. In *EACL*.

O. Uryupina and A. Moschitti. 2013. Multilingual mention detection for coreference resolution. In *IJCNLP*.

O. Uryupina and A. Moschitti. 2014. Coreference resolution for Italian: Assessing the impact of linguistic components. In *CLIC-it*.

O. Uryupina, S. Saha, A. Ekbal, and M. Poesio. 2011. Multi-metric optimization for coreference: The UniTN / IITP / Essex submission to the 2011 CONLL shared task. In *CoNLL*.

O. Uryupina, A. Moschitti, and M. Poesio. 2012. BART goes multilingual: The UniTN / Essex submission to the CoNLL-2012 Shared Task. In *CoNLL*.

A. van den Bosch, B. Busser, S. Canisius, and W. Daelemans. 2007. An efficient memory-based morphosyntactic tagger and parser for Dutch. In *CLIN*. Leuven, Belgium.

Y. Versley, S.P. Ponzetto, M. Poesio, V. Eidelman, A. Jern, J. Smith, X. Yang, and A. Moschitti. 2008. BART: a modular toolkit for coreference resolution. In *ACL*.

new/s/leak – Information Extraction and Visualization for Investigative Data Journalists

Seid Muhie Yimam[†] and **Heiner Ulrich**[‡] and **Tatiana von Landesberger**[◇] and
Marcel Rosenbach[‡] and **Michaela Regneri**[‡] and **Alexander Panchenko**[†] and
Franziska Lehmann[◇] and **Uli Fahrer**[†] and **Chris Biemann**[†] and **Kathrin Ballweg**[◇]

[†]**FG Language Technology**	[◇]**Graphic Interactive Systems Group**	[‡]**SPIEGEL-Verlag**
Computer Science Department	Computer Science Department	Hamburg, Germany
Technische Universität Darmstadt	Technische Universität Darmstadt	

Abstract

We present *new/s/leak*, a novel tool developed for and with the help of journalists, which enables the automatic analysis and discovery of newsworthy stories from large textual datasets. We rely on different NLP preprocessing steps such named entity tagging, extraction of time expressions, entity networks, relations and metadata. The system features an intuitive web-based user interface based on network visualization combined with data exploring methods and various search and faceting mechanisms. We report the current state of the software and exemplify it with the WikiLeaks PlusD (Cablegate) data.

1 Introduction

This paper presents *new/s/leak*[1], the *network of searchable leaks*, a journalistic software for investigating and visualizing large textual datasets (see live demo here[2]). Investigation of unstructured document collections is a laborious task: The sheer amount of content can be vast, for instance, the WikiLeaks PlusD[3] dataset contains around 250 thousand cables. Typically, these collections largely consist of unstructured text with additional metadata such as date, location or sender and receiver of messages. The largest part of these documents are irrelevant for journalistic investigations, concealing the crucial storylines. For instance, war crime stories in WikiLeaks were hidden and scattered among hundreds of thousands of routine conversations between officials. Therefore, if journalists do not know in advance what to look for in the document collections, they can only vaguely target all people and organizations (named entities) of public interest.

Currently, the discovery of novel and relevant stories in large data leaks requires many people and a large time budget, both of which are typically not available to journalists: If the documents are confidential like datasets from an informer, only a few selected journalists will have access to the classified data, and those few will have to carry the whole workload. On the other hand, if the documents are publicly available (e.g. a leak posted on the web), the texts have to be analyzed under enormous time pressure, because the journalistic value of each story decreases rapidly if other media publish it before.

There is a plethora of tools (see Section 2) for data journalist that automatically reveal and visualize interesting correlations hidden within large number-centric datasets (Janicke et al., 2015; Kucher and Kerren, 2014). However, these tools provide very limited automatic support with visual guidance through plain text collections. Some tools include shallow natural language processing, but mostly restricted to English. There is no tool that works for multiple languages, handles a large number of text collections, analyzes and visualizes named entities along with the relations between them and allows editing what is considered as an entity. Moreover, available software is usually not open source but rather expensive and often requires substantial training, which is unsuitable for a journalist under time pressure and no prior experience with such software.

---

[1]http://newsleak.io

[2]http://bev.lt.informatik.tu-darmstadt.de/newsleak/

[3]https://wikileaks.org/plusd/about

Proceedings of the 54th Annual Meeting of the Association for Computational Linguistics—System Demonstrations, pages 163–168,
Berlin, Germany, August 7-12, 2016. ©2016 Association for Computational Linguistics

The goal of *new/s/leak* is to provide journalists with a novel visual interactive data analysis support that combines the latest advances from natural language processing approaches and information visualization. It enables journalists to swiftly process large collections of text documents in order to find interesting pieces of information.

This paper presents the core concepts and architecture behind the *new/s/leak*. We also show an in-depth analysis of user requirements and how we implement and address these. Finally, we discuss our prototype, which will be made available in open source[4] under a lenient license.

2 Related work

Kirkpatrick (2015) states that investigative journalist should look at the facts, identify what is wrong with the situation, uncover the truth, and write a story that places the facts in context. This work explains traditional story discovery engine components which, on the technical side, consist of a knowledge base, an inference engine and an easy to use user interface for visualization.

Discussions with our partner journalists confirm this view: newsworthy stories are not evident from leaked documents, but following up on information from leaks might reveal relevant pointers for journalistic research.

Cohen et al. (2011) outline a vision for "a cloud for the crowd" system to support collaborative investigative journalism, in which computational resources support human expertise for efficient and effective investigative journalism.

The *DocumentCloud*[5] and the *Overview*[6] project are the most popular tools comparable to the *new/s/leak*, both designed for journalists dealing with large set of documents. *DocumentCloud* is a tool for building a document archive for the material related to an investigation. Similarly to our system, people, places and organizations are recognized in documents. We put additional focus on the UI by adding a graph-based visualization and better support for document browsing. *Overview* is designed to help journalists find stories in large number of documents by topical clustering. This is a complementary approach to ours: rather than keyword-based topics, our tool centers around entities and text-extracted relations. Fur-

ther, we added advanced editing capabilities for users to add entities and edit the whole network.

Aleph.grano.cc visualizes connections of people, places and organizations extracted from text documents, but leaves the relationship types underspecified. *Detective.io*, a platform for collaborative network analysis, does some of the visualizations and annotations we are working on. However, there is a crucial difference: *Detective.io* assumes a rigid data structure (e.g."corporate networks") and the user has to fill the underlying database entirely manually. Our tool targets on unstructured sources and extracts networks from text, enabling navigation to the sources. *Jigsaw*[7] extracts named entities from text collections and computes various plots from them, but received little attention from journalists due to its unintuitive user interface.

With *new/s/leak*, we want to develop existing tools a step further, by combining the automation of entity and relationship extraction with an intuitive and appealing visual interface.

New/s/leak is based on two prior systems developed namely from the works of (Benikova et al., 2014), *Network of the Day*[8] and (Kochtchi et al., 2014), *Network of Names*[9]. Both tools automatically analyze named entities and their relationships and present an interactive network visualization that allows to retrieve the original sources for displayed relations. In the current project, we add support for faceted data browsing, a timeline, a better access to source documents and a possibility to tag and edit visualizations.

3 Objectives and User Requirements

The objective of *new/s/leak* is to support investigative data journalists in finding important facts and stories in large unstructured text collections. The two key elements are an easy-to-use interactive visualization and linguistic preprocessing.

To gain a more precise focus for our development, we conducted structured interviews with potential users. They seek for an answer to the question "Who does what to whom?" – possibly amended with "When and where?". At the same time, they always need access to the source documents, to verify the machine-given answers. The

---

[4]http://github.com/tudarmstadt-lt/newsleak
[5]https://www.documentcloud.org/home
[6]https://https://www.overviewdocs.com

[7]http://www.cc.gatech.edu/gvu/ii/jigsaw
[8]http://tagesnetzwerk.de
[9]http://maggie.lt.informatik.tu-darmstadt.de/thesis/master/NetworksOfNames

outcome of these interviews are summarized in the following requirements.

1) Identify key persons, places and organizations.
2) Browse the collection, identify interesting documents and read documents in detail.
3) Analyze the connections between entities.
4) Assess temporal evolution of the documents.
5) Explore geographic distribution of events.
6) Annotate documents with findings as well as edit the data to enhance data quality.
7) Save and share selected documents.

While some of these requirements (like document browsing) are standard search features, others (like annotation and sharing) are usually not yet integrated in journalism tools. The final version of our system will include all of these features.

4 Implementation details

4.1 System

The *new/s/leak* tool consists of two major parts shown in Figure 1: The backend provides various NLP tools for document pre-processing and document analysis (Sec. 5), interactive visualization for investigative journalism (Sec. 6). The implementation of the backend and frontend components of *new/s/leak* are integrated in a modular way that allows e.g. adding a different relation extraction mechanism or support for multiple languages.

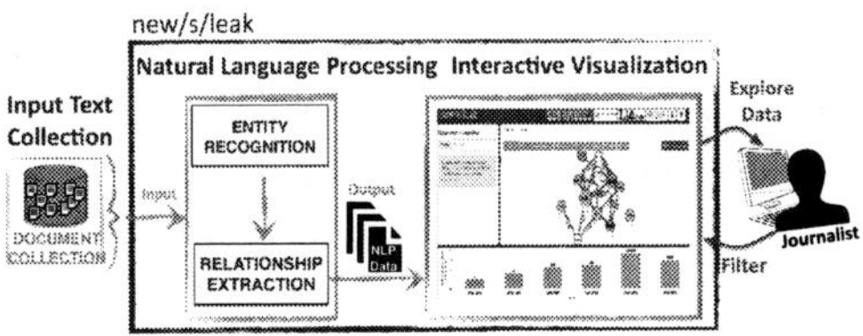

Figure 1: Schema of *new/s/leak* for visual support of investigative analysis in text collections.

4.2 Demo datasets

We demonstrate capabilities of our system on two well-known cases:

1) The well-investigated WikiLeaks PlusD "Cablegate" collection, a collection of diplomatic notes from over 45 years originating from US embassies all over the world.
2) The Enron email dataset (Klimt and Yang, 2004) is a collection of email messages which is available publicly from the Enron Corporation.

The dataset comprises over 600,000 messages between 158 employees. This example shows the tools' general applicability to email leaks.

5 Backend: information extraction

The *new/s/leak* backend uses different NLP tools for preprocessing and analysis, integrated with a relational database, a NoSQL document store and some specific retrieval methods. First, documents are pre-processed and converted to an intermediate *new/s/leak* document representation. This format is generic enough to represent collections from any possible source, such as emails, relational databases or XML documents.

In a second step, our NLP preprocessing extracts important entities, metadata (like time and location), term co-occurrences, keywords, and relationships among entities. We store relevant documents and extracted entities in a *PostgreSQL*[10] database and an *ElasticSearch*[11] index. We explain the following steps using the Wikileaks Cablegate dataset as an example, but the tool is not limited to this single dataset.

5.1 Preprocessing

The first step of *new/s/leak* workflow is preprocessing the input documents and represent them in *new/s/leak*'s intermediate document representation. Preprocessing of the Cablegate dataset requires truecasing the original documents which are mostly in capitals. The work of Lita et al. (2003) indicates that truecasing improves the F-score of named entity recognition by 26%. We used a frequency based approach for case restoring based on a very large true-cased background corpus. Once case is restored, we extract metadata from the document, including the document creation dates, subject, message sender document creator, and other metadata already marked in the dataset. Metadata is stored in a database as triples of (n, t, v) where n is the name, t is the data type (e.g. text or date) and v is the value of the metadata. The tool further supports manual identification of metadata during the analysis and production stages.

---

[10]http://www.postgresql.org
[11]https://www.elastic.co

Dataset	#Documents	#Entities	#Relations
WikiLeaks	251,287	1,363,500	163,138,000
Enron	255,636	613,225	81,309,499

Table 1: Statistics on WikiLeaks PlusD and Enron

5.2 Entity, relation, co-occurrence, keyword, and event time extractions

Recognition of named entities and related terms are key steps in the investigative data-driven journalistic process. For this purpose, we first automatically identify four classes of entities, namely person (PER), organization (ORG), location (LOC) and miscellaneous (MISC) using the named entity recognition tool from Epic[12]. We assume relationships between entities whenever the two entities co-occur in a document. In order to extract relevant keywords regarding two entities, we follow the approach by Biemann et al. (2007). Furthermore, we extract entity relation labels by computing document keywords using JTopia[13]. JTopia extracts relevant key terms for search based on part of speech information. To label the relationship between two entities, the most frequent keywords from the documents where the two entities appeared together is used. To extract temporal expressions, we use the Heideltime (Strötgen, 2015) tool, which disambiguates temporal expressions based on document creation times. For the WikiLeaks dataset, it is possible to extract and disambiguate more than 3.9 million temporal expressions.

All the extraction and processing work-flows of the *new/s/leak* components are implemented using the Apache Spark cluster computing framework for parallel computations. Table 1 shows the different statistics for the WikiLeaks PlusD and Enron datasets.

6 Frontend: interactive visualization

Journalists can browse through the document collection using an interactive visual interface (see Figure 2). It enables faceted document exploration within several views:
1) Graph view: shows named entities and their relations.
2) Map view: shows document distribution in geographic space.
3) Document timeline view: shows document fre-

---

[12]https://github.com/dlwh/epic
[13]http://github.com/srijiths/jtopia

quency over time.
4) Document view: is composed of a) document list and b) document text for reading.

The views are interactive so that the user can browse and explore the document collection on demand. The user starts with exploring entities and their connections in the graph view or by searching for entities and keywords. All interactions in the views define a filter that constrains the current document set, which in turn changes information displayed in the views. The user can assess document frequency in a map or in the timeline, drill down and select documents from the result list, and read them closely. User-selected entities are highlighted in the documents.

Graph view: entities and their co-occurrences
The graph view shows a set of entities as nodes and their connections as links. Node size denotes the frequency of an entity in the document collection, node color denotes the entity type. The co-occurrence of entities within the documents is shown by edge thickness and edge label.
The user can explore the entities and their connections via expanding the graph along the neighbors of a selected entity (plus button). The expanded entities are slowly faded in, so that the user can easily spot which entities appeared. Moreover, the user can drill down into the data by displaying the so-called *ego network* of a selected entity. Clicking on nodes and edges retrieves the respective documents.

Map view. The map view shows the document frequency distribution over the geographic space. Users can hover over a country to see the number of documents mentioning this geographic area, effectively using the map as faceted search.

Document timeline. The document timeline shows the number of documents over time. We use a bar chart with logarithmic scale as it better adheres to the exponential document distribution characteristics. The users can drill down in time to see the document distribution over years, months or days. It is also possible to select a time interval for which the corresponding documents are shown in the document view (see below).

Document view. The document view shows a list of documents with their title or subject as selected by the currently active filters. For large document collections, the documents are loaded

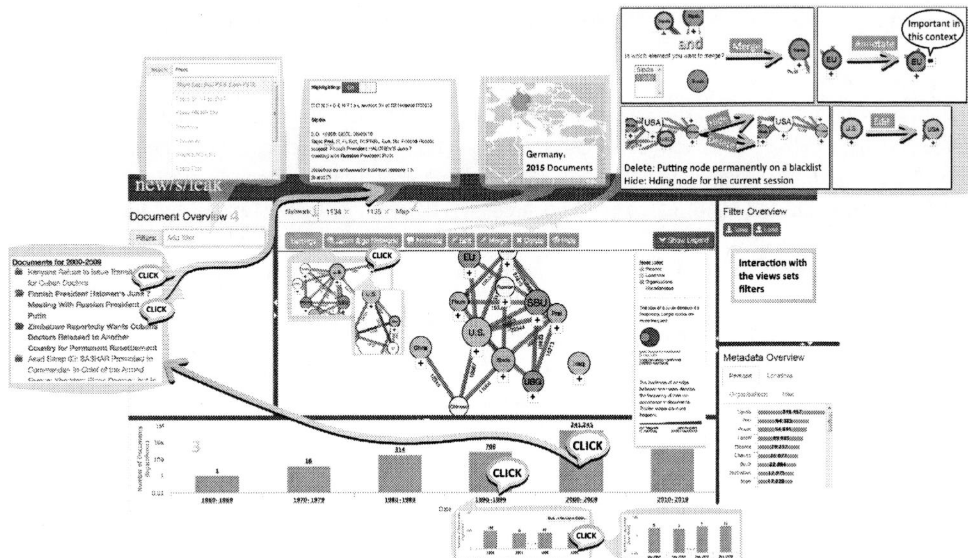

Figure 2: Interactive Visualization Interface composed of graph view on entities, document distribution over time, list of selected documents and a map of document geo-distribution.

on demand. The user can browse the list and identify documents for close reading (bold, open folder icon). The document text view shows the full text of the document, where the entities displayed in the graph are underlined. The underline color corresponds to the type of entity. If the user selected entities in the graph, these entities are highlighted with the background color of the entity. This "close reading" mode enables users to verify hypotheses they perceive in the "distant reading" (Moretti, 2007) visualizations.

6.1 Faceted search

The different levels of visualizations enable users to explore the dataset via *navigation* through document collection (Miller and Remington, 2004). Another highly complementary paradigm for information retrieval used in our system, and also one highly expected by users, is *searching*. During navigation, users explore the document collection interactively, browse with the help of the visualization interfaces, zoom in and out, gradually discovering topics, entities and facts mentioned in the corpus.

In contrast, searching in our system assumes that a user issues a conventional *faceted search* (Tunkelang, 2009) query being a free combination of a full text queries with filters on document metadata. The result of such a faceted search

is a set of documents that satisfy the specified facets, i.e. search conditions, formulated at query time, acting as a filter. Here facets can be any metadata initially associated with the document (e.g. date, sender or destination) extracted automatically (e.g. named entities or topics). Search results are presented to the user as a list of documents or in a form of a graph that corresponds to the document view of our system (see Figure 2).

Search and navigation compliment each other during a journalistic investigation. For instance, a user can get an idea about information available in the collection via interactive visualization interface (see Section 6). This navigation session may trigger a concrete journalistic hypothesis. In this case, during the next step a user may want to issue a specific search query to find documents that support or falsify the hypothesis. To implement this search functionality, we rely on *ElasticSearch*.

7 User Study

We conducted a user study to analyze the usability of the provided functions in the interactive visual interface. We asked 10 volunteer students of various major subjects to perform investigative tasks using our tool. The tasks covered all views. They included finding documents of a particular date, opening a document, selecting countries in a map, showing and expanding entity network, assessing entity type etc. We assessed subjective user experience.

The results showed that the implemented visualizations were intuitive and the interactive functions were easy to use for the requested tasks. The volunteers especially appreciated the drill down in the timeline, the fading in of newly appeared nodes and edges in the graph. The legend and tooltips were very often used as a guidance in the interface. Upon users' feedback, we extended zooming and panning functions in the graph and included highlighting of open documents in the document list. We improved the graph layout and look for reducing edge and node overplotting.

8   Conclusion and future work

In this paper, we presented *new/s/leak*, an investigative tool to support data journalists in extracting important storylines from large text documents. The backend of *new/s/leak* comprises of different NLP tools for preprocessing, analyzing and extracting objects such as named entities, relationships, term co-occurrences, keywords and event time expressions. In the frontend, *new/s/leak* provides network visualization with different views supporting navigating, annotating, and editing extracted information. We also developed a demo system presenting the current state of the *new/s/leak* tool and conducted a user study to evaluate the effectiveness of the system.

We are currently extending the tool to meet the remaining journalists' requirements. In particular, we include features for annotating entities and their relations with explanations, for saving a particular view to share it with colleagues or for later use. Moreover, we will provide journalists with the possibility to further edit this sharable view. Additional features for manual data curation will enhance data quality for analysis while ensuring protection of sources and compliance with legal issues. We will also integrate adaptive annotation machine learning approach (Yimam et al., 2016) into *new/s/leak* to automatically identify interesting objects based on the journalists' interaction and feedback. Further, we will investigate pulling in other information from linked open data and the web.

Acknowledgements

The authors are grateful to data journalists at Spiegel Verlag for their helpful insights into journalistic work and for the identification of tool requirements. The authors wish to thank Lukas Raymann, Patrick Mell, Bettina Johanna Ballin, Nils Christopher Boeschen, Patrick Wilhelmi-Dworski and Florian Zouhar for their help with system implementation and conduction of the user study. The work is being funded by Volkswagen Foundation under Grant Nr. 90 847.

References

D. Benikova, U. Fahrer, A. Gabriel, M. Kaufmann, S. M. Yimam, T. von Landesberger, and C. Biemann. 2014. Network of the day: Aggregating and visualizing entity networks from online sources. In *Proc. NLP4CMC Workshop at KONVENS*, Hildesheim, Germany.

C. Biemann, G. Heyer, U. Quasthoff, and M. Richter. 2007. The Leipzig Corpora Collection – monolingual corpora of standard size. In *Proc. Corpus Linguistics*, Birmingham, UK.

S. Cohen, C. Li, J. Yang, and C. Yu. 2011. Computational journalism: A call to arms to database researchers. In *Proc. CIDR-11)*, pages 148–151, Asilomar, CA, USA.

S. Janicke, G. Franzini, M. F. Cheema, and G. Scheuermann. 2015. On Close and Distant Reading in Digital Humanities: A Survey and Future Challenges. In *Proc. EuroVis*, Cagliari, Italy.

K. Kirkpatrick. 2015. Putting the data science into journalism. *Commun. ACM*, 58(5):15–17.

B. Klimt and Y. Yang. 2004. The Enron Corpus: A New Dataset for Email Classification Research. In *Proc. ECML 2004*, pages 217–226, Pisa, Italy.

A. Kochtchi, T. von Landesberger, and C. Biemann. 2014. Networks of names: Visual exploration and semi-automatic tagging of social networks from newspaper articles. *Computer Graphics Forum*, 33(3):211–220.

K. Kucher and A. Kerren. 2014. Text visualization browser: A visual survey of text visualization techniques. online textvis.lnu.se.

L.V. Lita, A. Ittycheriah, S. Roukos, and N. Kambhatla. 2003. tRuEcasIng. In *Proc. ACL '03*, Sapporo, Japan.

C. S. Miller and R. W Remington. 2004. Modeling information navigation: Implications for information architecture. *Human-computer interaction*, 19(3):225–271.

F. Moretti. 2007. *Graphs, maps, trees : abstract models for a literary history*. Verso, London, UK.

J. Strötgen. 2015. *Domain-sensitive Temporal Tagging for Event-centric Information Retrieval*. Ph.D. thesis, University of Heidelberg.

D. Tunkelang. 2009. Faceted search. *Synthesis lectures on information concepts, retrieval, and services*, 1(1):1–80.

S. Yimam, C. Biemann, L. Majnaric, Š. Šabanović, and A. Holzinger. 2016. An adaptive annotation approach for biomedical entity and relation recognition. *Brain Informatics*, pages 1–12.

Author Index